MULTILINGUAL LEXICON OF LINGUISTICS AND PHILOLOGY

МНОГОЯЗЫЧНЫЙ ЛЕКСИКОН ЛИНГВИСТИКИ И ФИЛОЛОГИИ

MEHRSPRACHIGES LEXIKON DER SPRACHWISSENSCHAFTEN

LEXIQUE MULTILINGUE DE LA LINGUISTIQUE ET DE LA PHILOLOGIE

ROSE NASH / РОЗА НЭШ

Multilingual Lexicon of Linguistics and Philology:

ENGLISH, RUSSIAN, GERMAN, FRENCH

Многоязычный лексикон лингвистики и филологии:
АНГЛИЙСКИЙ, РУССКИЙ, НЕМЕЦКИЙ, ФРАНЦУЗСКИЙ

Mehrsprachiges Lexikon der Sprachwissenschaften:
ENGLISCH, RUSSISCH, DEUTSCH, FRANZÖSISCH

Lexique multilingue de la linguistique et de la philologie:
ANGLAIS, RUSSE, ALLEMAND, FRANÇAIS

CONSULTANTS / СОТРУДНИКИ / BERATER / COLLABORATEURS:

MERVIN ALLEYNE (French, Französisch, Français)   По русскому языку   С. Судаков
GERD FRAENKEL (German, Deutsch, Allemand)   По немецкому языку   Г. Фрэнкель
STEPHEN SOUDAKOFF (Russian, Russisch, Russe)   По французскому языку   М. Аллейн

MIAMI LINGUISTICS SERIES NO. 3

UNIVERSITY OF MIAMI PRESS
CORAL GABLES, FLORIDA

Copyright © 1968 by
University of Miami Press
Library of Congress Catalog Card No.: 68-31044
Manufactured in the United States of America

to Carl / Карлу / für Karl / pour Carl

CONTENTS / СОДЕРЖАНИЕ / INHALT / TABLE DES MATIÈRES

PREFACE

THIS BOOK IS designed specifically for the linguist who wishes to read the works of foreign scholars. Selections for entries were made from a wide variety of sources on the basis of frequency, relevance, and potential difficulty of translation. Basic terminology was taken from existing dictionaries of technical terms, reference grammars, language teaching manuals, and indexes to introductory textbooks on linguistics; this was amplified with semi-technical specialized vocabulary extracted from several thousands of pages of running text in representative books and articles, and by close comparison of translations of important works with their originals; finally, standard dictionaries were scanned page by page for additional vocabulary which might be helpful. (See p. 385)

The following categories were considered in gathering material: traditional grammatical terms; well-established modern terms; terms in historical linguistics and dialectology; sources of language monuments; speech anatomy; articulatory and acoustic classifications; cultural and typological classifications; forms of communication other than speech; names of theoretical models of language; names of related disciplines; names of major languages; concepts associated with language; standard vocabulary frequently used in linguistic literature; signs and symbols in linguistic descriptions; speech styles and sub-types; idioms, colloquial expressions, and other common designations for vocabulary used in special situations; and terms of interest to the linguist relating to education, computers, publishing, recording equipment, etc.

There are slightly more than 5000 English entries. The complete list, including the Russian, German, and French equivalents, totals approximately 23,000. The majority of these were taken directly from the printed page, with minor normalizations for the sake of consistency. In cases where no specific term has been established in one of the languages, a short explanation of the meaning or usage is given. Occasionally, also, suitable terms suggested by the consultants are added, enclosed in angular brackets. (⟨ ⟩)

The choice of citation form as to number follows that used most frequently in the works consulted. Grammatical information is limited to number (plural indicated), gender (for all French entries, and in German and Russian where it is not predictable from an accompanying adjective), and part of speech (supplied for the English entry where necessary and assumed to be the same for other languages unless otherwise noted). Adjectives as separate entries are given in the masculine singular form for Russian and French, and in the uninflected form for German. Russian verbs are given in the imperfective aspect unless usage requires the perfective.

English homonyms having distinctly different meanings are listed separately, with clarifications added in parentheses. Where there are multiple foreign equivalents for an English entry, the preferred, or most frequent equivalent is listed first. In German and Russian, there is a tendency to replace native terms with international terms of Greek and Latin origin, and in many cases the native terms are semiobsolete; they are included here, however, for reference. It should be understood, of course, that as in any dictionary, multiple equivalents are possible correspondences to the English entry, and are not necessarily equivalent to each other in meaning and usage outside of actual context.

Except for the list of distinctive features (D 203), all English entries are in strict alphabetical order without regard to grouping. The first character in each index reference code is identical to the first letter of the corresponding English entry in the main section of the book. Thus the Russian entry *slovo*, for example, has the code W 034, which refers to the English entry *word* with the same code.

In the German and Russian indexes, adjective-plus-noun phrases and compound words containing head words corresponding to *consonant, vowel, sound, language, speech, sentence,* and *model,* are listed both alphabetically and grouped under the appropriate head word. Thus, the German entry *Fragesatz,* for example, appears also under the entry for *Satz.* Usual word order made this automatic for the French index.

The lexicographer working in a modern field of specialization is faced with a number of thorny problems. Not the least of these is a rapidly expanding subject matter, which, however, does not expand at the same rate and in the same direction in every language. It should be emphasized, therefore, that the lexicon in its present form is intended to be useful rather than exhaustive, and linguists with special research interests will find deficiencies in the overall choice of entries. Many new concepts and recently created terms which have not yet crossed the language barrier, and even some which have, had to be excluded in order to limit the choices to those most essential to the intended purpose of the lexicon. Work is in progress on a greatly expanded and more comprehensive compilation, to include entries in Spanish. Users of this lexicon are warmly invited to contribute their suggestions for additional entries.

Many friends and colleagues helped in the preparation of this book. Special thanks are due Pierre Cintas of Harvard University and Jens Peters of Kiel University, who assisted in the early stages of gathering material; to Morris Halle of the Massachusetts Institute of Technology for checking the accuracy of the distinctive feature equivalents; to Wolfgang Wölck of Indiana University, who supplied many of the German terms; to Adolf Hieke and Genevieve Benjamin of Inter American University for their help in checking proofs; to the Indiana University Research Computing Center for the use of their facilities in preparing the indexes; and to Jaakko Ahokas, John Krueger, Samuel Rosenberg, Cornelis Van Schooneveld, Elaine Hagstrom, and A. Pfeffer, all of whom provided valuable sources and much needed encouragement.

ROSE NASH

San Juan, Puerto Rico
February, 1968

ПРЕДИСЛОВИЕ

Настоящая книга предназначена в помощь лингвистам, интересующимся работами иностранных учёных в области языкознания. Выбор статей был сделан в соответствии с тем, как часто они встречаются, насколько они важны, насколько труден перевод. Причём выбор был сделан из большого числа разнообразных источников, наиболее употребительные из которых поименованы на странице 385.

Основная терминология была взята из существующих словарей, технических терминов, справочников по грамматике, руководств для преподавания языков, а также индексов, взятых из разных учебников введения в общую лингвистику. Словарный состав был пополнен полутехнической и специальной терминологией. Выборка терминологии была произведена при просмотре тысяч страниц текстуального материала соответствующих книг и статей, и путём сравнения переводного материала выдающихся работ с оригиналами. И, наконец, были просмотрены и сделаны выборки из обыкновенных словарей с целью подбора добавочного словарного материала, который в той или иной мере может оказаться полезным.

При подборе материала особое внимание уделялось и обращалось на следующие категории: на традиционную грамматическую терминологию, на твёрдо установившуюся современную терминологию, на терминологию исторической лингвистики и диалектологии; на терминологию, относящуюся к историческим языковым памятникам, на анатомию речи, артикуляционные и акустические классификации, на неречевые формы общения, на названия теоретических моделей языка; на названия смежных дисциплин, имеющих то или иное отношение к лингвистике; на названия главных языков; на понятия, связанные с языком; на стандартный запас слов, часто встречающихся в литературе по лингвистике. Обращалось внимание на знаки и символы, употребляемые в лингвистических описаниях; на стили речи и говоры; на идиомы, разговорные выражения и другие термины общесловарного запаса, которые могут быть употреблены в особых случаях; на иные выражения, могущие интересовать лингвиста, занимающегося педагогикой, областью вычислительных машин, относящимся к издательству, звукозаписывающим оборудованием, и.т.д.

Настоящий сборник включает немногим больше пяти тысяч английских статей. Полный перечень, включая русские, немецкие и французские эквиваленты, насчитывает примерно двадцать три тысячи статей. Большинство из них было взято непосредственно из печатного текста с незначительными, минимальными изменениями или поправками для блага цели. В тех случаях, когда соответствующего термина в данном языке не обнаруживалось, давались краткие объяснения значения и применения слова или выражения. Иногда вносились в угловые скобки (⟨ ⟩) подходящие термины, указанные специалистами.

Выбор грамматического числа данной формы в словаре определяется в большинстве случаев той формой числа, которая чаще всего употребляется в пересмотренных источниках. Грамматические сведения ограничиваются указанием числа (только множественного), рода (во всех франзцузких, а в русских и немецких статьях в тех случаев, если род не определен прилагательным), и, где нужно, части речи английского слова. Части речи других языков даются лишь только в тех случаях, когда часть речи данного слова не соответствует английской. Прилагательные, как отдельные единицы, даны в единственном числе мужского рода в русских и франзцузких, а в немецких статьях в основной форме без окончания. Русские глаголы даны в несовершенном виде, исключая случаев, когда при употреблении необходим совершенный вид глагола.

Английские омонимы, включающие в себя явно различные понятия, даны отдельно, а объяснения к ним даны в круглых скобках ( ). В случае, если на соответствующее английское выражение существует несколько выражений-эквивалентов на иностранном языке, самое употребительное из них даётся первым. В немецком и русском языках наблюдается тенденция к замене терминов родного языка интернациональными греческого и латинского происхождения и довольно часто соответствующие термины родного языка становятся полуустаревшими. Такие термины, однако, включены в качестве подсобного справочного материала. Конечно, само собой разумеется, что в данном, как и в любом словаре, иностранные эквиваленты соответствуют английскому слову лишь при определённых условиях, но взятые из других контекстов они могут не соответствовать друг другу.

За исключением списка различных признаков (Д203) все английские слова и выражения даны в строго алфавитном порядке, а не по смысловым группам. Первый знак индексного кода совпадает с первой буквой соответствующего английского выражения в главной части словаря. Выражения состоящие из прилагательных и существительных и сложные слова даются в индексах не только по алфавиту, но для удобства сгруппированы под индексом немецкие и русские эквиваленты в следующем порядке: согласная, гласная, звук, предложение, язык, речь, модель. Обычный порядок слов во французском языке исключил дополнительный характер такой группировки.

В настоящее время составитель словаря, работая в определённой области, сталкивается с рядом затруднений. Из них немаловажным является быстро накапливающиеся данные и материалы, которые, однако, не прогрессируют равномерно в соответствующем направлении в разных языках. Уместно подчеркнуть, что словарь в его настоящей форме рассчитан на то, чтобы извлечь максимум пользы при работе с ним и не рассчитан на всеобъемлемость охвата материала. Поэтому лингвисты со специальными интересами в определённой области языкознания и исследовательской работы столкнутся с пробелами в подборе материалов.

Необходимо заметить, что многие новые понятия и недавно возникшие выражения, которые ещё прочно не прижились и даже некоторые уже прижившиеся должны были быть исключены из списка, чтобы ограничиться самыми важными. В настоящее время ведётся работа над расширенным, дополненным словарём, в который войдут, кроме уже включённых, и испанский язык. Покорнейше просим лиц, работающих со словарём, вносить предложения в виде добавочных статей для включения в новое издание.

При подготовке к печати настоящего издания нам была оказана большая услуга друзьями и коллегами.

Особую благодарность выражаем Пьеру Синтасу (Гарвардский у-тет), и Енсу Петерсу (Килский у-тет) за помощь в начальной стадии работы; Морису Халле (МИТ) за проверку точности переводов различительных признаков; Вольфгангу Вольку (Индианский у-тет), давшему большое число

немецких терминов; А. Хайку и
Г. Бенямине Меж-Американского у-га
за помощь при чтении коррективов;
Вычислительному центру Индианс-
кого у-та предоставление обору-
дования для составления индексов;
Яакко Ахокасу, Джону Крюгеру,
Самуилу Розенбергу, Корнелису ван
Сконефельу, Элейн Хагстром, А.

Пфефферу за предоставление соста-
вителям ценных материалов и источников, а также за моральную
поддержку и добрые советы.

Роза Нэш

г. Сан Хуан, о. Пуэрто Рико
Февраль, 1968

VORWORT

Dieses Buch soll insbesondere dem
Linguisten helfen, der die Arbeiten aus-
ländischer Wissenschaftler lesen möchte.
Beiträge wurden unter dem Gesichtspunkt
von Häufigkeit, Wichtigkeit und denkbarer
Übersetzungsschwierigkeit auf Grund von
verschiedenen Quellen ausgewählt. Die
nützlichsten sind auf Seite 385 aufgeführt.
Die Grundterminologie wurde aus beste-
henden Fachlexika, Handgrammatiken,
Sprachlehren und Sachverzeichnissen in
die Linguistik einführender Lehrbücher
entnommen. Sie wurde mit halbtechni-
schem Fachvokabular aus hierfür ein-
schlägigen Büchern erweitert, von denen
mehrere Seiten fortlaufenden Textes geprüft wurden; ferner wurden Übersetzung-
en bedeutender Arbeiten genau mit ihren
Originalen verglichen, und schliesslich
wurden Standardlexika Seite für Seite auf
zusätzliches Vokabular hin geprüft.

Die folgenden Kategorien wurden bei
der Materialsammlung berücksichtigt: herkömmliche grammatikalische Termini; fest
begründete moderne Termini; Termini
aus der historischen Linguistik und Dia-
lektlehre; Quellen von Sprachdenkmä-
lern, Sprachanatomie, Einteilungen nach
Aussprache und Akustik; kulturelle und
typologische Einteilungen, weitere Kom-
munikationsformen neben der Sprache;
Namen theoretischer Sprachmodelle; Begriffe verwandter Disziplinen; Namen der
Hauptsprachen; Begriffe, die mit der
Sprache verbunden sind; Standardvoka-
bular, das häufig in linguistischer Literatur
angewandt wird; Zeichen und Symbole in
linguistischen Darstellungen; Sprachstile
und Unterarten; idiomatische Redewen-
dungen, umgangssprachliche Ausdrücke
und andere allgemeingültige Bezeichnungen
für Vokabular, das in besonderen Situa-

tionen verwandt wird; sowie für den Linguisten interessante Termini, die sich auf Erziehungswesen, Rechenmaschinen, Verlagswesen, Aufnahmegeräte etc. beziehen.

Die Zahl der englischen Stichworte liegt leicht über 5,000. Die vollständige Liste, die die russischen, deutschen und französischen Stichworte einschliesst, enthält annähernd 23,000 Ausdrücke, welche zum grössten Teil direkt aus Büchern ausgewählt wurden, mit geringen Verbesserungen zum Zweck der Übereinstimmung. In den Fällen, in denen sich kein besonderer Terminus in einer der Sprachen herausgebildet hat, ist eine Umschreibung der Bedeutung angegeben. Gelegentlich sind auch Termini hinzugefügt, die von den beratenden Fachleuten vorgeschlagen wurden. Diese Termini sind in Winkelklammern ⟨ ⟩ eingeschlossen.

Die Zitierungsweise hinsichtlich der Zahl stimmt im allgemeinen mit der überein, die am häufigsten in der Fachliteratur gefunden wurde. Grammatikalische Angaben sind auf Wortarten (die für das englische Stichwort angemerkt sind und von denen angenommen wird, dab sie die gleichen für die anderen Sprachen sind, wenn nicht anders angegeben), Zahl und Geschlecht (im Russischen und Deutschen, falls nicht von dem begleitenden Adjektiv ersichtlich), beschränkt. Adjektive als gesonderte Stichworte sind fur französisch und russisch im Masculin singular und für deutsch in der Grundform angegeben. Russische Verben stehen im imperfekten Aspekt, wenn der perfekte Aspekt nicht verlangt wird.

Englische Homonyme, die deutliche Bedeutungsunterschiede aufweisen, sind gesondert aufgeführt; Erklärungen hierzu sind in runde Klammern ( ) angegeben. Hat das Stichwort in der fremden Sprache mehrere entsprechende Ausdrücke, so wurde das am häufigsten angewendete oder das vorzuziehende gewählt. Im Deutschen und Russischen neigt man sehr dazu, Termini der Muttersprache durch internationale Termini griechischen und lateinischen Ursprungs zu ersetzen; in vielen Fällen sind die älteren Termini der Muttersprache halbwegs neraltet. Sie sind jedoch zur Verweisung hier mit aufgeführt. Es versteht sich natürlich, dass mehrere Ausdrücke, wie in jedem Wörterbuch, nur mögliche Entsprechungen des englischen Stichwortes im eigentlichen Fachgebrauch sind. In anderen Zusammenhängen haben sie nicht unbedingt die gleiche Bedeutung.

Ausser der Liste von "relevanten Merkmalen" (D 203) sind alle englischen Worte ohne Rücksicht auf Einteilung in streng alphabetischer Ordnung aufgeführt. Der erste Buchstabe in jeder Indexeintragsverweisung ist mit dem ersten Buchstaben des entsprechenden englischen Wortes im Hauptteil des Buches identisch. So führt z. B. das russische Wort *slovo* die Verweisungsnummer W 034, welche auf das englische Wort *word* verweist.

In der deutschen und russischen Stichwortverzeichnissen sind aus Adjektiv und Hauptwort zusammengesetzte Phrasen so wie zusammengesetzte Worte, die den englischen Termini *consonant*, *vowel*, *sound*, *language*, *speech*, *sentence* und *model* entsprechen, sowohl alphabetisch sowie unter dem Hauptwort der Zusammensetzung angeführt. Zum Beispiel das deutsche Wort *Fragesatz* erscheint ebenfalls unter den Stickwort *Satz*. Im französischen Stichwortverzeichnis ist dies eine automatische Begleiterscheinung der normalen Satzstellung.

Der Verfasser eines Wörterbuches, der in einem modernen, spezialisierten Bereich arbeitet, sieht sich einer Reihe schwieriger Probleme gegenübergestellt. Eines der grössten ist ein sich schnell ausbreitendes Wissensgebiet, das sich jedoch in den verschiedenen Sprachen nicht mit der gleichen Geschwindigkeit und in die gleiche Richtung hin ausdehnt.

Ich möchte betonen, dass das Lexikon in seiner vorliegenden Form eher nützlich als erschöpfend sein soll; Linguisten mit besonderen Forschungsinteressen werden Mängel hinsichtlich der Gesamtauswahl der Stichworte finden. Viele neue Begriffe und jüngst gebildete Termini, die noch nicht die Sprachschranke passiert haben und sogar einige, denen das gelungen ist, mubten ausgelassen werden, um die Anzahl der Stichworte auf die wichtigsten zu beschränken. Es wird zur Zeit an einer erweiterten und umfassenderen Sammlung gearbeitet, die spanische Ausdrücke mit einschliessen soll, und deren Veröffentlichung für die Zukunft geplant ist. Leser dieses Buches sind freundlichst aufgefordert, ihre Vorschläge zur Aufnahme zu unterbreiten.

Viele Freunde und Kollegen haben bei den Vorbereitungen für dieses Buch geholfen. Besonderer Dank gilt Pierre Cintas von der Harvard University und Jens Peters von der Universität Kiel, die im Anfang bei der Materialsammlung behilflich waren; Morris Halle von dem Massachusetts Institute of Technology dafür, dass er die Genauigkeit der Übersetzungen der "relevante Merkmale" geprüft hat; Wolfgang Wölck von der Indiana University, der viele deutsche Termini beisteuerte; Adolf Hieke und Genevieve Benjamin von der Inter American University, für ihre Hilfe beim Lesen und Korrigieren der Korrekturbogen; dem Indiana Research Computing Center für die Benutzung seiner Komputer bei der Vorbereitung der verschiedenen Register; und Jaakko Ahokas, John Krueger, Samuel Rosenberg, Cornelis Van Schooneveld, Elaine Hagstrom und A. Pfeffer, die alle wertvolle Quellen und unentbehrliche Aufmunterung beisteurten.

ROSE NASH

San Juan, Puerto Rico
Februar, 1968

PRÉFACE

Le présent ouvrage a été conçu spécifiquement pour rendre accessibles au linguiste les travaux de savants étrangers. Le choix des termes a été fait selon l'importance, la fréquence d'usage et les difficultés de traduction potentielles. Nous avons consulté un nombre considérable de sources diverses dont les plus utiles ont été énumérées sur les pages 385. La terminologie de base a été choisie dans des dictionnaires techniques déjà existants, dans des grammaires de référence, des manuels d'enseignement des langues et enfin dans l'index des manuels de linguistique générale. Nous y avons ajouté un vocabulaire de termes mi-techniques mais d'usage spécialisé et que nous avons recueilli en dépouillant plusieurs milliers de pages dans des ouvrages qui relèvent de la linguistique et en faisant une comparaison minutieuse entre les versions traduites d'importants ouvrages et les textes originaux. Enfin des dictionnaires bilingues et sémantiques ont été étudiés page par page à la recherche de vocabulaire supplémentaire utile.

En recueillant ce matériel, nous avons considéré les catégories suivantes: terminologie de la linguistique historique et de la dialectologie, terminologie de la grammaire traditionnelle, terminologie moderne d'usage courant, sources de monuments historiques linguistiques, anatomie de l'appareil phonatoire, classification articulatoire et acoustique, classification culturelle et typologique, autres formes de communication que le langage, désignations de modèles théoriques de la langue, noms de disciplines apparentées, noms des langues principales, concepts ayant rapport avec l'étude des langues, vocabulaire général d'usage fréquent en littérature linguistique, signes et symboles utilisés dans la description linguistique, styles du discours, idiotismes, expressions du langage quotidien et d'autres éléments du vocabulaire courant employés dans des contextes spéciaux. Enfin il a été relevé des termes pour le linguiste spécialiste en matière d'éducation, de calculatrices électroniques, de publication, et d'équipement enrégistreur.

Plus de 5000 articles anglais paraissent dans cet ouvrage. La liste complète, y compris les termes équivalents en russe, en allemand et en français, remonte à environ 23000 termes. La plupart de ces termes ont été relevés directement des ouvrages divers et une sorte de normalisation a été suivie pour réaliser une uniformité de forme. Une brève explication du sens ou de l'usage est donnée pour certains termes qui n'ont pas été établis dans l'une ou l'autre des langues. Pour certains d'autres encore de cette même catégorie, les linguistes collaborateurs, eux-mêmes, ont suggéré des expressions convenables, lesquelles ont été ajoutées à l'ouvrage et apparaissent entre parenthèses angulaires (⟨ ⟩).

La forme citée dans chaque article est, en ce qui concerne le nombre, celle qui est la plus courante dans les ouvrages consultés

L'explication grammaticale est limitée au nombre (le pluriel étant indiqué spécifiquement), au genre (indiqué pour tous les termes français, et pour ces termes russes et allemands où le genre n'est pas reconnaissable à la forme d'un adjectif qui accompagne un nom) et aux parties du discours (que nous identifions, au besoin, dans les articles anglais et que nous supposons être les mêmes pour les autres langues, sauf si autrement indiquées). Les adjectifs indépendemment relevés se trouvent sous forme du singulier masculin en russe et en français, et sous la forme sans flexion en allemand. Les verbes russes sont donnés à l'aspect imperfectif, à moins que l'usage n'exige le perfectif.

Les homonymes anglais sont présentés individuellement avec des définitions entre parenthèses, vu l'acception distincte donnée à chacun des termes. Pour les articles anglais à plusieurs équivalents en langues étrangères, le terme d'usage le plus courant est donné en premier.

En allemand et en russe, les termes autochtones tendent à être remplacés par des termes internationaux d'origine grecque ou latine, et, dans plusieurs cas, ceux-là sont devenus à peu près hors d'usage; malgré ce fait, ces termes ont été inscrits dans cet ouvrage pour faciliter la recherche ou la référence.

Il est important de tenir compte, comme il en est toujours le cas dans l'usage des dictionnaires, de la multiplicité des équivalents qui peuvent correspondre à un seul terme anglais mais qui ne s'équivalent nécessairement pas entre eux du point de vue de la définition ou de l'usage hors de contexte.

A l'exception de la liste des traits distinctifs (D 203), tous les articles anglais sont en ordre alphabétique sans tenir compte du groupement sémantique. La première lettre dans chaque code de référence est identique à la première lettre du terme anglais correspondant dans la partie principale de l'ouvrage. Par exemple, le mot russe *slovo* prend le code W 034, correspondant au mot anglais *word* avec le même code.

Pour rendre l'ouvrage encore plus pratique, certaines locutions formées d'adjectifs et de noms et certains termes composés ont été groupés, en plus de leur apparition dans les listes alphabétiques de l'index, sous les équivalents russes et allemands pour les termes suivants: consonne, voyelle, son, phrase, langue, parole, modèle. L'ordre usuel des mots en français a rendu ce groupement automatique pour l'index français.

Le lexicographe qui se spécialise dans un domaine moderne se trouve en face d'un nombre de problèmes difficiles; parmi les plus difficiles, il y a le probléme d'un vocabulaire technique qui ne fait que s'amplifier. Ce vocabulaire, pourtant, ne se développe pas à la même vitesse ou dans la même direction pour toutes les langues. Il faut souligner que ce lexique, sous le format actuel, est destiné à être un ouvrage plutôt utile qu'approfondi. Ainsi, les linguistes, dont le domaine est les recherches d'intérêt tout spécial, trouveront cet ouvrage incomplet sinon insuffisant dans le choix des termes donnés. Il a été nécessaire de s'abstenir de relever des termes récemment innovés ou encore des idées nouvelles qui n'ont, pour ainsi dire, pas encore franchi l'obstacle linguistique; et même s'ils l'ont franchi, l'élmination de ces termes de ce lexique a été nécessaire pour n'ajouter que les termes les plus essentiels.

Le présent ouvrage n'est qu'une introduction à une oeuvre en préparation, oeuvre plus complète et plus détaillée, englobant des données en langue espagnole, et qui sera publiée à une date ultérieure. Nous invitons nos lecteurs à soumettre leurs suggestions pour l'inclusion dans l'oeuvre en préparation.

Plusieurs amis et collègues ont contribué au présent ouvrage. Nous remercions en particulier MM. Pierre Cintas de l'Université Harvard et Jens Peters de l'Université de Kiel, qui ont collaboré aux premières étapes du matériel; M. Morris Halle de l'Institut de Technologie de Massachussets d'avoir vérifié l'exactitude de la traduction des traits distinctifs; M. Wolfgang Wölck de l'Université d'Indiana d'avoir relevé plusieurs des termes allemands; M. Adolf Hieke et Mme. Genevieve Benjamin de l'Université Inter American d'avoir pris part dans la vérification des épreuves; le Research Computing Center de l'Université de Indiana d'avoir mis à notre disposition l'usage des appareils nécessaires pour la préparation des index, et MM. Jaakko Ahokas, John Krueger, Samuel Rosenberg, Cornelis Van Schooneveld, A. Pfeffer, et Mme. Elaine Hagstrom, qui ont tous offert d'importants renseignements et surtout nous ont soutenu par leur encouragement inlassable.

Rose Nash

San Juan, Puerto Rico
Février, 1968

BIOGRAPHICAL NOTES

MERVIN ALLEYNE, a native of Trinidad, is Associate Professor in the Department of Spanish at the University of West Indies, where he received his Bachelors Degree in Honors French. His graduate work was done in France at the Institut de Linguistique Romane under the direction of Monseigneur P. Gardette, and he completed his doctorate at the University of Strasbourg. He has been a Research Fellow at Yale University under a grant from the Rockefeller Foundation, and during 1965-66 served as Exchange Professor in Linguistics at Indiana University. His published works include a monograph, *Les Noms des Vents en Galloroman,* a teaching manual of the Creole language of Sierra Leone, which he co-authored, and several papers on his chief research interests, bilingualism and language contacts.

GERD FRAENKEL is Associate Professor of Linguistics at Peabody College in Nashville, Tennessee. He was born in Germany and received his early education in Mainz. After emigration to Israel he continued his studies at Hebrew University, receiving the M.A. Degree in Languages and Pedagogy. In 1956 he came to the United States and, after earning the Ph.D. Degree in Linguistics at Indiana University in 1961, joined the faculty of the University of Pittsburgh. He is author of several books and articles, including a high school text series entitled *New Aspects of Language,* a textbook on Israel, several papers on international and constructed languages, and linguistic terminology in Turkish and Hebrew. He has taught English, German, Hungarian, and Hebrew, and done research in a variety of uncommon languages. During 1961-65 he was Staff Linguist for Applied Hebrew Linguistics at the NDEA Summer Institute for Secondary School Teachers at Yeshiva University.

ROSE NASH, a native Chicagoan, earned degrees in Music at Northwestern University and in Soviet Area Studies at Middlebury College before entering the field of Linguistics in 1960. After several years as supervisory linguist with the Indiana University Intensive Language Center directing the teaching of Russian, she resumed graduate work at Indiana University, and completed the Ph.D. Degree in Linguistics with dissertation research on Turkish intonation. She was associated with the Indiana University Research Center in Anthropology, Folklore, and Linguistics on the preparation for publication of *Current Trends in Linguistics, Volume I: Soviet and East European Linguistics,* and also compiled the Index of Terms for *Volume III: Theoretical Foundations.* She has done research in the Soviet Union and in England, and has held several NDEA Title VI Fellowships for the study of modern languages. During 1966 she served as staff linguist at the Foreign Service Institute in Washington, D.C. At the present time she is Assistant Professor of Linguistics at Inter American University in San Juan, Puerto Rico.

STEPHEN SOUDAKOFF was born in China of Russian parents, and came to the United States in 1939. He received the Bachelors Degree in Far East Studies at the University of California in Berkeley, and the Masters Degree in Slavic Lanuages and Literatures at Indiana University. He has taught Russian at the University of California, the Army Language School in Monterey, and Indiana University, and has done extensive work as a technical translator. In 1962 he was selected as a participant in the International Seminar for Teachers of Russian held at Moscow University, where he met with leading Soviet linguists and language specialists. In 1962-67 he was senior administrative tour leader for Russian language summer study groups from the Indiana University Slavic Workshop. He is presently completing doctoral studies in Slavic Linguistics at Indiana University.

БИОГРАФИЧЕСКИЕ ЗАМЕТКИ

МЕРВИН АЛЛЕЙН, уроженец Тринидада. Закончил Вест-Индийский Университет. Специализировался во французском языке. Работал в аспирантуре во франции в Институте Романской Лингвистики под руководством II. Гардет. Докторскую степень получил в Страсбургском Университете. Работал Научным сотрудником при Ейльском Университете. В 1965-1966 годах преподавал в Индианском Университете. Был представителем группы профессоров по линии обмена научными работниками. В настоящее время-профессор факультета испанского языка Вест Индийского Университета (Ямайка). Профессор Аллейн является автором монографии *Les noms des vents en galloroman;* учебного пособия креольского языка

Сиерра-Леоне и ряда работ по специальности, а именно: двуязычие и языковой контакт.

ГЕРД ФРЕНКЕЛЬ. профессор лингвистики Пибоди Коллелжа в Нашвиле (штат Теннеси). Родился в Германии; начальное образование получил в Мейнце. В Израиле продолжал образование в Еврейском Университете, где ему была присвоена магистерская степень в области языкознания и педагогики. С 1956 года проживает в США. В 1961 году защитил докторскую диссертацию по лингвистике в Индианском Университете. Преподаватель Питсбургского Университета. Профессор Френкель является автором ряда статеи и книг, включая учебник на тему страны Израиля, серия научных памфлетов для средных школ под названием *New Aspects of Language,* и ряда статей из области его специализации — международные и составленные языки, лингвистическая терминология турецкого и еврейского яеыков. В прошлом профессор Френкель преподавал английский, немецкий, венгерский и еврейский языки параллельно работая в области малоизученных языков. В 1961-1965 годах работал штатным лингвистом прикладной лингвистики еврейского языка на летних курсах в Ешивском Университете (Нью-Йорк).

РОЗА НЗШ, уроженка города Чикаго. Окончила консерваторию Нордвестерн-ского Университета. Магистерскую степень получила в Мидлберском Колледже. Специализировалась в области советологии. Работая в качестве ответственного лингвиста на курсах ускоренного изучения русского языка при Индианском Университете, начала изучать теоретическую лингвистику и алтайские языки. Получив государственную стипендию для изучения языков успешно защитила докторскую диссертацию на тему *Turkish Intonation: An Instrumental Study* на кафедре лингвистики при Индианском Университете. Р. Нэш работала научным сотрудником Института Антрополгии, Фольклора и Лингвистики при Индианском Университете по подготовке *Current Trends 1: Soviet and East European Linguistics,* составила индекс к третьему тому *Theoretical Foundations.* В связи с научной работой Р. Нэш ездила в СССР. В 1966 году, как специалистка по лингвистике была причислена к школе Министерства Иностранных Дел. В настоящее время преподает на Лингвистическом факультете Меж-Американского Университета в Сан Хуан (о. Пуэрто Рико).

С. СУДАКОВ, родился в Китае. С 1939 года постоянно проживает в США. Окончил Калифорнийский Университет(Берклей). Специализировался в области дальневосточных наук. Магистерскую степень получил в Индианском Университете по славянским языкам и литературе. Опытный переводчик технической литературы с многолетним стажем. Преподаватель русского языка в Калифорнийском и Индианском Университетах. В 1962 году был участником семинара русского языка в Московском Университете для преподавателей зарубежных стран. В 1962-67 годах был руководителем экскурсии по Советскому Союзу группы студентов, изучавших русский язык на летних курсах в Индианском Университете. В настоящее время заканчивает работу на докторскую степень по славянским языкам.

BIOGRAPHISCHE ANMERKUNGEN

MERVIN ALLEYNE aus Trinidad ist Associate Professor in der spanischen Fakultät an der University of West Indies, an der er seinen Bachelors Degree in Honors French erhielt. Im Anschluss daran studierte er in Frankreich am Institut de Linguistique Romane unter der Leitung von P. Gardette; er erwarb seinen Doktortitel an der Universität Strasbourg. Er war wissenschaftlicher Assistent an der Yale University mit Unterstützung der Rockefeller Stiftung. 1965/66 wirkte er als Austauschprofessor fur Linguistik an der Indiana University. Zu seinen Veröffentlichungen gehört die Monographie *"Les Noms des Vents en Galloroman,"* ein Lehrbuch fur die kreolische Sprache in Sierra Leone, das er mitverfasste, und mehrere Aufsätze über sein Hauptforschungsgebiet, Zweisprachigkeit und Sprachberührungen.

GERD FRAENKEL ist Associate Professor für Linguistik am Peabody College in Nashville/Tenn. Er wurde in Deutschland geboren und begann seine akademische Ausbildung in Mainz. Nachdem er nach Israel ausgewandert war, setzte er sein Studium an der Hebräischen Universität fort und erhielt dort den Masters Titel für Sprachen und Pädagogik. 1956 kam er in die Vereinigten Staaten und erwarb 1961 seinen Doktortitel in Linguistik an der Indiana University; danach trat er der Fakultät der University of Pittsburgh bei. Er hat mehrere Bücher und Aufsätze verfasst, darunter eine Mittelschulbücherreihe unter dem Namen *"New Aspects of Language,"* ein Lehrbuch über Israel und mehrere Artikel über sein Spezialgebiet, internationale und konstruierte Sprachen, und linguistische Terminologie in Türkisch und Hebräisch. Er hat Englisch, Deutsch, Ungarisch und Hebräisch unterrichtet und an einer Anzahl ungeläufiger Sprachen Forschungsarbeiten betrieben. Von 1961 bis 1965 unterrichtete er angewandte hebräische Linguistik im NDEA Sommerinstitut für Lehrer höherer Schulen an der Yeshiva University.

ROSE NASH stammt aus Chicago und legte Examen in Musik an der Northwestern University und in Soviet Area Studies am Middlebury College ab, bevor sie sich der Linguistik zuwandte. Nachdem sie mehrere Jahre als Linguistin den Russischunterricht im Indiana University Intensive Language Center geleitet hatte, setzte sie ihre Promotionsarbeit an der Indiana University fort und schloss ihren Doktortitel mit einer Dissertation über Intonation der türkischen Sprache ab.

Sie war Mitarbeiterin im Indiana University Research Center for Anthropology, Folklore and Linguistics bei der Vorbereitung der Veröffentlichung: *"Current Trends, Band I: Soviet and East European Linguistics";* ferner stellte sie das Terminiverzeichnis für Band III: *"Theoretical Foundations"* auf. Sie betrieb wissenschaftliche Studien in der Sowjetunion und England, und hat mehrere NDEA Title VI Stipendien für das Sprachenstudium erhalten. 1966 trat sie als Linguistin in das Foreign Service Institute des Äussenministeriums der Vereinigten Staaten ein. Zur Zeit ist sie Assistant Professor der Linguistik an der Inter American University in San Juan, Puerto Rico.

STEPHEN SOUDAKOFF wurde in China als Sohn russischer Eltern geboren und kam 1939 in die Vereinigten Staaten. Er erhielt den Bachelors Titel für Far East Studies an der University of California in Berkeley und erwarb den Masters Titel für slavische Sprachen und Literatur an der Indiana University. Er unterrichtete Russisch an der University of California, an der Army Language School in Monterey und an der Indiana University und hat sehr häufig als Fachübersetzer gearbeitet. 1962 wurde er als Teilnehmer für das internationale Russischlehrerseminar ausgewählt, das an der Universität Moskau stattfand. Dort traf er führende sowjetische Linguisten und Sprachspezialisten. Von 1962 bis 1967 war er Exkursionsleiter für Sommerexkursionen für die russische Sprache von dem slavischen Arbeitskreis der Indiana University. Im Augenblick ist er dabei, seine Doktorarbeit für slavische Linguistik an der Indiana University abzuschliessen.

NOTES BIOGRAPHIQUES

MERVIN ALLEYNE, né à Trinidad est Professeur-Adjoint au Départment d'Espagnol de l'Université des Antilles, où d'ailleurs il a obtenu sa licence-ès-Lettres avec grade 'Honoris Causa en Français. Il a ensuite complété ses études supérieures à l'Institut de Linguistique Romane en France sous la direction de Mgr. P. Gardette. C'est à l'Université de Strasbourg qu'il a obtenu le Doctorat.

Muni d'une bourse de la Rockefeller Foundation, Alleyne a fait des recherches avancées à l'Université de Yale; et au cours de l'année 1965-1966, il a été Professeur de Linguistique à l'Université d'Indiana (échange professorial).

Les ouvrages de M. Alleyne, comprennent, entre autres, une monographie intitulée *Les Noms des Vents en Galloroman,* et un manuel d'enseignement du Créole de la Sierra Léone écrit en collaboration. Il est aussi l'auteur de plusieurs articles sur ses recherches principales auxquelles il porte un intérêt tout spécial: le bilingisme et le contact des langues.

GERD FRAENKEL est Professeur-Adjoint de Linguistique à Peabody College à Nashville, Tennessee. Il est né en Allemagne et a fait ses études à Mainz. Ayant émigré en Israël, il a poursuivi ses études à l'Université Hebreuse et a obtenu le M. A. en Langues et Pédagogie. Il est arrivé aux États-Unis en 1956 et il a réçu le Doctorat-ès-Lettres en Linguistique de l'Université d'Indiana en 1961. A la suite, il s'est joint au corps enseignant de l'Université de Pittsburgh.

M. Fraenkel est l'auteur de plusiers livres et articles, y compris une série de manuels intitulée *Aspects Nouveaux du Langage* à l'usage de l'enseignement secondaire, un manuel sur Israél et divers articles qui se rapportent à des sujets d'intérêt spécial pour lui: Langues Internationales et Auxiliaires Construites et la terminologie linguistique en Turc et Hébreu. Il a enseigné l'Anglais, l'Allemand, l'Hongrois et le Hébreu tout en poursuivant des recherches dans diverses langues peu connues.

Entre 1961 et 1965, Fraenkel a été Linguiste de Groupe pour la Linguistique Appliquée du Hébreu au Congrès des Maîtres d'Écoles Sécondaires de la N.D.E.A. (Organisation gouvernementale des États-Unis) tenue à l'Université de Yéshiva (Israél).

ROSE NASH est née à Chicago et a reçu des diplômes en Musique à Northwestern University (Illinois) et en Étude des Affaires Soviétiques à Middlebury Collège (Vermont) avant de poursuivre ses études de la Linguistique.

Madame Nash a été pendant plusieurs années Linguiste-Administrateur au Centre de l'Étude Intensive des Langues de l'Université d'Indiana (Intensive Language Center, I. U.), chargée de l'enseignement du Russe. Elle a repris des études supérieures a l'Université d'Indiana et a obtenu le Doctorat ci-après. Le sujet de sa dissertation a été *Turkish Intonation: An Instrumental Study.*

Madame Nash a entrepris, en collaboration avec le Centre de Recherches d'Anthropologie de Folk-lore et de Linguistique de la même Université, la préparation de la publication de *Current Trends in Linguistics,* Volume I: *Soviet and East European Linguistics;* de même pour l'Index des Termes pour Volume III: *Theoretical Foundations.* Elle a fait de recherches dans l'Union Sovietique et en Angleterre et a tenu plusieurs bourses pour l'étude des langues modernes.

En 1966, elle a fait partie du corps enseignant de l'Institut du Service Étranger du Départment d'État (FSI) à Washington, D.C.

A présent, elle est Professeur-Adjoint de Linguistique à l'Université Interaméricaine à San Juan, Puerto Rico.

STEPHEN SOUDAKOFF est né en Chine de parents russes et s'est établi aux États-Unis à partir de 1939. Il a fait ses études sur les Affaires de l'Extrême Orient et a obtenu la Licence de l'Université de California à Berkeley, et le M.A. du Département des Langues et Littératures Slaves de l'Université d'Indiana. Il a enseigné le Russe successivement à l'Université de California, à l'École Militaire des Langues à Monterey (California) et enfin à l'Université d'Indiana. Il a traduit un grand nombres de travaux en matière technique. En 1962, M. Soudakoff a fait partie en tant que Participant du Séminar (Réunion) International(e) de l'Instruction du Russe à l'Université de Moscou. Au cours de ces réunions, il a fait la connaissance des principaux spécialistes de langues et linguistes Soviétiques. Entre 1962 et 1967 il a été administrateur pour l'étude de la langue russe pour les groupes d'été des étudiants des Études Slaves de l'Université d'Indiana.

M. Soudakoff se prépare en ce moment à compléter ses études du Doctorat en Linguistique Slave à l'Université d'Indiana.

ABBREVIATIONS / СОКРАЩЕНИЯ / ABKÜRZUNGEN

In an entry of more than one word in length, the abbreviation refers to the head word of the construction.

В многословных выражениях сокращения относятся к главному слову.

Für Stichworte, die mehr als ein Wort umfassen, bezieht sich die Abkürzung auf das Kernwort.

Notez bien que l'abréviation se rapporte au mot-souche quand il s'agit de plus d'un mot dans une entrée donnée.

adj. adjective / прилагательное / Adjektiv / adjectif
adv. adverb / наречие / Adverb / adverbe
f. *feminine gender* / *женский род* / *Femininum* / *féminin*
m. *masculine gender* / *мужской род* / *Maskulinum* / *masculin*
n. *neuter gender* / *средний род* / *Neutrum* / *neutre*
n. noun / существительное / Substantiv / substantif
pl. plural / множественное число / Plural / pluriel
s. *masculine or feminine gender* /
     мужской или женский род /
     Maskulinum oder Femininum /
     masculin ou féminin
sg. singular / единственное число / Singular / singulier
v. verb / глагол / Verb / verbe

MULTILINGUAL LEXICON OF LINGUISTICS AND PHILOLOGY

МНОГОЯЗЫЧНЫЙ ЛЕКСИКОН ЛИНГВИСТИКИ И ФИЛОЛОГИИ

MEHRSPRACHIGES LEXIKON DER SPRACHWISSENSCHAFTEN

LEXIQUE MULTILINGUE DE LA LINGUISTIQUE ET DE LA PHILOLOGIE

THE LEXICON / ЛЕКСИКОН / DAS LEXIKON / LE LEXIQUE

No.	English	Russian	German	French

A

No.	English	Russian	German	French
001	A B C book	букварь, *m.*	Fibel, *f.*	abécédaire, *m.*
002	abbreviated speech (style)	телеграфный стиль	Telegrammstil, *m.*/ abgekürzte Redeweise	langage télégraphique, *m.*
003	abbreviation, n.	сокращение, *n.*	Abkürzung, *f.*	abbréviation, *f.*
004	ability, n.	способность, *f.*	Fähigkeit, *f.*	capacité, *f.*
005	ablative case	аблатив, *m.*	Ablativ, *m.*	ablatif, *m.*
006	ablaut, n.	аблаут, *m.*	Ablaut, *m.*/Abstufung, *f.*	apophonie, *f.*
007	abrupt onset	сильный приступ	fester Einsatz/ scharfer Einsatz	attaque dure, *f.*/attaque forte, *f.*/début abrupt, *m.*
008	abruptive consonants, pl.	мгновенные согласные, pl.	Momentanlaute, *m.*, pl.	consonnes momentanées, *f.*, pl.
009	absence, n.	отсутствие, *n.*	Fehlen, *n.*/ Nichtvorhandensein, *n.*	absence, *f.*
010	absence of a grammatical category	отсутствие грамматической катагории, *n.*	Nichtvorhandensein einer grammatischen Kategorie, *n.*	absence de catégorie grammaticale, *f.*
011	absence of articles	отсутствие артикля, *n.*	Artikellosigkeit, *f.*	absence de l'article, *f.*
012	absence of gender	отсутствие рода, *n.*	Genuslosigkeit, *f.*	absence de genre, *f.*
013	absence of inflection	отсутствие флексии, *n.*	Flexionslosigkeit, *f.*	absence de flexion, *f.*
014	absence of prefixes	отсутствие приставок, *n.*	Präfixlosigkeit, *f.*	absence de préfixes, *f.*

No.	English	Russian	German	French
015	absence of suffixes	отсутствие суфф-иксов, *n.*	Suffixlosigkeit, *f.*	absence de suffixes, *f.*
016	absolute case	абсолютный падеж	absoluter Kasus	cas absolu, *m.*
017	absolute construction	абсолютная конструкция	absolute Konstruktion	construction absolue, *f.*
018	absolute final	абсолютный исход	absoluter Auslaut/Schluss, *m.*	finale absolue, *f.*
019	absolute form	абсолютная форма	absolute Form	forme absolue, *f.*
020	absolute pitch (of sound)	абсолютная высота тона	absolute Tonhöhe	hauteur absolue, *f.*
021	absolute pitch (of person)	абсолютный слух	absolutes Gehör	oreille absolue, *f./*ouïe parfaite, *f.*
022	absolute position	абсолютное положение	absolute Stellung	position absolue, *f.*
023	absorption, n.	абсорбция, *f./*поглощение, *n.*	Absorption, *f.*	absorption, *f.*
024	abstract, v.	делать выдержки	resumieren/zusammenfassen	résumér
025	abstract, n.	конспект, *m./*резюме, *n.*	Abriss, *m./*Resumee, *n./*Zusammenfassung, *f.*	abrégé, *m./*extrait, *m./*résumé, *m.*
026	abstract, adj.	отвлеченный	abstrakt	abstrait
027	abstract noun	имя существительное отвлеченное	Abstraktum, *n./*Begriffswort, *n.*	nom abstrait, *m.*
028	abstraction, n.	абстракция, *f.*	Abstraktion, *f.*	abstraction, *f.*
029	academic year	учебный год	akademisches Jahr/Schuljahr, *n.*	année scolaire, *f.*
030	acceleration, n.	ускорение, *n.*	Beschleunigung, *f.*	accélération, *f.*
031	accent, n.	акцент, *m.*	Akzent, *m.*	accent, *m.*
032	accent shift	перемещение ударения, *n.*	Akzentverschiebung, *f./*Akzentumschwung, *f.*	déplacement de l'accent, *m.*
033	accentual unit	ударная единица	Akzenteinheit, *f.*	unité accentuelle, *f.*

No.	ENGLISH	RUSSIAN	GERMAN	FRENCH
034	accentuation, n.	акцентуация, *f.*	Akzentuierung, *f.*/ Betonung, *f.*	accentuation, *f.*
035	acceptable, adj.	приемлемый	annehmbar	acceptable
036	acceptable to a native speaker, adj.	приемлемый для носителя языка	annehmbar für einen Sprecher der Muttersprache	acceptable à un locuteur /acceptable à un sujet parlant du pays
037	accessory word	служебное слово	Hilfswort, *n.*/ Nebenwort, *n.*	mot accessoire, *m.*
038	accidence, n.	морфология, *f.*	Formenlehre, *f.*/ Morphologie, *f.*	flexion, *f.*
039	accident, n.	случайность, *f.*	Zufall, *m.*	chance, *f.*
040	accidental, adj.	случайный	zufällig	accidentel/fortuit
041	accompaniment, n.	сопровождение, *n.*	Begleitung, *f.*	accompagnement, *m.*
042	accomplishment, n.	достижение, *n.*	Erreichung, *f.*/ Vollendung, *f.*	réalisation, *f.*
043	accountability, n.	объяснимость, *f.*	Erklärbarkeit, *f.*	degré de comprehension, *m.*
044	accretion, n.	приращение, *n.*	Wachstum, *n.*	accroissement, *m.*
045	acculturation, n.	культурная ассимиляция	Akkulturation, *f.*/ kulturelle Anpassung	assimilation culturelle, *f.*
046	accuracy, n.	точность, *f.*/ правильность, *f.*	Genauigkeit, *f.*	exactitude, *f.*
047	accusative case	винительный падеж	Akkusativ, *m.*/Wenfall, *m.*/vierter Fall	accusatif, *m.*
048	acknowledgments, n., pl.	признательность, *f.*	Anerkennung(en), *f.* (pl.) dankende Erwähnung, *f.*	reconnaissance, *f.*
049	acoustic, adj.	акустический/ слуховой	akustisch	acoustique
050	acoustic analysis	акустический анализ	akustische Analyse	analyse acoustique, *f.*
051	acoustic classification	акустическая классификация	akustische Klassifizierung	classement acoustique, *m.*

No.	English	Russian	German	French
052	acoustic effect	акустический эффект	akustische Wirkung/ Klangwirkung, *f.*/ Schallwirkung, *f.*	effet acoustique, *m.*
053	acoustic features, pl.	акустические признаки, *m.*, pl.	akustische Eigenschaften, *f.*, pl.	traits acoustiques, *m.*, pl.
054	acoustic image	акустический образ	Lautbild, *n.*	image acoustique, *f.*
055	acoustic phonetics	акустическая фонетика	akustische Phonetik	phonétique acoustique, *f.*
056	acoustic signal	акустический сигнал	akustiches Signal	signal acoustique, *m.*
057	acoustics, n.	акустика, *f.*	Akustik, *f.*/Schallehre, *f.*	acoustique, *f.*
058	acquaintance, n.	знакомство, *n.*	Bekanntschaft, *f.*	connaissance, *f.*
059	acquired, adj.	приобретенный	erlernt/erworben	acquis/appris
060	acquired behavior	приобретенное поведение	erlerntes Verhalten	comportement acquis, *m.*
061	acquired knowledge	приобретенное знание	erlerntes Wissen/ erworbenes Wissen	connaissance acquise, *f.*
062	acquisition, n.	приобретение, *n.*	Erwerbung, *f.*	acquisition, *f.*
063	acronym, n.	акроним, *m.*	Akronym, *n.*	acronyme, *m.*/ abbréviation, *f.*
064	acrophony, n.	акрофония, *f.*	Akrophonie, *f.*	acrophonie, *f.*
065	acrostic, n.	акростих, *m.*	Akrostichon, *n.*	acrostiche, *m.*
066	action, n.	действие, *n.*	Aktion, *f.*/Handlung, *f.*	action, *f.*
067	action noun	имя действия, *n.*	Aktionssubstantiv, *n.*	nom d'action, *m.*
068	action verb	глагол действия, *m.*	Tatverb(um), *n.*	verbe d'action, *m.*
069	active, adj.	активный/ действующий	aktiv/tätig	actif
070	active participle	причастие действительного залога, *n.*	aktives Partizip	participe actif, *m.*
071	active sentence	активное предложение	Aktivsatz, *m.*	phrase à la voix active, *f.*
072	active vocabulary	активный словарь	aktiver Wortschatz	vocabulaire actif, *m.*

No.	English	Russian	German	French
073	active voice	действительный залог	Aktiv, *n.*	voix active, *f.*
074	actor, n.	деятель, *m.*	Agens, *n.*	agent, *m.*
075	actual, adj.	актуальный/ действительный	tatsächlich	réel
076	actualization, n.	актуализация, *f.*/ реализация, *f.*/ фонетическая форма	Realisierung, *f.*/ Verwirklichung, *f.*	réalisation, *f.*
077	acuity of hearing	острота слуха, *f.*	Gehörsschärfe, *f.*	acuité d'ouïe, *f.*
078	acute accent	акут/острый тон	Akut, *m.*	accent aigu, *m.*
079	ad, n.	объявление, *n.*	Anzeige, *f.*	petite annonce, *f.*
080	adage, n.	поговорка, *f.*	Sprichwort, *n.*/ Maxime, *f.*	adage, *m.*
081	adaptation, n.	приспособление, *n.*	Anpassung, *f.*	adaptation, *f.*
082	adaptability, n.	приспособляемость, *f.*	Anpassungsfähigkeit, *f.*	faculté d'adaptation, *f.*
083	addition, n.	прибавление, *n.*/ присоединение, *n.*/ сложение, *n.*	Hinzufügung, *f.*/ Beifügung, *f.*/ Zusatz, *m.*	addition, *f.*
084	addition sign	знак сложения, *m.*	Additionszeichen, *n.*	signe d'addition, *m.*
085	address (location), n.	адрес, *m.*	Adresse, *f.*/Anschrift, *f.*	adresse, *f.*
086	address (to person), n.	обращение, *n.*	Anrede, *f.*	allocution, *f.*
087	adequacy, n.	адекватность, *f.*/ соразмерность, *f.*	Angemessenheit, *f.*/ Zulänglichkeit, *f.*	suffisance, *f.*/ exactitude, *f.*
088	adjacent, adj.	соседний/ смежный/ соприкасающийся/ прилегающий	benachbart/ danebenstehend	adjacent/contigu
089	adjectival, adj.	прилагательный	adjektivisch	adjectival
090	adjective, n.	прилагательное, *n.*	Adjektiv(um), *n.*/ Eigenschaftswort, *n.*	adjectif, *m.*
091	adjective used as noun	субстантированное прилагательное	substantiviertes Adjektiv	adjectif substantif
092	adjectively, adjectivally, adv.	как прилагательное	adjektivisch	adjectivement

No.	ENGLISH	RUSSIAN	GERMAN	FRENCH
093	adjoining, adj.	соседний	benachbart	attenant
094	adjunct, n.	определение, *n.*/ обстоятельственное слово	Attribut, *m.*/Zusatz, *n.*	mot accessoire, *m.*/ complément, *m.*
095	adjunction, n.	присовокупление, *n.*	Beifügung, *f.*/Zusatz, *m.*	adjonction, *f.*
096	adnominal, adj.	приименный	nominal	adnominal
097	adoption, n.	принятие, *n.*	Annahme, *f.*/ Übernahme, *f.*	adoption, *f.*
098	admissible, adj.	приемлемый/ допустимый	annehmbar/zulässig	acceptable
099	adolescent speech	язык подростков, *m.*	Jugendsprache, *f.*	langage des adolescents, *m.*
100	adult education	обучение взрослых, *n.*	Erwachsenenbildung, *f.*	enseignement post-scolaire, *m.*
101	adult speech	язык взрослых, *m.*	Erwachsenensprache, *f.*	langage adulte, *m.*
102	advantage, n.	преимущество, *n.*	Vorteil, *m.*/Vorzug, *m.*	avantage, *m.*
103	adverb, n.	наречие, *n.*	Adverb(ium), *n.*/ Umstandswort, *n.*	adverbe, *m.*
104	adverbal (from verb), adj.	приглагольный	verbal	adverbal
105	adverbial (of adverb), adj.	наречный	adverbial/adverbiell	adverbial
106	adverbial clause	обстоятельственное предложение	Adverbialsatz, *m.*	proposition adverbiale, *f.*
107	adverbial modifier	обстоятельство, *n.*	adverbiale Bestimmung/ Umstandsbestimmung, *f.*	complément circonstanciel, *m.*
108	adverbial modifier of cause	обстоятельство причины, *n.*	kausale Umstandsbestimmung	complément circonstanciel de cause, *m.*
109	adverbial modifier of manner	обстоятельство образа действия, *n.*	adverbiale Bestimmung der Art und Weise	complément circonstanciel de manière, *m.*
110	adverbial modifier of place	обстоятельство места, *n.*	adverbiale Bestimmung des Ortes	complément circonstanciel de lieu, *m.*

No.	ENGLISH	RUSSIAN	GERMAN	FRENCH
111	adverbial modifier of purpose	обстоятельство цели, *n.*	adverbiale Bestimmung des Zwecks/finale adverbiale Bestimmung	complément circonstanciel de but, *m.*
112	adverbial modifier of time	обстоятельство времени, *n.*	adverbiale Bestimmung der Zeit	complément circonstanciel de temps, *m.*
113	adverbial phrase	обстоятельственный оборот	adverbialer Ausdruck	locution adverbiale, *f.*
114	adverbially, adv.	как наречие	adverbial	adverbialement
115	advertisement, n.	реклама, *f.*	Reklame, *f.*/Anzeige, *f.*	annonce, *f.*/réclame, *f.*
116	advertising style, advertising language	рекламный стиль/ рекламный язык	Reklamesprache, *f.*	langage publicitaire, *m.*/ style publicitaire, *m.*
117	aesthetic, adj.	эстетический	ästhetisch	esthétique
118	aesthetics, n.	эстетика, *f.*	Ästhetik, *f.*	esthétique, *f.*
119	affective speech	аффективная речь	affektive Rede/ gefühlsbetonte Bede	langage affectif, *m.*
120	affective stress	аффективное ударение /эмоциональное ударение	Affektbetonung, *f.*	accent affectif, *m.*
121	affinity, n.	родственность, *f.*/ близость, *f.*	Affinität, *f.*/ Verwandtschaft, *f.*	affinité, *f.*
122	affirmation, n.	утверждение, *n.*	Bejahung, *f.*/ Bestätigung, *f.*	affirmation, *f.*
123	affirmative sentence	утвердительное предложение	bejahender Satz	phrase affirmative, *f.*
124	affix, n.	аффикс, *m.*	Affix, *n.*	affixe, *m.*
125	affixation, n.	аффиксация, *f.*	Hinzufügung von Affixen, *f.*	affixation, *f.*
126	affixing languages, pl.	аффиксирующие языки, *m.,* pl.	affixierende Sprachen, *f.,* pl.	langues affixantes, *f.,* pl.
127	affricate consonants, pl.	аффрикаты, *f.,* pl./ смычно-щелевые согласные, *m.,* pl.	Affrikaten, *f.,* pl.	consonnes affriquées, *f.,* pl.

No.	ENGLISH	RUSSIAN	GERMAN	FRENCH
128	aftereffect, n.	последствие, *n.*	Nachwirkung, *f.*	contrecoup, *m.*
129	age (in time), n.	период, *m.*/эпоха, *f.*	Epoche, *f.*/Zeitalter, *n.*	age, *m.*/époque, *f.*/ période, *f.*
130	age (of person), n.	возраст, *m.*	Alter, *n.*	age, *m.*
131	age expression	выражение возраста, *n.*	Altersangabe, *f.*	expression d'âge, *f.*/ locution d'âge, *f.*
132	agent, n.	действующее лицо/ деятель, *m.*	Agens, *n.*/ handelnde Person, *f.*	agent, *m.*
133	agglutinating languages, pl.	агглютинирующие языки, *m.*, pl.	agglutinierende Sprachen, *f.*, pl.	langues agglutinantes, *f.*, pl.
134	aggregate, n.	совокупность, *f.*/ состав, *m.*	Anhäufung, *f.*/Summe, *f.*	ensemble, *m.*
135	agreement (grammatical), n.	согласование, *n.*	Kongruenz, *f.*/ Übereinstimmung, *f.*	accord, *m.*
136	agreement in case	согласование в падеже, *n.*	Kasuskongruenz, *f.*/ Übereinstimmung im Fall, *f.*	accord de cas, *m.*
137	agreement in gender	согласование в роде, *n.*	Genuskongruenz, *f.*/ Übereinstimmung im Geschlecht, *f.*	accord de genre, *m.*
138	agreement in number	согласование в числе, *n.*	Numeruskongruenz, *f.*/ Übereinstimmung in der Zahl, *f.*	accord de nombre, *m.*
139	agreement in person	согласование в лице, *n.*	Kongruenz in der Person, *f.*/ Übereinstimmung in der Person, *f.*	accord de personne, *m.*
140	air chamber	воздушная камера	Luftraum, *m.*	chambre à air, *f.*
141	airstream, n.	поток воздуха, *m.*	Luftstrom, *m.*	colonne d'air, *f.*/ courant d'air, *m.*
142	algebra, n.	алгебра, *f.*	Algebra, *f.*	algèbre, *f.*
143	algorithm, n.	алгоритм, *m.*	Algorithm, *m.*	algorithme, *m.*
144	allegory, n.	аллегория, *f.*/ иносказание, *n.*	Allegorie, *f.*	allégorie, *f.*

No.	English	Russian	German	French
145	alliteration, n.	аллитерация, *f.*	Alliteration, *f.*/ Stabreim, *m.*	allitération, *f.*
146	allograph, n.	аллограф, *m.*	Allograph(ie), *m.*/ Graphemvariante, *f.*	variante de graphème, *f.*
147	allomorph, n.	алломорфа, *f.*/ морфемный альтернант/ морфемный вариант	Allomorph, *n.*/ Morphemvariante, *f.*	variante de morphème, *f.*
148	allophone, n.	аллофон, *m.*/вариант, *m.*	Allophon, *n.*/ Phonemvariante, *f.*	variante de phonème, *f.*/ réalisation de phonème, *f.*
149	allowable, adj.	допустимый/ законный	zulässig	permis
150	allusion, n.	ссылка, *f.*	Anspielung, *f.*	allusion, *f.*
151	almanac, n.	альманах, *m.*/ календарь, *m.*	Almanach, *m.*/ Jahrbuch, *n.*	almanach, *m.*/ calendrier, *m.*
152	alphabet, n.	алфавит, *m.*/азбука, *f.*	Alphabet, *n.*	alphabet, *m.*
153	alphabetic(al) order	алфавитный порядок	alphabetische Anordnung	ordre alphabétique, *m.*
154	alphabetic script	буквенное письмо	Buchstabenschrift, *f.*	écriture alphabétique, *f.*
155	alteration, n.	изменение, *f.*/ перемена, *f.*	Veränderung	modification, *f.*/ changement, *m.*
156	alternant, n.	вариант, *m.*	Alternante, *f.*/Variante, *f.*	variante, *f.*
157	alternation, n.	чередование, *n.*	Alternanz, *f.*/Wechsel, *m.*	alternance, *f.*
158	alternative solutions, pl.	возможные решения, *n.*, pl.	mögliche Lösungen, *f.*, pl.	solutions de rechange, *f.*, pl.
159	alveolar consonants, pl.	альвеолярные согласные, pl.	alveolare Konsonanten, *m.*, pl./Zahnrandlaute, *m.*, pl.	consonnes alvéolaires, *f.*, pl.
160	alveolus, n.	альвеола, *f.*/ячея, *f.*	Zahnrand, *m.*/ Zahnhöhle, *f.*/ Zahnscheide, *f.*	alvéole, *m.*
161	amalgam, n.	амальгама, *f.*/ сращение, *n.*	Amalgam, *n.*/ Verschmelzung, *f.*	amalgame, *m.*

No.	ENGLISH	RUSSIAN	GERMAN	FRENCH
162	amalgamating languages, pl.	амальгамирующие языки, *m.*, pl.	amalgamierende Sprachen, *f.*, pl.	langues amalgamantes, *f.*, pl.
163	ambidexterity, n.	одинаковое владение обеими руками	Rechts- und Linkshändigkeit, *f.*	ambidextérité, *f.*
164	ambiguity, n.	двусмысленность, *f.*	Zweideutigkeit, *f.*	ambiguïté, *f.*
165	amplification, n.	усиление, *n.*/ расширение, *n.*	Verstärkung, *f.*	amplification, *f.*
166	amplifier, n.	усилитель, *m.*	Verstärker, *m.*	amplificateur, *m.*
167	amplitude, n.	амплитуда, *f.*/размах, *m.*	Amplitude, *f.*/ Schwingungsweite, *f.*	amplitude, *f.*
168	anacoluthon, n.	анаколуф, *m.*	Anakoluth, *m.*	anacoluthe, *f.*
169	anagram, n.	анаграмма, *f.*	Anagramm, *n.*	anagramme, *m.*
170	analogical change	аналогическое изменение	analoge Veränderung	changement analogique, *m.*
171	analogical languages, pl.	аналогические языки, *m.*, pl.	analogische Sprachen, *f.*, pl.	langues analogiques, *f.*, pl.
172	analogical levelling	выравнивание по аналогии, *n.*	analoger Ausgleich	harmonisation par analogie, *f.*
173	analogous, adj.	аналогичный	analog	analogue
174	analogous forms, pl.	аналогичные формы, *f.*, pl.	analoge Formen, *f.*, pl./ sich entsprechende Formen, *f.*, pl.	formes analogues, *f.*, pl.
175	analogous relationships, pl.	аналогичные отношения, *n.*, pl.	analoge Beziehungen, *f.*, pl.	rapports analogues, *m.*, pl.
176	analogue, n.	аналог, *m.*	Analogon, *n.*	analogue, *m.*
177	analogy, n.	аналогия, *f.*	Analogie, *f.*	analogie, *f.*
178	analytical comparison	аналитическое сравнение	analytischer Vergleich, *m.*	comparaison analytique, *f.*
179	analytical grammar	аналитическая грамматика	analytische Grammatik	grammaire raisonnée
180	analytical languages, pl.	аналитические языки, *m.*, pl.	analytische Sprachen, *f.*, pl.	langues analytiques, *f.*, pl.

No.	ENGLISH	RUSSIAN	GERMAN	FRENCH
181	analysis, n.	анализ, *m.*	Analyse, *f.*/ Zergliederung, *f.*	analyse, *f.*
182	anaphora, n.	анафора, *f.*	Anapher, *f.*	anaphore, *f.*
183	anaptyxis, n.	анаптиксис, *m.*/ вставка звука, *f.*	Anaptyxis, *f.*/ Vokalentfaltung, *f.*	anaptyxe, *m.*
184	anatomy, n.	анатомия, *f.*	Anatomie, *f.*	anatomie, *f.*
185	ancestor, n.	прародитель, *m.*/ предок, *m.*	Vorfahr, *m.*	ancêtre, *m.*/aïeul, *m.*
186	ancestral language	праязык, *m.*/ язык-предок, *m.*	Ursprache, *f.*/ sprachlicher Vorläufer	langue-mère, *f.*
187	ancient languages, pl.	древние языки, *m.*, pl.	alte Sprachen, *f.*, pl.	langues anciennes, *f.*, pl.
188	anecdote, n.	анекдот, *m.*	Anekdote, *f.*	anecdote, *f.*
189	angular brackets, pl. (⟨⟩)	угловые скобки, *f.*, pl.	spitze Klammern, *f.*, pl.	crochets, *m.*, pl.
190	animal language	язык животных, *m.*	Tiersprache, *f.*	langue des animaux, *f.*
191	animal names, pl.	названия животных, *n.*, pl.	Tiernamen, *m.*, pl.	noms des animaux, *m.*, pl.
192	animate, adj.	одушевленный	belebt/lebend	animé
193	animation, n.	оживление, *n.*	Personifizierung, *f.*/ Beseelung, *f.*	animation, *f.*
194	anomalous, adj.	неправильный	anomal/unregelmässig	anormal
195	anomalous sentence	неправильное предложение	unregelmässiger Satz	phrase anormale, *f.*
196	anomalous verb	неправильный глагол	unregelmässiges Verb	verbe irrégulier, *m.*
197	anomaly, n.	аномалия, *f.*	Anomalie, *f.*/ Unregelmässigkeit, *f.*	anomalie, *f.*
198	anonymous, adj.	анонимный/ безымянный	anonym	anonyme
199	answer (to problem), n.	решение, *n.*/ответ, *m.*	Lösung, *f.*/	solution, *f.*
200	answer (to question), n.	ответ, *m.*	Antwort, *f.*	réponse, *f.*

No.	ENGLISH	RUSSIAN	GERMAN	FRENCH
201	antecedent, adj.	предыдущий/ предшествующий	vorhergehend	antérieur
202	antecedent	предыпущий член	Beziehungswort, *n.*	antécédent, *m.*
203	anthology, n.	антология, *f.*	Anthologie, *f.*	anthologie, *f.*
204	anthropological linguistics	⟨антропологическая лингвистика⟩/ изучение бесписьменных языков, *n.*	⟨anthropologische Sprachwissenschaft⟩/ Erforchung schriftloser Sprachen, *f.*	linguistique anthropologique, *f.*/étude des langues non écrites, *f.*
205	anthropology, n.	антропология, *f.*	Anthropologie, *f.*	anthropologie, *f.*
206	anticipatory, adj.	вводящий/ предваряющий	vorbereitend/ vorwegnehmend	anticipatif
207	antinomy, n.	антиномия, *f.*/ парадокс, *m.*	Antonomie, *f.*/ Paradox(on), *n.*	antinomie, *f.*
208	antithesis, n.	антитеза, *f.*/ противоположение, *n.*	Antithese, *f.*/ Gegensatz, *m.*	antithèse, *f.*
209	antonym, n.	антоним, *m.*	Antonym, *n.*/entgegengesetzter Begriff	antonyme, *m.*
210	aorist, n.	аорист, *m.*	Aorist, *m.*	aoriste, *m.*
211	aorist aspect	аористический вид	aoristische Aktionsart	aspect aoristique, *m.*
212	aperture, n.	отверствие, *n.*/ открытие, *n.*/ раствор, *m.*	Öffnung, *f.*	aperture, *f.*/ouverture, *f.*
213	aphasia, n.	афазия, *f.*	Aphasie, *f.*	aphasie, *f.*
214	aphorism, n.	афоризм, *m.*/краткое изречение	Aphorismus, *m.*/Gedankensplitter, *m.*/kurzer Denkspruch/kurzer Lehrspruch	aphorisme, *m.*
215	apical consonants, pl.	апикальные согласные, pl.	apikale Konsonanten, *m.*, pl./Zungenspitzenlaute, *m.*, pl.	consonnes apicales, *f.*, pl.
216	apocope, n.	апокопа, *f.*/отпадение, *n.*	Apokope, *f.*/Abfall, *m.*	apocope, *f.*

No.	ENGLISH	RUSSIAN	GERMAN	FRENCH
217	apophony, n.	апофония, *f.*	Ablaut, *m.*/Abstufung, *f.*	apophonie, *f.*
218	aposiopesis, n.	апозиопесис, *m.*	Aposiopese, *f.*	aposiopèse, *f.*
219	apostrophe, n.	апостроф, *m.*	Apostroph, *n.*/Auslassungszeichen, *n.*	apostrophe, *f.*
220	apparatus, n.	аппарат, *m.*	Apparat, *m.*/Gerät, *n.*	appareil, *m.*
221	apparent, adj.	видимый/очевидный	offensichtlich	apparent
222	apparent subject	кажущееся подлежащее	Scheinsubjekt, *n.*	sujet apparent, *m.*
223	appearance (occurrence), n.	появление, *n.*/ возникновение, *n.*	Erscheinung, *f.*/ Auftreten, *n.*	manifestation, *f.*
224	appearance (outer form), n.	вид, *m.*/облик, *m.*	äussere Form	aspect, *m.*
225	appellative, n.	имя существительное нарицательное	Appellativ(um), *n.*/ Benennung, *f.*/ 〈Anredeform〉, *f.*	nom commun, *m.*
226	appendix, n.	приложение, *n.*	Appendix, *m.*/ Anhang, *m.*	appendice, *m.*
227	application, n.	применение, *n.*	Anwendung, *f.*	application, *f.*
228	application of a theory	применение теории, *n.*	Anwendung einer Theorie, *f.*	application d'une théorie, *f.*
229	application of a transformation	набор трансформации, *m.*	Anwendung der Transformationsregel, *f.*	application d'une transformation, *f.*
230	applied linguistics	прикладная лингвистика	angewandte Linguistik/ angewandte Sprachwissenschaft	linguistique appliquée, *f.*
231	apposition, n.	приложение, *n.*	Apposition, *f.*/ Beifügung, *f.*	apposition, *f.*
232	appropriate, adj.	соответствующий/ уместный	zugehörig/passend/ treffend	approprié
233	approximation, n.	приближение, *n.*	Annäherung, *f.*	approximation, *f.*
234	arbitrary, adj.	произвольный	arbiträr/willkürlich	arbitraire

No.	English	Russian	German	French
235	arbitrary sign	произвольный знак	arbiträres Zeichen/ willkürliches Zeichen	signe arbitraire, *m.*
236	archaeology, n.	археология, *f.*	Archäologie, *f.*/ Altertumswissenschaft, *f.*	archéologie, *f.*
237	archaic, adj.	архаический/ устарелый	archäisch/veraltet	archaïque
238	archaism, n.	архаизм, *m.*	Archäismus, *m.*	archaïsme, *m.*
239	archetype, n.	архетип, *m.*/ прототип, *m.*	Archetypus, *m.*/Urbild, *n.*/Urform, *f.*/Vorbild, *n.*	archetype, *m.*/ prototype, *m.*
240	archiphoneme, n.	архифонема, *f.*	Archiphonem, *n.*	archiphonème, *m.*
241	archives, n., pl.	архив, *m.*	Archiv, *n.*	archives, *f.,* pl.
242	area, n.	область, *f.*	Bereich, *m.*/Gebiet, *n.*	aire, *f.*/domaine, *m.*/ région, *f.*
243	areal characteristic	областная характеристика/ областной признак	geographische Eigenheit	caractéristique géographique, *f.*
244	areal group	ареальная группа	geographische Sprachgruppe	confédération de langues, *f.*
245	areal linguistics	ареальная лингвист-ика	Areallinguistik, *f.*/ Sprachgeographie, *f.*	linguistique géographique, *f.*
246	arrangement, n.	аранжировка, *f.*/ расположение, *n.*	Anordnung, *f.*/Muster, *n.*	agencement, *m.*/ arrangement, *m.*
247	arrow, n.	стрелка, *f.*	Pfeil, *m.*	flèche, *f.*
248	art, n.	исскуство, *n.*	Kunst, *f.*	art, *m.*
249	article (in journal), n.	статья, *f.*	Artikel, *m.*/Aufsatz, *m.*	article, *m.*
250	article (part of speech), n.	артикль, *m.*/член, *m.*	Artikel, *m.*/ Geschlechtswort, *n.*	article, *m.*
251	articulated language	членораздельный язык	Lautsprache, *f.*	langage articulé, *m.*
252	articulation, n.	артикуляция, *f.*/ образование звуков, *n.*/членение, *n.*	Artikulation, *f.*/ Aussprache, *f.*/ Lautbildung, *f.*	articulation, *f.*

No.	English	Russian	German	French
253	articulator, n.	активный орган	Artikulationsorgan, *n.*/ Sprachorgan, *n.*	articulateur, *m.*
254	articulatory classification	артикуляторная клас-сификация	artikulatorische Klassifizierung	classement articulatoire, *m.*
255	articulatory phonetics	артикуляторная фонетика	artikulatorische Phonetik	phonétique articulatoire, *f.*
256	artifact, n.	изделья, *f.*	Machwerk, *n.*	produit ouvré, *m.*/ objet façonné, *m.*
257	artificial languages, pl.	исскуственные языки, *m.*, pl.	künstliche Sprachen, *f.*, pl./Kunstsprachen, *f.*, pl.	langues artificielles, *f.*, pl.
258	ascending tone	восходящий тон	steigender Ton	ton ascendant, *m.*
259	aspect, n.	вид, *m.*	Aspekt, *m.*/Aktionsart, *f.*	aspect, *m.*
260	aspirated consonants, pl.	придыхательные согласные, pl.	aspirierte Konsonanten, *m.*, pl./behauchte Konsonanten, *n.*, pl.	consonnes aspirées, *f.*, pl.
261	aspiration, n.	аспирация, *f.*/ придыхание, *n.*	Aspiration, *f.*/ Behauchung, *f.*	aspiration, *f.*
262	assignment, n.	классификация, *f.*/ распределение, *n.*	Klassifizierung, *f.*/ Zuteilung, *f.*	classification, *f.*
263	assimilation, n.	ассимиляция, *f.*/ уподобление, *n.*	Assimilation, *f.*/ Assimilierung, *f.*/ Angleichung, *f.*	assimilation, *f.*
264	associated meaning	ассоциативное значение/связанное значение	assozierte Bedeutung	sens associé, *m.*
265	associated words, pl.	связанные слова, *n.*, pl.	assozierte Wörter, *n.*, pl.	mots associés, *m.*, pl.
266	associative field	ассоциативное поле	Assoziationsfeld, *n.*	champ associatif
267	association of ideas	связь идей, *f.*	Ideenassoziation, *f.*/ Gedankenverbindung, *f.*	association d'idées, *f.*
268	assonance, n.	ассонанс, *m.*/ созвучие, *n.*	Assonanz, *f.*/ Gleichklang, *m.*/ Stimmreim, *m.*	assonance, *f.*

No.	ENGLISH	RUSSIAN	GERMAN	FRENCH
269	assumption, n.	допущение, *n.*/ предположение, *n.*	Annahme, *f.*/ Vermutung, *f.*	supposition, *f.*
270	asterisk, n., (*)	звездочка, *f.*	Sternchen, *n.*	astérisque, *m.*
271	astonishment, n.	удивление, *n.*	Erstaunen, *n.*	étonnement, *m.*
272	asymmetric(al), adj.	асимметричный	asymmetrisch/ unsymmetrisch/ ungleichförmig	asymétrique
273	asymmetry, n.	асимметрия, *f.*	Asymmetrie, *f.*	asymétrie, *f.*
274	asyndetic, adj.	бессоюзный	asyndetisch/ unverbunden	en asyndète
275	atlas, n.	атлас, *m.*	Atlas, *m.*	atlas, *m.*
276	atonic, adj.	атонический/ безударный	unbetont/tieftönig	atone
277	attached, adj.	прикрепленный	verknüpft	lié
278	attack, n.	начальный приступ/ экскурсия, *f.*	Einsatz, *m.*	attaque, *f.*
279	attainment, n.	достижение, *n.*	Gewinnung, *f.*	aboutissement, *m.*/ réalisation, *f.*
280	attempt, n.	попытка, *f.*	Versuch, *m.*	essai, *m.*
281	attention, n.	внимание, *n.*	Aufmerksamkeit, *f.*	attention, *f.*
282	attested form	засвидетельствованная форма	bezeugte Form/ belegte Form	forme attestée, *f.*
283	attitude, n.	склад ума, *m.*	Einstellung, *f.*/Haltung, *f.*	état d'esprit, *m.*
284	attraction, n.	выравнивание по смежности, *n.*	syntaktischer Ausgleich	assimilation syntaxique, *f.*
285	attribute, n.	определение, *n.*	Attribut, *n.*	épithète, *f.*
286	attributive adjective	определительное прилагательное	attributives Adjektiv	adjectif qualificatif, *m.*
287	attributive clause	определительное предложение	Attributsatz, *m.*	proposition qualificative, *f.*

No.	ENGLISH	RUSSIAN	GERMAN	FRENCH
288	atypical, adj.	нетипичный	atypisch/untypisch	non caractéristique
289	audibility, n.	слышимость, *f.*	Hörbarkeit, *f.*	audibilité, *f.*
290	audible, adj.	слышимый	hörbar	audible
291	audio-lingual method	слуховой-повторитель-ный метод	audio-linguistische Methode	méthode audio-linguale, *f.*
292	audio-visual method	наглядно-слуховой метод	audio-visuelle Methode	méthode audio-visuelle, *f.*
293	auditory language	слуховой язык	Gehörsprache, *f.*	langage auditif, *m.*
294	auditory nerve	слуховой нерв	Gehörnerv, *m.*	nerf acoustique, *m.*
295	auditory phonetics	слуховая фонетика	auditive Phonetik/ Ohrenphonetik, *f.*/ Gehörlehre, *f.*	phonétique auditive, *f.*
296	auditory sign	слуховой знак	Gehörsignal, *n.*	signe auditif, *m.*
297	augment, n.	приращение, *n.*	Augment, *n.*	augment, *m.*
298	augmentative, n.	увеличительное, *n.*	Verstärkungsform, *f.*	augmentatif, *m.*
299	auricle, n.	внешнее ухо	ausseres Ohr/ Ohrmuschel, *f.*	auricle, *f.*
300	author, n.	автор, *m.*/писатель, *m.*	Autor, *m.*/Verfasser, *m.*	auteur, *m.*
301	autobiography, n.	автобиография, *f.*	Autobiographie, *f.*/ Selbstbiographie, *f.*	mémoires, *m., pl.*
302	automatic alternation	автоматическое чередование	automatischer Wechsel	alternance automatique, *f.*
303	automatic speech recognition	машинное распознавание речи	maschinelle Spracherkennung	identification mécanique du langage parlé, *f.*
304	automatic translation	машинный перевод	maschinelle (Sprach)-übersetzung	traduction automatique, *f.*
305	autonomous system	автономная система	autonomes System	système autonome, *m.*
306	auxiliary, adj.	вспомогательный	Hilfs-	auxiliaire
307	auxiliary languages, pl.	вспомогательные языки, *m., pl.*	Hilfssprachen, *f., pl.*	langues auxiliaires, *f., pl.*

No.	ENGLISH	RUSSIAN	GERMAN	FRENCH
308	auxiliary verb	вспомогательный глагол	Hilfsverb(um), *n.*/Hilfszeitwort, *n.*	verbe auxiliaire, *m.*
309	average, n.	среднее число/средняя величина	Durchschnitt, *m.*	moyenne, *f.*
310	awareness, n.	сознательность, *f.*	Bewusstsein, *n.*	conscience, *f.*
311	axis, n.	ось, *f.*	Achse, *f.*	axe, *m.*

B

No.	ENGLISH	RUSSIAN	GERMAN	FRENCH
001	babbling, n.	лепетание, *n.*	Geplapper, *n.*	bafouillage, *m.*
002	baby talk	детская речь	Babysprache, *f.*/Lallwörter, *n.*, pl.	langage enfantin, *m.*
003	baccalaureate, n.	степень бакалавра, *f.*	Bakkalaureat, *n.*	baccalauréat, *m.*
004	back consonants, pl.	задние согласные, pl.	hintere Konsonanten, *m.*, pl./Gaumenlaute, *m.*, pl.	consonnes postérieures, *f.*, pl.
005	back formation	обратное словообразование,	Rückbildung, *f.*	régression, *f.*
006	back of tongue	спинка языка, *f.*	Zungenrücken, *m.*	dos de la langue, *m.*
007	back vowels, pl.	гласные заднего ряда, pl./задние гласные, pl.	hintere Vokale, *m.*, pl.	voyelles postérieures, *f.*, pl.
008	background noise	шумовой фон	Hintergrundsgeräusch, *n.*	bruit de fond, *m.*
009	backing (articulation), n.	передвижение назад, *n.*	Velarisierung, *f.*	reculement, *m.*
010	backward dictionary	обратный словарь	rückläufiges Wörterbuch	dictionnaire inverse, *m.*
011	backward letter	перевернутая буква	umgekehrter Buchstabe	lettre renversée, *f.*
012	backward writing	обратное написание	Spiegelschrift, *f.*	graphie inverse, *f.*
013	balance, n.	равновесие, *n.*	Gleichgewicht, *n.*	équilibre, *m.*
014	balanced system	уравновешенная система	ausgeglichenes System/symmetrisches System	système symétrique, *m.*

No.	English	Russian	German	French
015	ballad, n.	баллада, *f.*	Ballade, *f.*	ballade, *f.*
016	ball-point pen	шариковая ручка	Kugelschreiber, *m.*	stylo à bille, *m.*
017	barbarism, n.	варваризм, *m.*	Barbarismus, *m.*/ Sprachwidrigkeit, *f.*	barbarisme, *m.*
018	base, n.	база, *f.*/основа, *f.*	Basis, *f.*/Grundlage, *f.*	base, *f.*
019	basic allophone	основной вид фонемы/основная разновидность фонемы	Grundvariante, *f.*	première réalisation d'un phonème, *f.*
020	basic concept	основное понятие	Grundbegriff, *m.*	concept de base, *m.*/ concept fondamental
021	basic form	основная форма/ основной вид	Grundform, *f.*	forme de base, *f.*
022	basic function	основная функция	Grundfunktion, *f.*	fonction de base, *f.*
023	basic meaning	прямое значение	Grundbedeutung, *f.*	acception première, *f.*/ sens premier, *m.*
024	basic principle	основной принцип	Grundprinzip, *n.*	principe fondamental, *m.*
025	basic sentence	основное предложение	zugrundeliegender Satz	phrase de base, *f.*
026	basic unit	исходная единица/ основная единица	Grundeinheit, *f.*	unité fondamentale, *f.*
027	basic vocabulary	основной словарный состав/основной словарный фонд	Grundwortschatz, *m.*	vocabulaire élémentaire, *m.*
028	basis, n.	база, *f.*/основа, *f.*	Basis, *f.*/Grundlage, *f.*	base, *f.*
029	basis of articulation	артикуляционная база	Artikulationsbasis, *f.*	base d'articulation, *f.*
030	battery operated, adj.	работающий на батареях	batteriebetrieben	à pils
031	beginning, n.	начало, *n.*	Anfang, *m.*	commencement, *m.*/ début, *m.*
032	behavior, n.	поведение, *n.*	Verhalten, *n.*	comportement, *m.*
033	behaviorism, n.	бихевиоризм, *m.*	Behaviorismus, *m.*	behaviorisme, *m.*

No.	ENGLISH	RUSSIAN	GERMAN	FRENCH
034	benediction, n.	благословение, *n.*	Segensspruch, *m.*	bénédiction, *f.*
035	Bible, n.	библия, *f.*	Bibel, *f.*	bible, *f.*
036	Bible translations, pl.	переводы библии, *m.*, pl.	Bibelübersetzungen, *f.*, pl.	traductions de la bible, *f.*, pl.
037	biblical language	библейский язык	Bibelsprache, *f.*/ Sprache der Bibel, *f.*	langue biblique, *f.*
038	bibliography, n.	библиография, *f.*	Literaturververzeichnis, *n.*/Schriftenverzeichnis, *n.*/ Bibliographie, *f.*	bibliographie, *f.*
039	bilabial consonants, pl.	билабиальные согласные, pl./ губно-губные согласные, pl./ двугубные согласные, pl.	bilabiale Konsonanten, *m.*, pl./Lippenlaute, *m.*, pl.	consonnes bilabiales, *f.*, pl.
040	bilateral, adj.	двусторонний	doppelseitig/zweiseitig	bilatéral
041	bilingualism, n.	двуязычие, *n.*	Bilinguismus, *m.*/ Zweisprachigkeit, *f.*	bilinguisme, *m.*
042	billboard, n.	афиша, *f.*	Anschlagbrett, *n.*/Litfassäule, *f.*/ Plakatsäule, *f.*	panneau d'affichage, *m.*
043	binarity, n.	бинарность, *f.*	Binärität, *f.*/ Zweigliedrigkeit, *f.*	binarité, *f.*
044	binary, adj.	бинарный/двоичный/ двойной	binär/zweigliedrig	binaire
045	binary code	двоичный код	Binärcode, *m.*	code binaire, *m.*
046	binary construction	бинарная конструкция	binäre Konstruktion	construction binaire, *f.*
047	binary opposition	бинарная оппозиция	binärer Gegensatz	opposition binaire, *f.*
048	binary scale	двоичная шкала	Binärskala, *f.*	échelle binaire, *f.*
049	binary sentence	двусоставное предложение	binärer Satz	phrase dirème, *f.*
050	binary symbol	двоичный символ	binäres Symbol	symbole binaire, *m.*

No.	ENGLISH	RUSSIAN	GERMAN	FRENCH
051	binary system	бинарная система/ двоичная система	Binärsystem, *n.*	système binaire, *m.*
052	binary unit	двоичная единица/ двоичный знак	Binäreinheit, *f.*/ Binärziffer, *f.*/Bit, *n.*	chiffre binaire, *m.*/ monade, *f.*
053	biography, n.	биография, *f.*	Biographie, *f.*	biographie, *f.*
054	biolinguistics, n.	биолингвистика, *f.*	Biolinguistik, *f.*	biolinguistique, *f.*
055	biology, n.	биология, *f.*	Biologie, *f.*	biologie, *f.*
056	birth, n.	рождение, *n.*	Geburt, *f.*	naissance, *f.*
057	birthplace, n.	место рождения, *n.*	Geburtsort, *m.*	lieu de naissance, *m.*
058	bit (also binit), n.	двоичная единица/ двоичный знак	Bit, *n.*/Binarziffer, *f.*/ Binarstelle, *f.*	monade, *f.*
059	bi-uniqueness, n.	двусторонняя единственность	Ein-Eindeutigkeit, *f.*	caractère d'être bi-unique, *m.*
060	blade of the tongue	передняя часть языка	Zungenblatt, *n.*	partie antérieure de la langue, *f.*
061	blank space between words	пропуск между словами, *m.*/пустое место между словами	Wortzwischenraum, *m.*	espace entre mots, *m.*/ blanc entre mots, *m.*
062	blank verse	белый стих	Blankvers, *m.*/ reimloser Vers	vers blanc, *m.*/ vers sans rime, *m.*
063	blend, n.	смесь, *m.*/смешение, *f.*/ сплав, *n.*	Mischbildung, *f.*/ Verschmelzung, *f.*	fusionnement, *m.*/ mélange, *m.*
064	blessing, n.	благословение, *n.*	Segen, *m.*	bénédiction, *f.*
065	blind, adj.	слепой	blind	aveugle
066	blindness, n.	слепота, *f.*	Blindheit, *f.*	cecité, *f.*
067	block letters, pl.	прописные печатные буквы, *f.,* pl.	Blockschrift, *f.*	majuscules, *f.,* pl.
068	blunder, n.	промах, *m.*	Schnitzer, *m.*	bévue, *f.*
069	boarding school	школа-интернат, *m.*	Internat, *n.*/ Heimschule, *f.*	pensionnat, *m.*/pension, *f.*

No.	ENGLISH	RUSSIAN	GERMAN	FRENCH
070	boldface type	жирный шрифт	Fettdruck, *m.*	caractère gras, *m.*
071	book, n.	книга, *f.*	Buch, *n.*	livre, *m.*
072	booklet, n.	книжечка, *f.*	Broschüre, *f.*/ Büchlein, *n.*	livret, *m.*/opuscule, *m.*
073	book jacket	отделная обложка	Schutzumschlag, *m.*	jaquette, *f.*
074	book learning	книжные знания, *n.,* pl./теоретические знания, *n.,* pl.	Buchgelehrsamkeit, *f.*	savoir livresque, *m.*/ savoir théorique, *m.*
075	book publisher	книжное издательство	Verleger, *m.*	éditeur, *m.*
076	book store	книжный магазин	Buchhandlung, *f.*	librairie, *f.*
077	border region	пограничная область	Grenzgebiet, *n.*	région frontière, *f.*
078	borrowed word	заимствованное слово	Lehnwort, *n.*	emprunt lexical, *m.*
079	borrowing, n.	заимствование, *n.*	Entlehnung, *f.*/ Lehngut, *n.*	emprunt, *m.*
080	bound form	связанная форма	gebundene Form	morphème non-libre, *m.*
081	boundary, n.	граница, *f.*/придел, *m.*	Grenze, *f.*	frontière, *f.*/limite, *f.*
082	boundary markers, pl.	пограничные сигналы, *m.,* pl.	Grenzsignale, *n.,* pl.	signes de démarcation, *m.,* pl.
083	bow-wow theory	теория аф-аф, *f.*	wau-wau-Theorie, *f.*	théorie toutou, *f.*
084	braces, pl. ({ })	фигурные скобки, *f.,* pl.	geschweifte Klammern, *f.,* pl.	accolades, *f.,* pl.
085	brackets, pl. ([ ])	скобки, *f.,* pl./ квадратные скобки, *f.,* pl.	eckige Klammern, *f.,* pl.	accolades, *m.,* pl./ crochets, *m.,* pl.
086	braille, n.	шрифт для слепых, *m.*	Braille, *n.*/ Blindenschrift, *f.*	braille, *m.*
087	brain, n.	мозг, *m.*	Gehirn, *n.*	cerveau, *m.*
088	branch, n.	ветвь, *f.*/ветка, *f.*/ отрасль, *f.*	Zweig, *m.*	branche, *f.*

No.	English	Russian	German	French
089	branch of knowledge	отрасль знания, *f.*	Disziplin, *f.*/Fach, *n.*/ Wissensgebiet, *n.*	discipline, *f.*
090	branch of language family	ветвь языковой семьи, *f.*	Zweig einer Sprachfamilie, *m.*	branche de famille linguistique, *f.*
091	branching, n.	разветвление, *n.*/ развертывание, *n.*/ ответвление, *n.*	Abzweigung, *f.*/ Verzweigung, *f.*	embranchement, *m.*
092	break, n.	пауза, *f.*	Unterbrechung, *f.*/ Zäsur, *f.*	point de suspension, *m.*
093	break up (into parts), v.	разбивать	zerlegen	décomposer
094	breath, n.	вздох, *m.*/дыхание, *n.*	Atem, *m.*/Hauch, *m.*	haleine, *f.*/souffle, *m.*
095	breath group	дыхательная группа	Sprechtakt, *m.*	groupe respiratoire, *m.*
096	breathed consonants, pl.	воздушные согласные, pl.	Anblaselaute, *m.*, pl./ Hauchlaute, *m.*, pl.	consonnes soufflantes, *f.*, pl.
097	breathing, n.	дыхание, *n.*	Atmen, *n.*/Atmung, *f.*	aspiration, *f.*
098	breathing apparatus	дыхательный аппарат	Atmungsorgane, *n.*, pl.	appareil respiratoire, *m.*
099	bright vowels, pl.	светлые гласные, pl./ яркие гласные, pl.	helle Vokale, *m.*, pl.	voyelles claires, *f.*, pl.
100	broad transcription	приблизительная транскрипция	annähernd phonematische Transkription/ annähernd phonematische Umschrift	notation large, *f.*
101	broadcast, n.	передача, *f.*	Sendung, *f.*	radiodiffusion, *f.*
102	brochure, n.	брошюра, *f.*	Broschüre, *f.*	brochure, *f.*
103	brogue, n.	ирландский акцент	irischer Akzent	accent irlandais, *m.*
104	bronchial tubes, pl.	бронхи, pl.	Bronchien, *f.*, pl./ Luftröhren, *f.*, pl.	bronches, *f.*, pl.
105	bulletin, n.	объявление, *n.*	Mitteilung, *f.*	bulletin, *m.*/ communiqué, *m.*
106	bulletin board	доска для объявлений, *f.*	Anschlagtafel, *f.*	tableau d'affichage, *m.*

No.	ENGLISH	RUSSIAN	GERMAN	FRENCH
107	Bulgarian, adj.	болгарский	bulgarisch	bulgare
108	bundle, n.	пучок, *m.*	Bündel, *m.*	faisceau, *m.*
109	bundle of distinctive features	пучок различительных признаков, *m.*	Bündel von distinktiven Merkmalen, *n.*	faisceau de traits distinctifs, *m.*
110	bundle of isoglosses	пучок изоглосс, *m.*	Isoglossenbündel, *n.*	faisceau d'isoglosses, *m.*
111	burial place	место погребения, *n.*/ кладбище, *n.*	Grabstätte, *f.*	cimetière, *m.*
112	burial service	заупокойная служба/ погребальная служба	Tötenfeier, *f.*/ Trauerfeier, *f.*	service funèbre, *m.*/ office des morts, *m.*
113	burring, n.	картавость, *f.*	Zäpfchenlaut, *m.*	grasseyement, *m.*
114	byword, n.	поговорка, *f.*	Maxime, *f.*/ Sprichwort, *n.*	dicton, *m.*

C

No.	ENGLISH	RUSSIAN	GERMAN	FRENCH
001	cacophony, n.	какофония, *n.*/ неблагозвучие, *f.*	Kakophonie, *f.*/ Missklang, *m.*	cacophonie, *f.*
002	cadence, n.	каденция, *f.*	Kadenz, *f.*	cadence, *f.*
003	calculation, n.	вычисление, *n.*/ расчет, *m.*	Berechnung, *f.*/ Rechnung, *f.*	calcul, *m.*
004	calculus, n.	исчисление, *n.*	Rechnen, *n.*	calcul, *m.*
005	calendar, n.	календарь, *m.*	Kalender, *m.*	calendrier, *f.*
006	call, n.	призыв, *m.*	Anruf, *m.*	appel, *m.*
007	calligraphy, n.	каллиграфия, *f.*	Kalligraphie, *f.*/ Schönschreibekunst, *f.*	calligraphie, *f.*
008	calque, n.	калька, *f.*	Abbild, *n.*/Abklatsch, *m.*/ Calque, *n.*/ Lehnübersetzung, *f.*/ Übersetzungs- entlehnung, *f.*	calque, *m.*

No.	ENGLISH	RUSSIAN	GERMAN	FRENCH
009	canonic form	каноническая форма	Kanonform, *f.*	forme canonique, *f.*
010	cant, n.	жаргон, *m.*	Jargon, *m.*	argot, *m.*/jargon, *m.*
011	canto, n.	песнь, *f.*	Gesang, *m.*	chant, *m.*
012	capability, n.	способность, *f.*/ возможность, *f.*	Fähigkeit, *f.*	possibilité, *f.*
013	capital letter	прописная буква/ заглавиая буква	grosser Buchstabe/ Majuskel, *f.*	majuscule, *f.*
014	caption, n.	заголовок, *m.*	Bildtext, *m.*/Überschrift, *f.*/Unterschrift, *f.*	légende, *f.*
015	card file, card index	картотека, *f.*	Kartothek, *f.*/Kartei, *f.*/ Zettelarchiv, *n.*	fichier, *m.*
016	cardinal number	количественное числительное	Kardinalzahl, *f.*/ Grundzahl, *f.*	nombre cardinal, *m.*
017	cardinal vowels, pl.	кардинальные гласные, pl.	Kardinalvokale, *m.*, pl./ Grundvokale, *m.*, pl.	voyelles cardinales, *f.*, pl.
018	carryover, n.	перенос, *m.*	Übertrag, *m.*	report, *m.*/transfert, *n.*
019	cartilage, n.	хрящ, *m.*	Knorpel, *m.*	cartilage, *m.*
020	case, n.	падеж, *m.*	Fall, *m.*/Kasus, *m.*	cas, *m.*
021	catalogue, n.	каталог, *m.*	Katalog, *m.*/ Verzeichnis, *n.*	catalogue, *m.*
022	catch-word, n.	крылатое слово	Schlagwort, *n.*/ Stichwort, *n.*	mot-souche, *m.*/ mot-vedette, *m.*
023	categorial grammar, categorial model	⟨категориальная грамматика⟩/ категориальная модель	Kategorialgrammatik, *f.*/ Kategorialmodell, *n.*	grammaire catégoriale/ modèle de langue catégorial, *f.*
024	category, n.	категория, *f.*/разряд, *m.*	Kategorie, *f.*	catégorie, *f.*
025	catenation, n.	сцепление, *n.*	Kettung, *f.*/Verkettung, *f.*	enchaînement, *m.*
026	causality, n.	причинность, *f.*	Kausalität, *f.*	causalité, *f.*
027	causative, n.	каузатив, *m.*	Kausativ, *m.*/ veranlassendes Verb	causatif, *m.*

No.	ENGLISH	RUSSIAN	GERMAN	FRENCH
028	cause, n.	причина, *f.*	Grund, *m.*/Ursache, *f.*	cause, *f.*
029	cause and effect	причина и следствие	Ursache und Wirkung	effet et cause
030	cave-man, cave-dweller, n.	троголит, *m.*/ пещерный житель	Höhlenmensch, *m.*/ Höhlenbewohner, *m.*	homme des cavernes, *m.*
031	cavity, n.	полость, *f.*	Höhle, *f.*	cavité, *f.*/fossé, *f.*
032	cedilla, n. (ç)	седиль, *m.*	Cedille, *f.*	cédille, *f.*
033	cemetery, n.	кладбище, *n.*/место погребения, *n.*	Friedhof, *m.*/Gottes- acker, *m.*/Kirchhof, *m.*	cimetière, *m.*
034	Celtic, adj.	кельтский	keltisch	celtique
035	censorship, n.	цензура, *f.*	Zensur, *f.*	censure, *f.*
036	center, n.	центр, *m.*/ середина, *f.*/ средоточие, *n.*	Zentrum, *n.*/Mitte, *f.*	centre, *m.*/milieu, *m.*
037	central, adj.	центральный	zentral	central
038	century, n.	век, *m.*	Jahrhundert, *n.*	siècle, *m.*
039	cerebral sound	церебральный звук	zerebraler Laut	son cacuminal, *m.*
040	ceremonial speech	формальная речь/ перемониальный стиль	Zeremonialsprache, *f.*	discours de circon- stance, *m.*
041	certainty, n.	несомненность, *f.*/ уверенность, *f.*	Gewissheit, *f.*	certitude, *f.*
042	chain, n.	цепь, *f.*/цепочка, *f.*	Kette, *f.*	chaîne, *f.*
043	chance occurrence	случайное явление/ случайность, *f.*	zufälliges Auftreten	cas fortuit, *m.*
044	chance resemblance	случайное сходство	zufällige Ähnlichkeit	ressemblance fortuite, *f.*
045	change, n.	изменение, *n.*/ перемена, *f.*	Änderung, *f.*/ Veränderung, *m.*/Wan- del, *m.*/Wechsel, *m.*	changement, *m.*
046	channel, n.	канал, *m.*/путь, *m.*/ тракт, *m.*	Kanal, *m.*/Weg, *m.*	voie, *f.*

No.	English	Russian	German	French
047	chant, n.	монотонное песнопение	eintöniges Lied	mélopée, *f.*
048	chapter, n.	глава, *f.*	Kapitel, *n.*	chapitre, *m.*
049	chapter heading	заглавие главы, *n.*	Kapitelüberschrift, *f.*	intitulé de chapitre, *m.*
050	character, n.	знак, *m.*/иероглиф, *m.*/ литера, *f.*	Schriftzeichen, *n.*	caractère, *m.*
051	characteristic, adj.	характерный/ типичный	charakteristisch/ kennzeichnend/ eigenartig	caractéristique
052	characteristic, n.	характерная черта/ особенность, *f.*/ свойство, *n.*	Charakteristik, *f.*/ Eigenschaft, *f.*/ Kennzeichen, *n.*	caractéristique, *f.*/ marque dominante, *f.*/ note dominante, *f.*/ propre, *m.*
053	charade, n.	шарада, *f.*	Scharade, *f.*	charade, *f.*
054	chart, n.	учебный плакат/ схема, *f.*	Skizze, *f.*/Tabelle, *f.*/ Tafel, *f.*	tableau, *m.*
055	chatter, n.	болтовня, *f.*	Geplauder, *n.*	bavardage, *m.*/ papotage, *m.*
056	check, n.	проверка, *f.*	Kontrolle, *f.*	contrôle, *m.*
057	check mark (✔)	контрольный знак/ птичка, *f.*	Kontrollmarke, *f.*	marque de contrôle, *f.*
058	checked vowels, pl.	замкнутые гласные, pl.	gedeckte Vokale, *m.,* pl.	voyelles entravées, *f.,* pl.
059	cheek, n.	щека, *f.*	Backe, *f.*/Wange, *f.*	joue, *f.*
060	chest, n.	грудная клетка/ грудь, *f.*	Brust, *f.*	poitrine, *f.*
061	chest pulse	пульс дыхания, *m.*	Lungenstoss, *m.*	souffle pulmonaire, *m.*
062	child language	детский язык	Kindersprache, *f.*	langage enfantin, *m.*
063	child vocabulary	словарный состав детей	Kinderwortschatz, *m.*	vocabulaire enfantin, *m.*
064	Chinese, adj.	китайский	chinesisch	chinois

No.	English	Russian	German	French
065	choice, n.	отбор, *m.*/выбор, *m.*	Auswahl, *f.*/Wahl, *f.*	choix, *m.*/option, *f.*
066	choral speaking	хоровая речь	Sprechen im Chor, *n.*	récitation collective. *f.*
067	chronogram, n.	хронограмма, *f.*	Chronogramm, *n.*	chronogramme, *m.*
068	chronological order	хронологический порядок	chronologische Reihen-folge	ordre chronologique, *m.*
069	chronology, n.	хронология, *f.*	Chronologie, *f.*	chronologie, *f.*
070	cipher, n.	шифр, *m.*	Ziffer, *f.*/Chiffre, *f.*	chiffre, *m.*
071	circle, n.	круг, *m.*	Kreis, *m.*	cercle, *m.*
072	circumflex accent (ˆ)	циркумфлекс, *m.*	Zirkumflex, *m.*	accent circonflexe, *m.*
073	circumlocution, n.	иносказание, *n.*/ парафраза, *f.*	Umschreibung, *f.*	circonlocution, *f.*/ périphrase, *f.*
074	circumscribed, adj.	ограниченный	umschrieben	circonscrit
075	circumstance, n.	обстоятельство, *n.*	Umstand, *m.*	circonstance, *f.*
076	citation, n.	цитата, *f.*	Zitat, *n.*	citation, *f.*
077	citation form	словарная форма	Zitatform, *f.*	forme d'entrée, *f.*
078	clarity, n.	ясность, *f.*	Klarheit, *f.*	clarté, *f.*
079	class, n.	класс, *m.*	Klasse, *f.*	classe, *f.*
080	class concept	понятие класса, *n.*	Klassenbegriff, *m.*/ Mengenbegriff, *m.*	concept de classe, *m.*
081	class inclusion	включение в класс, *n.*	Klassenzugehörigkeit, *f.*	inclusion dans la classe, *f.*
082	class marker	классный показатель	Klassenindikator, *m.*/ Klassenanzeiger, *m.*	indice de classe, *m.*/ classificateur, *m.*
083	class member	член класса, *m.*	Glied der Klasse, *n.*	membre de classe, *m.*
084	classic example	классический пример	klassisches Beispiel/ mustergültiges Beispiel	exemple classique, *m.*
085	classical languages, pl.	классические языки, *m.*, pl./ древние языки, *m.*, pl.	klassische Sprachen, *f.*, pl./alte Sprachen, *f.*, pl.	langues classiques, *f.*, pl.

No.	ENGLISH	RUSSIAN	GERMAN	FRENCH
086	classical philology	классическая филология	klassische Philologie	philologie classique, *f.*
087	classification, n.	классификация, *f.*	Klassifikation, *f.*/ Klassifizierung, *f.*/ Einteilung, *f.*	classification, *f.*
088	classified advertise-ments, pl.	газетные объявления по категориям, *n.*, pl.	Anzeigen, *f.*, pl./ Kleinanzeigen, *f.*, pl./ Annoncen, *f.*, pl.	petites annonces, *f.*, pl.
089	classify, v.	классифицировать	klassifizieren	classifier
090	clause, n.	предложение, *n.*	Satzglied, *n.*/Satzteil, *m.*	membre de phrase, *m.*/ proposition, *f.*
091	clause structure	строй предложения, *m.*	Satzstruktur, *f.*	structure des proposi-tions, *f.*
092	clause terminal (marker)	знак конца предложения, *m.*	Satzschluss, *m.*/ Satzende, *n.*	fin de proposition, *f.*/ indice de la fin de la phrase, *m.*
093	cleft palate	волчья пасть, *f.*	Gaumenspalte, *f.*	palais fendu, *m.*
094	cliche, n.	клише, *n.*	Gemeinplatz, *m.*/ Platitüde, *f.*	cliché, *m.*
095	click, n.	кликс, *m.*/щелкающий звук	Sauglaut, *m.*/ Schnalzlaut, *m.*	clic, *m.*/claquement, *m.*
096	climate, n.	климат, *m.*	Klima, *n.*	climat, *m.*
097	close, n.	конец, *m.*	Schluss, *m.*	fin, *f.*
098	close	близкий	nah	proche
099	close relationship	тесная связь	enge Verwandtschaft	rapport étroit, *m.*
100	close resemblance	близкое сходство	grosse Ähnlichkeit	ressemblance étroite, *f.*
101	close transition	закрытый переход	enge Verbindung/ geschlossenes Sandhi	liaison étroite, *f.*
102	close translation	точный перевод	wortgetreue Übersetzung, *f.*	traduction fidèle, *f.*
103	closed, adj.	закрытый	geschlossen	fermé
104	closed class	закрытый класс/ замкнутый класс	geschlossene Klasse	classe fermée, *f.*

No.	ENGLISH	RUSSIAN	GERMAN	FRENCH
105	closed loop	замкнутый контур	geschlossene Schleife/ geschlossener Kreis	boucle fermée, *f.*
106	closed syllable	закрытый слог	geschlossene Silbe	syllabe fermée, *f.*/ syllabe entravée, *f.*
107	closed vowels, pl.	закрытые гласные, pl.	geschlossene Vokale, *m.,* pl.	voyelles fermées, *f.,* pl.
108	closure, n.	смычка, *f.*/ смыкание, *n.*/ затвор, *m.*/ закрытие, *n.*	Schliessung, *f.*/ Verschluss, *m.*	fermeture, *f.*
109	clue, n.	показание, *n.*/ключ, *m.*	Hinweis, *m.*/Finger- zeig, *m.*/Andeutung, *f.*	fil directeur, *m.*/indice, *m.*
110	cluster, n.	группа, *f.*/скопление, *n.*/стечение, *n.*/ стяжение, *n.*	Gruppe, *f.*/Gefüge, *n.*/ Folge, *f.*	groupe, *m.*/complexe, *m.*
111	code, n.	код, *m.*	Code, *m.*	code, *m.*
112	code and message	код и сообщение	Code und Nachricht	code et message
113	code character	кодовой знак	Chiffre, *f.*	caractère de code, *m.*/ chiffre de code, *m.*
114	code switching	перемена кода, *f.*	Codewechsel, *m.*	changement de code, *m.*
115	code word	кодовое слово	Deckwort, *n.*	mot de code, *m.*
116	coding, n.	кодирование, *n.*	Chiffrieren, *n.*/ Verschlüsseln, *n.*	codage, *m.*
117	co-existent, adj.	сосуществующий	gleichzeitig vorhanden	coexistant
118	cognate words, pl.	родственные слова, *n.,* pl.	verwandte Wörter, *n.,* pl.	mots apparentés, *m.,* pl.
119	cognition, n.	познание, *n.*	Erkenntnis, *f.*/ Erkennung, *f.*	cognition, *f.*
120	cohesive, adj.	связующий	zusammenhangend	cohésif
121	coincide, v.	совпадать	zusammenfallen/ übereinstimmen	coïncider
122	coincidental, adj.	случайный	zufällig	de coïncidence

No.	ENGLISH	RUSSIAN	GERMAN	FRENCH
123	coined word	неологизм, *m.*	geprägtes Wort	création, *f.*
124	collaboration, n.	сотрудничество, *n.*	Zusammenarbeit, *f./* Mitarbeit, *f.*	collaboration, *f.*
125	collaborator, n.	сотрудник, *m.*	Mitarbeiter, *m.*	collaborateur, *m.*
126	colleague, n.	коллега, *m.*	Kollege, *m.*	collègue, *m.*
127	collection, n.	собрание, *n.*	Sammlung, *f.*	collection, *f./*recueil, *m.*
128	collection of articles	сборник статей, *m.*	Aufsatzsammlung, *f.*	ensemble d'articles, *f.*
129	collective noun	имя существительное собирательное	Kollektivum, *n./* Sammelbegriff, *m.*	nom collectif, *m.*
130	collective numeral	собирательное числительное	zusammenfassendes Zahlwort	nombre collectif, *m.*
131	college (in US), n.	вуз, *m./*институт, *m./* отдел университета, *m.*	Hochschule, *f./* Akademie, *f./* Universität, *f.*	collège, *f./*division de l'université, *f./*école supérieure, *f.*
132	collision, n.	столкновение, *n.*	Zusammenstoss, *m.*	collision, *f./*rencontre, *f.*
133	colloquial speech	разговорная речь	Umgangssprache, *f./* Alltagssprache, *f.*	parler d'usage, *m.*
134	colloquialism, n.	просторечие, *n.*	umgangssprachlicher Ausdruck	expression familière, *f./* tournure familière, *f.*
135	colon, n. (:)	двоеточие, *n.*	Doppelpunkt, *m.*	deux points, *m.,* pl.
136	color, n.	цвет, *m.*	Farbe, *f.*	couleur, *f.*
137	color names, pl.	названия цветов, *n.,* pl.	Farbnamen, *m.,* pl.	noms de couleurs, *m.,* pl.
138	color symbolism	символизм красок, *m.*	Farbensymbolismus, *m.*	symbolisme des couleurs, *m.*
139	colored hearing	цветовой слух	farbiges Hören	ouïe colorée, *f.*
140	colorful language	красочный стиль языка	bildhafte Sprache	langage pittoresque, *m.*
141	column, n.	столбец, *m.*	Spalte, *f.*	colonne, *f.*
142	column and row	столбец и ряд	Spalte und Reihe	rangée et colonne

No.	ENGLISH	RUSSIAN	GERMAN	FRENCH
143	combination, n.	комбинация, *f./* сочетание, *n.*	Kombination, *f./* Zusammensetzung, *f./* Gefüge, *n./* Verbindung, *f.*	combinaison, *f.*
144	combinatory variant	комбинаторный вариант/ обусловленный вариант	kombinatorische Variante	variante combinatoire, *f.*
145	combining form	сочитаемая форма	Kombinationswort, *n.*	élément de combinaison, *m.*
146	comic strip, comics, pl.	рассказ в кари- катурахь *m.*	Karikaturstreifen, *m.*	dessin humoristique, *m.*
147	comical, adj.	смешной	komisch	comique
148	comitative case	совместный падеж	Komitativus, *m.*	comitatif, *m.*
149	comma, n. (,)	запятая, *f.*	Komma, *n./*Beistrich, *m.*	virgule, *f.*
150	command, n.	приказ, *m.*	Befehl, *m.*	ordre, *m.*
151	command of a language	владение языком, *n.*	Sprachbeherrschung, *f.*	maîtrise d'une langue, *f.*
152	commensurable, adj.	соизмеримый/ пропорциональный	kommensurabel/ verleichbar	commensurable
153	comment, n.	замечание, *n.*	Bemerkung, *f.*	remarque, *f.*
154	commentary, n.	комментарий, *m.*	Kommentar, *m./* Bemerkung, *f./* Randbemerkung, *f./* Reportage, *f.*	commentaire, *m.*
155	commercial (radio, TV), n.	коммерческое объявление	Reklame(sendung), *f.*	annonce publicitaire, *f.*
156	commercial language	торговый язык	Handelssprache, *f./* Geschäftssprache, *f.*	langage du commerce, *m.*
157	committee	комитет, *m.*	Ausschuss, *m.*	comité, *m.*
158	common expressions, pl.	полезные выражения, *n.,* pl./бытовые выражения, *n.,* pl.	gebräuchliche Ausdrücke, *m.,* pl./ geläufige Ausdrücke, *m.,* pl.	expressions usuelles, *f.,* pl.

No.	ENGLISH	RUSSIAN	GERMAN	FRENCH
159	common feature	общая черта	gemeinsame Eigenschaft/ gemeinsamer Zug	trait commun, *m.*
160	common gender	общий род	doppeltes Geschlecht/ Genus communis	genre commun, *m.*
161	common language	общий язык	Gemeinsprache, *f.*	langue commune, *f.*
162	common noun	имя существительное нарицательное	Gattungsname, *m.*	nom commun, *m.*
163	common origin of languages	общее возникновение языков	gemeinsamer Ursprung von Sprachen	monogenèse des langues, *f.*
164	common sense	здравый смысл	gesunder Menschenverstand	bon sens, *m.*
165	common spelling	обыкновенное правописание	normale Schreibweise	orthographe habituelle, *f.*
166	common usage	общее употребление	allgemeiner Gebrauch	usage courant, *m.*
167	common word	обыкновенное слово	gebräuchliches Wort	mot usuel, *m.*
168	commonplace, adj.	банальный/избитый	alltäglich	banal
169	communication, n.	коммуникация, *f.*/ общение, *n.*	Kommunikation, *f.*/ Verständigung, *f.*	communication, *f.*
170	communication channel	путь общения, *m.*/ коммуникационная линия	Kommunikationskanal, *m.*/ ⟨Nachrichtenweg⟩, *m.*	moyen de communication, *m.*
171	communication system	система коммуникации, *f.*	Kommunikationssystem, *n.*	système de communication, *m.*
172	communication theory	теория связи, *f.*	Kommunikationstheorie, *f.*/Informationstheorie, *f.*	théorie de l'information, *f.*/théorie des communications, *f.*
173	commutation, n.	коммутация, *f.*/ замена, *f.*	Kommutation, *f.*/ Vertauschung, *f.*	commutation, *f.*/ échange, *m.*
174	commutation test	коммутационное испытание	Verschiebeprobe, *f.*/ Einsetzungstest, *m.*	test de substitution, *m.*
175	community, n.	община, *f.*	Gemeinschaft, *f.*	communauté, *f.*

No.	ENGLISH	RUSSIAN	GERMAN	FRENCH
176	comparative degree	сравнительная степень	komparative Stufe/ Vergleichsstufe, *f.*	degré de comparaison, *m.*
177	comparative grammar	сравнительная грам- матика	vergleichende Grammatik	grammaire comparée, *f.*
178	comparative method	сравнительный метод	vergleichende Methode, *f.*	méthode comparative, *f.*
179	comparative-historical method	сравнительно- исторический метод	historisch-vergleichende Methode	méthode historico- comparative, *f.*
180	comparative linguistics	сравнительная лингвистика	vergleichende Sprachwissenschaft	linguistique comparative, *f.*
181	comparative mythology	сравнительная мифология	vergleichende Mythologie	mythologie comparée, *f.*
182	comparative philology	сравнительная филология	vergleichende Philologie/ vergleichende Sprach- wissenschaft	philologie comparée, *f.*
183	comparative sentence	сравнительное предложение	Komparativsatz, *m.*/ Vergleichssatz, *m.*	phrase comparative, *f.*
184	comparative stylistics	сравнительная стилистика	vergleichende Stilistik	stylistique comparée, *f.*
185	comparison, n.	сравнение, *n.*	Vergleich, *m.*	comparaison, *f.*
186	compatible, adj.	совместимый	angemessen	compatible
187	compendium, n.	компендиум, *m.*/ конспект, *m.*	Leitfaden, *m.*	abrégé, *m.*
188	compensatory, adj.	компенсирующий/ уравнивающий	ausgleichend	compensatoire
189	compensatory lengthen- ing of vowels	заменительное протяжение гласных	Ersatzdehnung bei Vokalen, *f.*	allongement compensa- toire des voyelles, *m.*
190	competence, n.	способность, *f.*/ умение, *n.*	Fähigkeit, *f.*	aptitude, *f.*
191	compilation, n.	составление, *n.*	Zusammenstellung, *f.*/ Zusammenfassung, *f.*/ Sammlung, *f.*	compilation, *f.*

No.	ENGLISH	RUSSIAN	GERMAN	FRENCH
192	complement, n.	дополнение, *n.*	Ergänzung, *f.*	complément, *m.*
193	complementary distribution	дополнительное распределение	komplementäre Verteilung	distribution complémentaire, *f.*
194	complete, adj.	полный	voll/ganz/vollständig	complet/plein
195	complete assimilation	полная ассимиляция	vollständige Assimilation	assimilation totale, *f.*
196	complete closure	полная смычка	vollständiger Verschluss	fermeture complète, *f.*
197	complete sentence	полная фраза/полное предложение	ganzer Satz	phrase complète, *f.*
198	completion, n.	завершение, *n.*	Vollendung, *f.*	achèvement, *m.*
199	complex, adj.	сложный	komplex/kompliziert	complexe
200	complex sentence	сложноподчиненное предложение	Satzgefüge, *n.*	phrase complexe, *f.*
201	complexity, n.	сложность, *f.*	Komplexheit, *f.*/ Verflechtung, *f.*/ Verwicklung, *f.*	complexité, *f.*/ complication, *f.*
202	complicated sentence	осложненное предложение	kompliziertes Satzgefüge	phrase compliquée, *f.*
203	component, n.	компонент, *m.*/ составляющий, *m.*	Komponente, *f.*/ Bestandteil, *m.*	composant, *m.*
204	componential analysis	анализ по компонентам, *m.*	Komponentenanalyse, *f.*	analyse des composants, *f.*
205	composite, n.	композит, *m.*/смесь, *f.*/ составное, *n.*	Kompositum, *n.*/ Zusammensetzung, *f.*	composé, *m.*
206	composition, n.	сочинение, *n.*	Zusammensetzung, *f.*/ Zusammenstellung, *f.*	composition, *f.*
207	compound, adj.	составной/ сложносочиненный	zusammengesetzt	composé
208	compound grapheme	составная графема	zusammengesetztes Graphem/zusammengesetztes Schriftzeichen	graphème composé, *m.*

No.	ENGLISH	RUSSIAN	GERMAN	FRENCH
209	compound noun	составное существительное	zusammengesetztes Substantiv	nom composé, *m.*
210	compound phoneme	сложная фонема	zusammengesetztes Phonem	phonème composé, *m.*
211	compound predicate	составное сказуемое	zusammengesetztes Prädikat	attribut composé, *m.*
212	compound sentence	сложносочиненное предложение	zusammengesetzter Satz/Satzreihe, *f.*	phrase complexe, *f.*
213	compound sound	сложный звук/ составной звук	zusammengesetzter Laut	son composé, *m.*
214	compound subject	составное подлежащее	zusammengesetztes Subjekt	sujet composé, *m.*
215	compound tense	сложное время	zusammengesetzte Zeit	temps composé, *m.*
216	compound verb	составной глагол	zusammengesetztes Verb(um)	verbe composé, *m.*
217	compound word	сложное слово/ составное слово	Kompositum, *n.*/zusammengesetztes Wort	mot composé, *m.*
218	compounding, n.	сложение, *n.*	Zusammensetzung, *f.*	composition, *f.*
219	comprehension, n.	понятливость, *f.*/ понимание, *n.*	Verständnis, *n.*/ Verstehen, *n.*	compréhension, *f.*
220	comprehensive, adj.	исчерпывающий	umfassend/ zusammenfassend	compréhensif
221	compression, n.	сжатие, *n.*	Zusammendrückung, *f.*	compression, *f.*
222	computational linguistics	математическая лингвистика	maschinelle Linguistik	linguistique mathématique, *f.*
223	computer, n.	электронная вычислительная машина	Komputer, *m.*/elektronische Rechenanlage/elektronische Rechenmaschine/ Elektronenrechner, *m.*/ Elektronengehirn, *n.*	calculatrice électronique, *f.*/ordinateur, *m.*
224	computing center	вычислительный центр	Rechenzentrum, *n.*	centre de calcul, *m.*

No.	ENGLISH	RUSSIAN	GERMAN	FRENCH
225	concatenation, n.	сцепление, *n.*	Verkettung, *f.*	enchaînement, *m.*
226	concealed, adj.	скрытый	verdeckt	caché
227	concentration, n.	концентрация, *f.*/ сосредоточение, *n.*	Konzentration, *f.*	concentration, *f.*
228	concept, n.	понятие, *n.*	Begriff, *m.*	concept, *m.*
229	conceptual category	понятийная категория	Begriffskategorie, *f.*	catégorie conceptuelle, *f.*
230	concessive clause	уступительное предложение	Konzessivsatz, *m.*/ Einräumungssatz, *m.*	proposition concessive, *f.*
231	concise, adj.	сжатый	zusammengefasst/knapp	concis
232	conclusion (end), n.	конец, *m.*/ заключение, *n.*	Ende, *n.*/Schluss, *m.*/ Abschluss, *m.*	conclusion, *f.*/fin, *f.*/ issue, *f.*
233	conclusion (deduction), n.	вывод, *m.*/ заключение, *n.*	Folgerung, *f.*/ Schluss(folgerung), *f.*	conclusion, *f.*
234	conclusive, adj.	заключительный	entscheidend	conclusif/concluant
235	concord, n.	согласование, *n.*	Kongruenz, *f.*/ Übereinstimmung, *f.*	accord, *m.*
236	concordance, n.	указатель встечающихся в книге слов или изречений, *m.*	Konkordanz, *f.*	concordance, *f.*
237	concrete, adj.	конкретный/ вещественный	konkret	concret
238	concrete noun	конкретное существительное / неотвлеченное существительное	Konkretum, *n.*/ Dingwort, *n.*/ Gegenstandswort, *n.*	nom concret, *m.*
239	concrete number	именованное число	bestimmtes Zahlwort	nombre concret, *m.*
240	concurrence, n.	одновременное действие/ совпадение, *n.*	Zusammenlaufen, *n.*/ Zusammentreffen, *n.*	rencontre, *f.*/ coïncidence, *f.*
241	concurrent, adj.	одновременный/ совпадающий	zusammentreffend/ zusammenlaufend/ gleichzeitig	concourant/coexistant/ coïncidant

No.	ENGLISH	RUSSIAN	GERMAN	FRENCH
242	condensation, n.	резюме, *n.*	Zusammenfassung, *f.*/ Abkürzung, *f.*/ Resümee, *n.*	résumé, *m.*
243	condition, n.	состояние, *n.*/ условие, *n.*	Zustand, *m.*/Verfass-ung, *f.*/Bedingung, *f.*	condition, *f.*/état, *m.*
244	conditional clause	условное предложение	Konditionalsatz, *m.*/ Bedingungssatz, *m.*	proposition condi-tionnée, *f.*
245	conditional mood	условное наклонение	Konditional, *m.*	conditionnel, *m.*
246	conditional probability	условная вероятность	bedingte Wahrschein-lichkeit	probabilité condition-nelle, *f.*
247	conditional sentence	условное предложение	Konditionalsatz, *m.*/ Bedingungssatz, *m.*	phrase conditionnelle, *f.*
248	conditioned, adj.	обусловленный	bedingt	conditionné
249	conditioned allophone	обусловленный вариант	kombinatorische Variante/umge-bungsbestimmte Variante	variante combinatoire, *f.*
250	conditioned reflex	условный рефлекс	bedingter Reflex	réflexe conditionné, *m.*
251	conditioned response	условная реакция	bedingte Reaktion	réaction conditionnée, *f.*
252	conditioned sound change	обусловленное изменение звука	bedingte Lautveränderung, *f.*/ kombinatorischer Lautwandel	changement phonétique conditionné, *m.*
253	conditioning, n.	обусловление, *n.*	Bedingung, *f.*	conditionnement, *m.*
254	conference, n.	конференция, *f.*/ совещание, *n.*/ съезд, *m.*	Konferenz, *f.*	congrès, *m.*
255	configuration, n.	конфигурация, *f.*/ очертание, *n.*	Gestaltung, *f.*/ Anordnung, *f.*	configuration, *f.*
256	configurational features, pl.	конфигуративные признаки, *m.,* pl.	prosodische Eigen-schaften, *f.,* pl.	traits prosodiques, *m.,* pl.
257	confirmation, n.	подтверждение, *n.*	Bestätigung, *f.*	confirmation, *f.*

No.	ENGLISH	RUSSIAN	GERMAN	FRENCH
258	confirmative question	подтвердителыный вопрос	bestätigende Frage	demande d'assentiment, *f.*
259	conflict, n.	конфликт, *m.*/ столкновение, *n.*	Konflikt, *m.*/ Zusammenstoss, *m.*	lutte, *f.*
260	confluence, n.	слияние, *n.*/ соединение, *n.*	Zusammenfluss, *m.*	confluence, *f.*
261	conformity, n.	соответствие, *n.*	Anpassung, *f.*/ Entsprechung, *f.*	conformité, *f.*/ ressemblance, *f.*
262	congress, n.	конгресс, *m.*/съезд, *m.*	Kongress, *m.*/Tagung, *f.*/ Versammlung, *f.*	congrès, *m.*
263	congruence, n.	конгруэнтность, *f.*	Kongruenz, *f.*	congruence, *f.*
264	congruent, adj.	соответствующий	entsprechend/ zusammengehörig	conforme/convenable/ d'accord
265	conjecture, n.	предположение, *n.*	Vermutung, *f.*	conjecture, *f.*
266	conjoining, n.	соединение, *n.*	Verbindung, *f.*	association, *f.*
267	conjugation, n.	спряжение, *n.*	Konjugation, *f.*	conjugaison, *f.*
268	conjunction, n.	союз, *n.*	Konjunktion, *f.*/ Bindewort, *n.*	conjonction, *f.*
269	conjunctive adverb	соединительное наречие	Konjunktionaladverb, *n.*/ verbindendes Adverb	adverbe conjonctif, *m.*
270	conjunctive mood	сослагательное наклонение	Konjunktiv, *m.*/ Möglichkeitsform, *f.*	mode conjonctif, *m.*
271	connected speech	связанная речь	fortlaufende Rede	discours suivi, *m.*
272	connecting, adj.	союзный/ соединительный/ связующий	verbindend	connectif/de liaison
273	connecting morpheme	соединительная морфема	Verbindungsmorphem, *n.*	terme de líaison, *m.*
274	connecting vowel	соединительная гласная	Bindevokal, *m.*/ Einschubvokal, *m.*	voyelle de liaison, *f.*

No.	ENGLISH	RUSSIAN	GERMAN	FRENCH
275	connective, n.	соединительное слово	verbindendes Wort	mot de liaison, *m.*
276	connotation, n.	сопутствующее значение/ дополнительное значение	Nebenbedeutung, *f.*	implication, *f.*/ sens suggéré, *m.*
277	conscious choice	сознательный отбор	bewusste Auswahl	choix conscient, *m.*
278	conciousness, n.	сознательность, *f.*	Bewusstsein, *f.*	conscience, *f.*
279	consecutive, adj.	последовательный	aufeinander folgend/konsekutiv	consécutif
280	consequence, n.	следствие, *n.*/ последствие, *n.*	Folge, *f.*	conséquence, *f.*
281	consequent, adj.	последующий	folgend	conséquent
282	consideration, n.	рассмотрение, *n.*	Betrachtung, *f.*/Erwägung, *f.*/Überlegung, *f.*	examen, *m.*
283	consistent, adj.	согласующийся/ последовательный	übereinstimmend/ konsequent	logique
284	consonance, n.	созвучие, *n.*	Einklang, *m.*	assonance, *f.*
285	consonant, n.	согласная, *f.*/ согласный звук	Konsonant, *m.*/ Mitlaut, *m.*	consonne, *f.*
286	consonant alternation	чередование согласных, *n.*	Konsonantenwechsel, *m.*	alternance consonantique, *f.*
287	consonant change	изменение согласных, *n.*	Konsonantenwandel, *m.*	changement consonantique, *m.*
288	consonant classification	классификация согласных, *f.*	Konsonantenklassifikation, *f.*/ Konsonanteneinteilung, *f.*	classement des consonnes, *m.*
289	consonant cluster	стяжение согласных, *n.*/ скопление согласных, *n.*/ стечение согласных, *n.*/слияние согласных, *n.*	Konsonantengefüge, *m.*/ Konsonantengruppe, *f.*/ Konsonantenfolge, *f.*/ Konsonantenverbindung	groupe de consonnes, *m.*/ complexe de consonnes, *m.*
290	consonant formation	образование согласных, *n.*	Konsonantenbildung, *f.*	formation des consonnes, *f.*

No.	ENGLISH	RUSSIAN	GERMAN	FRENCH
291	consonant insertion	вставка согласного, *f.*	Konsonanteneinschub, *m.*/Konsonantenein-schiebung, *f.*	insertion de consonne, *f.*
292	consonant length	длительность согласных, *f.*	Länge von Konsonanten, *f.*	longueur des consonnes, *f.*
293	consonant omission	пропуск согласного, *m.*	Konsonantenauslassung, *f.*/Konsonantenverlust, *m.*	omission de consonne, *f.*
294	consonant(al) phoneme	согласная фонема	konsonantisches Phonem	phonème consonantique, *m.*
295	consonant(al) script	консонантное письмо	Konsonantenschrift, *f.*	écriture consonantiqe, *f.*
296	consonant series	согласный ряд	Konsonantenreihe, *f.*	série de consonnes, *f.*
297	consonant shift	передвижение согласных, *n.*	Konsonantenverschie-bung, *f.*/Lautverschie-bung, *f.*	mutation consonantique, *f.*
298	consonant sound	согласный звук	Konsonant, *m.*/ Mitlaut, *m.*	son consonantique, *m.*
299	consonant system	система согласных, *f.*	Konsonantensystem, *n.*	système consonantique, *m.*
300	consonantism, n.	консонантизм, *m.*	Konsonantismus, *m.*	consonantisme, *m.*
301	constant, adj.	постоянный	konstant	constant
302	constituent, n.	составляющее, *n.*	Konstituente, *f.*/ Bestandteil, *m.*	élément constitutif, *m.*
303	constituent structure	структура составляющих, *f.*	Konstituentenstruktur, *f.*	structure élémentaire, *f.*
304	constraint, n.	ограничение, *n.*	Beschränkung, *f.*/ Einschränkung, *f.*	limitation, *f.*
305	constriction, n.	смыкание, *n.*	Zusammenziehung, *f.*	rétrécissement, *m.*
306	construction, n.	конструкция, *f.*	Konstruktion, *f.*	construction, *f.*
307	contact, n.	контакт, *n.*/ соприкосновение, *m.*	Kontakt, *m.*	rencontre, *f.*/contact, *m.*
308	contamination, n.	контаминация, *f.*/ смешение, *n.*	Kontamination, *f.*/ Mischbildung, *f.*	contamination, *f.*

No.	ENGLISH	RUSSIAN	GERMAN	FRENCH
309	contemporaneous, adj.	современный	gleichzeitig/zeitge-nössisch/derzeitig	contemporain
310	contemporary languages, pl.	современные языки, *m.*, pl.	lebende Sprachen, *f.*, pl./ Sprachen der Gegenwart, *f.*, pl.	langues contemporaines, *f.*, pl.
311	contempt, n.	презрение, *n.*	Verachtung, *f.*	mépris, *m.*
312	content, n.	содержание, *n.*	Inhalt, *m.*	contenu, *m.*
313	content analysis	анализ содержания, *m.*	Inhaltsanalyse, *f.*	analyse intérieure, *f.*
314	content system	план содержания, *m.*	Inhaltssystem, *n.*	plan du contenu, *m.*
315	content words, pl.	конкретные слова, *n.*, pl.	Inhaltswörter, *n.*, pl.	mots signifiants, *m.*, pl.
316	context, n.	контекст, *m.*/ содержание, *n.*	Kontext, *m.*/ Zusammenhang, *m.*	contexte, *m.*
317	context-free grammar	грамматика без контекстуальных ограничений, *f.*	kontextfreie Grammatik/ kontextunabhängige Grammatik	grammaire indépendante du contexte, *f.*
318	context-restricted grammar (also: context-sensitive grammar)	грамматика с контекстуальными ограничениями, *f.*	kontextbedingte Grammatik/kontextbestimmte Grammatik	grammaire dépendante du contexte, *f.*
319	contextual meaning	контекстное значение	Kontextbedeutung, *f.*/ Bedeutung im Zusammenhang, *f.*	sens contextuel, *m.*/sens relatif au contexte, *m.*
320	contextually conditioned neutralization	обусловленная контекстом нейтрализация	kontextbedingte Neutralisation	neutralisation conditionnée par le contexte, *f.*
321	contigu/adjacent	смежный/соседний	benachbart	contigu/adjacent
322	contiguous assimilation	контактная ассимиляция	Nahassimilation, *f.*/ unmittelbare Assimilation	assimilation de contact, *f.*/assimilation organique, *f.*
323	contiguous sounds, pl.	смежные звуки, *m.*, pl./ соседние звуки, *m.*, pl.	benachbarte Laute, *m.*, pl.	sons contigus, m., pl.
324	contingent, adj.	условный	bedingt	dépendant
325	continual, adj.	непрерывный	ununterbrochen	continuel

No.	ENGLISH	RUSSIAN	GERMAN	FRENCH
326	continuant consonants, pl.	протяженные согласные, pl./ длительные согласные, pl.	Dauerlaute, *m.,* pl.	consonnes continues, *f.,* pl.
327	continuation, n.	продолжение, *n.*	Weiterführung, *f./* Verlängerung, *f./* Fortsetzung, *f.*	prolongation, *f./* prolongement, *m.*
328	continuity, n.	непрерывность, *f./* постоянство, *n.*	Stetigkeit, *f.*	continúite, *f.*
329	continuous, adj.	непрерывный/ постоянный	stetig/fortlaufend	continu
330	continuous process	непрерывный процесс	stetiger Vorgang	processus continu, *m.*
331	continuum, n.	континуум, *m.*	Kontinuum, *n.*	continu, *m.*
332	contour, n.	контур, *m./*оболочка, *f.*	Kontur, *f./*Umriss, *m./* Umrisslinie, *f.*	profil, *m.*
333	contracted expression	стяжение, *n./* сокращение, *n.*	verkürzter Ausdruck/ Kurzform, *f.*	expression contractée, *f.*
334	contracted sentence	слитное предложение	verkürzter Satz	phrase elliptique, *f.*
335	contraction, n.	сокращение, *n./* стяжение, *n.*	Verkürzung, *f./* Kontraktion, *f.*	contraction, *f.*
336	contradiction, n.	противоречие, *n.*	Widerspruch, *m.*	contradiction, *f.*
337	contrast, n.	контраст, *m./* противопоставление, *n.*	Kontrast, *m./* Opposition, *f./* Gegensatz, *m.*	contraste, *m.*
338	contrastive analysis	сопоставительный анализ	kontrastive Analyse	analyse contrastive, *f.*
339	contrastive distribution	контрастирующая дистрибуция/ сопоставительное распределение	kontrastive Verteilung	distributon contrastive, *f.*
340	contrastive grammar	сопоставительная грамматика	kontrastive Grammatik	grammaire contrastive, *f.*
341	contribution, n.	вклад, *m.*	Beitrag, *m.*	contribution, *f.*
342	control, n.	контроль, *m.*	Kontrolle, *f.*	contrôle, *m.*

No.	ENGLISH	RUSSIAN	GERMAN	FRENCH
343	control group	контрольная группа	Kontrollgruppe, *f.*	groupe de contrôle, *m.*
344	controlled vocabulary	отобранная лексика	ausgewählter Wortschatz	vocabulaire contrôlé, *m.*
345	controversy, n.	спорный вопрос	Kontroverse, *f.*/ Streitfrage, *f.*	controverse, *f.*
346	conundrum, n.	загадка, *f.*/ головоломка, *f.*	Scherzfrage, *f.*	devinette, *f.*
347	convenient, adj.	удобный/пригодный	bequem/geeignet	pratique
348	convention, n.	общее согласие/ условность, *f.*	Übereinkommen, *n.*/ allgemeines Überein- kommen, *n.*	convention, *f.*
349	conventional, adj.	условный	konventionell	conventionnel
350	conventional sign	общепринятый знак/ условный знак	konventionelles Zeichen	signe conventionnel, *m.*
351	convergence, n.	конвергенция, *f.*/ схождение, *n.*	Konvergenz, *f.*/ Zusammenlaufen, *n.*	convergence, *f.*
352	convergent development of languages	сходящееся развитие языков	konvergente Sprachent- wicklung	développement conver- gent des langues, *m.*
353	conversation, n.	разговор, *m.*/беседа, *f.*	Gespräch, *n.*/ Unterhaltung, *f.*	conversation, *f.*
354	conversationalists, pl.	собеседники, *m.,* pl.	Gesprächspartner, *m.,* pl.	causeurs, *m,* pl.
355	converse, n.	обратное положение	Gegensatz, *m.*/Gegenteil, *n.*/Umkehrung, *f.*	converse, *f.*
356	conversion, n.	конверсия, *f.*/ превращение, *n.*	Konversion, *f.*/ Umstellung, *f.*	conversion, *f.*
357	convertible, adj.	заменимый/ превращаемый	umkehrbar/umwandelbar	interchangeable
358	co-occurrence, n.	совместная встречаемость	Zusammentreffen, *n.*	co-apparition, *f.*
359	cooing, n.	воркование, *n.*	Girren, *n.*	roucoulement, *m.*
360	cookbook style	стиль поваренной книги, *m.*	Kochbuchstil, *m.*	style de livre de cuisine, *m.*

No.	ENGLISH	RUSSIAN	GERMAN	FRENCH
361	cooked data, pl.	проработанные данные, pl.	bearbeitetes Material	données truquées, *f.*, pl.
362	cooperation, n.	сотрудничество, *n.*	Mitwirkung, *f.*/ Zusammenarbeit, *f.*	coopération, *f.*
363	coordinating conjunction	сочинительный союз	beiordnende Konjunktion	conjonction de coordination, *f.*
364	coordination, n.	координация, *f.*/ соподчинение, *n.*/ сочинение, *n.*	Beiordnung, *f.*	coordination, *f.*
365	copula, n.	связка, *f.*	Kopula, *f.*/ Verbindungswort, *n.*	copule *f.*
366	copy (of a book), n.	экземпляр, *m.*	Exemplar, *n.*	exemplaire, *m.*
367	copyright, n.	авторское право	Urheberrecht, *n.*	droits d'auteur, *m.*, pl.
368	corollary, n.	следствие, *n.*	Folge, *f.*/Folgesatz, *m.*	corollaire, *m.*
369	corpus, n.	совокупность высказываний, *f.*	Corpus, *m.*	corpus, *m.*
370	correct, adj.	правильный	richtig	exact
371	correct pronunciation	правильное произношение	richtige Aussprache	prononciation exacte, *f.*
372	correct spelling	правильное правописание	richtige Schreibweise	orthographe exacte, *f.*
373	correct usage	правильное употребление	richtiger Gebrauch	bon usage, *m.*
374	correct word order	правильный порядок слов	richtige Wortstellung	ordre normal des mots, *m.*
375	correction, n.	исправление, *n.*/ поправка, *f.*	Korrektur, *f.*/ Verbesserung, *f.*	correction, *f.*
376	correlate, n.	коррелят, *m.*	Korrelat(ivum), *n.*	corrélatif, *m.*
377	correlated pair	коррелятивная пара	Korrelationspaar, *n.*	paire corrélative, *f.*
378	correlation, n.	корреляция, *f.*/ соотношение, *n.*	Korrelation, *f.*	corrélation, *f.*

No.	English	Russian	German	French
379	correlative series	коррелятивная серия	korrelative Reihe	série corrélative, *f.*
380	correspondence (between items), n.	соответствие, *n.*	Entsprechung, *f.*	correspondance, *f.*
381	correspondence (between people), n.	переписка, *f.*	Korrespondenz, *f.*/ Briefwechsel, *m.*	correspondance, *f.*
382	corresponding, adj.	соответствующий/ соотносительный	entsprechend	correspondant
383	corrupted word	исковерканное слово/ искаженное слово	verderbtes Wort	mot corrompu, *m.*
384	cost, n.	стоимость, *f.*	Kosten, *f.*, pl.	coût, *m.*
385	count noun	имя существительное обозначающее считаемый предмет	zählbares Substantiv	substantif capable de former un pluriel, *m.*
386	counteraction, n.	противодействие, *n.*	Gegenwirkung, *f.*	opposition, *f.*
387	counter-term, n.	антоним, *m.*	Antonym, *n.*/entgegenge-setzter Begriff	antonyme, *m.*
388	counting, n.	счет, *m.*	Zahlen, *n.*	dénombrement, *m.*
389	couplet, n.	рифмованное двустишие	Reimpaar, *n.*/Distichon, *n.*/Zweizeiler, *m.*	distique, *m.*
390	course of developments	ход событий, *m.*	Gang der Dinge, *m.*	développment des événements, *m*
391	course of study (leading to degree)	программа обучения, *f.*	Studienplan, *m.*	programme d'enseignement, *m.*
392	covariation, n.	⟨одновременная вариация⟩	gleichzeitige Veränderung/ Mitveränderung, *f.*	variation coïncidante, *f.*
393	covert, adj.	скрытый	verdeckt/verborgen	couvert
394	creation, n.	создание, *n.*	Schöpfung, *f.*	création, *f.*
395	creolized languages, pl.	креолизированные языки, *m.*, pl./ креольские языки, *m.*, pl.	kreolische Sprachen, *f.*, pl.	parlers créoles, *m.*, pl.

No.	English	Russian	German	French
396	crest, n.	вершина, *f.*	Gipfel, *m.*	sommet, *m.*
397	criterion, n.	критерий, *m.*	Kriterium, *n.*	critère, *m.*
398	criticism, n.	критика, *f.*	Kritik, *f.*	critique, *f*
399	cross-cultural studies, pl.	межкультурные исследования, *n.,* pl.	⟨Interkulturstudien⟩, *f.,* pl.	étude et comparaison des cultures, *f.,* sg.
400	cross-reference, n.	ссылка на другое место, *f./* ⟨перекрестная ссылка⟩	Kreuzverweis, *m./* Querverweis, *m.*	renvoi, *m.*
401	cross-section, n.	поперечный разрез	Querschnitt, *m.*	coupe transversale, *f*
402	crossing theory	теория скрещивания, *f.*	Kreuzungstheorie, *f.*	théorie de croisement, *f.*
403	crossword puzzle	крестословица, *f./* кроссворд, *m.*	Kreuzworträtsel, *n.*	mots-croisés, *m.,* pl.
404	crucial test	решающий опыт	Feuerprobe, *f.*	test décisif, *m.*
405	crying, n.	плач, *m.*	Weinen, *n.*	pleurs, *m.,* pl.
406	cryptanalysis, n.	криптографический анализ	Kryptoanalyse, *f.*	analyse cryptographique, *f.*
407	cryptogram, n.	криптограмма, *f./* шифрованный документ	Kryptogramm, *n.*	cryptogramme, *m.*
408	cryptography, n.	криптография, *f./* тайнопись, *f.*	Kryptographie, *f./* Geheimschrift, *f.*	cryptographie, *f.*
409	culmination, n.	завершение, *n.*	Vollendung, *f.*	culmination, *f.*
410	cultivated speech	воспитанная речь	Hochsprache, *f.*	langage des gens cultivés, *m*
411	cultural change	культурное изменение	kulturelle Veränderung	changement culturel, *m.*
412	cultural determination	культурное определение	kulturelle Bestimmung/ kulturelle Bedingtheit	conditionnement culturel, *m.*
413	cultural diffusion	культурное распространение	kulturelle Verbreitung	diffusion culturelle, *f.*

No.	ENGLISH	RUSSIAN	GERMAN	FRENCH
414	cultural distribution	культурная дистрибуция/ культурное распределение	kulturelle Verteilung	distribution suivant les cultures, *f.*
415	cultural exchange	культурный обмен	Kulturaustausch, *m.*	échange culturel, *m.*
416	cultural lag	культурная отсталость	kulturelle Verzögerung	attardement culturel, *m.*
417	cultural transmission	культурная передача	kulturelle Überlieferung/ kulturelle Übertragung	transmission culturelle, *f.*
418	culture, n.	культура, *f.*	Kultur, *f.*/Zivilisation, *f.*	culture, *f.*
419	culture area	район культурного влияния, *m.*	Kulturgebiet, *n.*	zone d'influence culturelle, *f.*
420	cuneiform writing	клинопись, *f.*	Keilschrift, *f.*	écriture cunéiforme, *f.*
421	current problem	текущая проблема	gegenwärtiges Problem/ aktuelles Problem/ Gegenwartsfrage, *f.*	problème d'actualité, *m.*
422	curriculum, n.	учебный план	Lehrplan, *m.*	programme, *m.*
423	curse, n.	проклятие, *n.*	Fluch, *m.*	malédiction, *f.*
424	cursive writing	рукописный шрифт	Kursivschrift, *f.*	écriture cursive, *f.*
425	curved line	кривая линия	gebogene Linie/ geschwungene Linie	ligne courbe, *f.*
426	custom, n.	обычай, *m.*/ привычка, *f.*	Gewohnheit, *f.*/Sitte, *f.*	coutume, *m.*
427	customary, adj.	обычный/привычный	gewohnheitsmässig/ gewöhnlich	habituel/usuel/coutumier
428	cut, n.	сечение, *n.*	Schnitt, *m.*	coupe, *f.*
429	cybernetics, n.	кибернетика, *f.*	Kybernetik, *f.*	cybernétique, *f.*
430	cycle, n.	цикл, *m.*	Zyklus, *m.*	cycle, *m.*
431	cycles per second, pl.	герц, *m.*	Frequenz, *f.*/Hertz, *n.*	fréquence, *f.*
432	cyclic, adj.	циклический	zyklisch	cyclique
433	Cyrillic alphabet	кириллица, *f.*	kyrillisches Alphabet	alphabet cyrillique, *m.*
434	Czech, adj.	чешский	tschechisch	tchèque

No.	ENGLISH	RUSSIAN	GERMAN	FRENCH

D

No.	ENGLISH	RUSSIAN	GERMAN	FRENCH
001	Danish, adj.	датский	dänisch	danois
002	dark 1	темное л/велярное л/ заднее л	dunkles L/hinteres L/ velares L	l creux, *m.*/l postérieur, *m.*/l velaire, *m.*
003	dark vowels, pl.	темные гласные, pl.	dunkle Vokale, *m.,* pl.	voyelles sombres, *f.,* pl.
004	dash, n.	тире, *n.*/черточка, *f.*	Gedankenstrich, *m.*	tiret, *m.*
005	data, pl.	данные, pl.	Daten, *f.,* pl./Material, *n.* /Unterlagen, *f.,* pl.	données, *f.,*pl.
006	data processing	обработка данных, *f.*	Datenverarbeitung, *f.*	ordination, *f.*
007	date, n.	дата, *f.*/число, *n.*	Datum, *n.*	date, *f.*
008	dating, n.	датирование, *n.*	Datierung, *f.*	dâte à laquelle remonte..., *f.*
009	dative case	дательний падеж	Dativ, *m.*/Wemfall, *m.*/ dritter Fall	datif, *m.*
010	daughter language	язык-потомок, *m.*	Tochtersprache, *f.*	langue fille, *f.*
011	dead languages, pl.	мертвые языки, *m.,* pl.	tote Sprachen, *f.,* pl.	langues mortes, *f.,* pl.
012	deaf, adj.	глухой	taub	sourd
013	deafness, n.	глухота, *f.*	Taubheit, *f.*/ Gehörlosigkeit, *f.*	surdité, *f.*
014	debate, n.	дебаты, pl./прения, *f.*	Debatte, *f.*	débat, *m.*/ conférence contradictoire, *f.*/ parlote, *f.*
015	decade, n.	десятилетие, *n.*	Jahrzehnt, *n.*	décennie, *f.*
016	decay, n.	распад, *m.*	Verfall, *m.*	dégradaton, *f.*
017	decimal, adj.	десятичный	dezimal	décimal
018	decipher, v.	расшифровывать	entziffern	décoder
019	decision, n.	решение, *n.*	Entscheidung, *f.*	décision, *f.*
020	decision procedure	решающая процедура	Entscheidungsverfahren, *n.*	methode pour faire un choix, *f.*

No.	ENGLISH	RUSSIAN	GERMAN	FRENCH
021	decisive, adj.	решительный	entscheidend	définitif
022	declarative sentence	повествовательное предложение	Aussagesatz, *m.*	phrase déclarative, *f.*/ phrase assertive, *f.*
023	declension, n.	склонение, *n.*	Deklination, *f.*/ Beugung, *f.*	déclinaison, *f.*
024	declinable, adj.	склоняемый	deklinierbar/ beugungsfähig	déclinable
025	decoding, n.	декодирование, *n.*/ расшифровка, *f.*	Dekodierung, *f.*/ Dechiffrierung, *f.*/ Entschlüsselung, *f.*/ Entzifferung, *f.*	décodage, *m.*
026	decrease, n.	снижение, *n.*/ уменьшение, *n.*	Abnahme, *f.*/Schwund, *n.* /Schwinden, *n.*	diminution, *f.*
027	dedication, n. (of book)	посвящение, *n.*	Zueignung, *f.*/ Widmung, *f.*	dédicace, *f.*
028	deduction, n.	дедукция, *f.*/вывод, *m.*	Deduktion, *f.*/Folgerung, *f.*/Herleitung, *f.*	déduction, *f.*
029	deductive reasoning	дедуктивное рассуждение	deduktives Urteil	raisonnement déductif, *m.*
030	deep structure	структура ядерных предложений, *f.*	Tiefenstruktur, *f.*	structure sous-jacente, *f.*
031	defective, adj.	недостаточный	defektiv/lückenhaft/ unvollständig	défectif
032	defective distribution	дефективная дистрибуция	defektive Verteilung	distribution défective, *f.*
033	defective verb	недостаточный глагол	defektives Verb(um)	verbe défectif, *m.*
034	deficiency, n.	недостаток, *m.*	Unzulänglichkeit, *f.*	insuffisance, *f.*
035	definite, adj.	определенный	bestimmt	défini
036	definite article	определенный артикль	bestimmter Artikel	article défini, *m.*
037	definite tense	определенное время	bestimmte Zeitform	temps défini, *m.*
038	definition, n.	определение, *n.*	Definition, *f.*/ Begriffsbestimmung, *f.*	définition, *f.*

No.	ENGLISH	RUSSIAN	GERMAN	FRENCH
039	definitive, adj.	решительный/ определяющий	bestimmend/definitiv/ endgültig	défini
040	degree, n.	степень, *f.*	Grad, *m.*/Stufe, *f.*	degré, *m.*
041	degree of aperture	степень открытия, *f.*	Öffnungsgrad, *m.*	degré d'ouverture, *m.*
042	degree of closure	степень закрытия, *f.*	Verschlussgrad, *m.*/ Engengrad, *m.*	degré de fermeture, *m.*
043	degree of comparison	степень сравнения, *f.*	Steigerungsstufe, *f.*/ Vergleichungsgrad, *m.*	degré de comparaison, *m.*
044	degree of grammaticality, degree of grammaticalness	степень грамматичности, *f.*	Grad der Grammatizität, *m.*/Grad der grammatischen Richtigkeit, *m.*	degré de grammaticalité, *m.*
045	degree of stability	степень устойчивости, *f.*	Stabilitätsgrad, *m.*	degré de stabilité, *m.*
046	degree of tension	степень напряженности, *f.*	Spannungsgrad, *m.*	degré de tension, *m.*
047	deictic, adj.	показательный/ указательный	deiktisch/hinweisend	démonstratif
048	deity, n.	божество, *n.*	Gott, *m.*/Gottheit, *f.*	déité, *f.*/divinité, *f.*
049	deletion, n.	пропуск, *m.*	Löschung, *f.*/Tilgung, *f.*	suppression, *f.*
050	delimitation, n.	разграничение, *n.*/ ограничение, *n.*	Abgrenzung, *f.*	délimitation, *f.*
051	delineation, n.	очертание, *n.*/ описание, *n.*	Entwurf, *m.*	esquisse, *f.*/description, *f.*
052	demand, n.	требование, *f.*	Forderung, *f.*	exigence, *f.*
053	demarcation, n.	отграничение, *n.*	Abgrenzung, *f.*	démarcation, *f.*
054	demarcative feature	диарема, *f.*/ разграничительный сигнал	Grenzsignal, *n.*	diaréma, *m.*/signe démarcatif, *m.*
055	demography, n.	демография, *f.*	Demographie, *f.*	démographie, *f.*
056	demonstrative article	указательный артикль	Demonstrativartikel, *m.*	article indicatif, *m.*

No.	English	Russian	German	French
057	demonstrative pronoun	указательное местоимение	Demonstrativpronomen, *n.*/hinweisendes Fürwort	pronom démonstratif, *m.*
058	demonstrative word	указательное слово	Demonstrativ(um), *n.*	mot démonstratif, *m.*
059	denominative, n.	производное от существительного	Denominativ(um), *n.*	dénominatif, *m.*
060	denotation, n.	обозначение, *n.*	Bedeutung, *f.*	sens, *m.*
061	density, n.	плотность, *f.*	Dichte, *f.*	densité, *f.*
062	density of isoglosses	плотность изоглосс, *f.*	Dichte der Isoglossen, *f.*	densité des isoglosses, *f.*
063	density of population	плотность населения, *f.*	Bevölkerungsdichte, *f.*	densité de population, *f.*
064	dental consonants, pl.	дентальные согласные, pl./ зубные согласные, pl.	dentale Konsonanten, *m.*, pl./Zahnlaute, *m.*, pl.	consonnes dentales, *f.*, pl.
065	department of university	факультет, *m.*/ кафедра, *f.*	Fakultät, *f.*/Institut der Universität, *n.*/Seminar der Universität, *n.*	section d'une faculté, *f.*
066	dependability, n.	надежность, *f.*	Zuverlässigkeit, *f.*	sécurité, *f.*
067	dependence, n.	зависимость, *f.*	Abhängigkeit, *f.*	dépendance, *f.*
068	dependent element	зависимый элемент	abhängiges Element	élément subordonné, *f.*
069	dependent clause	подчиненное предложение	abhängiger Satz/ Nebensatz, *m.*	proposition subordonné, *f.*
070	dependent variable	зависимая переменная	abhängige Variable	variable subordonnée, *f.*
071	depth, n.	глубина, *f.*	Tiefe, *f.*	profondeur, *f.*
072	derivation, n.	деривация, *f.*/ происхождение, *n.*	Ableitung, *f.*	dérivation, *f.*
073	derivational affix	деривационный аффикс/слово-образовательный аффикс	Ableitungsaffix, *n.*/ derivatives Affix/ Wortbildungselement, *n.*	affixe dérivatif, *m.*
074	derivative, adj.	производный	derivativ/abgeleitet	dérivé

No.	English	Russian	German	French
075	derivative, n.	производное, *n.*	Derivatum, *n.*/ abgeleitetes Wort	dérivé, *m.*
076	derived, adj.	производный	abgeleitet	dérivé
077	derived meaning	производное значение	abgeleitete Bedeutung	sens dérivé, *m.*
078	derived stem	производная основа	abgeleiteter Stamm	radical dérivé, *m.*
079	derived word	производное слово	abgeleitetes Wort	mót dérivé, *m.*
080	descent, n.	происхождение, *n.*/ родословная, *f.*	Abstammung, *f.*/ Herkunft, *f.*	descendance, *f.*
081	description, n.	описание, *n.*	Beschreibung, *f.*	description, *f.*
082	descriptive adjective	описательное прилагательное	deskriptives Adjektiv	adjectif descriptif, *m.*
083	descriptive attribute	описательное определение	deskriptives Attribut	épithéte descriptif, *m.*
084	descriptive linguistics	дескриптивная лингвистика	deskriptive Linguistik	linguistique descriptive, *f.*
085	design, n.	модель, *f.*	Bauplan, *m.*/Modell, *n.*	schéma, *m.*
086	designating, adj.	обозначающий	designant/bezeichnend	designant
087	designation, n.	обозначение, *n.*	Benennung, *f.*/ Bezeichnung, *f.*	désignation, *f.*
088	designator, n.	десигнатель, *m.*	Designator, *m.*/ Bezeichner, *m.*	désignateur, *m.*/ signifiant, *m.*
089	designatum, n.	десигнат, *m.*	Signifikatum, *n.*	signifié, *m.*
090	destination, n.	цель, *f.*	Bestimmungsort, *m.*/ Ziel, *n.*	but, *f.*/destination, *m.*
091	detached, adj.	отделенный/ обособленный	gelöst/getrennt/losgelöst	séparé
092	detail, n.	подробность, *f.*/ детали, pl.	Detail, *n.*/Einzelheit, *f.*	détail, *m.*
093	detection, n.	обнаружение, *n.*/ раскрытие, *n.*	Entdeckung, *f.*	répérage, *m.*
094	determiner, n.	определяющее, *n.*	Determinante, *f.*	déterminant, *m.*

No.	ENGLISH	RUSSIAN	GERMAN	FRENCH
095	development, n.	развитие, *n.*	Entwicklung, *f.*	développement, *m.*
096	deverbal, adj.	глагольный/ отглагольный	deverbativ	verbal
097	deviation, n.	отклонение, *n.*	Abweichung, *f.*	écart, *m.*
098	device (mechanical), n.	механизм, *m.*	Anlage, *f.*/Gerät, *n.*	procédé, *m.*
099	device (linguistic), n.	способ, *m.*	Mittel, *n.*/Verfahren, *n.*	moyen, *m.*
100	devoicing, n.	оглушение, *n.*	Stimmloswerden, *n.*	assourdissement, *m.*
101	diachronic, adj.	диахронический	diachronisch	diachronique
102	diachronic analysis	диахронический анализ	diachronische Analyse	analyse diachronique, *f.*
103	diachronic linguistics	диахроническая лингвистика	diachronische Sprach- wissenschaft	linguistique évolutive, *f.*
104	diachronic phonology	диахроническая фонология	diachronische Phonologie	phonologie diachronique, *f.*
105	diachronic syntax	диахронический синтаксис	diachronische Syntax	syntaxe diachronique, *f.*
106	diachrony, n.	диахрония, *f.*	Diachronie, *f.*	diachronie, *f.*
107	diacritical mark	диакритический знак	diakritisches Zeichen	signe diacritique, *m.*
108	diaeresis, n.	диэреза, *f.*/трема, *f.*	Dihärese, *f.*/Trema, *n.*	diérèse, *f.*
109	diagonal line	диагональная линия	diagonale Linie	ligne diagonale, *f.*
110	diagram, n.	диаграмма, *f.*/ схема, *f.*/график, *m.*	Diagramm, *n.*/graphische Darstellung/Skizze, *f.*	diagramme, *m.*
111	dialect, n.	диалект, *m.*/наречие, *n.*	Dialekt, *m.*/Mundart, *f.*	dialecte, *m.*
112	dialect area	диалектная область/ территория распространения диалекта, *f.*	Dialektgebiet, *n.*	aire dialectale, *f.*
113	dialect atlas	диалектологический атлас	Dialektatlas, *m.*	atlas linguistique, *m.*
114	dialect geography	диалектальная география	Dialektgeographie, *f.*	géographie dialectale, *f.*

No.	ENGLISH	RUSSIAN	GERMAN	FRENCH
115	dialectology, n.	диалектология, *f.*/ изучение диалектов, *n.*	Dialektologie, *f.*/Mund- artenforschung, *f.*	dialectologie, *f.*
116	dialogue, n.	диалог, *m.*	Dialog, *m.*/ Zwiegespräch, *n.*	dialogue, *m.*
117	diaphone, n.	диафон, *m.*	Diaphon, *n.*	diaphone, *m.*
118	diaphragm, n.	диафрагма, *f.*/ грудобрюшная преграда	Zwerchfell, *n.*	diaphragme, *m.*
119	diapason (of voice), n.	диапазон, *m.*	Stimmumfang, *f.*	diapason, *m.*
120	diary, n.	дневник, *m.*	Tagebuch, *m.*	journal intime, *m.*
121	diasystem, n.	диасистема, *f.*	Diasystem, *n.*/ Gesamtsystem, *n.*	diasystème, *m.*
122	dichotomy, n.	дихотомия, *f.*	Dichotomie, *f.*	dichotomie, *f.*
123	dichotomous phonology	дихотомическая фонология	dichotome Phonologie	phonologie dicotomique, *f.*
124	dichotomy scale	дихотомическая шкала	Dichotomie-Skala, *f.*	échelle de dichotomie, *f.*
125	dictaphone, n.	диктофон, *m.*	Diktaphon, *n.*/ Diktiergerät, *n.*	dictaphone, *m.*
126	dictation, n.	диктовка, *f.*	Diktat, *n.*	dictée, *f.*
127	diction, n.	дикция, *f.*	Ausdrucksweise, *f.*	diction, *f.*
128	dictionary, n.	словарь, *m.*	Wörterbuch, *n.*	dictionnaire, *m.*
129	dictionary entry	словарная статья	Stichwort, *n.*/ Wörterbucheintrag, *m.*	entrée de dictionnaire, *f.*/ article de dictionnaire, *m.*
130	difference, n.	отличие, *n.*/различие, *n.*/разница, *f.*	Unterschied, *m.*	différence, *f.*
131	difference in form	различие в форме, *n.*	Formunterschied, *m.*	différence de forme, *f.*
132	difference in meaning	различие в значении, *n.*	Bedeutungsunterschied, *m.*	différence de sens, *f.*
133	difference of opinion	разногласие, *n.*	Meinungsverschieden- heit, *f.*	différence d'opinion, *f.*

No.	English	Russian	German	French
134	differentiation, n.	дифференциация, *f.*/ различение, *n.*	Unterscheidung, *f.*	différenciation, *f.*
135	difficulty, n.	трудность, *f.*/ затруднение, *n.*	Schwierigkeit, *f.*	difficulté, *f.*
136	difficulty in translation, n.	трудность перевода, *f.*	Übersetzungsschwierig- keit, *f.*	difficulté de traduction, *f.*
137	diffusion, n.	распространение, *n.*	Verbreitung, *f.*/ Streuung, *f.*	diffusion, *f.*
138	digest, n.	краткий обзор	Resumée, *n.*/Abriss, *m.*	condensé, *m.*
139	digit, n.	цифра, *f.*	Ziffer, *f.*/Stelle, *f.*	chiffre, *m.*
140	digraph, n.	диграф, *m.*	Ligatur, *f.*/ Doppelzeichen, *n.*	digramme, *m.*
141	dimension, n.	размерность, *f.*	Dimension, *f.*	dimension, *f.*
142	diminutive, n.	уменьшительное, *n.*	Diminutiv, *n.*/Verkleine- rungsform, *f.*	diminutif, *m.*
143	diminutive name	уменьшительное имя	Kosename, *m.*/ Kurzname, *m.*	nom abrégé, *m.*
144	ding-dong theory	теория динь-динь, *f.*	bim-bim Theorie, *f.*	théorie ding-dang-dong, *f.*
145	diphthong, n.	дифтонг, *m.*/ двугласный, *m.*	Diphthong, *m.*/Doppel- vokal, *m.*/Zweilaut, *m.*	diphtongue, *f.*
146	diphthongization, n.	дифтонгизация, *f.*	Diphthongierung, *f.*	diphtongaison, *f.*
147	diploma, n.	диплом, *m.*	Diplom, *n.*/Zeugnis, *n.*	diplôme, *m.*
148	direct address	прямое обращение	direkte Anrede	adresse directe, *m.*
149	direct discourse	прямая речь	direkte Rede	discours direct, *m.*
150	direct meaning	прямое значение	direkte Bedeutung/ eigentliche Bedeutung	sens premier, *m.*
151	direct method (language teaching)	прямой метод	direkte Methode	méthode directe, *f.*
152	direct object	прямое дополнение	direktes Objekt	complément direct, *m.*

No.	ENGLISH	RUSSIAN	GERMAN	FRENCH
153	direct quotation	цитата, *f.*	Zitat, *n.*/ wörtliches Zitat	citation, *f.*
154	direction, n.	направление, *n.*	Richtung, *f.*	direction, *f.*
155	direction of isoglosses	направление изоглосс, *n.*	Verlauf der Isoglossen, *m.*	direction des isoglosses, *f.*
156	direction of motion	направление движения, *n.*	Bewegungsrichtung, *f.*	sens de déplacement, *m.*
157	direction of sound changes	направление звуковых изменений, *n.*	Richtung des Lautwandels, *f.*	direction des changements phonétiques, *f.*
158	direction sign	указатель направления, *m.*	Richtungsanzeiger, *m.*/ Richtungsweiser, *m.*	flèche de direction, *f.*
159	directions, pl.	распоряжения, *n.,* pl./ указания, *n.,* pl.	Anweisungen, *f.,* pl.	instructions, *f.,* pl.
160	directory, n.	адресная книга	Adressbuch, *n.*	annuaire, *m.*
161	disadvantage, n.	ущерб, *m.*	Nachteil, *m.*	désavantage, *m.*
162	disadvantageous, adj.	невыгодный	nachteilig/ungünstig	désavantageux
163	disagreement, n.	разногласие, *n.*	Unstimmigkeit, *f.*	désaccord, *m.*
164	disappearance, n.	исчезновение, *n.*	Verschwinden, *n.*	disparition, *f.*
165	discernible, adj.	распознающий	erkennbar	perceptible
166	discipline, n.	дисциплина, *f.*	Disziplin, *f.*/Fach, *n.*/ Studienfach, *n.*	discipline, *f.*
167	disclosure, n.	раскрытие, *n.*	Veröffentlichung, *f.*/ Verlautbarung, *f.*	révélation, *f.*
168	disconnected, adj.	разрывный	unterbrochen	séparé
169	discontiguous, adj.	несмежный/несоприкасающийся	nicht aneinander grenzend	discontinu
170	discontinuance, n.	прекращение, *n.*	Unterbrechung, *f.*	interruption, *f.*/ discontinuation, *f.*
171	discontinuous constituent	прерванный составлющий	unterbrochene Konstituente	élément constitutif discontinu, *m.*

No.	English	Russian	German	French
172	discontinuous morpheme	разрывная морфема	unterbrochenes Morphem	morphème discontinu, *m.*
173	discourse, n.	беседа, *f.*/разговор, *m.*/ речь, *f.*	Gespräch, *n.*/Rede, *f.*	discours, *m.*
174	discourse analysis	анализ речи, *m.*	Analyse gesprochener Rede, *f.*	analyse de langage, *f.*
175	discovery, n.	открытие, *n.*	Entdeckung, *f.*	découverte, *f.*
176	discovery procedure	процедура для установления единиц, *f.*	Entdeckungsprozess, *m.*	méthode de découverte, *f.*
177	discrepancy, n.	несоответствие, *n.*	Widerspruch, *m.*	discordance, *f.*
178	discrete unit	дискретная единица, *f.*	diskrete Einheit, *f.*	unité discrète, *f.*
179	discrimination, n.	различение, *n.*	Unterscheidung, *f.*	discrimination, *f.*
180	discussion, n.	обсуждение, *n.*	Diskussion, *f.*	discussion, *f.*
181	disintegration, n.	распадение, *n.*	Zerfall, *m.*	désagrégation, *f.*
182	disjunct, adj.	разъединенный	getrennt	séparé
183	disjunctive, adj.	разделительный	disjunktiv	disjonctif
184	dislocation, n.	дислокация, *f.*/ перемещение, *n.*	Verschiebung, *f.*	disloquement, *m.*/ déplacement, *m.*
185	disparity, n.	несоответствие, *n.*	Ungleichheit, *f.*	disparité, *f.*
186	dispersion, n.	распространение, *n.*	Verbreitung, *f.*	dispersion, *f.*
187	displacement, n.	смешение, *n.*	Verschiebung, *f.*	déplacement, *m.*
188	disproportion, n.	диспропорция, *f.*	Missverhältnis, *n.*	disproportion, *f.*
189	disputed, adj.	спорный	umstritten	discuté
190	disregarded, adj.	незамеченный/ пропущенный	unbeachtet/ vernachlässigt	négligé
191	dissatisfaction, n.	неудовольствие, *n.*	Unzufriedenheit, *f.*	méconentement, *m.*
192	dissemination, n.	распространение, *n.*	Verbreitung, *f.*	dissémination, *f.*
193	dissertation, n.	диссертация, *f.*	Dissertation, *f.*/ Doktorarbeit, *f.*	mémoire, *m.*/dissertation, *f.*

No.	ENGLISH	RUSSIAN	GERMAN	FRENCH
194	dissimilarity, n.	несходство, *n.*	Unähnlichkeit, *f.*	dissemblance, *f.*
195	dissimilation, n.	диссимиляция, *f.*/ расподобление, *n.*	Dissimilation, *f.*	dissimilation, *f.*
196	dissonance, n.	диссонанс, *m.*/ неблагозвучие, *n.*	Dissonanz, *f.*	dissonance, *f.*
197	distance, n.	расстояние, *n.*	Entfernung, *f.*	éloignement, *m.*
198	distant, adj.	дальний	entfernt/fern	éloigné
199	distant future	далекое будущее	ferne Zukunft	avenir lointain, *m.*
200	distich, n.	дистих, *m.*/двустишие, *n.*	Distichon, *n.*/ Doppelvers, *m.*	distique, *m.*
201	distinction, n.	различие, *n.*	Unterscheidung, *f.*	distinction, *f.*
202	distinctive, adj.	отличительный/ различительный	distinktiv/ Unterscheidungs-	distinctif
203	distinctive features, pl.	дифференциальные признаки, *m.*, pl./ различительные признаки, *m.*, pl.	distinktive Merkmale, *n.*, pl./Unterscheidungs- merkmale, *n.*, pl	traits distinctifs, *m.*, pl.
	acute-grave	высокой тональн- ости — низкой тональности	akut-gravis/dunkel-hell	aigu-grave
	checked-unchecked	абруптивный — неабруптивный	gehemmt-ungehemmt	entravé-non-entravé
	compact-diffuse	компактный — диффузный	kompakt-diffus	compact-diffus
	consonantal-non- consonantal	согласный — несогласный	konsonantisch-nicht konsonantisch	consonantique-non- consonantique
	interrupted-con- tinuant	прерванный — непрерывный	abrupt-kontinuierlich	interrompu-continu
	flat-plain	бемольный — простой	gesenkt-normal/ erniedrigt- nichterniedrigt	bémol-normal
	nasal-oral	носовой — ртовый	nasal-oral	nasal-oral
	sharp-plain	диезный — прострой	erhöht-normal/ erhöhtnichterhöht	dièse-normal

No.	ENGLISH	RUSSIAN	GERMAN	FRENCH
203	— *continued*			
	strident-mellow	резкий—нерезкий	scharfklingend-sanftklingend	strident-mat
	tense-lax	напряженный—ненапряженный	gespannt-entspannt/ gespannt-ungespannt	tendu-relâché
	vocalic-nonvocalic	гласный—негласный	vokalisch-nicht vokalisch	vocalique-non-vocalique
	voiced-voiceless	звонкий—глухой	stimmhaft-stimmlos	sonore-sourd
204	distinctly, adv.	отчетливо	deutlich	distinctement
205	distinguish, v.	различать	unterscheiden	distinguer
206	distinguishable, adj.	различимый	unterscheidbar	reconnaissable
207	distortion, n.	искажение, *n.*	Verzerrung, *f.*	déformation, *f.*
208	distribution, n.	дистрибуция, *f./* распределение, *n.*	Verteilung, *f.*	distribution, *f./* répartition, *f.*
209	distribution class	дистрибутивный класс	Verteilungsklasse, *f.*	classe distributionnelle, *f.*
210	distributional analysis	дистрибутивный анализ	Verteilungsanalyse, *f.*	analyse par la distribution, *f.*
211	distributional pattern	дистриьутивная модель	Verteilungsmuster, *n./* Verteilungsschema, *n.*	modèle de distribution, *m./*patron de distribution, *m./*schéma de distribution, *m.*
212	distributional restrictions, pl.	дистрибутивные ограничения, *n.,* pl.	distributionelle Beschränckungen, *f.,* pl.	limitations distribution-nelles, *f.,* pl.
213	distributional similarity	дистрибутивное сходство	Ähnlichkeit in der Verteilung, *f./*distributionelle Ähnlichkeit	similitude dans la distribution, *f.*
214	distributive, adj.	разделительный	distributiv	distributif
215	distributive adjective	разделительное прилагательное	distributives Adjektiv	adjectif distributif
216	distributive numeral	распределительное числительное	distributive Zahl	nombre distributif

No.	ENGLISH	RUSSIAN	GERMAN	FRENCH
217	distributive pronoun	разделительное местоимение	distributives Pronomen	pronom distributif
218	disturbance, n.	возмущение, *n.*	Störung, *f.*	perturbation, *f.*
219	disyllabic, adj.	двусложный	zweisilbig	dissyllabique
220	ditto mark (″)	повторный знак	Wiederholungszeichen, *n.*	idem
221	divergence, n.	дивергенция, *f.*/ расхождение, *n.*/ отклонение, *n.*	Divergenz, *f.*	divergence, *f.*
222	diversity, n.	разнообразность, *f.*	Verschiedenheit, *f.*	diversité, *f.*
223	divided, adj.	разделенный	geteilt	divisé
224	dividing line	черта разграничения, *f.*	Trennungslinie, *f.*/ Scheidelinie, *f.*	ligne de séparaton, *f.*
225	divisible, adj.	делимый	teilbar	divisible
226	division, n.	деление, *n.*	Einteilung, *f.*	répartition, *f.*
227	doctrine, n.	доктрина, *f.*/учение, *n.*	Doktrin, *f.*/Grundsatz, *m.* /Lehre, *f.*	doctrine, *f.*
228	document, n.	документ, *m.*	Dokument, *n.*/ Urkunde, *f.*	document, *m.*
229	documentation, n.	документация, *f.*	Dokumentation, *f.*	documentation, *f.*
230	domain, n.	область, *f.*/сфера, *f.*	Bereich, *m.*/Gebiet, *n.*	domaine, *m.*
231	domal, adj.	небный	kakuminal/zerebral	cacuminal
232	dominant, adj.	господствующий	herrschend/ vorherrschend	dominant
233	dominant feature	господствующий признак	vorherrschende Eigenschaft	trait dominant, *m.*
234	dominant language	господствующий язык	Hauptsprache, *f.*	langue principale, *f.*
235	dominating node	доминирующий узел	dominierender Knoten	noeud dominant, *m.*
236	dorsal, adj.	дорсальный/ заднеязычный	Hinterzungen-	dorsal

No.	ENGLISH	RUSSIAN	GERMAN	FRENCH
237	dot and dash	тире и точка/ точка и черточка	Strich und Punkt	point et trait
238	dotted line (····)	пунктирная линия	punktierte Linie	ligne pointillée, *f.*
239	double arrow (↔)	двойная стрелка	Doppelpfeil, *m.*	flèche double, *f.*
240	double articulation	двухфокусная артикуляция	Doppelartikulation, *f.*/ zweifache Artikulation	articulation double, *f.*
241	double base transformation	генерализованная трансформация/ двухбазная трансформация	Zwei-Satz-Transformation, *f.*	transformation à base double, *f.*
242	double cross (#)	знак диэза, *m.*	Doppelkreuzzeichen, *n.*	croix double, *f.*
243	double letter	удвоенная буква	doppelter Buchstabe	lettre double, *f.*
244	double meaning	двоякое значение	zweifache Bedeutung	double sens, *m.*
245	double negative	двойное отрицание	doppelte Verneinung	double négation, *f.*
246	double possessive	двойное притяжательное	doppelte Possessiv-konstruktion	possessif double, *m.*
247	double space(d)	через строчку	doppelter Zwischenraum	interligne double, *f.*
248	double talk (meaningless chatter)	подражательная бессмысленная речь	sinnlose Sprachimitation	paroles creuses, *f., pl.*
249	doubled, adj.	сдвоенный	doppelt/verdoppelt	double
250	doubled consonant	двойнной согласный	Doppelkonsonant, *m.*	consonne géminée, *f.*
251	doublet, n.	дублет, *m.*	Dublette, *f.*	doublet, *m.*
252	doubling, n.	дублирование, *n.*/ удваивание, *n.*	Doppelung, *f.*/ Verdoppelung, *f.*	gémination, *f*
253	doubtful, adj.	сомнительный	zweifelhaft	douteux
254	doubtful phoneme	неопределенная фонема	fragliches Phonem	phonème ambigu, *m.*
255	drama, n.	драма, *f.*	Drama, *n.*/Schauspiel, *n.*	drame, *m.*
256	drawing, n.	рисунок, *m.*/чертеж, *m.*	Skizze, *f.*/Zeichnung, *f.*	dessin, *m.*

No.	ENGLISH	RUSSIAN	GERMAN	FRENCH
257	drawl, n.	протяженное произношение	schleppendes Sprechen	voix trainante, *f.*
258	drift, n.	течение, *п.*/тенденция, *f.*	Strömung, *f.*	voyage, *m.*
259	dropping, n.	выпадение, *п.*/отпадение, *п.*	Abfall, *m.*/Ausfall, *m.*/Fortfall, *m.*/Verlust, *m.*	syncope, *f.*
260	dropping of syllables	выпадение слогов, *п.*	Silbenabfall, *m.*/Silbenschwund, *m.*/Silbenverlust, *m.*	perte de syllabes, *f.*
261	dropping of case inflections	отпадение падежных флексий, *п.*	Verlust der Flexionsendung, *m.*	perte de flexions casuelles, *f.*
262	drum, n.	барабан, *m.*	Trommel, *f.*	tambour, *m.*
263	drum lanquage	барабанный язык	Trommelsprache, *f.*	langue de tambours, *f.*
264	dual, adj.	двойной/парный	doppelt/zweifach	double
265	dual gender	обоюдный род	doppeltes Genus	genre duel, *n.*
266	dual number	двойственное число	Dual, *m.*	nombre duel, *m.*
267	dual representation	двойное изображение	doppelte Darstellung	double representation, *f.*
268	duality, n.	двойственность, *f.*	Dualität, *f.*/Zweiheit, *f.*	dualité, *f.*
269	duality of patterning	двойное членение	zweifache Gliederung	deuxième articulation, *f.*
270	dumb, adj.	немой	stumm	muet
271	duplicate, n.	дупликат, *m.*/копия, *f.*	Duplikat, *n.*	duplicata, *m.*
272	duplication, n.	копирование, *п.*	Vervielfältigung, *f.*	duplication, *f.*
273	durative aspect	длительный вид	durativer Aspekt/durative Aktionsart	aspect duratif, *m.*
274	duration, n.	длительность, *f.*/продолжительность, *f.*	Dauer, *f.*	durée, *f.*
275	Dutch, adj.	голландский	holländisch/niederländisch	hollandais/néerlandais
276	dynamic, adj.	динамический	dynamisch	dynamique
277	dynamics, n.	динамика, *f.*	Dynamik, *f.*	dynamique, *m.*

No.	ENGLISH	RUSSIAN	GERMAN	FRENCH

E

No.	ENGLISH	RUSSIAN	GERMAN	FRENCH
001	ear, n.	ухо, *n.*	Ohr, *n.*	oreille, *f.*
002	eardrum, n.	барабанная перепонка	Trommelfell, *n.*	tympan, *m.*
003	earphones, pl.	наушники, pl.	Kopfhörer, *m.*	écouteurs, *m.,* pl.
004	ease of articulation	легкость артикуляции, *f.*	Leichtigkeit der Aussprache, *f.*	facilité d'articulation, *f.*
005	easily, adv.	легко	leicht	aisément
006	echo, n.	эхо, *n.*	Echo, *n.*/Nachklangser-scheinung, *f.*/Wider-hall, *m.*	écho, *m.*
007	economy, n.	экономия, *f.*	Ökonomie, *f.*/ Wirtschaft, *f.*/ Sparsamkeit, *f.*	économie, *f.*
008	economy in language	экономия в языке, *f.*	Ökonomie in der Sprache, *f.*	économie linguistique, *f.*
009	edict, n.	эдикт, *m.*/указ, *m.*	Edikt, *n.*/Verordnung, *f.*	édit, *m.*
010	edit, v.	подготовлять к печати	druckfertig machen	préparer pour la publica-tion
011	edition, n.	издание, *n.*	Auflage, *f.*/Ausgabe, *f.*	tirage, *m.*
012	editor, n.	редактор, *m.*	Herausgeber, *m.*/ Redakteur, *m.*	redacteur, *m.*/éditeur, *m.*
013	editorial, n.	редакционная статья/ передовая статья	Leitartikel, *m.*	éditorial, *m.*
014	educated speech	образованная речь	gebildete Sprache	langage cultivé, *m.*
015	education, n.	образование, *n.*	Erziehung, *f.*	enseignement, *m.*
016	effect, n.	следствие, *n.*	Wirkung, *f.*	effet, *m.*
017	effective, efficient, adj.	эффективный	wirksam	efficace
018	efficiency, n.	эффективность, *f.*	Wirkungsgrad, *m.*	efficacité, *f.*

No.	ENGLISH	RUSSIAN	GERMAN	FRENCH
019	elaboration, n.	уточнение, *n.*	Ausarbeitung, *f.*	élaboration, *f.*
020	electronic computer	электронная вычислительная машина	elektronische Rechen-maschine	calculatrice électronique, *m.*
021	electronic reading machine	электронная считывающая машина	elektronisches Lesegerät	lecteur électronique, *m.*
022	element, n.	элемент, *m.*	Element, *n.*	élément, *m.*
023	elementary, adj.	элементарный	elementar	élémentaire
024	elementary school	начальная школа	Grundschule, *f.*/ Volksschule, *f.*	école primaire, *f.*
025	eliciting procedure	техника собирания сырого материала, *f.*	Methode der Material-sammlung, *f.*	procédé d'enquêtes, *m.*/ technique d'enquêtes, *m.*
026	elimination, n.	исключение, *n.*	Ausschliessung, *f.*	exclusion, *f.*
027	elision, n.	элизия, *f.*	Elision, *f.*/ Vokalverschleifung, *f.*	élision, *f.*
028	elliptical, adj.	эллиптический	elliptisch	elliptique
029	elocution, n.	дикция, *f.*	Vortragskunst, *f.*	diction, *f.*/déclamation, *f.*
030	elongated, adj.	удлиненный	gestreckt	étiré/allongé
031	eloquence, n.	красноречие, *n.*	Beredsamkeit, *f.*	éloquence, *f.*
032	embedded, adj.	включаемый/ вложенный	eingebettet	inséré
033	embedded sentence	включаемое предложение	Zwischensatz	phrase insérée, *f.*
034	emergence, n.	появление, *n.*/ возникновение, *n.*	Erscheinung, *f.*	émergence, *f.*/ surgissement, *m.*
035	emotion, n.	эмоция, *f.*/чувство, *n.*	Gemütsbewegung, *f.*/ Gefühl, *n.*	émotion, *f.*/émoi, *m.*
036	emotional intonation	эмоциональная интонация	Gefühlsbetonung, *f.*	intonation émotive, *f.*

No.	English	Russian	German	French
037	emotive, adj.	чувствительный	gefühlsmässig	émotif/émouvant
038	emphasis, n.	эмфаза, *f.*/ударение, *n.*	Emphase, *f.*/ Nachdruck, *m.*	accent, *m.*
039	emphatic stress	эмфатическое ударение/ усилительное ударение	emphatische Betonung	accent d'insistence, *m.*/ accent d'intensité, *m.*
040	empirical, adj.	эмпирический	empirisch/auf Erfahrung beruhend	empirique
041	empirical sciences, pl.	эмпирические науки, *f.*, pl.	empirische Wissen- schaften, *f.*, pl.	sciences empiriques, *f.*, pl.
042	empiricism, n.	эмпиризм, *m.*	Empirismus, *m.*	empirisme, *m.*
043	empty, adj.	пустой	leer	vide
044	empty 'morpheme	пустая морфема	leeres Morphem	morphème vide, *m.*
045	empty position	пустая позиция	Leerstelle, *f.*	case vide, *f.*
046	empty slot	пустая клетка	leeres Feld	case vide, *f.*
047	empty word	пустое слово/ вспомогательное слово	leeres Wort/Hilfswort, *n.*	mot vide, *m.*/mot auxiliaire, *m.*
048	enclitic, n.	энклитика, *f.*	Enklise, *f.*/Enklitikum, *n.*	enclitique, *m.*
049	encoding, n.	кодирование, *n.*	Chiffrieren, *n.*/ Verschlüsselung, *f.*	encodage, *m.*
050	encyclopedia, n.	энциклопедия, *f.*	Enzyklopädie, *f.*	encyclopédie, *f.*
051	end, n.	конец, *m.*	Ende, *n.*/Schluss, *m.*	fin, *f.*
052	end of sentence	конец предложения, *m.*/конец фразы, *m.*	Satzschluss, *m.*	fin de la phrase, *f.*
053	end of word	конец слова, *m.*	Wortschluss, *m.*	fin de mot, *f.*
054	endearment form	ласкательная форма	Zärtlichkeitsform, *f.*/ Koseform, *f.*	terme d'attendrissement, *m.*
055	ending, n.	окончание. *n.*	Endung, *f.*/ Flexionsendung, *f.*	désinence, *f.*

No.	ENGLISH	RUSSIAN	GERMAN	FRENCH
056	endocentric, adj.	эндоцентрический	endozentrisch	endocentrique
057	energy, n.	энергия, *f.*	Energie, *f.*	énergie, *f.*
058	English, adj.	английский	englisch	anglais
059	enrichment, n.	обогащение, *f.*	Bereicherung, *f.*	enrichissement, *m.*
060	ensemble, n.	совокупность, *f.*/ состав, *m.*	Gesamtheit, *f.*	ensemble, *m.*
061	entire, adj.	целый/весь	gesamt	entier
062	entity, n.	существо, *n.*	Wesenheit, *f.*/Dasein, *n.*/ Wesen, *f.*	entité, *f.*
063	entrance examination	вступительное испытание	Aufnahmeprüfung, *f.*	examen d'entrée, *m.*
064	entropy, n.	энтропия, *f.*	Entropie, *f.*/ Wärmegewicht, *n.*	entropie, *f.*
065	entry, n.	статья, *f.*	Eintragung, *f.*/ Stichwort, *n.*	entrée, *f.*/article, *m.*
066	enumeration, n.	перечисление, *n.*	Aufzählung, *f.*	énumération, *f.*
067	enumerative intonation	перечислительная интонация	Intonation bei Aufzählung, *f.*	intonation énumérative, *f.*
068	enunciation, n.	дикция, *f.*	Aussprache, *f.*/Ausdrucksweise, *f.*/ Artikulation, *f.*	prononciation, *f.*/ articulation, *f.*
069	envelope (acoustic), n.	огибающая, *f.*/ оболочка, *f.*	Einhüllende, *f.*/ Enveloppe, *f.*	enveloppe, *f.*
070	environment, n.	окружение, *n.*/ окрестность, *f.*	Umgebung, *f.*/ Zusammenhang, *m.*	contexte, *m.*/entourage, *m.*/milieu, *m.*
071	epenthesis, n.	эпентеза, *f.*/вставка *f.*	Epenthese, *f.*/Einschub, *m.*/Sprossvokal, *m.*	épenthèse, *f.*
072	epic poem	эпическая поэма	Epos, *n.*/ Heldengedicht, *n.*	poème épique, *m.*/ épopée, *f.*
073	epicene, adj.	общего рода	beiderlei Geschlechts	épicène

No.	ENGLISH	RUSSIAN	GERMAN	FRENCH
074	epiglottis, n.	надгортанник, *m.*	Kehldeckel, *m.*	épiglotte, *m.*
075	epigram, n.	эпиграмма, *f.*	Epigramm, *n.*	épigramme, *f.*
076	epigraph, n.	эпиграф, *m.*	Inschrift, *f.*	épigraphe, *f.*
077	epilogue, n.	эпилог, *m.*	Nachwort, *n.*/ Schlusswort, *n.*	épilogue, *m.*
078	epitaph, n.	эпитафия, *f.*	Grabschrift, *f.*	épitaphe, *f.*
079	epithet, n.	эпитет, *m.*	Beiname, *m.*	épithète, *f.*
080	epoch, n.	эпоха, *f.*	Epoche, *f.*/ Zeitabschnitt, *m.*	époque, *f.*
081	eponym, n.	эпоним, *m.*	Eponym, *n.*/Urform, *f.*	éponyme, *m.*
082	epopee, epos, n.	эпопея, *f.*	episches Gedicht/ Epos, *n.*	épopée, *f.*
083	equal, adj.	равный	gleich	égal
084	equality, n.	равенство, *n.*	Gleichheit, *f.*	égalité, *f.*
085	equation, n.	уравнение, *n.*	Gleichung, *f.*	équation, *f.*
086	equational sentence	именное предложение	Gleichungssatz, *m.*	phrase copulative, *f.*
087	equative degree	тождественная степень	Aequativus, *n.*	équatif, *m.*
088	equilibrium, n.	равновесие, *n.*	Gleichgewicht, *n.*	équilibre, *m.*
089	equivalence, n.	эквивалентность, *f.*	Gleichwertigkeit, *f.*	équivalence, *f.*
090	equivalent, adj.	эквивалентный/ равный	gleichwertig/egal	égal
091	equivalent, n.	эквивалент, *m.*	Äquivalent, *n.*	équivalent, *m.*
092	ergative, n.	эргатив, *m.*	Ergativ, *m.*	ergatif, *m.*
093	erratum, n.	список шечаток, *m.*	Druckfehlerverzeichnis, *n.*/Berichtigung, *f.*	erratum, *m.*
094	erroneous, adj.	ошибочный/ неправильный	irrtümlich/falsch	erroné
095	error, n.	ошибка, *f.*	Fehler, *m.*/Irrtum, *n.*	faute, *f.*

No.	ENGLISH	RUSSIAN	GERMAN	FRENCH
096	erudition, n.	эрудиция, *f.*/ученость, *f.*	Gelehrsamkeit, *f.*/ Belesenheit, *f.*	érudition, *f.*
097	essay, n.	очерк, *m.*	Essay, *n.*	dissertation, *f.*
098	essential, adj.	существенный/ необходимый	wesentlich	essentiel
099	Estonian, adj.	эстонский	estnisch/estländisch	esthonien
100	et cetera, etc.	и так далее	und so weiter	et caetera
101	ethnic group	этническая группа	völkische Gruppe	groupe ethnique, *m.*
102	ethnography, n.	этнография, *f.*	Völkerbeschreibung, *f.*	ethnographie, *f.*
103	ethnolinguistics, n.	этнологическая лингвистика	völkerkundliche Linguistik	linguistique ethnologique, *f.*
104	ethnology, n.	этнология, *f.*	Völkerkunde, *f.*	ethnologie, *f.*
105	etymological dialect differences, pl.	этимологические диалектальные различия, *n.,* pl.	etymologische Dialektunterschiede, *m.,* pl.	différences dialectales étymologiques, *f.,* pl.
106	etymological doublet	этимологический дублет	etymologische Dublette	doublet étymologique, *m.*
107	etymological spelling	этимологическое правописание	etymologische Schreibung	orthographe étymologique, *m.*
108	etymology, n.	этимология, *f.*	Etymologie, *f.*/ Wortgeschichte, *f.*	étymologie, *f.*
109	etymon, n.	этимон, *m.*	Grundwort, *n.*	base étymologique, *f.*
110	eulogy, n.	панегирик, *m.*/ хвалебная речь	Lobrede, *f.*	panégyrique, *m.*
111	euphemism, n.	эвфемизм, *m.*	Euphemismus, *m.*	euphémisme, *m.*
112	euphony, n.	благозвучие, *n.*	Wohlklang, *m.*	euphonie, *f.*
113	evaluation, n.	оценка, *f.*	Abschätzung, *f.*/ Würdigung, *f.*	évaluation, *f.*
114	even distribution	равномерное распределение	ebenmässige Verteilung/ gleichmässige Verteilung/regelmässige Verteilung	distribution uniforme, *f.*

No.	English	Russian	German	French
115	even number	четное число	gerade Zahl	nombre pair, *m.*
116	even tone	ровный тон	ebener Ton	ton uni, *m.*
117	evenness, n.	равномерность, *f.*	Gleichmässigkeit, *f.*	égalité, *f.*
118	event, n.	событие, *n.*	Ereignis, *n.*	événement, *m.*
119	eventual, adj.	конечный	eventuell	définitif/final
120	eventuality, n.	возможность, *f.*	Möglichkeit, *f.*	éventualité, *f.*
121	eventually, adv.	в конце концов	am Ende/endlich/eventuell/schliesslich	finalement
122	everyday speech	бытовая речь	Alltagssprache, *f.*	langage quotidien, *m.*
123	evidence, n.	доказательство, *n.*	Beweis, *m.*/ Beweismaterial, *n.*	preuve, *f.*
124	evident, adj.	очевидный	klar	évident
125	evolution, n.	эволюция, *f.*/ развитие, *n.*	Entwicklung, *f.*	développement, *m.*
126	exact, adj.	точный	genau/richtig	exact/juste/précis
127	exact sciences, pl.	точные науки, *f., pl.*	exakte Wissenschaften, *f., pl.*	sciences exactes, *f., pl.*
128	exaggeration, n.	преувеличение, *n.*	Übertreibung, *f.*	exagération, *f.*
129	examination (in school), n.	экзамен, *m.*/ испытание, *n.*	Prüfung, *f.*	examen, *m.*
130	examination of the data	рассмотрение данных, *n.*	Untersuchung der Unterlagen, *f.*	étude des données, *f.*
131	example, n.	пример, *m.*	Beispiel, *n.*	exemple, *m.*
132	excavation, n.	раскопки, pl.	Ausgrabung, *f.*	excavation, *f.*
133	exception, n.	исключение, *n.*	Ausnahme, *f.*	exception, *f.*
134	excerpt, n.	отрывок, *m.*/выдержка, *f.*	Auszug, *m.*/Zitat, *n.*	extrait, *m.*
135	excessive, adj.	чрезмерный	übermässig	excessif

No.	ENGLISH	RUSSIAN	GERMAN	FRENCH
136	exchange, n.	обмен, *m.*/замена, *f.*	Austausch, *m.*/Vertauschung, *m.*/Wechsel, *f.*	échange, *m.*/ substitution, *f.*
137	exhortation, n.	увещание, *n.*	Ermahnung, *f.*	exhortation, *f.*
138	excitement, n.	возбуждение, *n.*/ волнение, *n.*	Erregung, *f.*	excitation, *f.*/agitation, *f.*
139	exclamation, n.	восклицание, *n.*	Ausruf, *m.*	exclamation, *f.*
140	exclamation mark (!)	восклицательный знак	Ausrufungszeichen, *n.*	point d'exclamation, *m.*
141	exclamatory sentence	восклицательное предложение	Ausrufungssatz, *m.*	phrase exclamative, *f.*
142	exclusion, n.	исключение, *n.*	Ausschliessung, *f.*/ Ausgrenzung, *f.*	exclusion, *f.*
143	exclusive choice	исключительный отбор	ausschliessende Wahl	choix exclusif, *m.*
144	exclusive first person	исключительное первое лицо	exklusive erste Person	première personne exclusive
145	excrescence, n.	развитие добавочного звука, *n.*	Sonderentwicklung, *f.*	développement excrescent, *m.*/excroissance, *f.*
146	execution, n.	выполнение, *n.*	Vollziehung, *f.*/ Vollstreckung, *f.*	exécution, *f.*
147	exegesis, n.	толкование, *n.*	Exegesis, *f.*/Auslegung, *f.*	exégèse, *f.*
148	exemplification, n.	пояснение примером, *n.*/иллюстрация, *f.*	Belegung durch Beispiele, *f.*	démonstration par l'exemple, *f.*
149	exercise, n.	упражнение, *n.*	Übung, *f.*	exercice, *m.*
150	exhaustive, adj.	исчерпывающий	erschöpfend	exhaustif/complet
151	existence, n.	существование, *n.*	Existenz, *f.*/Dasein, *n.*/ Vorhandensein, *n.*	être, *m.*/existence, *f.*
152	exocentric, adj.	экзоцентрический	exozentrisch	exocentrique
153	exotic languages, pl.	экзотические языки, *m.*, pl./иноземные языки, *m.*	exotische Sprachen, *f.*, pl.	langues exotiques, *f.*, pl.

No.	ENGLISH	RUSSIAN	GERMAN	FRENCH
154	expanded form	расширенная форма	erweiterte Form	forme étendue, *f.*
155	expansion, n.	расширение, *n.*	Ausdehnung, *f.*/Erweiterung, *f.*/Verbreitung, *f.*	élargissement, *m.*/ extension, *f.*
156	expected, adj.	ожидаемый	erwartet	attendu/prévu
157	experience, n.	опыт, *m.*	Erfahrung, *f.*/Praxis, *f.*	expérience, *f.*
158	experienced, adj.	квалифицированный/ опытный	erfahren	plein d'expérience/ expérimenté
159	experiment, n.	эксперимент, *m.*/ опыт, *m.*/проба, *f.*	Experiment, *n.*/Probe, *f.*/ Versuch, *m.*	expérience, *f.*
160	experimental model	экспериментальная модель	Versuchsmodell, *n.*	modèle expérimental, *m.*
161	experimental phonetics	экспериментальная фонетика	experimentelle Phonetik	phonétique expérimentale, *f.*
162	expiration, n.	выдох, *m.*/выдыхание, *n.*	Ausatmen, *n.*	expiration, *f.*
163	explanation, n.	объяснение, *n.*	Erklärung, *f.*	explication, *f.*
164	explanatory power	объяснительная сила	erklärende Kraft	puissance explicative, *f.*
165	expletive, n.	бранное выражение	Fluch, *m.*	explétif, *m.*
166	explication, n.	объяснение, *n.*	Erklärung, *f.*	explication, *f.*
167	explicit, adj.	точный/ясный	ausdrücklich/genau	précis
168	exploration, n.	исследование, *n.*	Erforschung, *f.*	recherche, *f.*
169	explosion, n.	взрыв, *m.*	Sprengung, *f.*	explosion, *f.*
170	explosive consonants, pl.	взрывные согласные, pl.	Explosivlaute, *m.*, pl./ Verschlusslaute, *m.*, pl.	consonnes explosives, *f.*, pl.
171	exposition, n.	изложение, *n.*	Exposition, *f.*/ Erklärung, *f.*	exposition, *f.*
172	exponent, n.	показатель степени, *m.*	Exponent, *m.*	exposant, *m.*
173	expression, n.	выражение, *n.*	Ausdruck, *m.*/Kundgabe, *f.*/Wendung, *f.*	expression, *f.*/locution, *f.*/ tournure, *f.*

No.	ENGLISH	RUSSIAN	GERMAN	FRENCH
174	expression system	план выражения, *m.*	Ausdruckssystem, *n.*	plan de l'expression, *m.*
175	expressive features, pl.	экспрессивные признаки, *m.,* pl.	expressive Merkmale, *n.,* pl.	traits expressifs, *m.,* pl.
176	expressive function	экспрессивная функция	Ausdrucksfunktion, *f./* expressive Funktion	fonction expressive, *f.*
177	expressive intonation	выразительная интонация	expressive Intonation	intonation expressive, *f.*
178	expressive language	выразительный язык	ausdrucksvolle Sprache	langage expressif, *m.*
179	expressivity, n.	выразительность, *f.*	Ausdruckhaftigkeit, *f.*	expressivité, *f.*
180	extended sentence	распространенное предложение	erweiterter Satz	phrase élargie, *f.*
181	extension, n.	расширение, *n./* распространение, *n.*	Ausdehnung, *f./* Erweiterung, *f.*	élargissement, *m.*
182	extension of meaning	расширение значения, *n.*	Bedeutungserweiterung, *f.*	élargissement de sens, *m.*
183	external, adj.	внешний	äusserlich	extérieur
184	external appearance	внешний вид	äusserer Schein	forme externe, *f.*
185	external change	внешнее изменение	äusserliche Veränderung	changement externe, *m.*
186	external inflection	внешняя флексия	äusserliche Flexion	inflexion externe, *f.*
187	external sandhi	внешнее сандхи	Anlauts-Sandhi, *n./*Auslauts-Sandhi, *n./*Satzphonetik, *f.*	sandhi externe, *m.*
188	extinct, adj.	вымерший	erloschen	éteint
189	extinct languages, pl.	мертвые языки, *m.,* pl.	tote Sprachen, *f.,* pl.	langues mortes, *f.,* pl.
190	extra-linguistic, adj.	внелингвистический	aussersprachwissenschaftlich	extra-linguistique
191	extract, n.	выдержка, *f./*цитата, *f.*	Auszug, *m./*Zitat, *n.*	extrait, *m.*
192	extraction, n.	происхождение, *n.*	Herkunft, *f.*	extraction, *f.*
193	extraneous, adj.	посторонний	unwesentlich	étranger

No.	ENGLISH	RUSSIAN	GERMAN	FRENCH
194	extraordinary, adj.	необычайный	ausserordentlich	extraordinaire
195	extrasensory perception	телепатия, *f.*/ непознаваемый чувствами	Telepathie, *f.*	télépathie, *f.*
196	eye, n.	глаз, *m.*	Auge, *n.*	oeil, *m.*

F

No.	ENGLISH	RUSSIAN	GERMAN	FRENCH
001	fable, n.	басня, *f.*	Fabel, *f.*	conte, *f.*/fable, *f.*
002	face, n.	лицо, *n.*	Gesicht, *m.*	visage, *m.*
003	facial expression	выражение на лице, *n.*	Gesichtausdruck, *m.*	mine, *f.*
004	facility in speaking	плавность речи, *f.*	Sprachgewandheit, *f.*	facilité de parler, *f.*
005	fact, n.	факт, *m.*	Tatsache, *f.*	fait, *m.*
006	factor, n.	фактор, *m.*	Faktor, *m.*	facteur, *f.*
007	facultative, adj.	факультативный	beliebig/möglich	facultatif
008	facultative pause	факультативная пауза	mögliche Pause	arrêt facultatif, *m.*
009	facultative variant	факультативный вариант	mögliche Variante	variante facultative, *f.*
010	faculty of speech	способность говорить, *f*.	Sprachfähigkeit, *f.*	faculté de langage, *f.*/ faculté de parler, *f.*
011	faculty of university	профессорско-преподовательский состав университета	Lehrkörper, *m.*	corps professoral d'université, *m.*
012	fading, n.	затухание, *n.*	Ausklingen, *n.*	évanouissement, *m.*
013	fairy tale	волшебная сказка	Märchen, *n.*	conte de fées, *f.*
014	fallacy, n.	ложный вывод	Trugschluss, *m.*	conclusion fallacieuse, *f.*
015	falling tone	нисходящий тон/ падающий тон	fallender Ton	ton descendant, *m.*
016	false, adj.	ложный/ неправильный	falsch	faux

No.	ENGLISH	RUSSIAN	GERMAN	FRENCH
017	false friends, pl.	⟨ложные друзья⟩, *m.,* pl./родственные слова схожие по форме а различные по значению, *n.,* pl.	⟨falsche Freunde⟩, *m.,* pl./verwandte Wörter, formal ähnlich aber bedeutungsweise verschieden, *n.,* pl.	faux amis, *m.,* pl.
018	falsehood, n.	ложь, *f.*/неправда, *f.*	Falschheit, *f.*/Lüge, *f.*/Unwahrheit, *f.*	mensonge, *f.*
019	falsetto, n.	фальцет, *m.*	Falsett, *n.*	fausset, *m.*
020	falsification, n.	искажение, *n.*/извращение, *n.*	Verfälschung, *f.*	falsification, *f.*
021	familiar form of address	интимная форма обращения	vertraute Anredeform	forme d'adresse familière, *f.*
022	familiarity with a language	хорошее знание языка	Sprachvertrautheit, *f.*	connaissance d'une langue, *f.*
023	familiarization, n.	ознакомление, *n.*	Gewöhnung, *f.*	familiarisation, *f.*
024	family, n.	семья, *f.*/гнездо, *n.*	Familie, *f.*	famille, *f.*
025	family name	фамилия, *f.*	Familienname, *m.*/Zuname, *m.*/Nachname, *m.*	nom de famille, *m.*
026	family of languages	семья языков, *f.*	Sprachfamilie, *f.*	famille de langues, *f.*
027	family tree	родословное дерево	Stammbaum, *m.*	arbre généalogique, *m.*
028	fantasy, n.	фантазия, *f.*	Phantasie, *f.*/Einbildung, *f.*	fantaisie, *f.*
029	far, adj.	далекий/дальний	fern/entfernt	lointain
030	fast speech	быстрая речь	schnelles Sprechen, *n.*	parler rapid, *m.*
031	favorable conditions, pl.	благоприятные условия, *n.,* pl.	günstige Bedingungen, *f.,* pl.	conditions favorables, *f.,* pl.
032	favorite sentence patterns, pl.	любимые построения предложений, *n.,* pl.	bevorzugte Satzgefüge, *n.,* pl./Lieblingssatzgefüge, *n.,* pl.	structures des phrases préférées, *f.,* pl.
033	feature, n.	признак, *m.*/черта, *f.*/свойство, *n.*/особенность, *f.*	Eigenschaft, *f.*/Merkmal, *n.*/Zug, *m.*	trait, *m.*

No.	English	Russian	German	French
034	feedback, n.	обратная связь	Rückführung, *f.*	régénération, *f.*/ effet de réaction, *m.*
035	feeling, n.	чувство, *n.*/эмоция, *f.*	Gefühl, *n.*	sentiment, *n.*
036	fellowship, n. (for study)	стипендия (в вузе), *f.*	Universitätsstipendium, *n.*	bourse de recherches, *f.*
037	feminine gender	женский род	Feminin(um), *n.*/ weibliches Genus/ weibliches Geschlecht	genre féminin, *m.*
038	feminine rhyme	женская рифма	weiblicher Reim	rime féminine, *f.*
039	fiction, n. (invention)	фикция, *f.*/вымысел, *m.*	Erdichtung, *f.*/ Erfindung, *f.*/ Einrede, *f.*	fiction, *f.*/invention, *f.*
040	fiction (literature), n.	беллетристика, *f.*/ художественная литература	Belletristik, *f.*/Prosadich-tung, *f.*/Romanlitera-tur, *f.*/schöne Literatur	ouvrage romanesque, *m.*
041	fictional, fictitious, adj.	фиктивный/ вымышленный	erdichtet	fictif/imaginaire
042	fictitious name	фиктивное имя	erfundener Name/ falscher Name	nom fictif, *m.*
043	field, n.	поле, *n.*/область, *f.*	Feld, *n.*/Gebiet, *n.*	champs, *m.*
044	field of observation	поле зрения, *n.*/поле наблюдения, *n.*	Untersuchungsfeld, *n.*/ Untersuchungsgebiet, *n.*	champs d'observation, *m.*
045	field trip	зкспедиция, *f.*/ поход, *m.*	Kundfahrt, *f.*/Exkursion, *f.*/Expedition, *f.*	tour d'enquêtes, *m.*
046	field work	полевая работа	Feldarbeit, *f.*/ Feldforschung, *f.*	enquêtes, *f.,* pl./travaux pratiques, *m.,* pl.
047	figuration, n.	контур, *m.*/форма, *f.*	Form, *f.*/Gestaltung, *f.*/ Kontur, *f.*	configuration, *f.*/forme, *f.*
048	figurative, adj.	фигуральный/ изобразительный	figürlich/sinnbildlich	figuré/imagé
049	figurative sense	переносный смысл/ переносное значение	übertragene Bedeutung/ übertragener Sinn	sens figuré, *m.*

No.	ENGLISH	RUSSIAN	GERMAN	FRENCH
050	figurative speech, figurative style	изобразительная речь/ образный стиль	Bildersprache, *f.*/ bilderreicher Stil	langage figuré/ style figuré
051	figure of speech	риторическая фигура	Ausdrucksweise, *f.*/ Metapher, *f.*/ Redewendung, *f.*	figure de rhétorique, *f.*/ figure de style, *f.*
052	file (index cards), n.	картотека, *f.*	Kartei, *f.*/Kartothek, *f.*	fichier, *m.*
053	filler, n.	заполняющий	Füller, *m.*	remplisseur, *m.*
054	film, n.	фильм, *m.*/пленка, *f.*	Film, *m.*	film, *m.*
055	film strip	учебный диафильм	Bildstreifen, *m.*	film fixe d'enseignement, *m.*
056	filthy talk, — language, — words	сквернословие, *n.*	Zotenreissen, *n.*	langage ordurier, *m.*
057	filtration, n.	фильтрация, *f.*	Filtrierung, *f.*	filtration, *f.*
058	final, adj.	конечный/ заключительный/ окончательный/ решающий	endlich/entscheidend/ letzt	final/ultime/définitif
059	final chapter	последняя глава	letzes Kapitel	chapitre ultime, *m.*
060	final clause	предложение цели, *n.*/ заключительное предложение	Absichtssatz, *m.*	proposition finale, *f.*
061	final consonant	конечная согласная	Endkonsonant, *m.*	consonne finale, *f.*
062	final examinations, pl.	выпускные экзамены, *m.*, pl.	Abschlussprüfung, *f.*, sg.	grands examens, *m.*, pl.
063	final glide	конечное скольжение	Abglitt, *m.*	détente, *f.*
064	final intonation	интонация точки, *f.*	Schlussintonation, *f.*	intonation finale, *f.*
065	final juncture	конечный стык	Endsignal, *n.*	point de jonction final, *m.*
066	final position	конечная позиция	Endstellung, *f.*	position finale, *f.*
067	final result	конечный результат/ заключительный результат	Endergebnis, *n.*	résultat final, *m.*

No.	ENGLISH	RUSSIAN	GERMAN	FRENCH
068	final sound	конечный звук	Auslaut, *m.*	son final, *m.*
069	final syllable	конечный слог	Endsilbe, *f.*/ Schlussilbe, *f.*	syllabe finale, *f.*
070	final vowel	конечная гласная	Endvokal, *m.*/ Schlussvokal, *m.*	voyelle finale, *f.*
071	find, v.	находить	finden	trouver
072	find, n.	находка, *f.*	Fund, *m.*	trouvaille, *f.*
073	findings, pl.	результаты, *m.*, pl./ полученные данные, pl.	Erbegnisse, *n.*, pl.	découvertes, *f.*, pl./ résultats, *m.*, pl.
074	fine distinction	тонкое различие	subtiler Unterschied	distinction subtile, *f.*
075	finger, n.	палец, *m.*	Finger, *m.*	doigt, *m.*
076	finger alphabet	азбука глухонемых, *f.*	Fingersprache, *f.*	alphabet des sourds-muets, *m.*
077	finish, v.	кончать/ заканчивать/ завершать	enden/beenden/ erledigen/fertigmachen abschliessen	finir/achever/terminer
078	finite, adj.	конечный/ ограниченный	endlich/begrenzt	fini
079	finite number	конечное число	endliche Zahl	nombre fini, *m.*
080	finite sequence	конечная последовательность	Schlussfolge, *f.*	séquence finale, *f.*
081	finite set	конечное множество	endliche Menge	ensemble fini, *m.*
082	finite state language	язык с конечным числом состояний, *m.*	endliche Zustandspra-che, *f.*/Sprache mit begrenzten Aussa-gemöglichkeiten, *n.*	langage à nombre fini d'états, *m.*
083	finite verb	личный глагол	Verbum finitum, *n.*	verbe fini, *m.*
084	Finnish, adj.	финский	finnisch	finnois
085	first, adj.	первый	erster	premier
086	first and foremost	в первую очередь/ прежде всего	in erster Linie/zualle-rerst/vor allem	avant tout

No.	English	Russian	German	French
087	first edition	первое издание	erste Auflage	édition première
088	first name	имя, *n.*	Vorname, *m.*	prénom, *m.*
089	first person	первое лицо	erste Person	première personne, *f.*
090	first word	начальное слово	Anfangswort, *n.*	mot premier, *m./* mot-début, *m.*
091	fit, n.	точное соответствие	genaues Passen	correspondance propre, *f.*
092	fixed, adj.	устойчивый	feststehend	fixe, fixé
093	fixed word combination	устойчивое словосочетание	feste Wortgruppe	locution fixe, *f.*
094	fixed stress	фиксированное ударение/ неподвижное ударение	feste Betonung	accent fixe, *m.*
095	fixed word order	неподвижный порядок слов	feste Wortfolge/ gebundene Wortfolge	ordre de mots fixe, *m.*
096	flap, n.	языковой удар	Zungenschlag, *m.*	son claqué, *m.*
097	flash card, n.	показная карточка	Wortkarte, *f.*	fiche, *f.*
098	flash language, flash lingo	воровское арго	Gaunersprache, *f.*	langue verte, *f.*
099	fleeting vowel	беглая гласная	flüchtiger Vokal/ schwindender Vokal	voyelle fugitive, *f.*
100	flexion, n.	флексия, *f.*	Flexion, *f.*	flexion, *f.*
101	flexibility, n.	гибкость, *f.*	Flexierbarkeit, *f.*	flexibilité, *f.*
102	florid style	витиеватый стиль	blumenreicher Stil	style fleuri, *m.*
103	flow, n.	течение, *n./*поток, *m.*	Fluss, *m./*Gang, *m.*	cours, *m.*
104	flow chart	блок-схема, *f./*схема логической программы, *f.*	Flussdiagramm, *n./* Strömungsdiagramm, *n.*	organigramme, *m.*
105	flower language	язык цветов, *m.*	Blumensprache, *f.*	langue des fleurs, *f.*
106	flowery style	цветистый слог/ витиеватый стиль	blumenreicher Stil/ schwülstiger Stil	style fleuri, *m.*

No.	English	Russian	German	French
107	fluctuation, n.	колебание, *n.*	Ebben, *n.*/Schweben, *n.*	fluctuation, *f.*
108	fluency, n.	беглость, *f.*	Sprachfertigkeit, *f.*/ Geläufigkeit, *f.*/ Fluss, *m.*	facilité d'élocution, *f.*
109	fluent speech	беглая речь	fliessende Rede/ fliessendes Sprechen	débit facile, *m.*
110	focal area	центральные районы, *m.*, pl.	Ausgangspunkt, *m.*/ Ausgangsgebiet, *n.*	centre de rayonnement, *m.*
111	focus, n.	средоточие, *n.*/фокус, *m.*/центр, *m.*	Brennpunkt, *m.*	foyer, *m.*/point de convergence, *m.*
112	folk etymology	народная этимология	Volksetymologie, *f.*	étymologie populaire, *f.*
113	folklore, n.	фольклор, *m.*	Volkskunde, *f.*	folklore, *m.*
114	folksong, n.	народная песня	Volkslied, *n.*	chanson folklorique, *f.*
115	folktale, n.	народная сказка	Volkserzählung, *f.*/ Volksmärchen, *n.*	conte folklorique, *f.*
116	following, adj.	следующий/ последующий	folgend	suivant
117	food names (prepared dishes), pl.	названия блюд, *n.*, pl./ пищевые названия, *n.*, pl.	Speisebezeichnungen, *f.*, pl./Speisenamen, *m.*, pl.	noms des plats, *m.*, pl.
118	footnote, n.	сноска, *f.*/ подстрочное замечание	Fussnote, *f.*	note en bas de page, *f.*
119	for example	например	zum Beispiel	par exemple
120	force, n.	сила, *f.*	Kraft, *f.*/Stärke, *f.*	force, *f.*
121	forefinger, n.	указательный палец	Zeigefinger, *m.*	index, *m.*
122	foregoing, adj.	предшествующий/ упомянутый выше	vorhergehend/früher erwähnt/obig/ oben erwähnt	précédent/ci-dessus
123	forehead, n.	лоб, *m.*	Stirn, *f.*	front, *m.*
124	foreign accent	иностранный акцент	ausländischer Akzent	accent étranger, *m.*

No.	ENGLISH	RUSSIAN	GERMAN	FRENCH
125	foreign born, adj.	родившийся в другой стране	fremdgeboren	né à l'étranger
126	foreign borrowing	иноязычное заимствование	fremdsprachliche Entlehnung	emprunt à une langue étrangère, m.
127	foreign country	зарубежная страна	Ausland, n.	pays étranger, n.
128	foreign influence	иностранное влияние	fremder Einfluss	influence étrangère, f.
129	foreign language	иностранный язык	Fremdsprache, f.	langue étrangère, f.
130	foreign parentage	иностранного происхождения	ausländische Abstammung	parenté étrangère, f.
131	foreign sound	чужой звук	Fremdlaut, m.	son étranger, m.
132	foreigner, n.	иностранец. m.	Ausländer, m.	étranger, m.
133	foreignism, n.	иностранное выражение	ausländischer Ausdruck	expression étrangère, f.
134	forementioned, adj.	вышеупомянутый	vorhererwähnt	susmentionné/ ci-dessus désigné
135	foreward, n.	предисловие, n.	Vorwort, n.	avant-propos, m.
136	forgetfulness, n.	забывчивость, f.	Vergesslichkeit, f.	manque de mémoire, m./ oubli chronique, m.
137	form (in European schools), n.	класс, m.	Klasse, f./Schulklasse, f.	classe, f.
138	form (linguistic), n.	форма, f.	Form, f.	forme, f.
139	form, v.	образовать/ составлять/ создавать	bilden	construire/former
140	form and concept	форма и понятие	Form und Begriff	forme et concept
141	form and content	форма и содержание	Form und Inhalt	forme et contenu
142	form and meaning	форма и значение	Form und Bedeutung	forme et sens
143	form and substance	форма и вещество	Form und Stoff	forme et substance
144	form association	аналогия по форме, f.	Formübertragung, f.	analogie, f.

No.	ENGLISH	RUSSIAN	GERMAN	FRENCH
145	form change	видоизменение, *n.*	Formwechsel, *m.*	changement de forme, *m.*
146	form class	формальный класс	Formklasse, *f.*	classe formelle, *f.*
147	form of address	форма обращения, *f.*	Anredeform, *f.*	titre d'adresse, *m.*
148	form of dictionary entry	форма словарной статьи, *f.*	Form des Wörterbucheintrags, *f.*	forme citée dans un dictionnaire, *f.*
149	formal, adj.	формальный	formal/formell	formel/de forme
150	formal criterion	формальный критерий	formales Kriterium	critère formel, *m.*
151	formal difference	формальное различие	Formunterschied, *m.*	différence formelle, *f.*
152	formal relationship	формальное отношение	formale Beziehung	rapport formel, *m.*
153	formal resemblance	внешнее сходство	Formähnlichkeit, *f.*	ressemblance formelle, *f.*
154	formal speech style	формальная речь/ официальный стил	formeller Stil	style formel, *m.*
155	formal system	формальная система	formales System	système formel, *m.*
156	formalism, n.	формализм, *m.*	Formalismus, *m.*	formalisme, *m.*
157	formant, n.	формант. *m.*	Formans, *m.*	formant, *m.*
158	format, n.	формат, *m.*	Format, *n.*	format, *m.*
159	formation, n.	образование, *n.*/ составление, *n.*/ конструкция, *f.*	Bildung, *f.*/ Konstruktion, *f.*	formation, *f.*/ construction, *f.*
160	former and latter	первый и последний	ersterer und letzterer	celui-là et celui-ci
161	formative, n.	образующий элемент/ словообразующий	formbildendes Element	élément formatif, *m.*
162	formula, n.	формула, *f.*	Formel, *f.*	formule, *f.*
163	formulation, n.	формулировка, *f.*	Formulierung, *f.*	formulation, *f.*
164	fossilized form	застывшая форма	erstarrte Form	forme figée, *f.*
165	foundation, n.	фундамент, *m.*/ основание, *n.*	Grundlage, *f.*	fondement, *m.*

No.	English	Russian	German	French
166	fountain pen	автоматическая ручка	Füllfeder, *f.*	stylo, *m.*
167	four-letter words, pl.	неприличные слова, *n.*, pl.	obszöne Wörter, *n.*, pl.	mots grossiers, *m.*, pl.
168	fourth estate	пресса, *f.*	Presse, *f.*/ Journalismus, *m.*	presse souveraine, *f.*
169	fraction, n.	дробь, *f.*	Bruch, *m.*	fraction, *f.*
170	fragment, n.	фрагмент, *m.*/ отрезок, *m.*	Fragment, *n.*	fragment, *m.*
171	fragmentary, adj.	фрагментарный/ отрывочный	fragmentarisch	fragmentaire
172	frame, n.	рама, *f.*	Rahmen, *m.*	système, *m.*
173	framework, n.	каркас, *m.*/остов, *m.*	Rahmen, *m.*	cadre, *m.*
174	free association	свободная ассоциация	freie Assoziation, *f.*	association libre, *f.*
175	free combination	свободное сочетание	freie Kombination/ freie Fügung	combinaison libre, *f.*
176	free form	свободная форма	freie Form	forme libre, *f.*
177	free morpheme	самостоятельная морфема	selbständiges Morphem	morphème libre, *m.*
178	free passage (of air)	свободный проход	freier Durchfluss/unge- hinderter Durchfluss/ ungehemmter Durchfluss	passage libre, *f.*
179	free translation	свободный перевод	freie Übersetzung/nicht wörtliche Übersetzung	traduction libre, *f.*
180	free variation	свободное варьирование	freie Variation	variation libre, *f.*
181	free verse	свободный стих	Blankvers, *m.*	vers libre, *m.*
182	free word order	свободный порядок слов	freie Wortstellung	ordre de mots libre, *m.*
183	French, adj.	французский	französisch	français
184	frequency, n.	частота, *f.*/ частотность, *f.*	Frequenz, *f.*/ Häufigkeit, *f.*	fréquence, *f.*

No.	ENGLISH	RUSSIAN	GERMAN	FRENCH
185	frequency count	подсчет частоты, *m.*	Frequenzzählung, *f.*/ Häufigkeitszählung, *f.*	cacul de fréquence, *m.*
186	frequency of occurrence	частота встречаемости, *f.*	Häufigkeit des Vorkommens, *f.*	fréquence d'emploi, *f.*
187	frequentative (verb), adj.	многократный	frequentativ	fréquentatif
188	frequently occurring, adj.	часто встречающийся/ частый	häufig vorkommend	fréquent
189	fricative consonants, pl.	фрикативные согласные, pl./ щелийные соглас-ные, pl./щелевые согласные, pl.	Frikative, *n.,* pl./ Reibelaute, *m.,* pl.	consonnes fricatives, *f.,* pl.
190	friction, n.	трение, *n.*	Reibung, *f.*	friction, *f.*
191	fringe area	переходная зона/ окраина, *f.*	Randzone, *f.*/ Randgebiet, *n.*	aire marginale, *f.*
192	front articulation	передняя артикуляция	Artikulation vorn, *f.*	articulation antérieure, *f.* /articulation d'avant, *f.*
193	front lingual, adj.	переднеязычный	Vorderzungen-	fronto-
194	front palatal, adj.	передненебный	Vorderpalatal-	palatal antérieur
195	front vowels, pl.	гласные переднего ряда, pl./передние гласные, pl.	vordere Vokale, *m.,* pl.	voyelles antérieres, *f.,* pl. /voyelles d'avant, *f.,* pl. /voyelles palatales, *f.,* pl.
196	fronting (of articulation), n.	передвижение вперед, *n.*	Palatalisierung, *f.*	articulation avancée, *f.*
197	full form	полная форма	Vollform, *f.*	forme pleine, *f.*
198	full meaning	полный смысл/ полное значение	Gesamtbedeutung, *f.*	sens global, *m.*
199	full sentence	полное предложение	vollständiger Satz/ ganzer Satz	phrase complète, *f.*
200	full stop	точка, *f.*	Punkt, *m.*	point, *m.*
201	function, n.	функция, *f.*	Funktion, *f.*	fonction, *f.*

No.	ENGLISH	RUSSIAN	GERMAN	FRENCH
202	function word	служебное слово	Hilfswort, *n.*/ Nebenwort, *n.*	mot-outil, *m.*/mot accessoire, *m.*
203	functional classification	функциональная классификация	funktionale Einteilung	classification fonctionnelle, *f.*
204	functional definition	функциональное определение	funktionale Definition	définition fonctionnelle, *f.*
205	functional load	функциональная нагрузка	funktionale Belastung	rendement fonctionnel, *m.*
206	functional marker	функциональный указатель	funktionales Merkmal	marquant fonctionnel, *m.*
207	functional relationship	функциональное соотношение	funktionale Beziehung	rapport fonctionnel, *m.*
208	functional role	функциональная роль	funktionale Rolle	rôle fonctionnel, *m.*
209	functional value	функциональное значение	funktionaler Wert	valeur fonctionnelle, *f.*
210	fundamental, adj.	основной/коренной	grundlegend	fondamental/de base
211	fundamental assumption	основное предположение	grundlegende Vermutung/grundlegende Voraussetzung	assomption de base, *f.*
212	fundamental frequency	основной тон	Grundfrequenz, *f.*	son fondamental, *m.*
213	fundamental principle	основной принцип	grundlegendes Prinzip	principe fondamental, *m.*
214	fundamental rule	основное правило	Grundregel, *f.*	règle fondamentale, *f.*
215	fundamentals, pl.	основы, *f., pl.*	Grundzüge, *m., pl.*	principes fondamentaux, *m., pl.*/éléments fondamentaux, *m., pl.*
216	funeral oration	погребальное слово	Trauerrede, *f.*	oraison funèbre, *f.*
217	funny, adj.	смешной	komisch	drôle
218	fusion, n.	фузия, *f.*/слияние, *n.*/сплав, *m.*	Schmelzung, *f.*/Verschmelzung, *f.*/Zusammenfall, *m.*	fusion, *f.*
219	future, n.	будущее, *n.*	Zukunft, *f.*	futur, *m.*

No.	ENGLISH	RUSSIAN	GERMAN	FRENCH
220	future participle	причастие будущего времени, *n.*	Partizip des Futurums, *n.*	participe futur, *m.*
221	future perfect	будущее предварительное	Futurum exactum, *n.*/ zweites Futur, *m.*	futur antérieur, *m.*
222	future tense	будущее время	Futur(um), *n.*	futur, *m.*

G

001	galley proof	гранка, *f.*	Fahnenkorrektur, *f.*	placard, *m.*
002	geminate consonants, pl.	двойные согласные, pl.	Doppelkonsonanten, *m.*, pl.	consonnes doubles, *f.*, pl. /consonnes géminées, *f.*, pl.
003	gender, n.	род, *m.*	Genus, *n.*/Geschlecht, *n.*	genre, *m.*
004	genderless, adj.	неродовой	genuslos/ geschlechtslos	insexué
005	genealogical classification	генеалогическая классификация	genealogische Klassifizierung	classement généalogique, *m.*
006	genealogical tree	родословное дерево	Stammbaum, *m.*	arbre généalogique, *m.*
007	genealogy, n.	генеалогия, *f.*/ родословная, *f.*	Genealogie, *f.*	généalogie, *f.*
008	general, adj.	общий	general/allgemein	général
009	general linguistics	общая лингвистика	allgemeine Sprachwissenschaft	sens général, *m.*
010	general meaning	общее значение	allgemeine Bedeutung	sens général
011	general phonetics	общая фонетика	allgemeine Phonetik	phonétique générale, *f.*
012	generality, n.	всеобщность, *f.*/ универсальность, *f.*	Allgemeingültigkeit, *f.*/ Allgemeinheit, *f.*	caractère général, *m.*/ généralité, *f.*
013	generalization, n.	обобщение, *n.*	Verallgemeinerung, *f.*	généralisation, *f.*
014	generate, v.	порождать	erzeugen	générer
015	generation (of people), n.	поколение, *n.*	Generation, *f.*	génération, *f.*

No.	English	Russian	German	French
016	generation (of sentences), n.	порождение, *n.*	Generierung, *f./* Erzeugung, *f.*	génération, *f.*
017	generative grammar, generative model	порождающая грамматика/ порождающая модель	generative Grammatik/ generatives Modell	grammaire générative, *f./* modèle de langue génératif, *m.*
018	generic name	общее название/ родовое обозначение	Gattungsname, *m.*	nom générique, *m.*
019	genesis, n.	генезис, *m./* возникновение, *n.*	Genesis, *f./* Ursprung, *m.*	genèse, *f.*
020	genetic relationship	родовое отношение	Verwandtschaft, *f.*	parenté, *f.*
021	genetics, n.	генетика, *f.*	Entstehungslehre, *f.*	génétique, *f.*
022	genitive case	родительный падеж	Genetiv, *m./*Wesfall, *m./* zweiter Fall	génitif, *m.*
023	genre, n.	жанр, *m.*	Genre, *n.*	genre, *m.*
024	genuine, adj.	подлинный	authentisch	authentique
025	geographical barrier	географическое препятствие	geographisches Hindernis	barrière géographique, *f.*
026	geographical classification	географическая классификация	geographische Klassifizierung	classement géographique, *m.*
027	geographical convergence	географическое схождение	geographische Konvergenz	convergence géographique, *f.*
028	geographical distribution	географическое расположение	geographische Verteilung	distribution géographique, *f.*
029	geographical linguistics	географическая лингвистика	geographische Linguistik/ Sprachgeographie, *f.*	linguistique géographique, *f.*
030	geographical name	географическое название/ топоним, *m.*	geographischer Name	nom géographique, *m.*
031	geographical variation	географическое разнообразие	geographische Variation	variation géographique, *f.*

No.	ENGLISH	RUSSIAN	GERMAN	FRENCH
032	geography, n.	география, *f.*	Geographie, *f.*/ Erdkunde, *f.*	géographie, *f.*
033	geometry, n.	геометрия, *f.*	Geometrie, *f.*	géométrie, *f.*
034	German, adj.	немецкий	deutsch	allemand
035	germane, adj.	подходящий	passend/zutreffend	allié
036	gerund, n.	герундий, *m.*	Gerundium, *n.*	gérondif, *m.*
037	gesture, n.	жест, *m.*/ телодвижение, *n.*	Gebärde, *f.*	geste, *m.*
038	gesture language	язык жестов, *m.*	Gebärdensprache, *f.*/ Zeichensprache, *f.*	langage mimique, *m.*
039	ghost word	слово-призрак, *m.*	Phantomwort, *n.*	mot-fantôme, *m.*
040	gibberish, n.	белиберда, *f.*	Kauderwelsch, *n.*	baragouin, *m.*/ charabia, *m.*
041	giggling, n.	хихиканье, *n.*	Gekicher, *n.*	gloussement, *m.*
042	glide, n.	скольжение, *n.*/ промежуточный звук/переходный звук	Gleitlaut, *m.*	glissement, *m.*/son de transition, *m.*
043	gloss, n.	глосса, *f.*	Glosse, *f.*	glose, *f.*
044	glossary, n.	глоссарий, *m.*/ словник, *m.*	Glossar, *n.*/ Spezialwörterbuch, *n.*	glossaire, *m.*
045	glossematics, n.	глоссематика, *f.*	Glossematik, *f.*	glossématique, *f.*
046	glottal stop	глоттальная смычка/ гортанная смычка	Kehlkopfverschluss, *m.*/ Knacklaut, *m.*	coup de glotte, *m.*/ occlusion glottale, *f.*
047	glottalized consonants, pl.	глоттализованные согласные, pl.	glottalisierte Konsonanten, *m.*, pl.	consonnes glottalisées, *f.*, pl.
048	glottalization, n.	глоттализация, *f.*	Glottalisierung, *f.*	glottalisation, *f.*
049	glottis, n.	голосовая щель	Stimmritze, *f.*	glotte, *f.*
050	glottochronology, n.	глоттохронология, *f.*	Glottochronologie, *f.*	glottochronologie, *f.*
051	goal, n.	цель, *f.*	Ziel, *n.*/Zweck, *m.*	but, *m.*

No.	English	Russian	German	French
052	gobbledegook, n.	тарабарщина, *f.*	Kauderwelsch, *n.*/ geradebrechte Sprache	charabia, *m.*/palabre, *m.*
053	gossip, n.	болтовня, *f.*	Klatsch, *m.*/Geklatsch, *m.*/Nachrede, *f.*	bavardage, *m.*
054	government, n.	управление, *n.*	Rektion, *f.*	rection, *f.*/direction, *f.*
055	gradation, n.	аблаут, *m.*/ чередование гласных, *n.*	Ablaut, *m.*	alternance graduée, *f.*
056	grade (U.S. school), n.	класс, *m.*	Klasse, *f.*/Schulklasse, *f.*	classe élémentaire, *f.*
057	grade of ablaut	степень аблаута, *m.*	Ablautsstufe, *f.*/ Ablautsgrad, *m.*	degré apophonique, *m.*
058	grade school	начальная школа	Grundschule, *f.*/ Volksschule, *f.*	école primaire, *f.*
059	gradual change	постепенное изменение	allmähliche Veränderung	changement graduel, *m.*
060	graduate student	аспирант, *m.*/ кандидат, *m.*	Doktorand, *m.*	licencié, *m.*
061	graduate school	аспирантура, *f.*/ высшее учебное заведение	Hochschule, *f.*	école de hautes études, *f.*
062	grammar, n.	грамматика, *f.*	Grammatik, *f.*	grammaire, *f.*
063	grammar school (Europe)	средняя классическая школа	Gymnasium, *n.*/höhere Schule/Lateinschule, *f.* /Mittelschule, *f.*	collège, *m.*/lycée, *m.*
064	grammar school (U.S.)	начальная школа	Grundschule, *f.*/ Volksschule, *f.*	école primaire, *f.*
065	grammarian, n.	грамматик, *m.*	Grammatiker, *m.*	grammarien, *s.*
066	grammatical, adj.	грамматический/ грамматически правильный/ грамматичный	grammatikalisch/ grammatisch	grammatical
067	grammatical abstraction	грамматическая абстракция	grammatische Abstraktion	abstraction grammaticale, *f.*
068	grammatical agreement	согласование, *n.*	Kongruenz, *f.*	accord grammatical, *m.*

No.	English	Russian	German	French
069	grammatical alternation	грамматическое чередование	grammatischer Wechsel	alternance grammaticale, *f.*
070	grammatical analysis	грамматический анализ	grammatische Analyse/ Satzanalyse, *f.*	analyse grammaticale, *f.*
071	grammatical category	грамматическая категория	grammatische Kategorie	catégorie grammaticale, *f.*
072	grammatical constituent	грамматическое составляющее	Formationsteil der Grammatik, *m.*/ Konstituente der Grammatik, *f.*	composant grammatical, *m.*
073	grammatical construction	грамматическая конструкция	grammatische Konstruktion	construction grammaticale, *f.*
074	grammatical core	грамматическое ядро	grammatischer Kern	fond grammatical, *m.*
075	grammatical device	грамматический способ	grammatisches Hilfsmittel	moyen grammatical, *m.*
076	grammatical feature	грамматический признак	grammatische Eigenschaft	trait grammatical, *m.*
077	grammatical form	грамматическая форма	grammatische Form	forme grammaticale, *f.*
078	grammatical equivalent	грамматический эквивалент	grammatisches Äquivalent	équivalent grammatical, *m.*
079	grammatical gender	грамматический род	grammatisches Genus/ grammatisches Geschlecht	genre grammatical, *m.*
080	grammatical meaning	грамматическое значение	grammatische Bedeutung	sens grammatical, *m.*
081	grammatical mistake	грамматическая ошибка	Grammatikfehler, *m.*	faute de grammaire, *f.*
082	grammatical morpheme	грамматическая морфема	grammatikalisches Morphem	morphème grammatical, *m.*
083	grammatical order	грамматический порядок	grammatische Ordnung	ordre grammatical, *m.*
084	grammatical process	грамматический процесс	grammatischer Vorgang	procédé grammatical, *m.*

No.	ENGLISH	RUSSIAN	GERMAN	FRENCH
085	grammatical sentence	грамматически правильное предложение	grammatischer Satz	phrase grammaticale, *f.*
086	grammatical stress	грамматическое ударение	grammatische Betonung	accent grammatical, *m.*
087	grammatical system	грамматнческая система	grammatisches System	système grammatical, *m.*
088	grammatical structure	грамматическая структура/грамматический строй	grammatische Struktur	structure grammaticale, *f.*
089	grammatical terminology	грамматическая терминология	grammatische Terminologie	terminologie grammaticale, *f.*
090	grammatical voice	грамматический залог	grammatisches Genus des Verbs	voix grammaticale, *f.*
091	grammaticality, n.	грамматичность, *f.*	Grammatizität, *m.*	grammaticalité, *f.*
092	graph, n.	график, *m.*/ диаграмма, *f.*	Diagramm, *n.*	graphique, *m.*
093	grapheme, n.	графема, *f.*/буква, *f.*	Graphem, *n.*/ Buchstabe, *m.*	graphème, *m.*
094	graphemics, n.	графемика, *f.*	Graphemik, *f.*	graphémique, *f.*
095	graphic, adj.	графический	graphisch	graphique
096	graphic assimilation	графическая ассимиляция	graphische Angleichung	assimilation graphique, *f.*
097	graphic representation	графическая передача	graphische Darstellung	représentation graphique, *f.*
098	graphic word	графическое слово	graphisches Wort	mot graphique, *m.*
099	graphic writing	начертательное письмо	Abbildungsschrift, *f.*	écriture par images, *f.*
100	graphology, n.	графология, *f.*	Graphologie, *f.*/ Handschriftenkunde, *f.*	graphologie, *f.*
101	grave, n.	могила, *f.*	Grab, *n.*	tombe, *f.*/tombeau, *m.*
102	grave accent	тупое ударение	Gravis, *m.*	accent grave, *m.*

No.	English	Russian	German	French
103	gravestone, n.	могильная плитка/ надгробный камень	Grabstein, *m.*	pierre tombale, *f.*
104	graveyard, n.	кладбище, *n.*	Friedhof, *m.*/ Kirchhof, *m.*	cimetière, *m.*
105	gravitation, n.	притяжение, *n.*	Neigung, *f.*	attirance, *f.*
106	Greek, adj.	греческий	griechisch	grec
107	greeting, n.	приветствие, *n.*	Gruss, *m.*	salut, *m.*
108	greeting card	поздравительная корточка	Glückwunschkarte, *f.*	carte de félicitation, *f.*
109	group, n.	группа, *f.*	Gruppe, *f.*	groupe, *m.*
110	grouping, n.	группировка, *f.*	Gruppierung, *f.*	groupement, *m.*
111	growth, n.	развитие, *n.*/рост, *m.*	Entwicklung, *f.*	développement, *m.*
112	guess, n.	догадка, *f.*	Vermutung, *f.*	conjecture, *f.*
113	guiding principle	руководящий принцип	Leitprinzip, *n.*	principe directeur, *m.*
114	gums, pl.	десны, *f.*, pl.	Zahnfleisch, *n.*, sg.	gencives, pl.
115	gutteral consonants, pl.	горловые согласные, pl./гортанные согласные, pl./задненебные согласные, pl.	Gutturale, pl./ Kehlkopflaute, *m.*, pl.	consonnes gutturales, *f.*, pl.
116	Gypsy, adj.	цыганский	Zigeuner-	gitan/romanichel

H

001	habit, n.	привычка, *f.*	Gewohnheit, *f.*	habitude, *f.*
002	handbook, n.	справочник, *m.*	Handbuch, *m.*	manuel, *m.*
003	handwriting, n.	почерк, *m.*	Handschrift, *f.*	écriture, *f.*
004	haplology, n.	гаплология, *f.*	Haplologie, *f.*	haplologie, *f.*

No.	ENGLISH	RUSSIAN	GERMAN	FRENCH
005	hard consonants, pl.	твердые согласные, pl.	harte Konsonanten, *m.,* pl.	consonnes dures, *f.,* pl.
006	hard of hearing, adj.	тугой на ухо	schwerhörig	dur d'oreille
007	hard palate	твердое небо	harter Gaumen	palais dur, *m.*
008	hard sign	твердый знак	hartes Zeichen	signe dur, *m.*
009	harmonic, n.	частичный тон/ парциальный тон	Harmonik, *f.*/Oberton, *m.*/Oberwelle, *f.*	harmonique, *m.*
010	head word	главное слово	Kernwort, *n.*	mot-souche, *m.*
011	heading, n.	заглавие, *n.*/надпись, *f.*	Überschrift, *f.*	rubrique, *f.*
012	headline, n.	заголовок, *m.*	Schlagzeile, *f.*	manchette, *f.*
013	headphone, n.	наушники, pl.	Kopfhörer, *m.*	écouteur, *m.*
014	hearer, n.	слушатель, *m.*	Zuhörer, *m.*	auditeur, *m.*
015	hearing, n.	слух, *m.*	Gehör, *n.*/Hören, *n.*	ouïe, *f.*
016	hearing aid	усилитель для глухих, *m.*	Hörgerät, *n.*	aide-ouïe, *f.*
017	hearing defect	дефект слуха, *m.*	Hörfehler, *m.*	défaut auditif, *m.*
018	hearing mechanism	слуховой аппарат	Hörmechanismus, *m.*	mécanisme auditif, *m.*
019	Hebrew, Hebraic, adj.	еврейский	hebräisch	hébraïque/hébreu
020	height, n.	высота, *f.*/уровень, *m.*	Höhe, *f.*	hauteur, *f.*
021	height of tongue	подъем языка, *m.*	Zungenhöhe, *f.*	niveau de la langue, *m.*
022	heredity, n.	наследственность, *f.*	Erbe, *n.*/Vererbung, *f.*	hérédité, *f.*
023	heroic epic	героическая поэма/ героический эпос	Heldengedicht, *n.*/ Epos, *n.*	vers héroïque, *m.*/ chanson épique, *f.*/ épopée, *f.*
024	hesitation, n.	пауза, *f.*/остановка, *f.*	Zögern, *n.*	hésitation, *f.*
025	heterogeneity, n.	разнородность, *f.*	Verschiedenheit, *f.*	hétérogénéité, *f.*
026	heterogeneous, adj.	разнородный/ неоднородный	heterogen	hétérogène

No.	ENGLISH	RUSSIAN	GERMAN	FRENCH
027	heuristic, adj.	эвристический	heuristisch	heuristique
028	hiatus, n.	зияние, *n.*/пробел, *m.*/ пропуск, *m.*	Hiatus, *m.*	hiatus, *m.*
029	hierarchical levels, pl.	иерархические уровни, *m.*, pl.	Stufen der Rangordnung, *f.*, pl.	niveaux hiérachiques, *m.*, pl.
030	hierarchical structure	иерархическая структура	hierarchische Struktur	structure hiérarchique, *f.*
031	hierarchy, n.	иерархия, *f.*	Hierarchie, *f.*	hiérarchie, *f.*
032	hieroglyph, n.	иероглиф, *m.*	Hieroglyphe, *f.*	hiéroglyphe, *m.*
033	hieroglyphic writing	иероглифическое письмо	Hieroglyphenschrift, *f.*	écriture hiéroglyphique, *f.*
034	high, adj.	высокий	hoch	haut
035	high frequency	высокая частота	Hochfrequenz, *f.*	haute fréquence, *f.*
036	High German, adj.	верхненемецкий	hochdeutsch/ oberdeutsch	haut allemand
037	high level abstraction	абстракция высокого уровня, *f.*	höhere Abstraktionsstufe	abstraction à niveau élevé, *f.*
038	high pitched, adj.	высокой тональности	in höherer Tonlage	de ton haut
039	high school	средняя школа	höhere Schule	école secondaire, *f.*
040	high speed storage	быстродействующая память	schnell wirkender Speicher	mémoire à accès rapide, *f.*/mémoire rapide, *f.*
041	high tonal register	высокий регистр тона	hohe Tonlage/höher Tonumfang	registre à tons hauts, *m.*
042	high tone	высокий тон/ верхний тон	Hochton, *m.*	ton élevé, *m.*
043	high vowels, pl.	высокие гласные, pl./ верхние гласные, pl.	hohe Vokale, *m.*, pl./ enge Vokale, *m.*, pl.	voyelles hautes, *f.*, pl./ voyelles fermées, *f.*, pl.
044	higher, adj.	высший/верхний	höher/oberer	plus haut
045	hissing sound	свистящий звук	Zischlaut, *m.*/S-Laut, *m.*	son sifflant, *m.*

No.	ENGLISH	RUSSIAN	GERMAN	FRENCH
046	historical change	историческое изменение	historischer Wechsel	changement historique, *m.*
047	historical dialectology	историческая диалектология	historische Dialektologie	dialectologie historique, *f.*
048	historical documentation	историческая документация	historische Dokumentation	documentation historique, *f.*
049	historical linguistics	историческая лингвистика	historische Sprachwissenschaft	linguistique historique, *f.*/ linguistique évolutive, *f.*
050	historical method	исторический метод	historische Methode	méthode historique, *f.*
051	historical morphology	историческая морфология	historische Morphologie	morphologie historique, *f.*
052	historical phonemics	историческая фонология	historische Phonologie	phonologie historique, *f.*
053	historical phonetics	историческая фонетика	historische Phonetik/ Lautgeschichte, *f.*	phonétique historique, *f.*
054	historical phonology	историческая фонология	historische Phonologie	phonologie historique, *f.*
055	historical present	настоящее время повествовательное	historisches Präsens	présent historique, *m.*
056	historical process	исторический процесс	historischer Vorgang	processus historique, *m.*
057	historical reconstruction	историческая перестройка	historische Rekonstruktion	réconstruction historique, *f.*/restitution historique, *f.*
058	historical semantics	историческая семантика	historische Semantik	sémantique historique, *f.*
059	historical syntax	исторический синтаксис	historische Syntax	grammaire historique, *f.*
060	historiography, n.	историография, *f.*	Geschichtsschreibung, *f.*	historiographie, *f.*
061	history, n.	история, *f.*	Geschichte, *f.*	histoire, *f.*
062	hoarse voice	охрипший голос/ хриплый голос	heisere Stimme	voix rauque, *f.*

No.	English	Russian	German	French
063	hocus-pocus, n.	фокус, *m.*	Hokuspokus, *m.*	tour de passe-passe, *f.*
064	hodge-podge, n.	всякая всячина	Mischmasch, *m.*	salmigondis, *m.*
065	hole in the pattern	недостаток в системе, *m .*	Lücke im System, *f.*	case vide, *f.*
066	homeland, n.	родина, *f.*	Heimatland, *n.*	pays natal, *m.*/patrie, *f.*
067	homework, n.	домашняя работа	Hausaufgabe, *f.*/ Schulaufgabe, *f.*	devoirs à la maison, *m.*, pl.
068	homogeneous, adj.	однородный	homogen/gleichartig	homogène
069	homograph, n.	омограф, *m.*	Homogramm, *n.*	homogramme, *m.*
070	homonym, n.	омоним, *m.*	Homonym, *n.*/ gleichlautendes Wort	homonyme, *m.*
071	homonymy, n.	омонимия, *f.*	Homonymie, *f.*	homonymie, *f.*
072	homophone, n.	омофон, *m.*	Homophon, *n.*	homophone, *m.*
073	homorganic, adj.	гоморганный	homorgan	homorgane
074	honorific address	почтительное обращение	respektvolle Anrede	formule courtoise, *f.*
075	horizontal, adj.	горизонтальный	horizontal	horizontal
076	horizontal axis	горизонтальная ось	x-Achse, *f.*	axe horizontal, *m.*
077	horizontal line	горизонтальная линия	horizontale Linie	ligne horizontale, *f.*
078	horizontal writing	горизонтальное письмо	horizontale Schrift	écriture horizontale, *f.*
079	hortatory mood	побудительное наклонение	ermahnender Modus	exhortatif, *m.*
080	howling, n.	вопль, *m.*	Heulen, *n.*	hurlement, *m.*
081	hum, n.	жужжание, *n.*	Brummton, *m.*	chantonnement, *m.*/ fredon, *m.*
082	human, adj.	человеческий	menschlich	humain

No.	English	Russian	German	French
083	human language	человеческий язык	menschliche Sprache	langage humain, *m.*
084	human race	человеческий род	menschliche Rasse	genre humain, *m.*
085	human society	человеческое общество	menschliche Gesell-schaft	société humaine, *f.*
086	humanity, n.	человечество, *n.*	Menschengeschlecht, *n.*	humanité, *f.*
087	humor, n.	юмор, *m.*	Humor, *m.*	humour, *m.*
088	humorous, adj.	смешной	humoristisch/humorvoll	amusant/comique
089	hushing sound	шипящий звук	Rauschlaut, *m.*/ Sch-Laut, *m.*	son chuintant, *m.*
090	Hungarian, adj.	венгерский	ungarisch/magyarisch	hongrois/magyar
091	hybrid formation	смешанное образование	hybride Bildung/ Mischbildung, *f.*	formation hybride, *f.*
092	hybrid language	смешанный язык	Mischsprache, *f.*	langue hybride, *f.*
093	hyperbole, n.	гипербола, *f.*/ преувеличение, *n.*	Hyperbel, *f.*	hyperbole, *f.*
094	hyper-urbanism, n.	излишняя нормализация/ сверхпоправка, *f.*	Hyperurbanismus, *n.*	régression fausse, *f.*
095	hyphen, n.	дефис, *m.*/ соединительная черточка	Bindestrich, *m.*/ Trennungsstrich, *m.*	trait d'union, *m.*
096	hyphenated word	слово написанное через дефис	mit Bindestrich geschrie-benes Wort	mot avec trait d'union, *m.*
097	hypocoristic form	уменьшительная форма	Koseform, *f.*	forme d'affection, *f.*/ forme d'attendrisse-ment, *f.*
098	hypotaxis, n.	гипотаксис, *m.*	Hypotaxe, *f.*/ Unterordnung, *f.*	hypotaxe, *f.*
099	hypothesis, n.	гипотеза, *f.*	Hypothese, *f.*	hypothèse, *f.*
100	hypothetical data	гипотетические данные, pl.	hypothetische Unterla-gen, pl.	données hypothétiques, pl.

No.	English	Russian	German	French
101	hypothetical form	гипотетическая форма	hypothetische Form	forme hypothétique, *f.*
102	hypothetical construct	гипотетический конструкт	hypothetisches Gebilde	composition hypothétique, *f.*
103	hypothetical language	гипотетический язык	hypothetische Sprache	langue hypothétique, *f.*

I

001	ictus, n.	ритмическое ударение	Iktus, *m.*/rhythmischer Akzent/Starkton, *m.*	accent, *m.*
002	idea, n.	идея, *f.*/мысль, *f.*	Idee, *f.*	idée, *f.*
003	identical, adj.	одинаковый	identisch	identique
004	identification, n.	отождествление, *n.*/ опознание, *n.*	Identifizierung, *f.*	identification, *f.*
005	identity, n.	тождество, *n.*	Identität, *f.*	identité, *f.*
006	ideogram, ideograph, n.	идеограмма, *f.*/ идеограф, *m.*	Ideogramm, *n.*/ Begriffszeichen, *n.*	idéogramme, *m.*
007	ideographic writing	идеография, *f.*/письмо понятиями, *n.*	Begriffsschrift, *f.*	écriture idéographique, *f.*
008	ideolect, n.	идеолект, *m.*	Ideolekt, *n.*/individuelle Spracheigentümlich- keiten, *f.*, pl.	langage individuel, *m.*
009	idiom, n.	идиома, *f.*	Idiom, *n.*/Sprachei- gentümlichkeit, *f.*	idiome, *m.*
010	idiomatic expression	идиоматическое выражение	idiomatischer Ausdruck/ Redewendung, *f.*	idiotisme, *m.*
011	idiomatic usage	идиоматическое употребление	idiomatischer Sprachge- brauch	emploi idiomatique, *m.*
012	idiosyncrasy, n.	личная особенность	Idiosynkrasie, *f.*/ Eigentümlichkeit, *f.*	particularité individuelle, *f.*
013	ill-defined, adj.	плохо определенный	schlecht definiert	mal défini
014	illegible, adj.	неразборчивый	unleserlich	illisible

No.	ENGLISH	RUSSIAN	GERMAN	FRENCH
015	illiterate person	неграмотный человек	Analphabet, *m.*	illétré, *m.*/ analphabète, *m.*
016	illiteracy, n.	безграмотность, *f.*/ неграмотность, *f.*	Analphabetentum, *n.*	analphabétisme, *m.*
017	illogical, adj.	нелогичный	unlogisch	illogique
018	illusion, n.	иллюзия, *f.*/обман чувств, *m.*	Illusion, *f.*/ Sinnestäuschung, *f.*	illusion, *f.*
019	illustration, n.	иллюстрация, *f.*/ пример, *m.*	Veranschaulichung, *f.*/ Beispiel, *n.*	illustration, *f.*/ éclaircissement, *m.*/ exemple, *m.*
020	image, n.	изображение, *n.*	Bild, *n.*	image, *f.*
021	imagination, n.	воображение, *n.*	Einbildungskraft, *f.*	imagination, *f.*
022	imbalance, n.	отсутствие равновесия, *n.*	Unausgeglichenheit, *f.*	déséquilibre, *m.*
023	imitation, n.	подражание, *n.*	Nachahmung, *f.*	imitation, *f.*/pastiche, *m.*
024	immediate constituents, pl.	непосредственно составляющие, pl.	unmittelbare Bestand-teile, *m.,* pl.	constituants immédiats, *m.*, pl.
025	immediate future	будущее немедленное	nähere Zukunft/Tem-pus instans, *n.*	futur proche, *m.*
026	immigrant speech	речь переселенцев, *f.*	Einwanderersprache, *f.*	langage de l'immigré, *m.*
027	immigration, n.	иммиграция, *f.*	Einwanderung, *f.*	immigration, *f.*
028	immutable, adj.	неизменный	unveränderlich	immuable
029	impact, n.	воздействие, *n.*	Wirkung, *f.*	impact, *m.*
030	impediment, n.	препятствие, *n.*	Hindernis, *n.*	obstacle, *m.*
031	impediment in speech	заикание, *n.*	Sprachfehler, *m.*	difficulté de parole, *f.*
032	imperative mood	повелительное наклонение	Imperativ, *m.*/ Befehlsform, *f.*	impératif, *m.*
033	imperative sentence	повелительное предложение	Imperativsatz, *m.*	phrase impérative, *f.*
034	imperceptible, adj.	незаметный	unmerklich	imperceptible

No.	English	Russian	German	French
035	imperfective aspect	несовершенный вид	imperfektive Aktionsart	aspect imparfait, *m.* aspect imperfectif, *m.*
036	impermissible, adj.	недопускаемый/ недопустимый	unannehmlich/ unzulässig	intolérable non admissible
037	impermanence, n.	непостоянность, *f.*	Unbeständigkeit, *f.*	impermanence, *f.*
038	impersonal, adj.	безличный	unpersönlich	impersonnel
039	impersonal pronoun	безличное местоимение	unpersönliches Prono- men	pronom impersonnel, *m.*
040	impersonal sentence	безличное предложение	unpersönlicher Satz	phrase impersonnelle, *f.*
041	impersonal verb	безличный глагол/ одноличный глагол	unpersönliches Verb(um)	verbe impersonnel, *m.*/ verbe unipersonnel, *m.*
042	implication, n.	вовлечение, *n.*	selbstverständliche Folgerung	implication, *f.*
043	implosive consonants, pl.	имплозивные согласные, pl.	implosive Konsonanten, *m.,* pl.	consonnes implosives, *f.,* pl.
044	important, adj.	важный/ значительный	wichtig	important
045	impossible, adj.	невозможный	unmöglich	impossible
046	imprecise, adj.	неточный	ungenau	non exact
047	impression, n.	впечатление, *n.*	Eindruck, *m.*	impression, *f.*
048	imprint, n.	отпечаток, *m.*/ штамп, *m.*	Abdruck, *m.*/Stempel, *m.*	empreinte, *f.*
049	improbable, adj.	невероятный	unwahrscheinlich	improbable
050	improvement, n.	успех, *m.*	Verbesserung, *f.*	progrés, *m.*
051	improvisation, n.	импровизация, *f.*	Improvisation, *f.*	improvisation, *f.*
052	inability, n.	неспособность, *f.*	Unfähigkeit, *f.*	incapacité, *f.*
053	inaccessible, adj.	неприступный	unzugänglich	inaccessible
054	inaccuracy, n.	неточность, *f.*/ ошибочность, *f.*	Unexaktheit, *f.*/ Ungenauigkeit, *f.*	inexactitude, *f.*

No.	ENGLISH	RUSSIAN	GERMAN	FRENCH
055	inaccurate, adj.	ошибочный/ неправильный/ неточный	ungenau	inexact
056	inadequacy, n.	неудовлетворитель- ность, *f.*	Unangemessenheit, *f.*	insuffisance, *f.*
057	inadmissibility, n.	недопустимость, *f.*	Unzulässigkeit, *f.*	inadmissibilité, *f.*
058	inanimate, adj.	неодушевленный	leblos/sächlich/unbelebt	inanimé
059	inapplicable, adj.	неприменимый	unanwendbar/ nicht zutreffend	inapplicable
060	inaudible, adj.	неслышный	unhörbar	inaudible
061	incantation, n.	заклинание, *n.*/ магическая формула	Beschwörungsformel, *f.*/ Zauberspruch, *m.*	incantation, *f.*
062	incentive, n.	побудительный мотив	Anreiz, *m.*	stimulant, *m.*
063	inceptive aspect	начинательный вид	Inchoativum, *n.*	inchoatif, *m.*
064	inclusion, n.	включение, *n.*	Einschluss, *f.*	inclusion, *f.*
065	inclusive first person	включительное первое лицо	inklusive erste Person	première personne inclu- sive, *f.*
066	incoherent speech	нечленораздельная речь	unzusammenhängendes Sprechen	divagations, *f.,* pl.
067	incommensurable, adj.	несоразмерный	unvergleichbar	incommensurable
068	incompatable, adj.	несовместимый	unpassend/unvereinbar	incompatible
069	incomplete, adj.	неполный	unvollendet	incomplet
070	incomplete sentence	неполное предложение	unvollendeter Satz	phrase incompléte, *f.*
071	incompletive past	несовершенное прошедшее	unvollendete Vergangen- heit	imparfait, *m.*
072	inconclusive, adj.	нерешающий	ergebnislos	non décisif
073	incongruity, n.	несоответствие, *n.*	Nichtübereinstimmung, *f.*	manque d'harmonie, *m.*
074	inconsistent, adj.	несообразный	unvereinbar	inconsistant

No.	ENGLISH	RUSSIAN	GERMAN	FRENCH
075	incorrect, adj.	неправильный/ ошибочный	falsch/fehlerhaft/unrichtig	inexact/erroné/faux
076	increase, n.	увеличение, *n.*	Zunahme, *f.*	augmentation, *f.*
077	indecisive, adj.	нерешительный	unentschlossen	peu concluant
078	indeclinable, adj.	несклоняемый	indeklinabel/undeklinierbar/unbeugbar/ unbeugefahig	indéclinable
079	indefinite, adj.	неопределенный	unbestimmt	indéfini
080	indefinite article	неопределенный артикль	unbestimmter Artikel	article indéfini, *m.*
081	indefinite pronoun	неопределенное местоимение	Indefinitpronomen, *n.*/ unbestimmtes Fürwort	pronom indéfini, *m.*
082	indefinite tense	неопределенное время глагола	unbestimmte Zeitform des Verbums	temps indéfini du verbe, *m.*
083	indentation, n.	отступ, *m.*	Zeileneinrückung, *f.*	alinéa, *m.*
084	independence, n.	независимость, *f.*/ самостоятельность, *f.*	Selbständigkeit, *f.*/ Unabhängigkeit, *f.*	indépendance, *f.*
085	independent clause	самостоятельная фраза/ самостоятельное предложение	selbständiger Satz	proposition principale, *f.*
086	independent development	независимое развитие	selbständige Entwicklung	développement indépendant, *m.*
087	independent phoneme	независимая фонема	selbständiges Phonem	phonème indépendant, *m.*
088	independent variable	независимая переменная	unabhängige Variable	variable indépendante, *f.*
089	indeterminate, adj.	неопределенный	unbestimmt	indéterminé
090	index, n.	указатель, *m.*	Index, *m.*/Register, *n.*/ Verzeichnis, *n.*	index, *m.*
091	index card	каталожная карточка	Karteikarte, *f.*/ Indexkarteikarte, *f.*	fiche, *f.*

No.	ENGLISH	RUSSIAN	GERMAN	FRENCH
092	index finger	указательный палец	Zeigefinger, *m.*	index, *m.*
093	indication, n.	знак, *m.*/указание, *n.*	Hinweis, *m.*	indice, *m.*
094	indicative mood	изъявительное наклонение	Indikativ, *m.*/Wirklich-keitsmodus, *m.*	indicatif, *m.*
095	indicator, n.	показатель, *m.*	Kennzeichen, *n.*	indicateur, *m.*
096	indigenous languages, pl.	туземные языки, *m.*, pl./местные языки, *m.*, pl.	einheimische Sprachen, *f.*, pl.	langues indigènes, *f.*, pl./langues autochtones, *f.*, pl.
097	indirect discourse	косвенная речь	indirekte Rede	discours indirect, *m.*
098	indirect motion	неопределенное движение	unbestimmte Bewegung	mouvement indirect, *m.*
099	indirect object	косвенное дополнение	Dativobjekt, *n.*	complément indirect, *m.*
100	indirect question	косвенный вопрос	indirekte Frage	interrogation indirecte, *f.*
101	indirect quotation	косвенная речь	indirekte Rede	discours indirect, *m.*
102	indispensable, adj.	необходимый	unerlässlich	indispensable
103	indistinct, adj.	неотчетливый	undeutlich	indistinct
104	individual, n.	индивидуум, *m.*/человек, *m.*	Individuum, *n.*/Mensch, *m.*	individu, *m.*
105	individual, adj.	индивидуальный/отдельный	individuell	séparé
106	individual speech differences, pl.	индивидуальные оттенки речи, *m.*, pl.	individuelle Sprachei-gentümlichkeiten, *f.*, pl.	différences de langage individuelles, *f.*, pl.
107	individual sound	отдельный звук	einzelner Laut	son isolé, *m.*
108	individual word	отдельное слово	einzelnes Wort	mot séparé, *m.*
109	indivisible, adj.	неделимый	unteilbar	indivisible
110	Indo-European, adj.	индо-европейский	indo-germanisch	indo-européen
111	inductive, adj.	индуктивный	induktiv	inductif
112	inefficient, adj.	неэффективный	leistungsunfähig	inefficace

No.	ENGLISH	RUSSIAN	GERMAN	FRENCH
113	inequality, n.	неравенство, *n.*	Ungleichheit, *f.*	inégalite, *f.*
114	inertia, n.	инерция, *f.*	Trägheit, *f.*	inertie, *f.*
115	inevitable, adj.	неизбежный	unumgänglich/ unvermeidlich	inévitable
116	inexact, adj.	неточный	ungenau	inexact
117	inexplicable, adj.	необъяснимый	unerklärlich	inexplicable
118	inexpressible, adj.	невыразимый	unsagbar	inexprimable
119	infallible, adj.	безошибочный	unfehlbar	infaillible
120	infant speech	детская речь	Kindersprache, *f.*	langage enfantin, *m.*
121	inference, n.	вывод, *m.*	Folgerung, *f.*	déduction, *f.*
122	infiltration, n.	проникновение, *n.*	Eindringen, *n.*	infiltration, *f.*
123	infinite, adj.	бесконечный	unendlich	infini
124	infinite number	безконечное число	unendliche Zahl	nombre infini, *m.*
125	infinitive, n.	инфинитив, *m.*/ неопределенная форма глагола	Infinitiv, *m.*/Nennform, *f.*	infinitif, *m.*
126	infix, n.	инфикс, *m.*	Infix, *n.*	infixe, *m.*
127	inflectable, adj.	изменяемый	beugbar/beugefähig	inflexionnable
128	inflected languages, inflecting——, inflectional——, pl.	флективные языки, *m.,* pl.	flektierende Sprachen, *f.,* pl.	langues flexionnelles, *f.,* pl.
129	inflection, n.	флексия, *f.*/ словоизменение, *n.*	Flexion, *f.*/Beugung, *f.*	flexion, *f.*
130	inflectional affix	флективный аффикс	flexivisches Affix	affixe inflexionnel, *m.*
131	inflectional category	флективная категория/ категория слово- изменение, *f.*	Flexionskategorie, *f.*	catégorie flexionnelle, *f.*
132	inflectional ending	флективное окончание	Flexionsendung, *f.*	désinence, *f.*

No.	ENGLISH	RUSSIAN	GERMAN	FRENCH
133	influence, n.	влияние, *n.*	Einfluss, *m.*	influence, *f.*
134	informal speech	разговорный язык	ungezwungene Sprache	discours non-formel, *m.* discours quotidien, *m.*
135	informant, n.	информант, *m.*/ представитель языка, *m.*	Gewährsmann, *m.*	sujet parlant, *m.*
136	informant response	сведения полученные от информанта, *n.,* pl.	Auskunft des Gewährsmannes, *f.*	réponse du sujet parlant, *f.*
137	information, n.	информация, *f.*/ сведения, *n.,* pl.	Information, *f.*/Bericht, *m.*/Nachricht, *f.*/ Auskunft, *f.*	information, *f.*
138	information processing	вычислитетьная техника/ обработка информации, *f.*	Informationsverarbei-tung, *f.*	traitement numérique de l'information, *m.*
139	information retrieval	извлечение сведений, *n.*/поиски информации, *f.,* pl.	Informationsbeschaffung, *f.*/Wiederauffinden von Informationen, *n.*	dépistage des informa-tions, *m.*/rappel des informations, *m.*/ récupération des infor-mations, *f.*
140	information theory	теория информации, *f.*	Informationstheorie, *f.*	théorie de l'information, *f.*
141	information unit	единица информации, *f* .	Informationseinheit, *f.*	unité d'information, *f.*
142	infrequent, adj.	редкий	selten	peu fréquent
143	ingressive consonants, pl.	вдыхательные согласные, pl.	ingressive Konsonanten, *m.,* pl.	consonnes ingressives, *f.,* pl.
144	inhabitant, n.	житель, *m.*/ обитатель, *m.*	Einwohner, *m.*	habitant, *m.*
145	inherent features, pl.	внутренние признаки, *m.,* pl.	inhärente Merkmale, *n.,* pl.	traits inhérents, *m.,* pl.
146	inhibition, n.	сдерживание, *n.*	Hemmung, *f.*	inhibition, *f.*
147	initial, adj.	исходный / начальный	Anfangs-/anfanglich/ anlautend	initial/du début

No.	ENGLISH	RUSSIAN	GERMAN	FRENCH
148	initial (letter), n.	инициал, *m.*/ начальная буква	Anfangsbuchstabe, *m.*/ Versalbuchstabe, *m.*	initiale, *f.*/ première lettre, *f.*
149	initial sound	начальный звук	Anlaut, *m.*	son initial, *m.*
150	initial mutation	начальная перегласовка	Anlautswechsel, *m.*	mutation initiale, *f.*
151	initial position	начальная позиция	Anfangsstellung, *f.*	position initiale, *f.*
152	initial stress	начальное ударение	Anfangssilbenbetonung, *f.*	accent initial, *m.*
153	initial syllable	начальный слог	Anfangssilbe, *f.*	syllabe initiale, *f.*
154	ink, n.	чернила, *f.*	Tinte, *f.*	encre, *f.*
155	inner core of language	внутреннее языковое ядро	innerer Sprachkern	noyau de la langue, *m.*
156	inner ear	внутреннее ухо	inneres Ohr	oreille interne, *f.*
157	inner form	внутренняя форма	innere Form	forme intérieure, *f.*
158	innovation, n.	нововведение, *n.*/ новшество, *n.*	Neuerung, *f.*	innovation, *f.*/ nouveauté, *f.*
159	input and output	вход и выход	Eingabe und Ausgabe	entrée et sortie
160	inquiry, n.	расспрашивание, *n.*	Nachfrage, *f.*	enquête, *f.*
161	inscription, n.	надпись, *f.*/ посвящение, *n.*/ легенда, *f.*	Inschrift, *f.*/Widmung, *f.*/ Zueignung, *f.*	inscription, *f.*/légende, *f.*/ dédicace, *f.*
162	inseparable, adj.	неотделимый	untrennbar	inséparable
163	insertion, n.	вставка, *f.*	Einschub, *m.*/Einsatz, *m.*	insertion, *f.*
164	insight, n.	интуиция, *f.*/ понимание, *n.*	Einsicht, *f.*	pénétration, *f.*
165	insignificant, adj.	незначительный	unbedeutend	insignifiant
166	inspection, n.	осмотр, *m.*	Besichtigung, *f.*	inspection, *f.*
167	inspiration, n.	вдох, *m.*/вдыхание, *n.*	Einatmung, *f.*	inspiration, *f.*
168	instability, n.	неустойчивость, *f.*	Instabilität, *f.*/ Unbeständigkeit, *f.*	instabilité, *f.*

No.	English	Russian	German	French
169	instance, n.	случай, *m.*/пример, *m.*	Beispiel, *n.*/Fall, *m.*	cas, *m.*/exemple, *m.*
170	instantaneous, adj.	мгновенный	momentan	instantané
171	instinct, n.	инстинкт, *m.*/ природное чутье	Instinkt, *m.*	instinct, *m.*
172	instinctive behavior	инстинктивное поведение	instinktives Verhalten	comportement instinctif, *m.*
173	instruction, n.	обучение, *n.*/ преподавание, *n.*	Lehren, *n.*/Unterricht, *m.*	enseignement, *m.*/ instruction, *f.*
174	instructional film	учебный фильм	Unterrichtsfilm, *m.*	film d'enseignement, *m.*
175	instructions, pl.	наставление, *n.*/ руководство, *n.*	Unterweisung, *f.*	mode d'emploi, *m.*
176	instrumental case	творительный падеж	Instrumentalis, *m.*	instrumental, *m.*
177	instrumental phonetics	приборная фонетика	instrumentale Phonetik	phonétique instrumentale, *f.*
178	insufficient, adj.	недостаточный	unzulänglich	insuffisant
179	insult, n.	оскорбление, *n.*/ обида, *f.*	Beleidigung, *f.*/ Beschimpfung, *f.*	injure, *f.*/insulte, *f.*
180	intellect, n.	интеллект, *m.*/ум, *m.*	Intellekt, *m.*/ Verstand, *m.*	intellect, *m.*/ entendement, *m.*
181	intellective, adj.	смысловой/ умственный	intellektuell	intellectif
182	intelligence, n.	ум, *m.*/рассудок, *m.*	Intelligenz, *f.*/ Verstand, *m.*	intelligence, *f.*
183	intelligence test	испытание умственной способности, *n.*	Intelligenzprüfung, *f.*/ Intelligenztest, *m.*	test d'habilité mentale, *m.*
184	intelligentsia, pl.	интеллигенция, *f.*	gebildete Oberschicht	élite intellectuelle, *f.*
185	intelligibility, n.	понятность, *f.*	Verständlichkeit, *f.*	intelligibilité, *f.*
186	intelligible, adj.	понятный	verständlich	intelligible
187	intensification, n.	усиление, *n.*	Verstärkung, *f.*	renforcement, *m.*
188	intensifying plural	усилительное множественное	Intensitätsplural, *m.*	pluriel d'intensité, *m.*

No.	English	Russian	German	French
189	intensity, n.	интенсивность, *f.*	Intensität, *f.*	intensité, *f.*
190	intensive language course	ускоренные курсы языка, *m.,* pl.	Schnellkurs in einer Sprache, *m.*	cours de langue accéléré, *m.*
191	intention, n.	намерение, *n.*	Intention, *f.*/Absicht, *f.*	intention, *f.*/dessein, *m.*/ but, *m.*
192	intention of the speaker	намерение говорящего, *n.*	Intention des Sprechers, *f.*	intention de l'interlocuteur, *f.*
193	interaction, n.	взаимодействие, *n.*	Wechselwirkung, *f.*	action réciproque, *f.*
194	iterative aspect	многократный вид	Iterativ, *m.*	itératif, *m.*
195	interchangeable, adj.	взаимозаменяемый	austauschbar	interchangeable/ alternable
196	interconnection, n.	взаимосвязь, *f.*	gegenseitige Verbindung	rapport réciproque, *m.*
197	intercostal muscles, pl.	межреберные мускулы, *m.,* pl.	interkostale Muskeln, *f.,* pl.	muscles intercostaux, *m.,* pl.
198	interdental consonants, pl.	интердентальные согласные, pl./ межзубные согласные, pl.	interdentale Konso- nanten, *m.,* pl.	consonnes interdentales, *f.,* pl.
199	interdependence, n.	взаимозависимость, *f.*	gegenseitige Abhängigkeit	interdépendance, *f.*/ dépendance mutuelle, *f.*
200	interference, n.	помеха, *f.*	Störung, *f.*/Störsignal, *n.*	interférence, *f.*/ parasites, *m.,* pl.
201	interference in foreign language learning, n.	помеха в изучении неродного языка, *f.*	Störung im Erlernen einer Fremdsprache, *f.*	interférence dans l'apprentissage d'une langue étrangère, *f.*
202	interjection, n.	междометие, *n.*	Interjektion, *f.*/Ausruf, *m.*/Ausrufungswort, *n.*	interjection, *f.*
203	interlinear, adj.	междустрочный	Interlinear-/ zwischenzeilig	interlinéaire
204	interlocked, interlocking, adj.	сцепленный	verkettet/zusammen- geschlossen	engrené
205	interlineation, n.	приписка, *f.*	Dazwischenschreiben, *n,* /eingefügtes Wort	interlinéation, *f.*

No.	English	Russian	German	French
206	interlingual, adj.	межязычный	zwischensprachlich	interlingual
207	interlocution, n.	беседа, *f.*/диалог, *m.*	Zwiegespräch, *n.*	interlocution, *f.*
208	intermediate, adj.	промежуточный/ средний	dazwischen liegend/ Zwischen-	intermédiaire
209	intermediary language	язык-посредник, *m.*	Übergangssprache, *f.*	interlangue, *f.*
210	internal causality	внутренняя причин- ная связь	innere Kausalität	causalité interne, *f.*
211	internal conditions, pl.	внутренние условия, *n.*, pl.	innere Voraussetzungen, *f.*, pl.	conditions internes, *f.*, pl.
212	internal form	внутренняя форма	innere Form	forme interne, *f.*
213	internal hiatus	внутреннее зияние	innerer Hiatus	hiatus interne, *m.*
214	internal inflection	внутренняя флексия	innere Flexion	flexion interne, *f.*
215	internal law	внутренний закон	inneres Gesetz	loi interne, *m.*
216	internal open juncture	внутренний открытый стык	innere Füge	jonction interne, *f.*
217	internal reconstruction	внутренняя реконструкция	innere Rekonstruktion	restitution interne, *f.*
218	internal sandhi	внутреннее сандхи	Inlauts-Sandhi, *n.*	sandhi interne, *m.*
219	internal structure	внутренняя структура	innere Struktur	structure interne, *f.*
220	international languages, interlanguages, pl.	международные языки, *m.*, pl./ межнациональные языки, *m.*, pl.	internationale Sprachen, *f.*, pl./Weltsprachen, *f.*, pl.	langues internationales, *f.*, pl.
221	international phonetic alphabet	международный фонетический алфавит	internationales phoneti- sches Alphabet	alphabet phonétique international, *m.*
222	international word	интернациональное слово/ международное слово	internationales Wort	mot international, *m.*
223	interpenetration, n.	взаимо- проникновение, *n.*	gegenseitige Durchdrin- gung	interpénétration, *f.*

No.	ENGLISH	RUSSIAN	GERMAN	FRENCH
224	interplay, n.	взаимодействие, *n.*	Wechselwirkung, *f.*	effets combinés, *m.*, pl.
225	interpretation, n.	интерпретация, *f.*/ толкование, *n.*	Interpretation, *f.*/ Deutung, *f.*	interprétation, *f.*
226	interpreter, n.	переводчик, *m.*	Dolmetscher, *m.*	interprète, *m.*
227	interrelated, adj.	взаимосвязанный	untereinander wechsel- bezogen/untereinander zusammenhangend	en corrélation
228	interrelation, n.	взаимоотношение, *n.*/ соотношение, *n.*	gegenseitige Beziehung, *f.*/Wechselbeziehung, *f.*	corrélation, *f.*
229	interrogative, adj.	вопросительный	Frage-/Interrogativ-/ fragend	interrogatif
230	interrogative intonation	вопросительная интонация	Fragesatzintonation, *f.*/ Frageton, *m.*	intonation interrogative, *f.*
231	interrogative particle	вопросительная частица	Fragepartikel, *f.*	particule interrogative, *f.*
232	interrogative pronoun	вопросительное местоимение	Interrogativpronomen, *n.*/Fragefürwort, *n.*	pronom interrogatif, *m.*
233	interrogative sentence	вопросительное предложение	Fragesatz, *m.*/ Interrogativsatz, *m.*	phrase interrogative, *f.*
234	interrogative sign (?)	вопросительный знак	Fragezeichen, *n.*	point d'interrogation, *m.*
235	interrogative word	вопросительное слово	Fragewort, *n.*	mot interrogatif, *m.*
236	interruption, n.	прерывание, *n.*	Unterbrechung, *f.*	interruption, *f.*
237	intersection, n.	пересечение, *n.*	Schnittpunkt, *m.*	intersection, *f.*
238	interval, n.	интервал, *m.*/ промежуток; *m.*	Intervall, *n.*/ Abstand, *m.*	intervalle, *m.*
239	interview, n.	интервью, *n.*	Interview, *n.*	interview, *m.*/entrevue, *f.*
240	intervocalic, adj.	интервокальный/ междугласный	intervokalisch	intervocalique
241	intimate form of address	интимное обращение/ обращение на ты, *n.*	vertraute Anredeform	tutoiement, *m.*

No.	English	Russian	German	French
242	intonation, n.	интонация, *f./*мелодия речи, *f.*	Intonation, *f./* Sprechmelodie, *f./* Tonfall, *m.*	intonation, *f.*
243	intonation contour	интонационная оболочка	Intonationslinie, *f./* Tonhöhenkurve, *f.* Spannbogen, *m.*	ligne d'intonation, *f.*
244	intransitive verb	непереходный глагол	Intransitivum, *n./* nichtzielendes Verb	verbe intransitif, *m.*
245	introducer, n.	вводящее слово	Einleitungselement, *n.*	introducteur, *m.*
246	introduction, n.	введение, *n.*	Einführung, *f./* Einleitung, *f.*	introduction, *f.*
247	intuition, n.	интуиция, *f.*	Intuition, *f.*	intuition, *f.*
248	invariability, n.	неизменяаемость, *f.*	Unveränderlichkeit, *f.*	invariabilité, *f.*
249	invariable, adj.	неизменный/ неизменяемый	unveränderlich/ gleichbleibend	invariable
250	invariant, n.	инвариант, *m.*	Unveränderliche, *f.*	invariante, *f.*
251	invasion, n.	нашествие, *n.*	Einfall, *m./*Invasion, *f.*	invasion, *f.*
252	invective, n.	бранная речь	Schimpfrede, *f./* Schimpfwörter, *n.*, pl.	invective, *f./* vitupération, *f.*
253	inventory, n.	инвентарь, *m.*	Inventar, *n.*	inventaire, *m.*
254	inverse, adj.	обратный	umgekehrt	inverse
255	inversion, n.	инверсия, *f.*	Inversion, *f.*	inversion, *f.*
256	inverted commas, pl. (")	перевернутые запятые, *f.*, pl.	Anführungszeichen, *n.*, sg./Gansefüsschen, *n.*, pl.	guillemets, *m.*, pl.
257	inverted order	обратный порядок	umgekehrte Reihenfolge	ordre inverti, *m.*
258	investigation, n.	исследование, *n.*	Untersuchung, *f./* Erforschung, *f.*	investigation, *f./* examen, *m.*
259	involuted sentence	осложненное предложение	Schachtelsatz, *m.*	phrase entortillée, *f.*

No.	ENGLISH	RUSSIAN	GERMAN	FRENCH
260	Irish, adj.	ирландский	irisch	irlandais
261	irony, n.	ирония, *f.*	Ironie, *f.*	ironie, *f.*
262	irregular, adj.	неправильный	unregelmässig	irrégulier
263	irregular verb	неправильный глагол	unregelmässiges Verb	verbe irrégulier, *m.*
264	irregularity, n.	неправильность, *f.*/ нарушение нормы, *n.*	Unregelmässigkeit, *f.*/ Abweichung von der Norm, *f.*	irrégularité, *f.*
265	irrelevant, adj.	неразличительный	irrelevant	non pertinent
266	irreversible, adj.	необратимый	nicht umkehrbar	irréversible
267	isogloss, n.	изоглосса, *f.*	Isoglosse, *f.*	isoglosse, *f.*
268	isolable, adj.	изолироваемый/ отделяемый	isolierbar	isolable
269	isolated, adj.	изолированный/ отдельный	isoliert	isolé
270	isolated case	единичный случай	Einzelfall, *m.*	cas isolé, *m.*
271	isolated sentence	предложение вырванное из контекста	aus dem Zusammenhang gerissener Satz	phrase isolée, *f.*
272	isolating languages, pl.	изолирующие языки, *m., pl.*	isolierende Sprachen, *f., pl.*	langues isolantes, *f., pl.*
273	isolation of sentence parts	обособление членов предложения, *n.*	Isolierung von Satzteilen, *f.*	séparation des parties de la phrase, *f.*
274	isomorphism, n.	изоморфизм, *m.*	Isomorphie, *f.*	isomorphisme, *m.*
275	issue (publication), n.	выпуск, *m.*	Nummer, *f.*	numéro, *m.*/fascicule, *m.*/ livraison, *f.*
276	issue (subject of discussion), n.	спорный вопрос	Streitfrage, *f.*	question, *f.*
277	Italian, adj.	итальянский	italienisch	italien
278	italic type, italics	курсив, pl.	Kursivdruck, *m.*	italique, *m.*
279	item (in newspaper), n.	газетная заметка	Zeitungsnotiz, *f.*	écho, *m.*/faits divers, *m., pl.*

No.	ENGLISH	RUSSIAN	GERMAN	FRENCH
280	item (unit), n.	единица, *f.*	Einheit, *f.*	unité, *f.*
281	item and arrangement model	модель единиц и аранжировки, *f.*	⟨Modell der Einheit und Anordnung⟩, *n.*	modèle de la nature et répartition des éléments, *m.*
282	item and process model	модель единиц и процессов, *f.*	⟨Modell der Einheit und Entwicklung⟩, *n.*	modèle de la nature et évolution des éléments, *m.*

J

No.	ENGLISH	RUSSIAN	GERMAN	FRENCH
001	Japanese, adj.	японский	japanisch	japonais
002	jargon, n.	жаргон, *m.*	Jargon, *m.*	jargon, *m.*/ cafouillage, *m.*/ charabia, *m.*/ baragouin, *m.*
003	jaw, n.	челюсть, *m.*	Kiefer, *m.*	machoire, *f.*
004	jaw-breaker, n.	труднопроизносимое слово	Zungenbrecher, *m.*	mot difficile à prononcer, *m.*
005	joining, n.	присоединение, *n.*	Gefüge, *n.*/Verbindung, *f.*/Zusammenfügen, *n.*	assemblage, *m.*
006	joke, n.	шутка, *f.*	Scherz, *m.*/Witz, *m.*	plaisanterie, *f.*
007	journal, n.	журнал, *m.*	Zeitschrift, *f.*	journal, *m.*
008	journalese, n.	журнальный язык	journalistische Sprache	langage journalistique, *m.*
009	juncture, n.	стык, *m.*	Fuge, *f.*/Verbindung, *f.*/Übergang, *m.*	joncture, *f.*
010	justifiable, adj.	оправдаемый	berechtigt	motivé
011	justification, n.	оправдание, *n.*	Rechtfertigung, *f.*	justification, *f.*
012	juvenile literature	юношеская литература	jugendliche Literatur/Jugendschriften, *f.,* pl.	oeuvres littéraires pour la jeunesse, *f.,* pl.
013	juxtaposition, n.	сопоставление, *n.*	Nebeneinanderstellung, *f.*	juxtaposition, *f.*

No.	ENGLISH	RUSSIAN	GERMAN	FRENCH

K

No.	ENGLISH	RUSSIAN	GERMAN	FRENCH
001	kernel, n.	ядро, *n.*	Kern, *m.*	noyau, *m.*
002	kernel sentence	ядерное предложение	Kernsatz, *m.*	phrase noyau, *f.*
003	key word	слово-ключ, *n.*	Schlüsselwort, *n.*/ Kennwort, *n.*	mot-clé, *m.*
004	kind, n.	сорт, *m.*	Art, *f.*	espèce, *f.*/sorte, *f.*/ variété, *f.*
005	kindergarten, n.	детский сад	Kindergarten, *m.*	jardin d'enfants, *m.*
006	kinesics, n.	кинезика, *f.*/ изучение жестикуляций и телодвижений	Gestik, *f.*/Motorik, *f.*	étude des gestes linguistiques, *f.*
007	kinship, n.	родство, *n.*	Verwandtschaft, *f.*	parenté, *f.*
008	kinship terminology	терминология родства, *f.*	Verwandtschaftsnamen, *m., pl.*	terminologie de la parenté, *f.*
009	knowledge, n.	знание, *n.*	Kenntnis, *f.*/Wissen, *n.*	connaissance, *f.*/ savoir, *m.*
010	known languages, pl.	известные языки, *m., pl.*	bekannte Sprachen, *f., pl.*	langues connues, *f., pl.*

L

No.	ENGLISH	RUSSIAN	GERMAN	FRENCH
001	label, n.	ярлык, *m.*/ярлычок, *m.*	Bezeichnung, *f.*/Etikett, *n.*/Kennzeichen, *n.*	marque, *f.*/étiquette, *f.*
002	labial consonants, pl.	губные согласные, pl.	labiale Konsonanten, *m., pl.*/Lippenlaute, *m., pl.*	consonnes labiales, *f., pl.*
003	labialization, n.	лабиализация, *f.*	Labialisierung, *f.*	labialisation, *f.*
004	labialized, adj.	лабиализованный	labialisiert	labialisé
005	labiodental, adj.	губно-зубной	labiodental	labiodental
006	labiovelar, adj.	лабиовелярный	labiovelar	labiovélaire
007	lack, n.	недостаток, *m.*	Fehlen, *n.*/Mangel, *m.*	manque, *m.*

No.	ENGLISH	RUSSIAN	GERMAN	FRENCH
008	lambdacism, n.	ламбдацизм, *m.*	Lambdacismus, *n.*	lambdacisme, *m.*
009	language, n.	язык, *m.*	Sprache, *f.*	langue, *f.*/langage, *m.*
010	language acquisition	приобретение языка, *n.*	Sprachaneignung, *f.*/ Spracherlernung, *f.*	apprentissage du langage, *m.*
011	language affinity	родство языков, *n.*	Sprachverwandtschaft, *f.*	parenté des langues, *f.*
012	language alliance	языковой союз	Sprachbund, *m.*	relation linguistique, *f.*
013	language analysis	анализ языка, *m.*	Sprachanalyse, *f.*	analyse de la langue, *f.*
014	language and area studies, pl.	изучение языка и области, *n.*	Sprach- und Raumstudien, *f.*, pl.	étude des langues selon leur situation géographique, *f.*
015	language and civilization	язык и цивилизация	Sprache und Zivilization	langue et civilisation
016	language and climate	язык и климат	Sprache und Klima	langue et climat
017	language and cognition	язык и познание	Sprache und Erkenntnis	langue et cognition
018	language and communication	язык и общение	Sprache und Kommunikation	langue et communication
019	language and culture	язык и культура	Sprache und Kultur	langue et culture
020	language and dialect	язык и диалект	Sprache und Dialekt	langue et dialecte
021	language and geography	язык и география	Sprache und Geographie	langue et géographie
022	language and heredity	язык и наследственность	Sprache und Vererbung	langue et hérédité
023	language and linguistics	язык и лингвистика/ язык и языкознание	Sprache und Linguistik/ Sprache und Sprachwissenschaft	langue et linguistique
024	language and literature	язык и литература	Sprache und Literatur	langue et littérature
025	language and logic	язык и логика	Sprache und Logik	langue et logique
026	language and mathematics	язык и математика	Sprache und Mathematik	langue et mathématique
027	language and metalanguage	язык и мета-язык	Sprache und Metasprache	langue et métalangue
028	language and music	язык и музыка	Sprache und Musik	langue et musique

No.	ENGLISH	RUSSIAN	GERMAN	FRENCH
029	language and nationality	язык и национальность	Sprache und Nationalität	langue et nationalité
030	language and necessity	язык п потребность	Sprache und Bedürfnis	langue et nécessité
031	language and personality	язык и индивидуальность	Sprache und Persönlichkeit	langue et personnalité
032	language and philosophy	язык и философия	Sprache und Philosophie	langue et philosophie
033	language and physiology	язык и физиология	Sprache und Physiologie	langue et physiologie
034	language and politics	язык и политика	Sprache und Politik	langue et politique
035	language and psychology	язык и психология	Sprache und Psychologie	langue et psychologie
036	language and race	язык и раса	Sprache und Rasse	langue et race
037	language and reality	язык и действительность	Sprache und Realität/ Sprache und Wirklichkeit	langue et réalité
038	language and religion	язык и религия	Sprache und Religion	langue et religion
039	langage and science	язык и наука	Sprache und Wissenschaft	langue et science
040	language and society	язык и общество	Sprache und Gesellschaft	langue et société
041	language and speech	язык и речь	Sprache und Rede	langue et parole
042	language and symbolism	язык и символизм	Sprache und Symbolismus	langue et symbolisme
043	language and thought	язык и мышление	Sprache und Denken	langue et pensée
044	language and writing	язык и письмо	Sprache und Schrift	langue et écriture
045	language aptitude	способность к языкам, *f.*	Sprachbegabung, *f./* Sprachgefühl, *n.*	aptitude pour les langues, *f.*
046	language area	лингвистическая область/языковой район	Sprachbereich, *n./* Sprachgebiet, *m.*	aire linguistique, *f.*
047	language as social contract	язык по общему соглашению	Sprache als Gesellschaftsvertrag, *m.*	langage conventionnel, *f.*

No.	ENGLISH	RUSSIAN	GERMAN	FRENCH
048	language as system of signs	язык как система знаков/язык по сигнальной системе	Sprache als Zeichensystem, f.	langue comme un système de signes, f.
049	language barrier	отсутствие общего языка, n./⟨языковая преграда⟩	Fehlen einer gemeinsamen Sprache, n./ ⟨Sprachschranke⟩, f.	absence d'une langue commune, f./barrière linguistique, f.
050	language change	языковое изменение	Sprachveränderung, f./ Sprachwandel, m.	changements linguistiques, m., pl.
051	language classification	классииикация языков, f.	Sprachenklassifizierung, f./Spracheneinteilung, f.	classement des langues, m.
052	language code	языковой код	Sprachkode, m.	code linguistique, m.
053	language comparison	сравнение языков, n.	Sprachvergleich, m.	comparaison des langues, f.
054	language contacts, pl.	контакты между языками, m., pl.	Sprachberührungen, f., pl.	contacts des langues, m., pl.
055	language crossing	скрещивание языков, n.	Sprachkreuzung, f.	croisement des langues, m.
056	language data, pl.	лингвистические данные, pl.	Sprachmaterialien, n., pl. /sprachwissenschaftliche Daten, n., pl.	données linguistiques, f., pl.
057	language data processing	обработка лингвистических данных, f.	Sprachdatenverarbeitung, f.	traitement numérique des données linguistiques, m.
058´	language dating	датировка языков, f.	Sprachdatierung, f.	détermination de l'âge des langues, f.
059	language decay	языковой распад	Sprachverfall, m.	décadence des langues, f. /dégradation des langues, f./pathologie linguistique, f.
060	language depth	глубина языка, f.	Sprachtiefe, f.	profondeur d'une langue, f.
061	language design	узор языка, m.	Sprachbau, m.	dessin de langues, m.
062	language description	описание языков, n.	Sprachbeschreibung, f.	description des langues, f.

No.	ENGLISH	RUSSIAN	GERMAN	FRENCH
063	language development	развитие языка, *n.*/ эволюция языков, *f.*	Sprachentwicklung, *f.*	développement des langues, *m.*/évolution des langues, *f.*
064	language diversity	разнообразие языков, *n.*	Verschiedenheit der Sprachen, *f.*	diversité des langues, *f.*
065	language diffusion	распространение языков, *n.*	Sprachverbreitung, *f.*	diffusion des langues, *f.*
066	language economy	экономия в языке, *f.*	Sprachökonomie, *f.*	économie de la langue, *f.*
067	language evolution	развитие языков, *n.*/ эволюция языков, *f.*	Sprachentwicklung, *f.*	évolution des langues, *f.*/ développement des langues, *m.*
068	language family	языковая семья	Sprachfamilie, *f.*	famille de langues, *f.*
069	language functions, pl.	функции языка, *f.*, pl.	Sprachfunktionen, *f.*, pl.	fonctions de langues, *f.*, pl.
070	language genealogy	генеалогия языков, *f.*	Sprachgenealogie, *f.*	généalogie des langues, *f.*
071	language group	языковая группа	Sprachgruppe, *f.*	groupe de langues, *m.*
072	language hierarchy	языковая иерархия	Sprachenhierarchie, *f.*	hiérarchie des langues, *f.*
073	language history	история языка, *f.*/ языковая история	Sprachgeschichte, *f.*	histoire des langues, *f.*
074	language interference	языковая помеха	Sprachstörung, *f.*	interférence linguistique, *f.*
075	language laboratory	лингвистический кабинет	Sprachlaboratorium, *n.*	laboratoire des langues, *m.*
076	language learning	изучение языка, *n.*	Sprachenlernen, *n.*	apprentissage d'une langue, *m.*
077	language level	уровень языка, *m.*/ языковой уровень	Sprachebene, *f.*	niveau de la langue, *m.*
078	language mixture	смесь языков, *f.*	Sprachenmischung, *f.*	mélange linguistique, *m.*
079	language models, pl.	модели языка, *f.*, pl.	Sprachmodelle, *n.*, pl.	modèles de langue, *m.*, pl.
080	language monument	языковой памятник	Sprachdenkmal, *n.*	monument de langue, *m.*

No.	English	Russian	German	French
081	language names, pl.	названия языков, *n.*, pl.	Sprachennamen, *m.*, pl.	noms des langues, *m.*, pl.
082	language origin	происхождение языка, *n.*	Sprachentstehung, *f.*	origine des langues, *f.*/ origine du langage, *f.*
083	language policy	языковая политика	Sprachpolitik, *f.*	politique linguistique, *f.*
084	language power	степень выразительности языка, *f.*	Sprachaussagekraft, *f.*	puissance expressive d'une langue, *f.*
085	language proficiency	степень совершенства в языке, *f.*	Sprachfertigkeit, *f.*/ Sprachkenntnis, *f.*	maîtrise d'une langue, *f.*
086	language progress	прогресс в языке, *m.*	Sprachfortschritt, *m.*	progrès des langues, *m.*
087	language purity	чистота языка, *f.*	Purismus, *f.*/ Sprachreinheit, *n.*	pureté d'une langue, *f.*
088	language reform	языковая реформа	Sprachreform, *f.*	réforme de la langue, *f.*
089	language relationship	родство языков, *n.*	Sprachverwandtschaft, *f.*	parenté des langues, *f.*
090	language simulation	симуляция языка, *f.*	Sprachsimulieren, *n.*	simulation de langue, *f.*
091	language standardization	нормализация языка, *f.*	Sprachstandardisierung, *f.*	normalisation de la langue, *f.*
092	language structure	структура языка, *f.*/ языковой строй	Sprachstruktur, *f.*	structure de la langue, *f.*
093	language substitution	замена языка, *f.*	Sprachwechsel, *m.*	substitution de langue, *f.*
094	language system	языковая система	Sprachsystem, *f.*	système de la langue, *m.*
095	language teaching	преподавание языков, *n.*	Sprachunterricht, *m.*	enseignement des langues, *m.*
096	language threshold	языковой рубеж	Sprachgrenze, *f.*	seuil du langage, *m.*
097	languages of civilization, pl.	культурные языки, *m.*, pl.	Sprachen der Kulturvölker, *f.*, pl.	langues de civilisation, *f.*, pl.
098	languages of primitive peoples, pl.	языки примитивных народов, *m.*, pl.	Sprachen der primitiven Völker, *f.*, pl.	langues de peuples primitifs, *f.*, pl.
099	languages of the world, pl.	языки мира, *m.*, pl.	Sprachen der Erde, *f.*, pl.	langues du monde, *f.*, pl.

No.	English	Russian	German	French
100	laryngeal sound	ларингальный звук/ гортанный звук	Kehlkopflaut, *m.*	son laryngien, *m.*
101	laryngoscope, n.	ларингоскоп, *m.*	Kehlkopfspiegel, *m.*	laryngoscope, *m.*
102	larynx,, n.	гортань, *f.*	Kehlkopf, *m.*	larynx, *m.*
103	last name	фамилия, *f.*	Familienname, *m.*/ Zuname, *m.*	nom de famille, *m.*
104	last page (book)	последняя страница	letzte Seite	dernière page, *f.*
105	last word (sentence)	конечное слово/ последнее слово	Schlusswort, *n.*	mot terminal, *m.*
106	lasting, adj.	длительный	dauernd	durable
107	lateral consonants, pl.	латеральные согласные, pl./ боковые согласные, pl.	Lateralengelaute, *m.*, pl./ Seitenlaute, *m.*, pl.	consonnes latérales, *f.*, pl.
108	Latin, adj.	латинский	lateinisch	latin
109	Latvian, adj.	латвийский/ латышский	lettisch	lettonien
110	laughing, laughter, n.	смех, *m.*/хохот, *m.*	Gelächter, *n.*/Lachen, *n.*	rire, *m.*
111	law, n.	закон, *m.*	Gesetz, *n.*	loi, *f.*
112	lax, adj.	ненапряженный	entspannt/ungespannt	relâché
113	layer, n.	слой, *m.*	Schicht, *m.*	couche, *f.*
114	layer of structure	слой структуры, *m.*/ ярус структуры, *m.*	Strukturschicht, *f.*	couche structurale, *f.*
115	learned behavior	выученное поведение	erlerntes Verhalten	comportement acquis, *m.*
116	learned borrowing	книжное слово	Buchwort, *n.*	emprunt savant, *m.*/ mot savant, *m.*
117	learning, n.	изучение, *n.*	Lernen, *n.*	étude, *f.*
118	learning process	процесс изучения, *m.*	Lernvorgang, *m.*	processus d'apprentissage, *m*
119	least effort	наименьшее усилие	geringster Kraftaufwand	moindre effort, *m.*

No.	ENGLISH	RUSSIAN	GERMAN	FRENCH
120	lecture, n.	доклад, *f.*/лекция, *m.*	Vortrag, *m.*/ Vorlesung, *f.*	cours, *m.*/conférence, *f.*
121	left-handed person	левша, *f.*	Linkshänder, *m.*	gaucher, *m.*
122	left-to-right writing	письмо с лева на право, *n.*	von-links-nach-rechts Schreibweise, *f.*	écriture de gauche à droite, *f.*
123	legal language	юридический язык	Gerichtssprache, *f.*/ Kanzleisprache, *f.*	langage juridique, *m.*
124	legend, n.	легенда, *f.*/надпись, *f.*	Legende, *f.*/Inschrift, *f.*/ Unterschrift, *f.*	légende, *f.*
125	legible, adj.	удобочитаемый/ разборчивый/ четкий	leserlich/deutlich	lisible
126	length (of sound), n.	длительность, *f.*	Dauer, *f.*	durée, *f.*
127	length (of sentence), n.	длина, *f.*/долгота, *f.*	Länge, *f.*	longueur, *f.*
128	length phoneme	фонема долготы, *f.*	Dauerphonem, *n.*	phonème de durée, *m.*
129	lengthening, n.	протяжение, *n.*	Dehnung, *f.*/ Verlängerung, *f.*	allongement, *m.*
130	lesson, n.	урок, *m.*	Aufgabe, *f.*/ Lerngruppe, *f.*	leçon, *f.*/répétition, *f.*
131	letter (of alphabet), n.	буква, *f.*/литера, *f.*	Buchstabe, *m.*	lettre, *f.*
132	letter (to a person), n.	письмо, *n.*	Brief, *m.*	lettre, *f.*
133	letter conventions, letter formulas, pl.	формулы употребляемые в письмах, *f., pl.*	Briefanreden- und Grussformen, *f., pl.*	formules épistolaires, *f., pl.*
134	level, n.	уровень, *m.*	Ebene, *f.*	niveau, *m.*
135	level of analysis	уровень анализа, *m.*	Ebene der Sprachanalyse, *f.*	niveau d'analyse, *m.*
136	level of comparison	уровень сравнения, *m.*	Vergleichungsgrad, *m.*	niveau de comparaison, *m.*
137	level of tongue	подъем языка, *m.*	Zungenhöhe, *f.*	niveau de la langue, *m.*

No.	English	Russian	German	French
138	level of usage	уровень применения, *m.*/уровень употребления, *m.*	Gebrauchsebene, *f.*	niveau d'usage, *m.*
139	level stress	ровное ударение	gleichstarke Betonung/ schwebende Betonung	accent uni
140	level tone	ровный тон	ebener Ton/gleichblei- bender Ton	ton uni
141	levelling, n.	выравнивание, *n.*	Ausgleich, *m.*	nivellement, *m.*
142	levels of language, pl.	языковые уровни, *m.,* pl.	Sprachebenen, *f.,* pl.	plans de la langue, *f.,* pl.
143	lexeme, n.	лексема, *f.*	Lexeme, *f.*/Lexem, *n.*	lexème, *m.*
144	lexical, adj.	лексический	lexikalisch	lexical/lexicologique
145	lexical abstraction	лексическая абстракция	lexikalische Abstraktion	abstraction lexicologique, *f.*
146	lexical change	лексическое изменение	lexikalische Veränderung	changement lexicologique, *m.*
147	lexical creation	лексическая выдумка	lexikalische Schöpfung	création lexicologique, *f.*
148	lexical economy	лексическая экономия	lexikalische Ökonomie	économie lexicologique, *f.*
149	lexical expansion	лексическое расширение	Bedeutungserweiterung, *f.*	élargissement lexical
150	lexical innovation	лексическое нововведение	lexikalische Neuerung	nouveauté lexicologique, *f.*
151	lexical level	лексический уровень	lexikalische Ebene	niveau lexicologique, *m.*
152	lexical meaning	лексическое значение	lexikalische Bedeutung	sens lexicologique, *m.*
153	lexical narrowing	лексическое сужение	Bedeutungsverengerung, *f.*	rétrécissement lexico- logique, *m.*
154	lexical morpheme	лексическая морфема	lexikalisches Morphem	morphème lexical
155	lexical redundancy	многословие, *n.*/ лексическое излишество	lexikalischer Pleonasmus	redondance lexicologique, *f.*

No.	ENGLISH	RUSSIAN	GERMAN	FRENCH
156	lexical resemblance	лексическое сходство	lexikalische Ähnlichkeit	ressemblance lexicologique, *f.*
157	lexical typology	лексическая типология	lexikalische Typologie	typologie lexicologique, *f.*
158	lexicalization, n.	лексикализация, *f.*	Lexikalisierung, *f.*	lexicalisation, *f.*
159	lexicalized combination	лексикализованное сочетание	feste Wortgruppe/feste Wortverbindung/festes Wortgefüge	locution fixe, *f.*
160	lexicographer, n.	лексикограф, *m.*	Lexikograph, *m.*/ Wörterbuchverfasser, *m.*	lexicographe, *s.*
161	lexicography, n.	лексикография, *f.*	Lexikographie, *f.*	lexicographie, *f.*
162	lexicology, n.	лексикология, *f.*	Lexikologie, *f.*	lexicologie, *f.*
163	lexicon, n.	лексикон, *m.*/ лексика, *f.*	Lexikon, *n.*/ Wortschatz, *m.*	lexique, *m.*
164	lexicostatistics, n.	лексикостатистика, *f.*	Lexikostatistik, *f.*	lexicostatistique, *f.*
165	liaison, n.	льезон, *m.*/связь, *f.*	Bindung, *f.*	liaison, *f.*
166	library, n.	библиотека, *f.*	Bibliothek, *f.*	bibliothèque, *f.*
167	lie, n.	ложь, *f.*	Lüge, *f.*	mensonge, *m.*
168	life, n.	жизнь, *f.*	Leben, *n.*	vie, *f.*
169	lifetime, n.	продолжительность жизни, *f.*/целая жизнь/вся жизнь	Lebensdauer, *f.*	durée de la vie, *f.*
170	ligature, n.	лигатура, *f.*	Ligatur, *f.*	ligature, *f.*
171	like, adj.	подобный/сходный	ähnlich/gleich	pareil/semblable/tel
172	likelihood, n.	вероятность, *f.*	Wahrscheinlichkeit, *f.*	vraisemblance, *f.*/ probabilité, *f.*
173	limerick, n.	шуточное пяти-строчное стихотворение	Limerick, *m.*	poème humoristique et parfois scabreux en cinq vers, *m.*

No.	English	Russian	German	French
174	limit, n.	граница, *f.*	Grenze, *f.*	limite, *f.*/frontière, *f.*
175	limitation, n.	ограничение, *n.*	Begrenzung, *f.*	limitation, *f.*
176	line, n.	линия, *f.*/строка, *f.*	Linie, *f.*/Strich, *m.*/Zeile, *f.*	ligne, *f.*
177	line of demarcation	линия разграничения, *f.*	Trennungslinie, *f.*/Trennungsstrich, *m.*	ligne de démarcation, *f.*
178	line drawing	диаграмма, *f.*	Linienzeichnung, *f.*/Federzeichnung, *f.*	esquisse, *f.*
179	lineage, n.	происхождение, *n.*/родословная, *f.*	Abstammung, *f.*/Herkunft, *f.*	lignage, *m.*/lignée, *f.*
180	linear phoneme	линейная фонема	lineäres Phonem	phonème linéaire, *m.*
181	linear sequence	линейная последовательность	lineäre Folge	séquence linéaire, *f.*
182	linearity, n.	линейность, *f.*	Linearität, *f.*	linéarité, *f.*
183	lingual sound	язычный звук	Zungenlaut, *m.*	son lingual, *m.*
184	lingo, n.	жаргон, *m.*	Jargon, *m.*	jargon, *m.*
185	linguist, n.	лингвист, *m.*/языковед, *m.*	Sprachforscher, *m.*/Sprachwissenschaftler, *m.*	linguiste, *s.*
186	linguistic, adj.	лингвистический/языковедческий	linguistisch/sprachwissenschaftlich	linguistique
187	linguistic adequacy	адекватность лингвистической модели, *f.*	Angemessenheit des Sprachmodells, *f.*	suffisance du modèle linguistique, *f.*
188	linguistic affinity	языковое родство	Sprachverwandtschaft, *f.*	affinité linguistique, *f.*
189	linguistic analysis	лингвистический анализ	linguistische Analyse	analyse linguistique, *f.*
190	linguistic atlas	лингвистический атлас	linguistischer Atlas/Sprachatlas, *m.*	atlas linguistique, *m.*
191	linguistic autonomy	лингвистическая автономия	Sprachautonomie, *f.*	autonomie linguistique, *f.*

No.	ENGLISH	RUSSIAN	GERMAN	FRENCH
192	linguistic causality	лингвистическая причинность/ языковая причинность	Sprachkausalität, *f.*	causalité linguistique, *f.*
193	linguistic change	языковое изменение, *n.*	Sprachwandel, *m.*/ Sprachveränderung, *f.*	changement linguistique, *m.*
194	linguistic classification	лингвистическая классификация	linguistische Klassifikation/linguistische Einteilung	classification linguistique, *f.*
195	linguistic community	лингвистическая община/языковая общность	Sprachgemeinschaft, *f.*	communauté linguistique, *f.*
196	linguistic comparison	лингвистическое сравнение	linguistischer Vergleich/ Sprachvergleich, *m.*	comparaison linguistique, *f.*
197	linguistic consciousness	лингвистическая сознательность	Sprachbewusstsein, *n.*	conscience linguistique, *f.*
198	linguistic context	словесный контекст	linguistischer Zusammenhang	contexte linguistique, *m.*
199	linguistic data, pl.	лингвистические данные, pl.	Sprachmaterialien, *n.,* pl. /sprachwissenschaftliche Daten, *n.,* pl.	données linguistiques, *f.,* pl.
200	linguistic description	лингвистическое описание языка	linguistische Sprachbeschreibung	description linguistique, *f.*
201	linguistic development	языковое развитие	Sprachentwicklung, *f.*	développement linguistique, *m.*
202	linguistic documentation	лингвистическая документация	linguistische Dokumentation	documentation linguistique, *f.*
203	linguistic evolution	языковое развитие/ языковой рост	Sprachentwicklung, *f.*	évolution linguistique, *f.*
204	linguistic fact	лингвистический факт	linguistische Tatsache	fait linguistique, *m.*
205	linguistic form	лингвистическая форма	Sprachform, *f.*	forme linguistique, *f.*
206	linguistic function	лингвистическая функция	sprachliche Funktion	fonction linguistique, *f.*

No.	ENGLISH	RUSSIAN	GERMAN	FRENCH
207	linguistic geography	лингвистическая география	Sprachgeographie, f.	géographie linguistique, f.
208	linguistic habits, pl.	языковые навыки, pl.	Sprachgewohnheiten, f., pl.	habitudes linguistiques, f., pl.
209	linguistic intuition	языковая интуиция	Sprachgefühl, n.	intuition linguistique, f.
210	linguistic level	лингвистический уровень	linguistische Ebene	niveau linguistique, m./ plan linguistique, m.
211	linguistic minority	языковое меньшинство	Sprachminderheit, f./ Sprachminorität, f.	minorité linguistique, f.
212	linguistic opposition	лингвистическая оппозиция/ лингвистическое противопоста-вление	linguistische Opposition	opposition linguistique, f.
213	linguistic ontogeny	языковой онтогенез	sprachliche Ontogenese	ontogenié linguistique, f.
214	linguistic prehistory	языковая доистория	sprachliche Vorgeschichte	préhistoire linguistique, f.
215	linguistic prime	лингвистическая первичная	sprachliches Grundele-ment	élément primaire lin-guistique, m.
216	linguistic reality	лингвистическая реальность	Sprachwirklichkeit, f.	réalité linguistique, f.
217	linguistic relationship	лингвистическое отношение	linguistische Beziehung	rapport linguistique, m.
218	linguistic research	лингвистическое исследование	Sprachforschung, f.	recherches linguistiques, f., pl.
219	linguistic sign	языковой знак	sprachliches Zeichen	signe linguistique, m.
220	linguistic significance	лингвистическая значимость	sprachliche Bedeutung	signification linguistique, f.
221	linguistic stock	языковое происхождение	Sprachfamilie, f.	famille linguistique, f.
222	linguistic structure	лингвиятическая структура/ лингвистический строй	linguistischer Aufbau	structure linguistique, f.

No.	English	Russian	German	French
223	linguistic subgroup	языковая подгруппа	sprachliche Untergruppe	sous-groupement linguistique, *m.*
224	linguistic theory	лингвистическая теория	Sprachtheorie, *f.*	théorie linguistique, *f.*
225	linguistic typology	лингвистическая типология	sprachwissenschaftliche Typologie	typologie linguistique, *f.*
226	linguistic usage	языковое употребление	Sprachgebrauch, *m.*	usage linguistique, *m.*
227	linguistic unit	лингвистическая единица	Spracheinheit, *f.*	unité linguistique, *f.*
228	linguistic universals, pl.	лингвистические всеобщие, pl.	Sprachuniversalien, *f., pl.*	absolus linguistiques, *m., pl.*
229	linguistics, n.	лингвистика, *f./* языкознание, *n./* языковедение, *n.*	Linguistik, *f./*Sprachwissenschaft, *f./* Sprachforschung, *f.*	linguistique, *f.*
230	linguistics and anthropology	лингвистика и антропология	Linguistik und Menschenkunde	linguistique et anthropologie
231	linguistics and archaeology	лингвистика и археология	Linguistik und Altertumswissenschaft	linguistique et archéologie
232	linguistics and computers	лингвистика и вычислительные машины	Linguistik und Rechenmaschinen	linguistique et calculatrices
233	linguistics and ethnology	лингвистика и этнология	Linguistik und Völkerkunde	linguistique et ethnologie
234	linguistics and language teaching	лингвистика и преподавание языков	Linguistik und Sprachunterricht	linguistique et enseignement des langues
235	linguistics and literature	лингвистика и литература	Linguistik und Literatur	linguistique et littérature
236	linguistics and mathematical models	лингвиятика и математические модели	Linguistik und mathematische Modelle	linguistique et modèles mathématiques
237	linguistics and "Miss Fidich"	лингвистика и преподавание грамматики по-старому	Linguistik und altmodischer Grammatikunterricht	linguistique et grammaire traditionnelle normative

No.	ENGLISH	RUSSIAN	GERMAN	FRENCH
238	linguistics and philology	лингвистика и филология	Linguistik und Philologie	linguistique et philologie
239	linguistics and psychiatry	лингвистика и психиатрия	Linguistik und Psychiatrie	linguistique et psychiatrie
240	linguistics and psycho-therapy	лингвистика и психотерапия	Linguistik und Psychotherapie	linguistique et psychothérapie
241	linguistics and sociology	лингвистика и социология	Linguistik und Soziologie	linguistique et sociologie
242	linguistics in general	общая лингвистика	allgemeine Sprachwis-senschaft	linguistique générale, f.
243	linguistics of a specific language(s)	частная лингвистика	Sprachwissenschaft einer bestimmten Sprache, f.	linguistique d'une langue particulière, f.
244	link, n.	звено, n./связь f.	Verbindung, f./Glied, n.	liaison, f.
245	link verb	глагол-связка, m.	Kopula, f.	verbe copulatif, m.
246	link word	соединительное слово/ союзное слово	Bindewort, n.	mot de liaison, m.
247	linked, adj.	связанный	verbunden	lié
248	linking element	соединительный элемент	Verbindungselement, n.	élément de liaison, m.
249	lip, n.	губа, f.	Lippe, f.	lèvre, f.
250	lip movements, pl.	движения губ, n., pl.	Lippenbewegungen, f., pl.	mouvements des lèvres, m., pl.
251	lip position	положение губ, n.	Lippenstellung, f.	position des lèvres, f.
252	lip reading	чтение губных движений, n.	Lippenlesen, n.	lecture sur les lèvres, f.
253	lip rounding	округление губ, n.	Lippenrundung, f.	arrondissement des lèvres, m.
254	liquid consonants, pl.	плавные согласные, pl.	Liquida, f., pl.	consonnes liquides, f., pl.
255	lisping, n.	шепелявость, f.	Gelispel, n./Lispeln, n.	zézayement, m./ blésement, m.

No.	English	Russian	German	French
256	list, n.	список, *m.*	Liste, *f.*/Verzeichnis, *n.*	liste, *f.*
257	listening, n.	слушание, *n.*	Zuhören, *n.*	écoute, *f.*
258	literacy, n.	грамотность, *f.*	Schreib- und Lesefähigkeit, *f.*/ gelehrte Bildung	fait de savoir lire et écrire, *m.*
259	literal, adj.	буквальный	buchstäblich/wörtlich	littéral
260	literal meaning	буквальное значение/ дословное значение	wörtliche Bedeutung/ eigentliche Bedeutung	sens propre, *m.*
261	literal translation	дословный перевод	wörtliche Übersetzung	traduction littérale, *f.*
262	literary, adj.	литературный	literarisch	littéraire
263	literary criticism	литературная критика	Literaturkritik, *f.*	critique littéraire, *f.*
264	literary language	литературный язык	Gemeinsprache, *f.*/ Schriftsprache, *f.*	langue littéraire, *f.*
265	literary work	литературное произведение	literarisches Werk	oeuvre littéraire, *f.*
266	literate, adj.	грамотный/ образованный	gebildet/gelehrt	sachant lire et écrire
267	literature, n.	литература, *f.*	Literatur, *f.*	littérature, *f.*
268	Lithuanian, adj.	литовский	litauisch	lituanien
269	liturgical language	церковный язык	liturgische Sprache	langage liturgique, *m.*
270	live, adj.	живой	lebend	vivant
271	live issue	спорный вопрос	aktuelle Frage	questions du jour, *f.,* pl.
272	living languages, pl.	живые языки, *m.,* pl.	lebende Sprachen, *f.,* pl.	langues vivantes, *f.,* pl.
273	loan, n.	заимствование, *n.*	Entlehnung, *f.*/ Lehngut, *n.*	emprunt, *m.*
274	loan translation	калька, *f.*	Lehnübersetzung, *f.*/ Übersetzungs- entlehnung, *f.*	calque, *m.*
275	loanword, n.	заимствованное слово	Lehnwort, *n.*	mot d'emprunt, *m.*

No.	ENGLISH	RUSSIAN	GERMAN	FRENCH
276	local dialect	местный говор	Lokalsprache, *f.*	parler local, *m.*/patois, *m.*
277	localization, n.	локализация, *f.*	Lokalisierung, *f.*	localisation, *f.*
278	localism, n.	местное выражение	örtliche Sprachei-gentümlichkeit	provincialisme, *m.*/régionalisme, *m.*
279	location, n.	местонахождение, *n.*	Lage, *f.*/Stelle, *f.*	location, *f.*
280	locative case	местный падеж	Lokativ, *m.*	locatif, *m.*
281	locution, n.	выражение, *n.*	Redeweise, *f.*/Redewen-dung, *f.*/Sprechweise, *f.*	locution, *f.*/tournure, *f.*
282	logarithm, n.	логарифма, *f.*	Logarithmus, *m.*	logarithme, *m.*
283	logic, n.	логика, *f.*	Logik, *f.*	logique, *f.*
284	logical intonation	смысловая интонация	intellektuelle Betonung	intonation intellectuelle, *f.*
285	logical' operation	логическая операция	logische Operation/logisches Verfahren	opération logique, *f.*
.286	logical stress	логическое ударение	logischer Akzent	accent intellectuel, *m.*
287	logical syntax	логический синтаксис	logische Syntax	syntaxe logique, *f.*
288	logical system	логическая система	logisches System	système logique, *m.*
289	logogram, n.	логограмма, *f.*/стенографическая буква	Sigle, *f.*	sténogramme, *m.*
290	long consonants, pl.	долгие согласные, pl.	lange Konsonanten, *m.*, pl.	consonnes longues, *f.*, pl.
291	long vowels, pl.	долгие гласные, pl.	lange Vokale, *m.*, pl.	voyelles longues, *f.*, pl.
292	long word	длинное слово	langes Wort	mot long, *m.*
293	longhand, n.	курсив, *m.*	Kurrentschrift, *f.*/gewohnliche Schreibschrift	écriture ordinaire, *f.*
294	long-playing record	долгоиграющая пластинка	Langspielplatte, *f.*	disque de longue durée *m.*
295	loop, n.	петля, *f.*	Schleife, *f.*	boucle, *f.*
296	loss, n.	потеря, *f.*/утрата, *f.*	Verlust, *m.*	perte, *f.*

No.	ENGLISH	RUSSIAN	GERMAN	FRENCH
297	loss of consonants	утрата согласных, *f.*	Verlust von Konso- nanten, *m.*	perte de consonnes, *f.*
298	loss of syllables	утрата слогов, *f.*	Verlust von Silben, *m.*	perte de syllabes, *f.*
299	loss of vowels	утрата гласных, *f.*	Verlust von Vokalen, *m.*	perte de voyelles, *f.*
300	loud voice	громкий голос	laute Stimme	haute voix, *f.*
301	loudness, n.	громкость, *f.*	Lautstärke, *f.*	force d'un son, *f.*
302	loudspeaker, n.	громкоговоритель, *m.*	Lautsprecher, *m.*	haut-parleur, *m.*
303	love letter	любовное письмо	Liebesbrief, *m.*	lettre d'amour, *m./* billet doux, *m.*
304	love poem	стихотворение о любви, *n.*	Liebesgedicht, *n.*	poème d'amour, *m.*
305	love words, pl.	ласкательные слова, *n.,* pl.	Kosewörter, *n.,* pl.	mots d'affection, *m.,* pl.
306	low frequency	низкая частота	Niederfrequenz, *f.*	fréquence basse, *f.*
307	Low German, adj.	нижненемецкий	niederdeutsch/ plattdeutsch	bas allemand
308	low pitched, adj.	низкого тона	tieftönend	de ton bas
309	low tone	низкий тон	Tiefton, *m.*	ton bas, *m.*
310	low tonal register	низкий регистр тона	tiefe Tonlage	registre de ton bas, *m.*
311	low voice	низкий голос	tiefe Stimme	voix basse, *f.*
312	low vowels, pl.	низкие гласные, pl./ нижние гласные, pl.	tiefe Vokale, *m.,* pl./ breite Vokale, *m.,* pl.	voyelles basses, *f.,* pl./ voyelles ouvertes, *f.,* pl.
313	lower bound	нижняя граница/ нижняя грань	untere Grenze, *f.*	limite inferieure, *f.*
314	lower case	строчные литеры, *f.,* pl.	unterer Schriftkasten	bas de casse
315	lower case letter	строчная буква	kleiner Buchstabe, *m./* Minuskel, *f.*	minuscule, *f.*
316	lower jaw	нижняя челюсть	Unterkiefer, *m.*	sous-maxillaire, *m.*
317	lower lip	нижняя губа	Unterlippe, *f.*	lèvre inférieure, *f.*

No.	ENGLISH	RUSSIAN	GERMAN	FRENCH
318	lowering (of articulation), n.	передвижение вниз, n. /понижение, n.	Senkung, f.	abaissement, m.
319	lungs, pl.	легкие, pl.	Lungen, f., pl.	poumons, m., pl.
320	lyric poem	лирическое стихотворение	lyrisches Gedicht	poème lyrique, m.
321	lying, n.	вранье, n.	Lügen, n.	mensonge, m.

M

001	machine language	машинный язык	Maschinensprache, f.	langage de machine, m.
002	machine translation	машинный перевод	maschinelle (Sprach)-übersetzung	traduction automatique, f.
003	macrocosm, n.	макрокозм, m.	Makrokosmos, m./ Weltall, n.	macrocosme, m.
004	macron, n.	знак долготы над гласным, m.	Längezeichen über Vokalen, n.	macron, m.
005	macrosegment, n.	макросегмент, m.	Taktgruppe, f.	macrosegment, m.
006	macrostructure, n.	макроструктура, f.	Grossgefüge, n.	macrostructure, f.
007	magazine literature	периодика, f./ журнальная литература	Zeitschriftenliteratur, f.	littérature des revues populaires, f.
008	magic formula	заклинание, n.	Zauberformel, f./ Zauberspruch, m.	formule magique, f.
009	magnetic tape	магнитная лента	Magnetband, n.	bande magnétique, m./ ruban magnetique, f.
010	magnitude, n.	величина, f.	Ausmass, n./Grösse, f./ Umfang, m.	ampleur, f.
011	maiden name	девичья фамилия	Mädchenname, m.	nom de jeune fille, m.
012	mail, n.	почта, f.	Post, f.	courrier, m./poste, f.
013	main clause	главное предложение	Hauptsatz, m.	proposition principale, f.
014	majority, n.	большинство, n.	Mehrheit, f.	majorité, f.

No.	ENGLISH	RUSSIAN	GERMAN	FRENCH
015	majority group (population)	большинство, *n.*	Mehrheit, *f.*/ Hauptteil, *m.*	groupe majoritaire, *m.*
016	majuscule, n.	прописная буква/ заглавная буква	grosser Buchstabe/ Majuskel, *f.*	majuscule, *f.*
017	malapropism, n.	ошибочное использование слова	Wortentstellung, *f.*/Wort- verdrehung, *f.*	impropriété d'expression, *f.*
018	Manchu, adj.	маньчжурский	mandschurisch	mandchou
019	mandatory, adj.	обязательный	unumgänglich	obligatoire
020	manifestation, n.	проявление, *n.*	Offenbarung, *f.*	manifestation, *f.*
021	manipulation, n.	манипуляция, *f.*	Behandlung, *f.*/ Kunstgriff, *m.*	manipulation, *f.*
022	mankind, n.	человечество, *n.*	Menschengeschlecht, *n.*	genre humain, *m.*/ humanité, *f.*
023	manner, n.	манера, *f.*	Art und Weise, *f.*	manière, *f.*
024	manner of articulation	манера артикуляции, *f.*/выговор, *m.*	Artikulationsweise, *f.*/ Bildungsweise, *f.*	mode d'articulation, *f.*
025	manual, n.	пособие, *n.*	Handbuch, *n.*/ Leitfaden, *m.*	manuel, *m.*
026	manual alphabet	азбука глухонемых, *f.*	Fingersprache, *f.*	alphabet manuel, *m.*
027	manuscript, n.	рукопись, *f.*	Manuskript, *n.*/ Handschrift, *f.*	manuscrit, *m.*
028	many-to-one correspondence	соотношение многого к одному, *n.*	mehrgliedrige Entsprechung	correspondance inégale, *f.*
029	map, n.	карта, *f.*	Karte, *f.*	carte, *f.*
030	margin, n.	поля, *f.*/периферия, *f.*	Rand, *m.*	marge, *f.*
031	marginal, adj.	маргинальный/ побоуный/ переходный	Rand-	marginal
032	marginal area (dialectology)	переходная полоса	Grenzgebiet, *n.*	aire périphérique, *f.*

No.	ENGLISH	RUSSIAN	GERMAN	FRENCH
033	marginal language	переходный язык	Grenzsprache, *f.*	langue marginale, *f.*
034	marginal phenomenon	побоуное явление	Randerscheinung, *f.*	phénomène marginal, *m.*
035	marginal phoneme	маргинальная фонема /неустановленная фонема	Grenzphonem, *n.*	phonème marginal, *m.*
036	mark, n.	знак, *m.*/признак, *m.*/ пометка, *f.*/ значок, *m.*	Zeichen, *n.*/Merkmal, *n.*	marque, *f.*
037	marked, adj.	маркированный/ отмеченный	merkmaltragend	marqué
038	marker, n.	знак, *m.*/показатель, *m.* /указатель, *m.*	Merkmal, *n.*/ Kennzeichen, *n.*	marque, *f.*
039	masculine gender	мужской род	Maskulin(um), *n.*/ männliches Geschlecht	masculin, *m.*
040	mass communication media, pl.	средства массового сообщения, *n.*, pl.	Massenkommunikations- media, *n.*, pl.	techniques de diffusion, *f.*, pl.
041	mass noun	имя существительное вещественное	Stoffname, *m.*/ mengenbegriffliches Substantiv	substantif de masse, *m.*
042	master's degree, M.A.	магистерская степень/ кандидатская степень	Magister Artium	diplôme d'études súperieures/licencié ès lettres/maître des arts
043	mastery (of language), n.	владение, *n.*	Beherrschung, *f.*	maîtrise, *f.*
044	mathematical formula- tion	математическая формулировка	mathematische Formulierung	formulation mathématique, *f.*
045	mathematical linguistics	математическая лингвистика	mathematische Sprachforschung	linguistique mathematique, *f.*
046	mathematical logic	математическая логика	mathematische Logik	logique mathématique, *f.*
047	mathematical model	математическая модель	mathematisches Modell	modèle mathématique, *m.*
048	mathematical process	математический процесс	mathematischer Vorgang	processus mathématique *m.*

No.	ENGLISH	RUSSIAN	GERMAN	FRENCH
049	mathematical representation	математическое представление	mathematische Darstellung	représentation mathématique, *f.*
050	mathematical symbol	математический символ	mathematisches Symbol	symbole mathématique, *m.*
051	mathematical terminology	математическая терминология	mathematische Terminologie	terminologie mathématique, *f.*
052	mathematics, n.	математика, *f.*	Mathematik, *f.*	mathématique, *f.*
053	matrix, n.	матрица, *f.*	Matrix, *f.*	matrice, *f.*
054	maturation, n.	созревание, *n.*	Reifen, *n.*	maturation, *f.*
055	maturity, n.	зрелость, *f.*	Reife, *f.*	maturité, *f.*
056	maxim, n.	сентенция, *f.*	Maxime, *f.*/Grundsatz, *m.*/Denkspruch, *m.*	maxime, *f.*
057	maximal differentiation	максимальная дифференциация	maximale Differenzierung	différenciation maximum *f.*
058	meaning, n.	значение, *n.*/смысл, *m.*	Bedeutung, *f.*/Sinn, *m.*	sens, *m.*/signification, *f.*
059	meaning and form	значение и форма	Bedeutung und Form	sens et forme
060	meaning and image	значение и изображение	Bedeutung und Bild	sens et image
061	meaning change	изменение значения, *n.*	Bedeutungswandel, *m.*	changement sémantique, *m.*
062	meaning difference	различие в значении, *n.*	Bedeutungsunterschied, *m.*	différence de sens, *f.*
063	meaning-differentiating function	смысло-разделительная функция	bedeutungsunterscheidende Funktion	fonction de différencier le sens, *f.*
064	meaning extension	расширение значения, *n.*	Bedeutungserweiterung, *f.*	extension de sens, *f.*
065	meaning in context	значение в контексте, *n .*	Bedeutung im Zusammenhang	signification dans un contexte, *f.*
066	meaning in isolation	самостоятельное значение	Bedeutung ohne Zusammenhang	signification sans contexte, *f.*

No.	ENGLISH	RUSSIAN	GERMAN	FRENCH
067	meaning of a sentence	значение предложения, *n.*	Satzbedeutung, *f.*	sens d'une phrase, *m.*
068	meaning of a word	значение слова. *n.*	Wortbedeutung, *f.*	sens d'un mot, *m.*
069	meaning restriction	сужение значения, *n.*	Bedeutungsverengerung, *f.*	restriction de sens, *f.*
070	meaning transfer	перенос значения, *m.*	Bedeutungsübertragung, *f.*	transfert de sens, *m.*
071	meaningful unit	значимая единица	bedeutungstragende Einheit	unité significative, *f.*
072	meaningfulness, n.	осмысленность, *f.*	Bedeutsamkeit, *f.*	nature significative, *f.*
073	meaningless, adj.	бессмысленный	bedeutungslos	sans signification
074	means, pl.	способ, *m.*/средство, *n.*	Mittel, *n.*	moyen, *m.*
075	means of communication, pl.	средство общения, *n.*, sg./средство сообщения, *n.*, sg.	Art der Kommunikation, *f.*, sg./Kommunikationsart, *f.*	moyens de communication, *m.*, pl.
076	measurable, adj.	измеримый	messbar	mensurable/mesurable
077	measurement, n.	измерение, *n.*	Messung, *f.*	mesurage, *m.*
078	mechanical, adj.	механический	mechanisch	mécanique
079	mechanical analysis	механический анализ	mechanische Analyse	analyse mécanique, *f.*
080	mechanical procedure	механический процесс	mechanisches Verfahren	procédé mécanique, *m.*
081	mechanical translation	машинный перевод	maschinelle (Sprach)-übersetzung	traduction automatique, *f.*
082	mechanism, n.	механизм, *m.*/аппарат, *m.*/устройство, *n.*	Mechanismus, *m.*/Gerät, *n.*	mécanisme, *m.*
083	mechanistic conception	механистическое понятие	mechanistische Auffassung	conception mécanistique, *f.*
084	medial, adj.	средний/внутренний	mittlerer/inlautend	médial/médian
085	medial position (of tongue)	средний подъем	mittlere Zungenstellung	position médiale, *f.*

No.	ENGLISH	RUSSIAN	GERMAN	FRENCH
086	medial position (in word)	внутреннее положение	Zwischenstellung, *f.*	position intérieure, *f.*
087	medieval, adj.	средневековый	mittelalterlich	médieval
088	medio-palatal, adj.	средненебный/ среднеязычный	medio-palatal	médio-palatal
089	medio-passive mood	среднестрадательный залог	Mediopassivum, *n.*	médiopassif, *m.*
090	mellow, adj.	нерезкий	sanftklingend	mat
091	melodic, adj.	мелодический	melodisch	mélodique
092	melodic tones, pl.	мелодичные тоны, *m.,* pl.	Richtungstöne, *m.,* pl.	tons mélodiques, *m.,* pl.
093	melody, n.	мелодия, *f.*	Melodie, *f.*	mélodie, *f.*
094	member, n.	член, *m.*	Mitglied, *n.*	membre, *m.*
095	membership, n.	принадлежность, *f.*	Zugehörigkeit, *f.*	qualité de membre, *f.*
096	memoirs, pl.	мемуары, pl./ воспоминания, *n.,* pl.	Memoiren, *f.,* pl./ Lebenserrinerungen, *f.,* pl.	mémoires, *m.,* pl.
097	memorandum, n.	меморандум, *m./* записка, *f.*	Notiz, *f./*Vermerk, *m.*	mémorandum, *m.*
098	memorize, v.	запоминать наизусть	auswendig lernen	apprendre par coeur
099	memory, n.	память, *f.*	Gedächtnis, *m./* Speicher, *m.*	mémoire, *f.*
100	mental, adj.	умственный	geistig	mental
101	mental image	мысленный образ	geistiges Abbild	représentation mentale, *f.*
102	mental reservation	мысленная оговорка	geistiger Vorbehalt	restriction mentale, *f.*
103	mental telepathy	телепатия, *f.*	Telepathie, *f.*	télépathie, *f.*
104	mentalism, n.	ментализм, *m.*	Mentalismus, *m.*	mentalisme, *m.*
105	mentalistic concept	менталистическое понятие	mentalistische Auffassung	concept mentalistique, *m.*

No.	ENGLISH	RUSSIAN	GERMAN	FRENCH
106	mentality, n.	склад ума, *m.*	Mentalität, *f.*	mentalité, *f.*
107	mention, n.	упоминание, *n.*	Erwähnung, *f.*	mention, *f.*
108	merging, n.	слияние, *n./* смешение, *n.*	Verschmelzung, *f./* Zusammenfall, *m.*	fusion, *f./*confusion, *f.*
109	message, n.	сообщение, *n.*	Nachricht, *f.*	message, *m.*
110	message and code	сообщение и код	Nachricht und Code	message et code
111	meta-language, n.	мета-язык, *m.*	Metasprache, *f.*	métalangue, *f.*
112	metalinguistics, n.	металингвистика, *f.*	Metalinguistik, *f.*	métalinguistique, *f.*
113	metamorphosis, n.	метаморфоза, *f.*	Metamorphose, *f./* Umgestaltung, *f.*	métamorphose, *f.*
114	metaphor, n.	метафора, *f.*	Metapher, *f.*	métaphore, *f.*
115	metaphrase, n.	дословный перевод	wörtliche Übersetzung	traduction littérale, *f.*
116	metaphysics, n.	метафизика, *f.*	Metaphysik, *f.*	métaphysique, *f.*
117	metathesis, n.	метатеза, *f./* перестановка звуков, *f.*	**Metathesis**, *f./* **Lautversetzung**, *f.*	méthathèse, *f.*
118	method, n.	метод, *m./*прием, *m./* способ, *m.*	**Methode**, *f./* **Arbeitsweise**, *f.*	mèthode *f.*
119	method of procedure	образ действия, *m.*	Vorgehensweise, *f.*	méthodologie, *f.*
120	methodical, adj.	систематический	methodisch	méthodique
121	methodology, n.	методология, *f.*	Methodenlehre, *f./*Unterrichtsmethodik, *f.*	méthodologie, *f.*
122	metonymy, n.	метонимия, *f.*	**Metonymie**, *f./***Begriffs**vertauschung, *f.*	métonymie, *f.*
123	metrics, n.	метрика, *f.*	Metrik, *f./*Verslehre, *f.*	métrique, *f.*
124	medial sound	серединный звук/ внутренний звук	Inlaut, *m.*	son médial, *m.*
125	microcosm, n.	микрокозм, *m.*	Mikrokosmus, *m.*	microcosme, *m.*
126	microfilm, n.	микрофильм, *m.*	Mikrofilm, *m.*	microfilm, *m.*

No.	ENGLISH	RUSSIAN	GERMAN	FRENCH
127	microphone, n.	микрофон, *m.*	Mikrophon, *n.*	microphone, *m.*
128	microstructure, n.	микроструктура, *f.*	Kleingefüge, *n.*	microstructure, *f.*
129	mid-	средне-	**Mittel-**	mi-
130	midvowels, pl.	гласные среднего подъема, pl.	Mittelvokale, *m.,* pl.	voyelles mixtes, *f.,* pl.
131	middle, n.	середина, *f.*	Mitte, *f.*	milieu, *m.*
132	middle, adj.	средний	mittler	moyen/médial/ intermédiaire
133	middle voice	средний залог	Medium, *n.*	voix moyenne, *f.*
134	migration, n.	миграция, *f./* переселение, *n.*	Wanderung, *f.*	émigration, *f.*
135	military language	военный язык	Militärsprache, *f./* Soldatensprache, *f.*	langage militaire, *m.*
136	mimicry, n.	мимика, *f./* подражание, *n.*	Nachahmung, *f.*	imitation, *f.*
137	mimeograph machine	гектограф, *m./* мимеограф, *m.*	Vervielfältigungsapparat, *m.*	autocopiste, *m.*
138	mind, n.	ум, *m.*	Geist, *m./*Verstand, *m./* Sinn, *m.*	esprit, *m.*
139	mindless machine	⟨машина без разума⟩, *f.*	⟨geistlose Maschine⟩	⟨machine sans esprit⟩, *f.*
140	miniature, n.	миниатура, *f.*	Miniatur, *f.*	miniature, *f.*
141	minimal, adj.	минимальный/ наименьший	minimal/mindest/ kleinst	minimal
142	minimal contrast	минимальный контраст/ наименьший контраст	minimaler Kontrast	contraste minimal, *m.*
143	minimal free form	минимальная свободная форма	minimale freie Form	forme libre minimale, *f.*
144	minimal meaningful unit	кратчайшая значимая единица	kleinste bedeutungstra- gende Einheit	unité de sens minimale, *f.*

No.	English	Russian	German	French
145	minimal pair	минимальная пара	minimales Paar	paire à différence minimale, *m.*
146	minimal segment	минимальный сегмент	kleinstes Segment	segment minimum, *m.*
147	minimal utterance	минимальное высказывание	minimale Äusserung	énoncé minimale
148	minimum, n.	минимум, *m.*	Minimum, *n.*	minimum, *m.*
149	minority, n.	меньшинство, *n.*	Minderzahl, *f.*/ Minorität, *f.*	minorité, *f.*
150	minority group	национальное меньшинство	Minderheit, *f.*/ Minorität, *f.*	groupe minoritaire, *m.*
151	minus feature	признак минуса, *m.*	negatives Merkmal	trait négatif, *m.*
152	minus sign (-)	знак минуса, *m.*	Minuszeichen, *n.*	signe moins, *m.*
153	minuscule, n.	строчная буква	Minuskel, *f.*/ kleiner Buchstabe	minuscule, *f.*
154	minute, adj.	мелкий/подробный	minuziös	minutieux/minuscule/ menu
155	minutiae, pl.	детали, pl./мелочи, pl.	Einzelheiten, *f.*, pl.	infimes détails, *m.*, pl.
156	misapplication, n.	неправильное применение	falsche Anwendung	mauvaise application, *f.*/ emploi erroné, *m.*
157	misconception, n.	неправильное представление	falsche Auffassung	conception erronée, *f.*
158	misinformation, n.	ошибочные сведения, *n.*, pl.	falsche Anskunft	renseignement faux, *m.*
159	misinterpretation, n.	неправильное толкование	falsche Auslegung	fausse interprétation, *f.*
160	misleading, adj.	вводящий в заблуждение	irreführend	fallacieux
161	misnomer, n.	неподходящее название	falsche Benennung/ falsche Bezeichnung	faux nom, *m.*
162	misplaced, adj.	неправильно поставленный	falsch gestellt	mal placé/rangé

No.	ENGLISH	RUSSIAN	GERMAN	FRENCH
163	misprint, n.	опечатка, *f.*	Druckfehler, *m.*	faute d'impression, *f.*
164	mispronunciation, n.	ошибочное произношение/ неправильное произношение	falsche Aussprache	mauvaise prononciation, *f.*
165	misquotation, n.	неверное цитирование	falsches Zitat	fausse citation, *f.*
166	misrepresentation, n.	искажение, *n.*/ ложное представление	falsche Darstellung	présentation fausse, *f.*
167	missing, adj.	отсутствующий	fehlend	manquant
168	missing link	недостающее звено	fehlendes Glied	chaînon manquant, *m.*
169	missionary, n.	миссионер, *m.*	Missionar, *m.*	missionaire, *m.*
170	misspelling, n.	описка, *f.*/ орфографическая ошибка	Rechtschreibefehler, *m.*/ falsche Buchstabierung/fehlerhafte Buchstabierung	faute d'orthographe, *f.*
171	misstatement, n.	ложное заявление/ оговорка, *f.*	falsche Angabe	déclaration fausse, *f.*
172	mistake, n.	ошибка, *f.*	Fehler, *m.*	faute, *f.*
173	mistranslation, n.	неправильный перевод	falsche Übersetzung	traduction erronée, *f.*
174	misunderstanding, n.	недоразумение, *n.*	Missverständnis, *n.*	désaccord, *m.*/ malentendu, *m.*
175	misuse, n.	неправильное употребление/ злоупотребление, *n.*	Missbrauch, *m.*	emploi abusif, *m.*
176	mixed, adj.	смешанный	gemischt	mixte
177	mixed conjugation	смешанное спряжение	gemischte Konjugation	conjugaison mixte, *f.*
178	mixed declension	смешанное склонение	gemischte Deklination	déclinaison mixte, *f.*
179	mixed language	смешанный язык	Mischsprache, *f.*	langue mixte, *f.*
180	mixed type	смешанный тип	gemischter Typ	type mixte, *m.*

No.	ENGLISH	RUSSIAN	GERMAN	FRENCH
181	mixture, n.	смесь, *f.*/смешивание, *n.*	Mischung, *f.*	mélange, *m.*/confusion, *f.*
182	mnemonic verse	мнемический стих	Denkreim, *m.*	vers mnémonique, *m.*
183	mnemonics, n.	мнемоника, *f.*/ мнемонические правила, *n.*, pl.	Mnemotechnik, *f.*/ Gedächtniskunst, *f.*	mnémonique, *f.*/ mnémotechnique, *f.*
184	moaning, n.	стон, *m.*	Stöhnen, *n.*	gémissement, *m.*
185	mobility, n.	подвижность, *f.*	Beweglichkeit, *f.*	mobilité, *f.*
186	modal, adj.	модальный	modal	modal
187	modal auxiliary	модальный вспомо-гательный	modales Hilfswort	auxiliaire de modalité, *m.*
188	modal verb	модальный глагол	modales Zeitwort	verbe modal, *m.*
189	modality, n.	модальность, *f.*	Modalität, *f.*	modalité, *f.*
190	mode, n.	наклонение, *n.*	Modus, *n.*	mode, *m.*
191	model, n.	модель, *f.*	Modell, *n.*	modèle, *m.*
192	modelling, n.	моделирование, *n.*	Modellieren, *n.*	modelage, *m.*
193	modern languages, pl.	современные языки, *m.*, pl./ новые языки, *m.*, pl.	neuere Sprachen, *f.*, pl.	langues vivantes, *f.*, pl.
194	modernism, n.	неологизм, *m.*	Neuerung, *f.*	néologisme, *m.*
195	modification, n.	модификация, *f.*/ видоизменение, *n.*	Modifikation, *f.*/ Veränderung, *f.*	modification, *f.*
196	modifier, n.	определяющее, *n.*	Attribut, *n.*	modificatif, *m.*
197	modulation, n.	модуляция, *f.*	Tonabstufung, *f.*	modulation, *f.*
198	momentary, adj.	мгновенный	momentan	momentané
199	momentary aspect	мгновенный вид	momentane Aktionsart	aspect momentané, *m.*
200	momentary sound	мгновенный звук	Momentanlaut, *m.*	son momentané, *m.*
201	momentum, n.	движущая сила	Kraftwirkung, *f.*	force d'impulsion, *f.*
202	monogram, n.	монограмма, *f.*	Monogramm, *n.*	monogramme, *m.*

No.	ENGLISH	RUSSIAN	GERMAN	FRENCH
203	monograph, n.	монография, *f.*	Monographie, *f.*	monographie, *f.*
204	monolingual, adj.	одноязычный	einsprachig	unilingue
205	monologue, n.	монолог, *m.*	Monolog, *m.*	monologue, *m.*
206	monophthong, n.	монофтонг, *m./* простой гласный звук	Monophthong, *m./* einfacher Vokal	monophthongue, *f.*
207	monosyllabic, adj.	односложный	einsilbig	monosyllabique
208	monosemy, n.	моносемия, *f./* однозначность, *f.*	Eindeutigkeit, *f.*	monosémie, *f.*
209	monotone speech	монотонная речь	eintönige Rede/ eintöniges Sprechen	parler monotone, *m.*
210	monotonic languages, pl.	однотонные языки, *m.,* pl.	eintönige Sprachen, *f.,* pl.	langues monotoniques, *f.,* pl.
211	monument, n.	памятник, *m.*	Denkmal, *n.*	monument, *m.*
212	mood, n.	наклонение, *n.*	Modus, *n.*	mode, *m.*
213	mora, n.	мора, *f.*	More, *f.*	more, *f.*
214	morph, n.	морф, *m./* морфа, *f.*	Morph, *n.*	morphe, *m.*
215	morpheme, n.	морфема, *f.*	Morphem, *n.*	morphème, *m.*
216	morpheme alternant	морфемный вариант	Morphemvariante, *f.*	variante de morphème, *f.*
217	morpheme boundary	граница морфемы, *f.*	Morphemgrenze, *f.*	frontière de morphème, *f.*
218	morpheme class	морфемный класс	Morphemklasse, *f.*	classe de morphèmes, *f.*
219	morpheme combination	сочетание морфем, *n.*	Morphemkombination, *f.*	combinaison de morphèmes, *f.*
220	morpheme concept	понятие морфемы, *n.*	Morphembegriff, *m.*	concept de morphème, *m.*
221	morpheme definition	определение морфемы, *n.*	Morphemdefinition, *f./* Morphembegriffsbe-stimmung, *f.*	définition du morphème, *f.*
222	morpheme distribution	распределение морфем, *n.*	Morphemverteilung, *f.*	distribution de morphèmes, *f.*

No.	ENGLISH	RUSSIAN	GERMAN	FRENCH
223	morpheme frequency	частота морфем, *f.*	Morphemfrequenz, *f.*/ Morphemhäufigkeit, *f.*	fréquence des morphèmes, *f.*
224	morpheme sequence	последовательность морфем, *f.*	Morphemfolge, *f.*	succession de morphèmes, *f.*
225	morphemic, adj.	морфемный	morphemisch	morphémique
226	morphemic analysis	морфемный анализ	morphemische Analyse	analyse morphémique, *f.*
227	morphemic cut	морфемный разрез	Morphemschnitt, *m.*	coupe morphémique, *f.*
228	morphemic shape	морфемная форма	Morphemform, *f.*	forme morphémique, *f.*
229	morphemic writing	морфемное письмо	morphemisches Schreiben	écriture morphémique, *f.*
230	morphemics, n.	морфемика, *f.*	Morphemik, *f.*/ Morphemlehre, *f.*/ Formenlehre, *f.*	étude des morphèmes, *f.*/ morphémique, *f.*
231	morphological, adj.	морфологический	morphologisch	morphologique
232	morphological alternation	морфологическое чередование	morphologische Wechselreihe	alternance morphologique, *f.*
233	morphological analogy	морфологическая аналогия	morphologische Analogie	analogie morphologique, *f.*
234	morphological analysis	морфологический анализ	morphologische Analyse	analyse morphologique, *f.*
235	morphological change	морфологическое изменение	morphologische Veränderung	changement morphologique, *m.*
236	morphological classification	морфологическая классификация	morphologische Klassifizierung/ morphologische Einteilung	classification morphologique, *f.*
237	morphological composition of words	морфологический состав слов	morphologische Wortbildung	composition morphologique des mots, *f.*
238	morphological conditioning	морфологическое обусловление	morphologische Bedingung	conditionnement morphologique, *m.*
239	morphological correlation	морфологическое соотношение	morphologische Korrelation	corrélation morphologique, *f.*

No.	ENGLISH	RUSSIAN	GERMAN	FRENCH
240	morphological homo-nymy	морфологическая омонимия	morphologische Homonymie	homonymie morphologique, *f.*
241	morphological level	морфологический уровень	morphologische Ebene	niveau morphologique, *m.*
242	morphological matrix	морфологическая матрица	morphologische Matrix	matrice morphologique, *f.*
243	morphological process	морфологический процесс	morphologischer Vorgang	processus morphologique, *m.*
244	morphological system	морфологическая система	Morphemsystem, *n.*	système morphologique, *m.*
245	morphological typology	морфологическая типология	morphologische Typologie	typologie morphologique, *f.*
246	morphology, n.	морфология, *f.*	Morphologie, *f./* Formenlehre, *f./* Wortbildungslehre, *f.*	morphologie, *f.*
247	morphophoneme, n.	морфофонема, *f.*	Morphonem, *n.*	morphonème, *m.*
248	morphophonemic alter-nation	морфофонемное чередование	morphonemischer Wechsel	alternance morphono-logique, *f.*
249	morphophonemic level	морфофонемный уровень	morphonemische Ebene	niveau morphonolo-gique, *m.*
250	morphophonemic repre-sentation	морфофонемное представление	morphonemische Darstellung	représentation mor-phonologique, *f.*
251	morphophonemic rules, pl.	морфофонемные правила, *n., pl.*	morphonemische Regeln, *f., pl.*	règles morphonolo-giques, *f., pl.*
252	morphophonemics, mor-phophonology, n.	морфофонология, *f.*	Morphophonologie, *f.*	morphophonologie, *f.*
253	morphotactics, n.	морфотактика, *f./* комбинаторная морфемика	kombinatorische Morphemik	morphémique combinatoire, *f.*
254	mother tongue	родной язык	Muttersprache, *f.*	langue maternelle, *f.*
255	motion, n.	движение, *n.*	Bewegung, *f.*	mouvement, *m.*
256	motion picture	кинофильм, *m.*	Film, *m.*	cinéma, pl./film, *m.*

No.	ENGLISH	RUSSIAN	GERMAN	FRENCH
257	motivation, n.	побуждение, *n.*	Motivierung, *f.*	motivation, *f.*
258	motto, n.	девиз, *m.*	Motto, *n.*/ Wahlspruch, *m.*/ Devise, *f.*	épigraphe, *f.*/ devise, *f.*
259	mould, n.	форма, *f.*/шаблон, *m.*	Form, *f.*	moule, *m.*
260	mouth, n.	рот, *m.*	Mund, *m.*	bouche, *f.*
261	movable stress	разноместное ударение	bewegliche Betonung	accent mobile, *m.*
262	movement, n.	движение, *n.*	Bewegung, *f.*	mouvement, *m.*
263	movie, n.	фильм, *m.*/кино, *n.*	Film, *m.*	cinéma, pl./film, *m.*
264	multi-dimensional, adj.	многомерный	vielfach	à dimensions multiples
265	multilateral, adj.	многосторонний	vielseitig	multilatéral
266	multilingual dictionary	разноязычный словарь	mehrsprachiges Wörterbuch	dictionnaire polyglotte, *m.*
267	multiple, adj.	многократный/ многочисленный	mehrfach/vielfach	multiple
268	multiple complementa-tion	частично дополнительная дистрибуция	teilkomplementäre Verteilung	complémentarité partielle, *f.*
269	multiple meaning	множественное значение	mehrfache Bedeutung	sens multiple, *m.*
270	multiplicative numeral	множественное число	Multiplikativum, *n.*	nombre multiplicatif, *m.*
271	multiplicity, n.	многочисленность, *f.*/ разнообразие, *n.*	Vielfältigkeit, *f.*	multiplicité, *f.*
272	multisyllabic, adj.	многосложный	mehrsilbig	disyllabique
273	murmuring voice	приглушенный голос	Murmelstimme, *f.*	voix chuchée, *f.*
274	muscle, n.	мускул, *m.*/мышца, *f.*	Muskel, *f.*	muscle, *m.*
275	music, n.	музыка, *f.*	Musik, *f.*	musique, *f.*

No.	ENGLISH	RUSSIAN	GERMAN	FRENCH
276	musical, adj.	музыкальный/ мелодичный	musikalisch/ wohlklingend	musical/mélodieux
277	musical instrument	музыкальный инструмент	Musikinstrument, *n.*	instrument de musique, *m.*
278	musical interval	музыкальный интервал	Tonabstand, *m.*	intervalle musical, *m.*
279	musical notation	музыкальная нотация/ ноты, pl.	musikalische Bezeich- nung	notation musicale, *f.*
280	musical pitch	музыкальный тон	Tonhöhe, *f.*	ton musical, *n.*
281	musical scale	музыкальная шкала	Tonleiter, *f.*	échelle musicale, *f.*
282	musical stress	тональное ударение	melodische Betonung	accent mélodique, *m.*
283	mutation, n.	перегласовка, *f.*	Umlaut, *m.*	métaphonie, *f.*
284	mute consonant	немая согласная	stummer Konsonant	consonne sourde', *f.*
285	mute letter	непроизносимая буква	stummer Buchstabe	lettre muette, *f.*
286	mute person	немой (человек)	Stummer, *m.*	muet, *m.*
287	mute vowel	немая гласная	stummer Vokal/ Stummvokal, *m.*/ Schlussvokal, *m.*	voyelle muette, *f.*
288	mutual, adj.	взаимный	gegenseitig	réciproque
289	mutual intelligibility	взаимопонимание, *n.*	gegenseitige Verständlichkeit	intercompréhension, *f.*
290	mutual substitutability	взаимная заместительность	gegenseitige Austauschbarkeit	capacité de se substituer, *f.*
291	mutually dependent, adj.	взаимнозависимый	gegenseitig abhängig	réciproquement dépendant
292	mutually exclusive, adj.	взаимо- исклюуающий	gegenseitig ausschlies- send	réciproquement exclusif
293	myth, n.	миф, *m.*	Mythe, *f.*/Sage, *f.*	mythe, *f.*
294	mythology, n.	мифология, *f.*	Mythologie, *f.*	mythologie, *f.*

No.	ENGLISH	RUSSIAN	GERMAN	FRENCH

N

No.	ENGLISH	RUSSIAN	GERMAN	FRENCH
001	name (thing), n.	название, *n.*	Name, *m.*/Benennung, *f.*/ Bezeichnung, *f.*	nom, *m.*/appelation, *f.*/ dénomination, *f.*
002	name (person), n.	имя, *n.*	Name, *m.*	nom, *m.*
003	naming function	наименующая функция	Namensgebungsfunktion, *f.*	fonction de désigner, *f.*
004	narration, n.	повествование, *n.*	Erzählung, *f.*	relation, *f.*
005	narrative, n.	рассказ, *m.*	Erzählung, *f.*	récit, *m.*/conte, *m.*/ histoire, *f.*/narration, *f.*
006	narrative past	прошедшее повествовательное	erzählende Vergangenheit	passé de narration, *m.*
007	narrow, adj.	узкий	eng	étroit
008	narrow band filter	узкополосовой фильтр	Schmalbandfilter, *m.*	filtre étroit, *m.*
009	narrow transcription	точная запись	genaue Transkription	notation étroite, *f.*
010	narrow vowels, pl.	узкие гласные, pl.	enge Vokale, *m.*, pl./ dünne Vokale, *m.*, pl.	voyelles étroites, *f.*, pl.
011	narrowing, n.	сужение, *n.*	Verengerung, *f.*	rétrécissement, *m.*
012	nasal, adj.	назальный/носовой	Nasal-	nasal
013	nasal cavity	носовая полость	Nasenraum, *m.*	fosses nasales, *f.*, pl.
014	nasal consonants, pl.	назальные согласные, pl./носовые согласные, pl.	nasale Konsonanten, *m.*, pl./Nasallaute, *m.*, pl.	consonnes nasales, *f.*, pl.
015	nasal twang	гнусавость, *f.*	Näseln, *n.*	nasillement, *m.*
016	nasal vowels, pl.	назальные гласные, pl./носовые гласные, pl.	nasale Vokale, *m.*, pl.	voyelles nasales, *f.*, pl.
017	nasality, n.	назальность, *f.*	Nasalität, *f.*	nasalité, *f.*
018	nasalization, n.	назализация, *f.*	Nasalieren, *n.*	nasalisation, *f.*
019	national, adj.	национальный/народный	national/staatlich/Volks-/Landes-	national

No.	ENGLISH	RUSSIAN	GERMAN	FRENCH
020	national accent	национальный акцент	nationale Aussprache	accent national, *m.*
021	national character	национальный характер	Volkscharakter, *m.*	caractère national, *m.*
022	national consciousness	национальное самосознание	Nationalbewusstsein, *n.*	conscience nationale, *f.*
023	national languages, pl.	национальные языки, *m.*, pl.	nationale Sprachen, *f.*, pl.	langues nationales, *f.*, pl.
024	nationality, n.	национальность, *f.*/ гражданство, *n.*	Nationalität, *f.*/Staatsangehörigkeit, *f.*	nationalité, *f.*
025	native, adj.	родной	gebürtig	natal
026	native country	родина, *f.*	Vaterland, *n.*	pays natal, *m.*
027	native element	исходный элемент	ursprüngliches Element	élément originaire, *m.*
028	native language	родной язык	Muttersprache, *f.*	langue maternelle, *f.*
029	native speaker	говорящий на родном языке, *m.*/носитель языка, *m.*/ представитель языка, *m.*	Sprecher der Muttersprache, *m.*/ gebürtiger Sprecher/ einheimischer Sprecher	sujet parlant du pays, *m.*
030	native word	родное слово	einheimisches Wort	mot indigène, *m.*
031	natural, adj.	естественный/ природный	Natur- /natürlich	naturel
032	natural gender	естественный род	natürliches Geschlecht	genre naturel, *m.*
033	natural languages, pl.	естественные языки, *m.*, pl.	natürliche Sprachen, *f.*, pl.	langues naturelles, *f.*, pl.
034	natural sciences, pl.	естественные науки, *f.*, pl.	Naturwissenschaften, *f.*, pl.	sciences naturelles, *f.*, pl.
035	natural speech	непринужденная речь	ungezwungene Sprache	langage naturel, *m.*
036	nature, n.	натура, *f.*/природа, *f.*/ сущность, *f.*	Natur, *f.*/Wesen, *n.*	nature, *f.*
037	nautical language	морская речь	Seemannssprache, *f.*	langage nautique, *m.*
038	necessary, adj.	необходимый/ неизбежный	notwendig	nécessaire

No.	ENGLISH	RUSSIAN	GERMAN	FRENCH
039	necessary and sufficient conditions, pl.	необходимые и достаточные условия, *n.*, pl.	notwendige und hinreichende Bedingungen, *f.*, pl.	conditions nécessaires et suffisantes, *f.*, pl.
040	necessity, n.	нужда, *f.*/потребность, *f.*	Bedürfnis, *n.*/ Notwendigkeit, *f.*	nécessité, *f.*/besoin, *m.*
041	neck, n.	шея, *f.*	Hals, *m.*	cou, *m.*
042	necrology, n.	некролог, *m.*	Nekrolog, *m.*	nécrologie, *f.*
043	negation, n.	отрицание, *n.*	Negation, *f.*/ Verneinung, *f.*	négation, *f.*
044	negative, adj.	отрицательный	negativ	négatif
045	negative affix	отрицательный аффикс	negatives Affix	affixe négatif, *m.*
046	negative particle	отрицательная частица	negatives Partikel	particule négative, *f.*
047	negative pronoun	отрицательное местоимение	negatives Pronomen	pronom négatif, *m.*
048	negative question	отрицательный вопрос	negative Frage	phrase interro-négative, *f.*
049	negative sentence	отрицательное предложение	Negativsatz, *m.*/ verneinender Satz	phrase négative, *f.*
050	negative sign (−)	знак минуса, *m.*	Minuszeichen, *n.*	signe moins, *m.*
051	negative transformation	отрицательная трансформация	negative Transformation	transformation négative, *f.*
052	negative verb	отрицательный глагол	negatives Verb	verbe négatif, *m.*
053	neglected languages, pl.	заброшенные языки, *m.*, pl.	vernachlässigte Sprachen, *f.*, pl.	langues exotiques, *f.*, pl.
054	negligible, adj.	незначительный	unbedeutend	négligeable
055	neighboring, adj.	соседний/смежный	benachbart/angrenzend	avoisinant/voisin
056	neogrammarians, pl.	младограмматики, *m.*, pl.	Junggrammatiker, *m.*, pl.	néogrammairiens, *m.*, pl.
057	neologism, n.	неологизм, *m.*	Neologismus, *m.*/ Neuerung, *f.*	néologisme, *m.*

No.	ENGLISH	RUSSIAN	GERMAN	FRENCH
058	nerve, n.	нерв, *m.*	Nerv, *m.*	nerf, *m.*
059	nervous system	нервная система	Nervensystem, *n.*	système nerveux, *m.*
060	nest, n.	гнездо, *n.*	Serie, *f.*/Zahl, *f.*	série, *f.*/faisceau, *m.*
061	network, n.	сеть, *f.*/сетка, *f.*	Netz, *f.*	réseau, *m.*
062	neural, adj.	нервный	Nerven-	neural/nerval
063	neurology, n.	неврология, *f.*	Neurologie, *f.*	neurologie, *f.*
064	neurosis, n.	невроз, *m.*	Neurose, *f.*	névrose, *f.*
065	neuter gender	средний род	Neutrum, *n.*/sächliches Geschlecht	neutre, *m.*
066	neutral, adj.	нейтральный	neutral	neutre
067	neutral position	спокойное положение	Indifferenzlage, *f.*/ Ruhelage, *f.*	position d'indifférence, *f.*
068	neutral sound	нейтральный звук	Indifferenzlaut, *m.*	son neutre, *m.*
069	neutral vowel	нейтральный гласный звук	neutraler Vokal/ Murmellaut, *m.*	voyelle neutre, *f.*
070	neutralization, n.	нейтрализация, *f.*	Neutralisierung, *f.*/ Aufhebung, *f.*	neutralisation, *f.*
071	neutralization of phonemic oppositions	нейтрализация фонематических сопоставлений, *f.*	Aufhebung distinktiver phonematischer Gegensätze, *f.*	neutralisation des oppositions phonologiques, *f.*
072	neutralized, adj.	нейтрализованный	neutralisiert	neutralisé
073	new, adj.	новый	neu	nouveau/neuf
074	new formation	новое образование	Neubildung, *f.*	nouvelle création, *f.*
075	new function	новая функция	neue Funktion	fonction nouvelle, *f.*
076	new generation	молодое поколение	jüngere Generation	nouvelle génération, *f.*
077	new usage	новое использование	Neugebrauch, *m.*	usage nouveau, *m.*
078	new word	новое слово	neues Wort	mot nouveau, *m.*
079	newly created literary languages, pl.	младописьменные языки, *m.,* pl.	neugeschaffene Schriftsprachen, *f.,* pl.	langues littéraires récemment crées, *f.,* pl.

No.	ENGLISH	RUSSIAN	GERMAN	FRENCH
080	newness, n.	новизна, *f.*	Neuheit, *f.*	nouveauté, *f.*
081	news, pl.	новости, *f.,* pl.	Nachrichten, *f.,* pl.	informations, *f.,* pl.
082	news broadcast	радиопередача новостей, *f.*	Nachrichtensendung, *f.,* sg./Radionachrichten, *f.,* pl.	journal parlé, *m./* informations, *f.,* pl.
083	newspaper, n.	газета, *f.*	Zeitung, *f.*	journal, *m.*
084	newspaperese, *n.*	газетный стиль	Zeitungsstil, *m.*	style des journaux, *m.*
085	newsreel, n.	киножурнал, *m./* хроника, *f.*	Wochenschau, *f.*	film d'actualités, *m./* bande d'actualités, *f.*
086	next, adj.	следующий	folgend	suivant/prochain/voisin
087	nexus, n.	нексус, *m./*связь, *f.*	Verbindung, *f.*	connexion, *f.*
088	nickname, n.	прозвище, *n./* уменьшительное имя	Spitzname, *m./* Übername, *m.*	sobriquet, *m./*surnom, *m.*
089	node, n.	узел, *m.*	Knoten, *m.*	noeud, *m.*
090	noise, n.	шум, *m.*	Geräusch, *n./*Lärm, *m.*	bruit, *m.*
091	noise level	уровень шума, *m.*	Geräuschpegel, *m.*	niveau de bruit, *m.*
092	noise spectrum	шумовой спектр	Geräuschspektrum, *n.*	spectre de bruit, *m.*
093	noiseless, adj.	бесшумный/ беззвучный	geräuschlos	sans bruit
094	noisy, adj.	шумный	geräuschvoll/lärmend	bruyant
095	nomadic, adj.	кочевой	nomadisch	nomade
096	nom-de-plume, n.	псевдоним, *m.*	Pseudonym, *n./*Schrift- stellername, *m.*	pseudonyme, *m.*
097	nomemclature, n.	номенклатура, *f.*	Nomenklatur, *f.*	nomenclature, *f.*
098	nominal, adj.	именной	nominal	nominal
099	nominal class	именной класс	nominale Klasse	classe nominale, *f.*
100	nominal inflection	именная флексия	nominale Flexion	flexion nominale, *f.*
101	nominal sentence	именное предложение	Nominalsatz, *m.*	phrase nominale, *f.*

No.	English	Russian	German	French
102	nominalization, n.	номинализация, *f.*/ субстантивизация, *f.*	Nominalisierung, *f.*/ Substantivierung, *f.*	nominalisation, *f.*
103	nominative absolute	именительный абсолютный	absoluter Nominativ	nominatif absolu, *m.*
104	nominative case	именительный падеж	Nominativ, *m.*/ Werfall, *m.*/erster Fall	nominatif, *m.*/cas sujet, *m.*
105	nonce word	слово образованное на случай	für einen besonderen Fall geprägtes Wort	création verbale occasionnelle, *f.*
106	non-commutable, adj.	незамещаемый	nicht vertauschbar	impermutable
107	non-conformity, n.	неподчинение, *n.*	mangelnde Übereinstimmung	non-conformité, *f.*
108	non-contiguous, adj.	несмежный	nicht benachbart	non contigu
109	non-contiguous assimilation	дистактная ассимиляция/ гармоническая ассимиляция	Assimilation auf Abstand, *f.*/Fernas- similation, *f.*/mittelbare Assimilation	assimilation à distance, *f.* /assimilation harmonique, *f.*
110	non-contrastive, adj.	несоставляющий контраста	kontrastlos	non contrastif
111	non-directional, adj.	ненаправленный	nicht gerichtet	non directionnel
112	non-distinctive, adj.	неразличительный	nicht distinktiv/ irrelevant	non distinctif/ non pertinent
113	non-effective, adj.	недействительный	ungünstig	ineffectif
114	non-essential, adj.	несущественный	unwesentlich	non essentiel
115	non-finite, adj.	неконечный	nicht endlich	non fini
116	non-finite verb	неличный глагол	infinites Verb(um)	verbe non fini, *m.*
117	non-human, adj.	нечеловеческий	nicht menschlich	non humain
118	non-integrated phoneme	нецарная фонема	nicht integriertes Phonem	phonème non intégré, *m.*
119	non-intersecting, adj.	непересекающиеся	nicht schneidend	qui ne se croisent pas
120	nonlinear, adj.	нелинейный	nicht linear	non linéaire

No.	ENGLISH	RUSSIAN	GERMAN	FRENCH
121	non-linguistic, adj.	вне-лингвистический	nicht linguistisch/ aussersprachlich	non linguistique
122	non-paired phoneme	непарная фонема	unpaariges Phonem	phonème hors couple, *m.*/phonème non apparié, *m.*
123	non-past verb	непрошедший глагол	Nichtvergangenheits- verb(um), *n.*	verbe non passé, *m.*
124	non-prescriptive, adj.	непредписывающий	nicht präskriptiv	non prescriptif
125	non-productive, adj.	непродуктивный	unproduktiv	non productif
126	non-restrictive, adj.	неограничивающий	nicht einschränkend	non limitatif
127	nonsense language	заумный язык/ бессмысленный язык	burleske Sprache/ sinnlose Sprache	langue de non-sens, *f.*
128	nonsensical, adj.	бессмысленный	unsinnig	absurde
129	non-separable, adj.	неотъемлемый	untrennbar	indémontable
130	non-standard, adj.	нестандартный	nicht normal/ nicht standard	non courant/non-étalon
131	non-typical, adj.	нетипичный	atypisch/untypisch	non typique
132	non-uniqueness, n.	неединичность, *f.*	Uneinzigartigkeit, *f.*	caractère non-unique, *m*
133	nonverbal language	бессловный язык	ungesprochene Sprache	langage sans mots, *m.*
134	norm, n.	норма, *f.*	Norm, *f.*	norme, *f.*
135	normal, adj.	нормальный	normal	normal
136	normal breathing	нормальное дыхание	normales Atmen	respiration normale, *f.*
137	normal distribution	нормальное распределение	normale Verteilung	répartition normale, *f.*/ distribution normale
138	normal intonation	нейтральная интонация	normale Intonation	intonation normale, *f.*
139	normal pronunciation	обычное произношение	normale Aussprache/ gewöhnliche Aussprache/ regelrechte Aussprache	prononciation usuelle, *f.*

No.	ENGLISH	RUSSIAN	GERMAN	FRENCH
140	normal school	педагогическое училище	Lehrerbildungsanstalt, *f./* Lehrerseminar, *n.*	école normale, *f.*
141	normal spelling	обычное правописание	normale Buchstabierung	orthographe normale, *f.*
142	normal usage	обыкновенное употребление	normaler Gebrauch	emploi usuel, *m.*
143	normal word order	обычный порядок слов	normale Wortstellung	ordre de mots normal, *m.*
144	normalization, n.	нормализация, *f.*	Normalisierung, *f.*	normalisation, *f.*
145	normative grammar	нормативная грамматика	normative Grammatik	grammaire normative, *f.*
146	Norwegian, adj.	норвежский	norwegisch	norvégien
147	nose, n.	нос, *m.*	Nase, *f.*	nez, *m.*
148	nostril, n.	ноздря, *f.*	Nasenloch, *n.*	narine, *f.*
149	notation, n.	нотация, *f./*запись, *f.*	Notation, *f./* Bezeichnungsweise, *f.*	notation, *f.*
150	notebook, n.	записная книжка	Notizbuch, *n.*	cahier, *m./*calepin, *m./* carnet, *m.*
151	notes, pl.	записки, *f.,* pl.	Aufzeichnungen, *f.,* pl./ Notizen, *f.,* pl.	notes, *f.,* pl.
152	notice, n.	заметка, *f./* объявление, *n.*	Anzeige, *f.*	avis, *m.*
153	notice board	доска для объявлений, *f.*	Anschlagtafel, *f.*	écriteau, *m./*tableau d'affichage, *m.*
154	noticeable, adj.	заметный	bemerkenswert	notable
155	notion, n.	понятие, *n.*	Begriff, *m.*	notion, *f.*
156	noun, n.	имя существительное	Nomen, *n./*Hauptwort, *n.* /Substantiv, *n.*	nom, *m./*substantif, *m.*
157	noun class	класс существительных, *m.*	Nomenklasse, *f.*	classe de noms, *f.*

No.	English	Russian	German	French
158	noun phrase	именная группа/ именная фраза	Nominalgruppe, *f.*/ Nominalphrase, *f.*/ Substantivgefüge, *n.*	groupe nominal, *m.*
159	novel, adj.	новый	neu	nouveau
160	novel, n.	роман, *m.*	Roman, *m.*	roman, *m.*
161	novelette, n.	новелла, *f.*/повесть, *f.*	Novelle, *f.*	nouvelle, *f.*/bluette, *f.*
162	nuance, n.	оттенок, *m.*	Nuance, *f.*/Abtönung, *f.*/ Abstufung, *f.*	nuance, *f.*
163	nucleus, n.	ядро, *n.*	Kern, *m.*	noyau, *m.*
164	nucleus of syllable	слоговое ядро	Silbenkern, *m.*	noyau de syllabe, *m.*
165	null form	пустая форма	leere Form	forme vide, *f.*
166	number, n.	число, *n.*/количество, *n.*	Numerus, *m.*/Zahl, *f.*	nombre, *m.*/numéro, *m.*
167	number of units	число единиц, *n.*	Anzahl der Einheiten, *f.*	nombre des unités, *m.*
168	numbering, n.	нумерование, *n.*	Numerierung, *f.*	numérotage, *m.*
169	numeral, n.	имя числительное, *n.*/ цифра, *f.*	Zahlwort, *n.*/Ziffer, *f.*	numéral, *m.*/ nombre, *m.*/chiffre, *m.*
170	numerical, adj.	числовой/цифровой	numerisch/zahlenmässig	numérique
171	numerous, adj.	многочисленный	zahlreich	nombreux
172	nursery language	детский язык	Ammensprache, *f.*	langage de crèche, *m.*
173	nursery rhyme	детские стишки, pl.	Kinderreim, *m.*	vers rimés d'enfants, *m.*, pl.
174	nursery school	детский сад	Kleinkindergarten, *m.*	école maternelle, *f.*
175	nursery tale	детский рассказ	Märchen, *n.*	conte de nourrice, *m.*

O

No.	English	Russian	German	French
001	oath, n.	клятва, *f.*/присяга, *f.*	Schwur, *m.*/Eid, *m.*	serment, *m.*
002	obituary, n.	некролог, *m.*	Nekrolog, *m.*/Nachruf, *m.*	nécrologie, *f.*

No.	ENGLISH	RUSSIAN	GERMAN	FRENCH
003	object (grammatical), n.	дополнение, *n.*	Objekt, *n./*Ergänzung, *f.*	régime, *m./* complément, *m.*
004	object (thing), n.	предмет, *m./*вещь, *f.*	Objekt, *n./*Gegenstand, *m.*	objet, *m./*chose, *f.*
005	objection, n.	возражение, *n.*	Einwand, *m./* Einwendung, *f.*	objection, *f./* inconvenient, *m.*
006	objectionable, adj.	нежелательный	nicht zulässig	critiquable
007	objective, adj.	объективный	objektiv	objectif
008	objective, n.	цель, *f./*стремление, *n.*	Ziel, *n./*Zweck, *m.*	objectif, *m./*fin, *f./*but, *m.*
009	objective case	объективный падеж	Objektfall, *m.*	cas régime, *m.*
010	objectivity, n.	объективность, *f.*	Objektivität, *f.*	objectivité, *f.*
011	obligatory, adj.	обязательный	obligatorisch	obligatoire
012	obligatory transforma-tion	обязательная трансформация	obligatorische Transfor-mation	transformation obligatoire, *f.*
013	oblique case	косвенный падеж	abhängiger Fall/ Beugungsfall, *m./* Casus Obliquus, *m.*	cas oblique, *m.*
014	oblique line	косая линия	schräge Linie/ Schrägstrich, *m.*	ligne de biais, *f.*
015	obliteration, n.	стирание, *n./* уничтожение, *n.*	Vernichtung, *f.*	grattage, *m./*rature, *f.*
016	oblivion, n.	забвение, *n.*	Vergessenheit, *f.*	oubli, *m.*
017	obscenity, n.	неприличные выражения, *n.,* pl.	obszöne Ausdrücke, *m.,* pl./Zoten, *f.,* pl.	mots obscènes, *m.,* pl.
018	obscure, adj.	неясный/скрытый	undeutlich/unklar	obscur/peu clair
019	observation (visual), n.	наблюдение, *n.*	Beobachtung, *f.*	observation, *f.*
020	observation (verbal), n.	замечание, *n.*	Bemerkung, *f.*	observation, *f./*remarque, *f./*commentaire, *m.*
021	obsolete, adj.	устаревший	obsolet/altmodisch/ veraltet	inusité/vieilli

No.	ENGLISH	RUSSIAN	GERMAN	FRENCH
022	obstacle, n.	препятствие, *n.*	Hindernis, *n.*	obstacle, *m.*
023	obstruction, n.	преграждение, *n.*	Hindernis, *n.*/ Hinderung, *f.*	occlusion, *f.*
024	obstruent consonants, pl.	шумные согласные, pl.	Geräuschlaute, *m.,* pl.	consonnes bruits, *f.,* pl.
025	obvious, adj.	очевидный/явный	klar/deutlich/ einleuchtend	évident/clair/patent/ manifeste/visible
026	occasional, adj.	случайный	gelegentlich	intermittent
027	occlusion, n.	смычка, *f.*	Verschluss, *m.*	occlusion, *f.*/fermeture, *f.*
028	occlusive consonants, pl.	смычные согласные, pl.	Verschlusslaute, *m.,* pl.	consonnes occlusives, *f.,* pl.
029	occurrence, n.	появление, *n.*/ встречаемость, *f.*	Vorkommen, *n.*	apparition, *f.*
030	octal, adj.	восьмиричный	oktal	octal
031	octave, n.	октава, *f.*	Oktave, *f.*	octave, *f.*
032	odd number	нечетное число	ungerade Zahl	nombre impair, *m.*
033	oddity, n.	странность, *f.*	Seltsamkeit, *f.*/ Eigentümlichkeit, *f.*	bizarrerie, *f.*/étrangeté, *f.*
034	ode, n.	ода, *f.*	Ode, *f.*	ode, *f.*
035	off-glide, n.	рекурсия, *f.*	Abglitt, *m.*	détente, *f.*/métastase, *f.*
036	official language (style)	административный жаргон	Amtssprache, *f.*/ Kanzleisprache, *f.*	jargon administratif, *m.*
037	old, adj.	старый	alt	vieux
038	Old Church Slavic, Old Church Slavonic, adj.	старославянский/ церковнославянский	altkirchenslawisch	slavique ancien de l'église
039	old-fashioned, adj.	старомодний/ устарелый	altmodisch	démodé
040	older generation	старшее поколение	ältere Generation	génération antérieure, *f.*
041	olfactory language	обонятельный язык	Geruchssprache, *f.*	langage olfactif, *m.*
042	omission, n.	пропуск, *m.*	Auslassung, *f.*	omission, *f.*

No.	ENGLISH	RUSSIAN	GERMAN	FRENCH
043	on-glide, n.	экскурсия, *f.*	Anglitt, *m.*	catastase, *f.*/tenue, *f.*
044	one-case language	однопадежный язык	Einheitskasussprache, *f.*	langue à cas unique, *f.*
045	one-dimensional, adj.	одномерный	eindimensional	à dimension unique
046	one-to-one correspondence	взаимнооднозначное соответствие	eingliedrige Entsprechung	correspondance à termes simples, *f.*/correspondance uniforme, *f.*
047	one-word sentence	однословное предложение/ слово-предложение, *n.*	eingliedriger Satz	phrase composée d'un seul mot, *f.*
048	onomastics, n.	ономастика, *f.*	Namenkunde, *f.*	onomastique, *f.*
049	onomatopoeia, n.	ономатопея, *f.*/ звукоподражание, *n.*	Onomatopöie, *f.*/ Schallnachahmung, *f.*	onomatopée, *f.*
050	onset, n.	приступ, *m.*	Einsatz, *m.*	attaque, *f.*
051	ontology, n.	онтология, *f.*	Ontologie, *f.*	ontologie, *f.*
052	open, adj.	открытый	offen	ouvert
053	open list	открытый список/ неограниченный список	offene Liste/ unbegrenzte Liste	liste ouverte, *f.*/liste non limitée, *f.*
054	open syllable	открытый слог	offene Silbe	syllable ouverte, *f.*/ syllable libre, *f.*
055	open transition	открытый переход	offene Verbindung/ offener Übergang	transition ouverte, *f.*
056	open vowels, pl.	открытые гласные, pl.	offene Vokale, *m.*, pl.	voyelles ouvertes, *f.*, pl.
057	opening, n.	открытие, *n.*/ отверствие, *n.*/ раствор, *m.*	Öffnung, *f.*	aperture, *f.*/ouverture, *f.*
058	operation, n.	действие, *n.*	Vorgang, *m.*/ Verfahren, *n.*	opération, *f.*
059	operational definition	оперативное определение	Operationsdefinition, *f.*/ genügende Definition	définition suffisante, *f.*
060	opinion, n.	мнение, *n.*	Meinung, *f.*	opinion, *f.*

No.	ENGLISH	RUSSIAN	GERMAN	FRENCH
061	opposed, adj.	противоположенный/ противопоставлен- ный	entgegengesetzt	opposé
062	opposite, adj.	обратный/ противоположный	entgegengesetzt/ rückkehrend	opposé
063	opposition, n.	оппозиция. *f.*/ противоположение, *n.*/ противопоставление, *n.*	Gegenüberstellung *f.*/ Opposition, *f.*	opposition, *f.*
064	optative mood	оптатив, *m.*/ желательное наклонение	Optativ, *m.*/ Wunschmodus, *m.*	optatif, *m.*
065	optical sign	оптический знак	optisches Zeichen	signe optique, *m.*
066	optimal, optimum, adj.	оптимальный	optimum	optimum
067	optional, adj.	факультативный/ необязательный	fakultativ/beliebig/ wahlfrei	facultatif
068	optional transformation	факультативная трансформация	fakultative Transforma- tion	transformation facultative, *f.*
069	oral, adj.	устный/ротовой/ словесный	Mund- /mündlich	oral/buccal
070	oral-aural method (lan- guage teaching)	устно-слуховой метод	audio-linguistische Methode	méthode audio-linguale, *f.*
071	oral cavity	полость рта, *f.*	Mundhöhle, *f.*	cavité buccale, *f.*
072	oral closure	ротовая смычка	Mundverschluss, *m.*	fermeture buccale, *f.*
073	oral consonants, pl.	ротовые согласные, pl.	orale Konsonanten, *m.*, pl./mundliche Konsonanten, *m.*, pl.	consonnes orales, *f.*, pl.
074	oral reading	чтение вслух, *n.*	lautes Lesen	lecture à haute voix, *f.*
075	oral sound	ротовой звук	Mundlaut, *m.*	son buccal, *m.*
076	oral vowels, pl.	ротовые гласные, pl.	mündliche Vokale, *m.*, pl.	voyelles orales, *f.*, pl.
077	oratorical speech (style)	ораторская речь	rhetorische Sprache/ rhetorischer Stil	langage oratoire, *m.*

No.	ENGLISH	RUSSIAN	GERMAN	FRENCH
078	oration, n.	речь, *f.*	Ansprache, *f.*/Rede, *f.*	discours, *m.*
079	oratory, n.	красноречие, *n.*	Beredsamkeit, *f.*	oratoire, *m.*
080	order (command), n.	приказ, *m.*	Befehl, *m.*	commandement, *m.*
081	order (of items), n.	порядок, *m.*	Anordnung, *f.*/Ordnung, *f.*/Reihenfolge, *f.*	ordre, *m.*
082	ordered pair	упорядоченная пара	geordnetes Paar	couple ordonné, *m.*
083	ordered rules, pl.	упорядоченные правила, *m., pl.*	geordnete Regeln, *f., pl.*	règles ordonnées, *f., pl.*
084	ordering, n.	упорядочение, *n.*	Anordnung, *f.*	ordonnement, *m.*
085	ordinal numeral	порядковое числительное	Ordinalzahl, *f.*/Ordnungszahl, *f.*	nombre ordinal, *m.*
086	ordinary speech	обычная речь	gewöhnliche Rede	langage usuel, *m.*/langage habituel, *m.*/langage courant, *m.*
087	organization, n.	организация, *f.*/аранжировка, *f.*	Anordnung, *f.*	agencement, *m.*
088	organ, n.	орган, *m.*	Organ, *n.*	organe, *m.*
089	organism, n.	организм, *m.*	Organismus, *m.*	organisme, *m.*
090	oriental, adj.	азиатский/восточный	morgenländisch/oriental	oriental/de l'orient
091	orientation, n.	ориентация, *f.*/ориентировка, *f.*/ориентирование, *n.*	Orientierung, *f.*	orientation, *f.*
092	origin, n.	источник, *m.*/начало, *n.*/происхождение, *n.*	Ursprung, *m.*/Herkunft, *f.*/Entstehung, *f.*/Anfang, *m.*	origine, *f.*
093	originality, n.	оригинальность, *f.*/самобытность, *f.*	Originalität, *f.*	originalité, *f.*
094	originally, adv.	первоначально	anfangs/ursprünglich	originairement/originellement
095	orinasal, adj.	ротоносовой	nasalisiert	nasalisé

No.	ENGLISH	RUSSIAN	GERMAN	FRENCH
096	orthoepy, n.	орфоэпия, *n.*	Orthöepie, *f.*	orthoépie, *f.*
097	orthographic(al), adj.	орфографический	orthographisch/ Rechtschreibungs-	orthographique
098	orthographic change	орфографическое изменение	orthographische Veränderung	changement orthographique, *m.*
099	orthographic system	орфографическая система	orthographisches System	système orthographique, *m.*
100	orthography, n.	орфография, *f.*/ правописание, *n.*	Orthographie, *f.*/ Rechtschreibung, *f.*	orthographe, *f.*
101	oscillation, n.	колебание, *n.*	Schwankung, *f.*/Schwingung, *f.*	oscillation, *f.*
102	oscillogram, n.	осциллограмма, *f.*	Oszillogramm, *n.*	oscillogramme, *f.*
103	oscillograph, n.	осциллограф, *m.*	Oszillograph, *m.*	oscillographe, *m.*
104	oscilloscope, n.	осциллоскоп, *m.*	Oszilloskop, *m.*	oscilloscope, *m.*
105	other, adj.	другой/иной	ander	autre
106	otherness, n.	отличие, *n.*	Anderssein, *n.*	caractère d'être autre, *m.*
107	ouch-ouch theory	теория ай-ай-ай, *f.*	au-au Theorie, *f.*	théorie aïe-aïe, *f.*
108	out of print, adj.	давно не издававшаяся/давно не печатающийся	vergriffen	épuisé
109	outcry, n.	выкрик, *m.*	Ausruf, *m.*	clameur, *f.*
110	outer, adj.	внешний/наружный	äusserer	extérieur/externe
111	outgrowth, n.	отпрыск, *m.*/ отросток, *m.*	Auswuchs, *m.*/ Nebenprodukt, *n.*	aboutissement, *m.*/ conséquence, *f.*/ résultat, *m.*
112	outline, n.	схема, *f.*/план, *m.*/ конспект, *f.*/очерк, *m.*/набросок, *m.*/ очертание, *m.*	Entwurf, *m.*/Plan, *m.*/ Skizze, *f.*/Überblick, *m.*/Umriss, *m.*	esquisse, *f.*/ébauche, *f.*/ plan, *m.*/schéma, *m.*
113	outlook, n.	перспектива, *f.*	Ausblick, *m.*/ Aussicht, *f.*	perspective, *f.*/ horizon, *m.*

No.	ENGLISH	RUSSIAN	GERMAN	FRENCH
114	outmoded, adj.	старомодный	altmodisch/veraltet	démodé/passé
115	output, n.	выход, *m.*	Ausgabe, *f.*	sortie, *f.*
116	overcorrection, n.	сверхпоправка, *f.*/ излишняя нормализация	Hypernormalisierung, *f.*	hypercorrection, *f.*
117	overdifferentiated, adj.	излишне дифференцированный	überdifferenziert	sur-différencié
118	overlapping, n.	частичное совпадение	teilweise Überlagerung, *f.*	chevauchement, *m.*
119	overloading, n.	перегрузка, *f.*	Überbelastung, *f.*	surménage, *m.*
120	overlong, adj.	сверхдолгий	überlang	ultralongue
121	overstatement, n.	преувеличение, *n.*	Übertreibung, *f.*	exagération, *f.*
122	overt, adj.	неприкрытый/ открытый	offenbar/offensichtlich	non déguisé
123	overtone, n.	обертон, *m.*/ частичный тон	Oberton, *m.*	harmonique, *m.*
124	ownership, n.	принадлежность, *f.*	Besitz, *m.*	possession, *f.*

P

No.	ENGLISH	RUSSIAN	GERMAN	FRENCH
001	pace, n.	шаг, *m.*	Schritt, *m.*	pas, *m.*
002	page, n.	страница, *f.*	Seite, *f.*	page, *f.*
003	pagination, n.	нумерация страниц, *f.*	Paginierung, *f.*/ Seitenzählung, *f.*	pagination, *f.*
004	pair, n.	пара, *f.*	Paar, *n.*	couple, *m.*
005	paired phoneme	парная фонема	paariges Phonem	phonème apparié, *m.*/ phonème de couple, *m.*
006	paired words, pl.	парные слова, *n., pl.*	paarige Wörter, *n., pl.*	mots couples, *m.*
007	palaeography, n.	палеография, *f.*	Handschriftenkunde, *f.*/ Paläographie, *f.*	paléographie, *f.*

No.	ENGLISH	RUSSIAN	GERMAN	FRENCH
008	palatal consonants, pl.	палатальные согласные, pl./ небные согласные, pl.	palatale Konsonanten, *m.*, pl./ Vorderzungenlaute, *m.*, pl.	consonnes palatales, *f.*, pl.
009	palatal vowels, pl.	палатальные гласные, pl./ переднеязычные гласные, pl.	palatale Vokale, *m.*, pl./ Vorderzungenvokale, *m.*, pl.	voyelles palatales, *f.*, pl./ voyelles antérieures, *f.*, pl.
010	palatalization, n.	пататализация, *f.*/ смягчение, *n.*	Palatalisierung, *f.*/ Erweichung, *f.*/ Mouillierung, *f.*	palatalisation, *f.*/ mouillement, *m.*
011	palatalized, adj.	палатизованный/ смягченный	palatalisiert	mouillé
012	palate, n.	небо, *n.*	Gaumen, *m.*	palais, *m.*
013	palm, n.	ладонь, *f.*	Handfläche, *f.*	paume, *f.*
014	pamphlet, n.	брошюра, *f.*	Broschüre, *f.*/Flugblatt, *n.*/Flugschrift, *f.*	brochure, *f.*/opuscule, *m.*
015	pantomine, n.	пантомима, *f.*	Pantomime, *f.*/ Gebärdenspiel, *n.*	mime, *m.*
016	paper (for writing), n.	бумага, *f.*	Papier, *n.*	papier, *m.*
017	paper (scholarly work), n.	научный доклад/ статья, *f.*	wissenschaftlicher Aufsatz/Vortrag, *m.*	piéce, *f.*/mémoire, *m.*/ étude, *f.*/dissertation, *f.*
018	paperback book, n.	книга в бумажной обложке, *f.*	Paperback, *m.*/ Taschenbuch, *n.*	livre broché, *m.*/ livre de poche, *m.*
019	papyrus, n.	папирус, *m.*	Papyrus, *m.*	papyrus, *m.*
020	par, n.	равенство, *n.*	Gleichheit, *f.*	égalité, *f.*
021	parable, n.	притча, *f.*/ иносказание, *n.*/ аллегория, *f.*	Parabel, *f.*/Gleichnis, *n.*	parabole, *f.*
022	paradigm, n.	парадигма, *f.*	Paradigma, *n.*/ Musterbeispiel, *n.*	paradigme, *m.*
023	paradigmatic, adj.	парадигматический	paradigmatisch	paradigmatique

No.	English	Russian	German	French
024	paradigmatic alternation	парадигматическое чередование	paradigmatischer Wechsel	alternance paradigmatique *f.*
025	paradigmatic axis	парадигматическая ось	paradigmatische Achse	axe paradigmatique, *f.*
026	paradigmatic class	парадигматический класс	paradigmatische Klasse	classe paradigmatique, *f.*
027	paradigmatic relationships, pl.	парадигматические отношения, *n.,* pl.	paradigmatische Beziehungen, *f.,* pl.	rapports paradigmatiques, *m.,* pl.
028	paradox, n.	парадокс, *m.*	Paradox(on), *n.*/ Widerspruch, *m.*	paradoxe, *m.*
029	paragraph, n.	параграф, *m.*/абзац, *m.*	Paragraph, *m.*/Absatz, *m.*	alinéa, *m.*/paragraphe, *m.*
030	paralanguage, n.	параязык, *m.*	Parasprache, *f.*	paralangue, *f.*
031	parallel, adj.	параллельный	parallel/gleichlaufend	parallèle
032	parallel formations, pl.	параллельные образования, *n.,* pl.	parallele Bildungen, *f.,* pl.	formations parallèles, *f.,* pl.
033	parallel developments, pl.	параллельные развития, *n.,* pl.	Parallelentwicklungen, *f.,* pl.	développements parallèles, *m.,* pl.
034	parallelism, n.	параллелизм, *m.*	Parallelismus, *m.*	parallélisme, *m.*
035	parameter, n.	параметр, *m.*	Parameter, *n.*/ Umkreis, *m.*	paramètre, *m.*
036	paraphrase, n.	парафраза, *f.*/ пересказ, *m.*	Paraphrase, *f.*/ Umschreibung, *f.*	paraphrase, *f.*
037	parataxis, n.	паратаксис, *m.*/ бессоюзное сочинение	Parataxis, *f.*/Beiordnung, *f.*/Nebenordnung, *f.*	parataxe, *f.*
038	parchment, n.	пергамент, *m.*	Pergament, *n.*	parchemin, *m.*
039	parent language	праязык, *m.*/ язык-предок, *m.*	Ursprache, *f.*/ Grundsprache, *f.*	langue-mère, *f.*
040	parentage, n.	происхождение, *n.*	Abkunft, *f.*/Abstammung, *f.*/Herkunft, *f.*	parenté, *f.*
041	parentheses, pl. ( )	круглые сковки, *f.* pl.	runde Klammern, *f.,* pl.	parenthèses, *f.,* pl.

No.	ENGLISH	RUSSIAN	GERMAN	FRENCH
042	parenthesis (insertion), n.	внесение, *n.*	Zwischensatz, *m.*	parenthèse, *f.*
043	parenthetical clause	вводное предложение	Schaltsatz, *m.*/ Einschubsatz, *m.*/ Einschalten, *n.*	incidente, *f.*/proposition entre parenthèses, *f.*
044	parenthetical words, pl.	вводные слова, *n., pl.*	Klammerformen, *f., pl.*	mots entre parenthèses, *m., pl.*
045	parents, pl.	родители, *m., pl.*	Eltern, pl.	parents, *m.* pl.
046	parlance, n.	говор, *m.*	Redeweise, *f.*	langage, *m.*/parler, *m.*
047	parody, n.	пародия, *f.*	Parodie, *f.*	parodie, *f.*/pastiche, *m.*
048	paronym, n.	пароним, *m.*/ производное слово	stammverwandtes Wort	paronyme, *m.*
049	parse, v.	делать граммати- ческий разьор	zerlegen	faire l'analyse grammati- cale
050	parsing, n.	грамматический анализ	grammatische Analyse/ Satzgliederung, *f.*	analyse grammaticale, *f.*
051	part, n.	часть, *f.*	Teil, *m.*	partie, *f.*
052	part and whole	часть и совокупность	Teil und Ganzes	partie et tout
053	partial, adj.	частичный	teilweise	partiel
054	partial assimilation	частичная ассимиляция/ неполная ассимиляция	teilweise Assimilation	assimilation partielle, *f.*
055	partial inventory	частичный инвентарь	Teilinventar, *n.*	inventaire partiel, *m.*
056	partial overlapping	частичное совпадение	teilweise Überlagerung	chevauchement partiel, *m.*
057	partial reduplication	частичная редупликация	teilweise Reduplikation	redoublement partiel, *m.*
058	partially complementary distribution	частично дополнительная дистрибуция/ частично дополнительное распределение	teilkomplementäre Verteilung	complémentarité partielle

No.	English	Russian	German	French
059	participation, n.	участие, *n.*	Mitwirkung, *f.*/ Teilnahme, *f.*	participation, *f.*
060	participial, adj.	причастный/ деепричастный	partizipial	participial
061	participial construction	причастный оборот	Partizipialfügung, *f.*	construction participiale, *f.*
062	participle, n.	причастие, *n.*	Partizip(ium), *n.*	participe, *m.*
063	particle, n.	частица, *f.*	Partikel, *n.*/Teilchen, *n.*	particule, *f.*
064	particular, adj.	специфический	spezifisch	particulier
065	particularly, adv.	особенно	besonders	particulièrement
066	particulars, pl.	подробности, *f.*, pl.	Einzelheiten, *f.*, pl./ nähere Auskunft	détails, *m.*, pl.
067	partition, n.	разбиение, *n.*/ расчленение, *n.*	Teilung, *f.*	division, *f.*
068	partitive, n.	партитив, *m.*/ разделительное слово	Partitiv(um), *n.*	partitif, *m.*
069	partitive article	партитивный артикль/ частичный артикль	Teilungsartikel, *m.*	article partitif, *m.*
070	partitive genitive	родительный разделительный	Teilungsgenetiv, *m.*	génétif partitif, *m.*
071	partly, adv.	частично/до некоторой степени/ отчасти	teilweise	partiellement/en partie
072	parts of the body, pl.	части тела, *f.*, pl.	Körperteile, *m.*, pl.	parties du corps, *f.*, pl.
073	parts of speech, pl.	части речи, *f.*, pl.	Wortklassen, *f.*, pl.	parties du discours, *f.*, pl.
074	parts of the sentence, pl.	члены предложения, *m.*, pl.	Satzteile, *m.*, pl./ Satzglieder, *n.*, pl.	membres de la phrase, *m.*, pl.
075	pass (through data), n.	проход, *m.*	Durchgang, *m.*	passage, *m.*
076	passage (of air), n.	прохождение, *n.*	Durchfluss, *m.*	passage, *m.*
077	passage (out of book), n.	отрывок. *m.*	Passus, *m.*	passage, *m.*

No.	English	Russian	German	French
078	passage (movement), n.	ход, *m.*/течение, *n.*	Verlauf, *m.*	passage, *m.*
079	passing of time	полет времени, *m.*/ течение времени, *n.*	Zeitverlauf, *m.*	fuite de temps, *f.*
080	passive form	пассивная форма/ страдательная форма	passive Form/ Leideform, *f.*	forme passive, *f.*
081	passive organ	пассивный орган	Indifferenzorgan, *n.*	organe inactif, *m.*
082	passive participle	страдательное причастие	passives Partizip	participe passé, *m.*
083	passive sentence	пассивное предложение/ страдательное предложение	Passivsatz, *m.*	phrase à la voix passive, *f.*
084	passive vocabulary	пассивный словарь	passiver Wortschatz	vocabulaire inactif, *m.*
085	passive voice	страдательный залог	Passiv, *n.*	voix passive, *f.*
086	password, n.	пароль, *m.*/пропуск, *m.*	Losung, *f.*/Losungswort, *n.*/Erkennungswort, *n.*	mot de passe, *m.*
087	past, n.	прошлое, *n.*	Vergangenheit, *f.*	passé, *m.*
088	past absolute	прошедшее абсолютное	einfache Vergangenheit	passé simple, *m.*
089	past active participle	причастие прошедшего времени действительного залога, *n.*	aktives Partizip der Vergangenheit	participe passé de l'actif, *m.*
090	past definite	прошедшее определенное	bestimmte Vergangenheit	passé défini, *m.*
091	past indefinite	прошедшее неопределенное	unbestimmte Vergangenheit	passé indéfini, *m.*
092	past participle	причастие прошедшего времени, *n.*	Participium Perfecti/ Perfektpartizip, *n.*/ Mittelwort der Vergangenheit, *n.*	participe passé, *m.*

No.	ENGLISH	RUSSIAN	GERMAN	FRENCH
093	past passive participle	причастие прошедшего времени страдательного залога, *n.*	passives Participium Perfecti/passives Perfektpartizip	participe passif du passé, *m.*
094	past perfect	плюсквамперфект, *m./* давнопрошедшее время	Plusquamperfekt, *n.*	plus que parfait, *m.*
095	past tense	прошедшее время	Vergangenheit, *f.*	temps passé, *m.*
096	pathology, n.	патология, *f.*	Pathologie, *f./* Krankheitslehre, *f.*	pathologie, *f.*
097	patronymic, n.	отчество, *n.*	Vatersname, *m./* Geschlechtsname, *m.*	patronyme, *m.*
098	pattern, n.	модель, *f.*	Muster, *n.*	patron, *m.*
099	pattern congruity	согласование модели, *n.*	Musterübereinstimmung, *f.*	conformité à un modèle, *f.*
100	pattern drill	лексико-грамматическое упражнение	Musterübung, *f.*	exercice structural, *m.*
101	pattern recognition	распознавание образцов, *n.*	Mustererkennung, *f.*	reconnaissance de la structure, *f.*
102	patterning, n.	моделирование, *n.*	Anordnung, *f.*	agencement, *m.*
103	pause, n.	пауза, *f./*перерыв, *m.*	Pause, *f./*Ruhepunkt, *m./* Unterbrechung, *f.*	pause, *f./*arrêt, *m./* hésitation, *f.*
104	peak, n.	пик, *m./*вершина, *f.*	Gipfel, *m.*	sommet, *m.*
105	peculiarity, n.	особенность, *f.*	Eigentümlichkeit, *f.*	particularité, *f.*
106	pedagogic(al), adj.	педагогический	pädagogisch	pédagogique
107	pedagogy, n.	педагогика, *f.*	Pädagogik, *f.*	pédagogie, *f.*
108	pedantic, adj.	педантичный	pedantisch	pédantesque
109	pejorative, adj.	уничижительный	heruntermachend/ verschlechternd	péjoratif

No.	ENGLISH	RUSSIAN	GERMAN	FRENCH
110	pen, n.	перо, *n.*/ручка, *f.*	Schreibfeder, *f.*	plume, *f.*/stylo, *m.*/ crayon à bille, *m.*
111	pencil, n.	карандаш, *m.*	Bleistift, *m.*	crayon, *m.*
112	pen-name, n.	псевдоним, *m.*	Pseudonym, *n.*/ Schriftstellername, *m.*	pseudonyme littéraire, *m.*
113	penetration, n.	проникновение, *n.*	Durchdringung, *f.*	pénétration, *f.*
114	pentasyllable, n.	пятисложное слово	fünfsilbiges Wort	mot de cinq syllabes, *m.*
115	penultimate syllable	предпоследний слог	Penultima, *f.*/ vorletzte Silbe	syllabe pénultième, *f.*/ syllabe avant- dernière, *f.*
116	(a) people, n.	народ, *m.*	Volk, *n.*	peuple, *m.*
117	percent, percentage, n.	процент, *m.*	Prozent, *n.*/ Prozentsatz, *m.*	pourcentage, *m.*
118	perceptible, adj.	воспринимаемый	wahrnehmbar	perceptible/sensible
119	perception, n.	восприятие, *n.*	Wahrnehmung, *f.*	perception, *f.*/ sensibilité, *f.*
120	perceptual phonetics	слуховая фонетика	auditive Phonetik	phonétique auditive, *f.*
121	perfect, adj.	идеальный	vollkommen	complet/parfait
122	perfect pitch	абсолютный слух	absolutes Gehör	oreille absolue, *f.*
123	perfect tense	перфект, *m.*	Perfekt(um), *n.*	parfait, *m.*/ passé composé, *m.*
124	perfective aspect	совершенный вид	perfektive Aktionsart	aspect perfectif, *m.*
125	perforated card	перфокарта, *f.*	Lochkarte, *f.*	carte perforée, *f.*
126	perforated tape	перфолента, *f.*	Lochband, *m.*/Loch- streifen, *f.*	bande perforée, *f.*/ ruban perforé, *m.*
127	performance, n.	выполнение, *n.*/ исполнение, *n.*	Ausführung, *f.*/ Leistung, *f.*	exécution, *f.*
128	period (punctuation), n.	точка, *f.*	Punkt, *m.*	point, *m.*
129	period (phrase), n.	синтагма, *f.*	Periode, *f.*/Takt, *m.*	période, *f.*
130	period of development	период развития, *m.*	Entwicklungsperiode, *f.*	période de développement, *f.*

No.	ENGLISH	RUSSIAN	GERMAN	FRENCH
131	period of history	эпоха, *f.*/исторический период	Zeitalter, *n.*	époque, *f.*
132	period of time	промежуток времени, *m.*	Zeitspanne, *f.*/ Umlaufszeit, *f.*	espace de temps, *m.*
133	periodic, adj.	периодический	periodisch	périodique
134	periodical, n.	журнал, *m.*/ периодическое издание	Zeitschrift, *f.*	périodique, *m.*/publication périodique, *f.*
135	peripheral, adj.	периферический/ побочный	peripherisch/Rand-	périphérique
136	peripheral phenomenon	побочное явление	Randerscheinung, *f.*	phénomène périphérique, *m.*
137	peripheral system	побочная система	peripheres System/ Randsystem, *n.*	système périphérique, *m.*
138	periphery, n.	периферия, *f.*	Peripherie, *f.*	périphérie, *f.*
139	periphrasis, n.	перифраза, *f.*	Umschreibung, *f.*	périphrase, *f.*/ circonlocution, *f.*
140	periphrastic conjugation	перифрастическое спряжение	periphrastische Konjugation	conjugaison périphrastique, *f.*
141	permanence, n.	постоянность, *f.*/ устойчивость, *f.*	Beständigkeit, *f.*	permanence, *f.*
142	permanent, adj.	постоянный/ неизменный	dauernd/ständig/stetig	permanent
143	permanent storage	постоянная память	Permanentspeicher, *m.*/ Dauerspeicher, *m.*	mémoire permanent, *m.*
144	permansive aspect	устойчивый вид	Permansiv(um), *m.*	permansif, *m.*
145	permissible, adj.	допустимый	zulässig	tolérable
146	permission, n.	разрешение, *n.*/ позволение, *n.*	Erlaubnis, *f.*	permission, *f.*
147	permitted sequence	допустимое сочетание	zugelassene Anordnung	séquence admissible, *f.*
148	permutation, n.	перемещение, *n.*/ перестановка, *f.*	Permutation, *f.*	permutation, *f.*
149	perpendicular, adj.	перпендикулярный	senkrecht	perpendiculaire

No.	English	Russian	German	French
150	perpetual, adj.	вечный	ewig	perpétuel
151	perpetuation, n.	увековечение, *n.*	Verewigung, *f.*	perpétuation, *f.*
152	Persian, adj.	персидский/иранский	persisch	persan, *m.*
153	person, n.	лицо, *n.*/человек, *m.*	Person, *f.*/Mensch, *m.*	personne, *f.*
154	personal endings, pl.	личные окончания, *n.,* pl.	Person alendungen, *f.,* pl.	terminaisons personnelles, *f.,* pl.
155	personal name	лцчное имя	Personenname, *m.*	nom de personne, *m.*
156	personal opinion	личное мнение	eigene Meinung	opinion personnelle, *f.*
157	personal pronoun	личное местоимение	Personalpronomen, *n.*/ persönliches Fürwort	pronom personnel, *m.*
158	personality, n.	личность, *f.*/ индивидуальность, *f.*	Persönlichkeit, *f.*/ Individualität, *f.*	personnalité, *f.*
159	personification, n.	олицетворение, *n.*/ воплощение, *n.*	Personifizierung, *f.*/ Belebung, *f.*	personnification, *f.*
160	perspective, n.	перспектива, *f.*/ вид, *m.*	Perspektive, *f.*/Aussicht, *f.*/Ausblick, *m.*	perspective, *f.*
161	pertinent, adj.	подходящий/ уместный	treffend/zutreffend/ angemessen	à propos
162	perturbation, n.	возбуждение, *n.*	Erregung, *f.*/Störung, *f.*	perturbation, *f.*
163	petrified form	застывшая форма/ окаменевшая форма	erstarrte Form	forme figée, *f.*/ forme fixe, *f.*
164	petrification, n.	фиксация, *f.*/ окаменение, *n.*	Erstarrung, *f.*/ Versteinerung, *f.*	fixation, *f.*
165	phantasy, n.	фантазия, *f.*	Phantasie, *f.*	fantaisie, *f.*/illusion, *f.*/ chimère, *f.*
166	phantom word	слово-празрак, *n.*	Phantomwort, *m.*/ vox nihili	mot-fantôme, *m.*
167	pharyngeal consonants, pl.	фарингальные согласные, pl.	Kehlkopflaute, *m.,* pl.	consonnes pharyngiennes, *f.,* pl.
168	pharyngealization, n.	фарингализация, *f.*	Pharyngalisierung, *f.*	pharyngealisation, *f.*

No.	ENGLISH	RUSSIAN	GERMAN	FRENCH
169	pharynx, n.	глотка, *f./*зев, *m.*	Rachenhöhle, *f.*	pharynx, *m.*
170	phase, n.	фаза, *f./*стадия, *f.*	Entwicklungsstufe, *f./* Stadium, *n.*	phase, *f.*
171	phenomenon, n.	явление, *n.*	Phänomen, *n./* Erscheinung, *f.*	phénomème, *m.*
172	philological, adj.	филологический/ языковедческий	philologisch/sprachwis- senschaftlich	philologique
173	philology, n.	филология, *f./* языковедение, *n.*	Philologie, *f./*Sprachwis- senschaft, *f.*	philologie, *f.*
174	philosophy, n.	философия, *f.*	Philosophie, *f.*	philosophie, *f.*
175	phonation, n.	фонация, *f.*	Lauthervorbringung, *f./* Lautäusserung, *f.*	phonation, *f.*
176	phone, n.	фона, *f./*звук речи, *m./* фонетическая единица	Phon, *n./*phonetische Einheit/Sprechlaut, *m.*	son du langage, *m./* unité phonétique, *f.*
177	phoneme, n.	фонема, *f.*	Phonem, *n.*	phonème, *m.*
178	phoneme alternant	вариант фонемы, *m./* аллофон, *m.*	Phonemvariante, *f.*	variante de phonème, *f.*
179	phoneme alternation	чередование фонем, *n.*	Phonemwechsel, *m.*	alternance de phonèmes, *f.*
180	phoneme boundary	граница фонемы, *f.*	Phonemgrenze, *f.*	frontière de phonème, *f.*
181	phoneme class	фонемный класс	Phonemklasse, *f.*	classe de phonèmes, *f.*
182	phoneme cluster	группа фонем, *f.*	Phonemgruppe, *f.*	combinaison de phonèmes, *m.*
183	phoneme combination	сочетание фонем, *n.*	Phonemkombination, *f.*	combinaison de phonèmes, *f.*
184	phoneme component	компонент фонемы, *m.*	Phonemkomponente, *f.*	composant de phonème, *m.*
185	phoneme concept	понятие о фонеме, *n.*	Phonembegriff, *m.*	concept de phonème, *m.*
186	phoneme contrast	сопоставление фонем, *n* .	Phonemkontrast, *m.*	contraste de phonèmes, *m.*

No.	ENGLISH	RUSSIAN	GERMAN	FRENCH
187	phoneme definition	определение фонемы, *n.*	Phonemdefinition, *f./* Phonembegriffs-bestimmung, *f.*	définition du phonème, *f.*
188	phoneme distribution	распределение фонем, *n.*	Phonemverteilung, *f.*	distribution des phonèmes, *f.*
189	phoneme frequency	частота фонем, *f.*	Phonemfrequenz, *f./* Phonemhäufigkeit, *f.*	fréquence des phonèmes, *f.*
190	phoneme inventory	инвентарь фонем, *m.*	Phoneminventar, *n.*	inventaire de phonèmes, *m.*
191	phoneme juncture	стык фонем, *m.*	Phonemverbindung, *f.*	jonction de phonèmes, *f.*
192	phoneme length	длительность фонемы, *f.*	Phonemdauer, *f.*	durée d'un phonème, *f.*
193	phoneme member	вариант фонемы, *m./* член фонемы, *m.*	Phonemglied, *n./* Phonemvariante, *f.*	membre de phonème, *m./* variante de phonème, *f.*
194	phoneme merger	слияние фонем, *n.*	Phonemzusammenfall, *m.*	fusion de phonèmes, *f.*
195	phoneme neutralization	нейтрализация фонем, *f.*	Phonemaufhebung, *f.*	neutralisation de phonèmes, *f.*
196	phoneme opposition	противопоставление фонем, *n.*	Phonemopposition, *f.*	opposition entre phonèmes, *f.*
197	phoneme pair	фонемная пара	Phonempaar, *n.*	couple de phonèmes, *m.*
198	phoneme realization	реализация фонемы, *f./* актуализация фонемы, *f./* манифестация фонемы, *f.*	Phonemrealisierung, *f./* Phonemaktualisie-rung, *f.*	réalisation de phonème, *f.*
199	phoneme sequence	последовательность фонем, *f./*сочетание фонем, *n.*	Phonemfolge, *f./* Phonemgruppe, *f.*	groupe de phonèmes, *m./* succession de phonèmes, *f./*suite de phonèmes, *f.*
200	phoneme series	фонемный ряд	Phonemreihe, *f.*	série de phonèmes, *f.*
201	phoneme split	расподобление фонемы, *n.*	Phonemspaltung, *f.*	dédoublement de phonème, *m./* bifurcation de phonème, *f.*

No.	ENGLISH	RUSSIAN	GERMAN	FRENCH
202	phoneme stress	ударение фонемы, *n.*	Phonembetonung, *f.*	accent de phonème, *m.*
203	phoneme system	система фонем, *f.*	Phonemsystem, *n.*	système de phonèmes, *m.*
204	phoneme variant	вариант фонемы, *m./* аллофон, *m.*	Phonemvariante, *f.*	variante de phonèmes, *f.*
205	phonemic, adj.	фонематический/ фонемный/ фонологический	Phonem- /phonematisch/ phonologisch	phonèmique/ phonèmatique/ phonologique
206	phonemic alternation	фонемное чередование	phonematischer Wechsel	alternance phonémique, *f.*
207	phonemic alphabet	фонемный алфавит	phonematisches Alphabet	alphabet phonémique, *m.*
208	phonemic analysis	фонемный анализ	phonematische Analyse	analyse phonémique, *f.*
209	phonemic change	фонемное изменение	phonematische Veränderung	changement phonémique, *m.*
210	phonemic component	фонемный компонент	phonematische Komponente	composant phonémique, *m.*
211	phonemic conditioning	фонемное обусловление	phonematische Bedingung	conditionnement phonémique, *m.*
212	phonemic contrast	фонемное сопоставление	phonematischer Kontrast	contraste phonémique, *m.*
213	phonemic correlation	фонемное соотн- ошение	phonematische Korrelation	corrélation phonémique, *f.*
214	phonemic description	фонемное описание	phonematische Beschreibung	description phonémique, *f.*
215	phonemic dialect differ- ences, pl.	фонемные диалектальные различия, *n., pl.*	phonematische Dialekt- unterschiede, *f., pl.*	différences dialectales phonèmiques, *f., pl.*
216	phonemic distinction	фонемное различие	phonematischer Unterschied	distinction phonémique, *f.*
217	phonemic features, pl.	фонемные признаки, *m., pl.*	phonematische Merkmale, *n., pl.*	traits phonématiques, *m., pl.*
218	phonemic inventory	фонемный инвентарь	Phoneminventar, *n.*	inventaire phonémique, *m.*

No.	ENGLISH	RUSSIAN	GERMAN	FRENCH
219	phonemic juncture	фонемный стык	phonematische Verbindung	jonction phonémique, *f.*
220	phonemic length	фонемная длительность	phonematische Dauer	durée phonémique, *f.*
221	phonemic level	фонемный уровень	phonematische Ebene	niveau phonémique, *m.*
222	phonemic merging	фонемное слияние	phonematischer Zusammenfall	fusion phonémique, *f.*
223	phonemic neutralization	фонемная нейтрал-изация	phonematische Aufhebung	neutralisation phonémique, *f.*
224	phonemic opposition	фонемное противо-поставление	phonematische Opposition	opposition phonémique, *f.*
225	phonemic principle	фонемный принцип	phonematisches Prinzip	principe phonémique, *m.*
226	phonemic shape	фонемная форма	phonematische Form	forme phonémique, *f.*
227	phonemic splitting	фонемное расподобление	phonematische Spaltung	dédoublement phonémique, *m.*
228	phonemic stress	фонемное ударение	phonematische Betonung	accent phonémique, *m.*
229	phonemic system	фонемная сиятема	phonematisches System	système phonémique, *m.*
230	phonemic tone	фонемный тон	phonematischer Ton	ton phonémique, *m.*
231	phonemic transcription	фонемная транскрипция/ фонемная запись	phonematische Umschrift	transcription phonémique, *f.*
232	phonemic typology	фонемная типология	phonematische Typologie	typologie phonémique, *f.*
233	phonemically different, adj.	фонематически различный	phonematisch verschieden	phonémiquement différent
234	phonemically irrelevant, adj.	фонематически недифференциаль-ный	phonematisch belanglos/ redundant	non pertinent/redondant
235	phonemicization, n.	фонематизация, *f.*/ фонемизация, *f.*/ фонологизация, *f.*	Phonemisierung, *f.*/ Phonologisierung, *f.*/ Lautwertung, *f.*	phonémisation, *f.*/ phonologisation, *f.*
236	phonemics, n.	фонематика, *f.*/ фонемика, *f.*	Phonematik, *f.*	phonématique, *f.*/ phonémique, *f.*

No.	ENGLISH	RUSSIAN	GERMAN	FRENCH
237	phonetic, adj.	фонетический	phonetisch/Laut-	phonétique
238	phonetic abstraction	фонетическая абстракция	phonetische Abstraktion	abstraction phonétique, *f.*
239	phonetic alphabet	фонетический алфавит	phonetisches Alphabet	alphabet phonétique, *m.*
240	phonetic alternation	фонетическое чередование	phonetischer Wechsel	alternance phonétique, *f.*
241	phonetic analysis	фонетический анализ	phonetische Analyse	analyse phonétique, *f.*
242	phonetic change	фонетическое изменение	phonetische Veränderung	changement phonétique, *m.*
243	phonetic data, pl.	фонетические данные, pl.	phonetische Grundlagen, *f.*, pl.	données phonétiques, *f.*, pl.
244	phonetic description	фонетическое описание	phonetische Beschreibung	description phonétique, *f.*
245	phonetic dialect differences, pl.	фонетические диалектальные различия, *n.*, pl.	phonetische Dialektunterschiede, *m.*, pl.	différences dialectales phonétiques, *f.*, pl.
246	phonetic environment	фонетическое окружение	phonetische Umgebung	contexte phonétique, *m.*
247	phonetic law	фонетический закон	Lautgesetz, *n.*	loi phonétique, *f.*
248	phonetic level	фонетический уровень	phonetische Ebene	niveau phonétique, *m.*
249	phonetic process	фонетический процесс/звуковой процесс	phonetischer Vorgang	processus phonétique, *m.*
250	phonetic script	фонетическое письмо	Lautschrift, *f.*	écriture phonétique, *f.*
251	phonetic similarity	фонетическое сходство/фонетическая близость	phonetische Ähnlichkeit/ phonetische Verwandtschaft	ressemblance phonétique, *f.*
252	phonetic spelling	фонетическое правописание	phonetische Schreibung	graphie phonétique, *f.*
253	phonetic substitution	фонетическая замена	phonetische Ersetzung	substitution phonétique, *f.*

No.	ENGLISH	RUSSIAN	GERMAN	FRENCH
254	phonetic transcription	фонетическая транскрипция/ фонетическая запись	Lautschrift, *f./* phonetische Umschrift	transcription phonétique, *f.*
255	phonetic variation	фонетическая вариация	phonetische Variation	variation phonétique, *f.*
256	phonetic word	фонетичеякое слово	phonetisches Wort	mot phonétique, *m.*
257	phonetically similar, adj.	фонетически сходный /фонетически близкий	phonetisch verwandt/ phonetisch ähnlich	phonétiquement semblable
258	phonetics, n.	фонетика, *f.*	Phonetik, *f./*Lautlehre, *f.*	phonétique, *f.*
259	phonic, adj.	фонический/ акустический	lautlich/akustisch	phonique
260	phonograph, n.	граммофон, *m./* патефон, *m.*	Plattenspieler, *m./* Grammophon, *n.*	gramophone, *m./* phonographe, *m.*
261	phonograph record	патефонная пластинка	Schallplatte, *f.*	disque, *m.*
262	phonological, adj.	фонологический	phonologisch	phonologique
263	phonological change	фонологическое изменение	phonologische Veränderung	changement phonologique, *m.*
264	phonological conditioning	фонологическое обусловление	phonologische Bedingung	conditionnement phonologique, *m.*
265	phonological merging	фонологическое смешение	Zusammenfall phonologischer Einheiten, *m.*	fusion phonologique, *f.*
266	phonological opposition	фонологическая оппозиция/ фонологическое противопоставление	phonologische Opposition	opposition phonologique, *f.*
267	phonological splitting	фонологический распад	Phonemspaltung, *f.*	dédoublement phonologique, *m.*
268	phonological system	фонологическая система, *f.*	phonologisches System, *n.*	système phonologique, *m.*
269	phonologically different, adj.	фонологически различный	phonologisch unterschieden	phonologiquement différent
270	phonologically similar, adj.	фонологически сходный	phonologisch ähnlich	phonologiquement semblable

No.	ENGLISH	RUSSIAN	GERMAN	FRENCH
271	phonology, n.	фонология, *f.*	Phonologie, *f.*	phonologie, *f.*
272	phonometrics, phonometry, n.	фонометрия, *f.*	Phonometrie, *f.*	phonométrie, *f.*
273	phonotactics, n.	фонотактика, *f.*	kombinatorische Phonetik	phonétique combinatoire, *f.*
274	phrase, n.	оборот речи, *m./* словосочетание, *n.*	Redewendung, *f./* Wortgefüge, *n.*	locution, *f./*expression, *f.* /groupe de mots, *m.*
275	phrase book	фразеологический словарь	Buch mit Redewendungen, *n.*	recueil d'expressions, *m.*
276	phrase structure	фразеологическая структура	Satzgliederungsstruktur, *f./*Satzstruktur, *f.*	structure phraséologique, *f.*
277	phrase structure model	модель непосредственно составляющих, *f.*	Modell der unmittelbaren Bestandteile, *n.*	modèle de constituants immèdiats, *m.*
278	phraseology, n.	фразеология, *f.*	Phraseologie, *f.*	phraséologie, *f.*
279	physical characteristics, pl.	физические свойства, *n., pl.*	physiche Eigenschaften, *f., pl.*	traits physiques, *m., pl.*
280	physical fact	физический факт	physische Tatsache	fait physique, *m.*
281	physical nature	физическая природа	physische Welt/ Erscheinungswelt, *f.*	nature physique, *f.*
282	physical reality	физическая реальность	physische Wirklichkeit	réalité physiqe, *f.*
283	physics, n.	физика, *f.*	Physik, *f.*	physique, *f.*
284	physiological phonetics	физиологическая фонетика	physiologische Phonetik	phonétique physiologique, *f.*
285	physiology, n.	физиология, *f.*	Physiologie, *f.*	physiologie, *f.*
286	pictographic writing	пиктография, *f./* письмо рисунками, *n.*	Bilderschrift, *f.*	écriture pictographique, *f.*
287	picture, n.	картина, *f./* изображение, *n.*	Bild, *n.*	image, *f.*
288	pidgin languages, pl.	ломаные языки-посредники, *m., pl.*	Pidgin-Sprachen, *f., pl.*	langues dites "pidgin", *f., pl.*

No.	ENGLISH	RUSSIAN	GERMAN	FRENCH
289	pitch, n.	высота тона, *f.*	Tonhöhe, *f.*	hauteur de ton, *f.*
290	pitch accent	тональное ударение	melodische Betonung	accent de hauteur, *m.*/ accent mélodique, *m.*
291	pitch contour	тональная оболочка	Tonhöhenkurve, *f.*	contour des tons, *m.*
292	pitch sequence	тональная послеовательность	Tonhöhenfolge, *f.*	succession de tons, *f.*
293	placard, n.	афиша, *f.*/плакат, *m.*	Anschlagzettel, *m.*/ Plakat, *n.*	affiche, *f.*
294	place names, pl.	топономика, *f.*/ названия мест, *m.*, pl.	Ortsnamen, *m.*, pl.	noms de lieux, *m.*, pl.
295	place of articulation	место образования звука, *n.*	Artikulationsstelle, *f.*	région d'articulation, *f.*
296	place of juncture	место стыка, *n.*	Verbindungsstelle, *f.*	lieu de jonction, *m.*
297	place of stress	место ударения, *n.*	Betonungsstelle, *f.*	position de l'accent, *f.*
298	placement, n.	поставление, *n.*/ постановка, *f.*/ расстановка, *f.*	Stellung, *f.*	mise, *f.*
299	plagiarism, n.	плагиат, *m.*	Plagiat, *n.*/ Gedankenraub, *m.*/ literarischer Diebstahl	plagiat, *m.*/ démarquage, *m.*
300	plan, n.	план, *m.*/проект, *m.*	Entwurf, *m.*/Plan, *m.*	plan, *m.*/projet, *m.*
301	plane, n.	плоскость, *f.*/ уровень, *m.*	Ebene, *f.*/Flache, *f.*	plan, *m.*/niveau, *m.*
302	planned intervention in language development	умышленное вмешательство в развитие языка	planmässiger Eingriff in die Sprachentwicklung	interventions planifiées dans l'évolution des langues, *f.*, pl.
303	platitude, n.	банальность, *f.*	Platitude, *f.*/ Seichtheit, *f.*/ Gemeinplatz, *m.*	platitude, *f.*/ lieu commun, *m.*
304	plausible, adj.	правдоподобный/ вероятный	wahrscheinlich/ einleuchtend	plausible/vraisemblable
305	play on words	игра слов, *f.*	Wortspiel, *n.*	jeu de mots, *m.*/ calembour, *m.*

No.	ENGLISH	RUSSIAN	GERMAN	FRENCH
306	playback, n.	прослушивание, *n.*	Wiedergabe, *f.*	lecture de la bande, *f.*
307	pleonasm, n.	плеоназм, *m.*	Pleonasmus, *m.*/ Wortüberfluss, *m.*	pleonasme, *m.*
308	plosive consonants, pl.	взрывные согласные, *m.,* pl.	Explosivlaute, *m.,* pl.	consonnes explosives, *f.,* pl.
309	pluperfect tense	прюсквамперфект, *m.*/ давнопрошедшее время	Plusquamperfekt, *n.*	plus que parfait, *m.*
310	plural number	множественное число	Plural, *m.*/Mehrzahl, *f.*	pluriel, *m.*
311	plus feature	признак плюс, *m.*	positives Merkmal	trait positif, *m.*
312	plus juncture	открытый переход	offene Verbindung/ offener Übergang	transition ouverte, *f.*
313	plus sign (+)	знак плюса, *m.*	Pluszeichen, *n.*	signe plus, *m.*
314	poem, n.	поэма, *f.*/стихи, pl./ стихотворение, *n.*	Gedicht, *n.*	poème, *m.*
315	poet, n.	поэт, *m.*	Dichter, *m.*	poète, *m.*
316	poetic language	поэтический язык, *m.*	poetische Sprache/ Dicthersprache, *f.*	langage poétique, *m.*
317	poetic license	вольность поэта, *f.*	dichterische Freiheit	licence poétique, *f.*
318	poetic usage	поэтическое употребление	poetischer Gebrauch	emploi poétique, *m.*
319	poetics, n.	поэтика. *f.*	Poetik, *f.*	poétique, *f.*
320	poetry, n.	поэзия, *f.*/стихи, pl.	Dichtung, *f.*	poésie, *f.*
321	point, v.	показывать пальцем/ указывать	mit Fingern zeigen	montrer du doigt
322	point, n.	пункт, *m.*/точка, *f.*	Punkt, *m.*	point, *m.*
323	point of articulation	место образования звука, *n.*	Artikulationsstelle, *f.*/ Bildungsstelle, *f.*	point d'articulation, *m.*
324	point of view	точка зрения, *f.*	Ansicht, *f.*/Erachten, *n.*/ Meinung, *f.*/ Standpunkt, *m.*/ Gesichtspunkt, *m.*	point de vue, *m.*/ opinion, *f.*

No.	ENGLISH	RUSSIAN	GERMAN	FRENCH
325	polar expressions, pl.	полярные выражения, *n.*, pl.	polare Ausdrücke, *m.*, pl.	expressions polaires, *f.*, pl.
326	polarity, n.	полярность, *f.*	Polarität, *f.*	polarité, *f.*
327	polarization, n.	поляризация, *f.*	Polarisierung, *f.*	polarisation, *f.*
328	polemics, n.	полемика, *f.*	Polemik, *f.*	polémique, *f.*
329	policy, n.	политика, *f.*	Politik, *f.*	politique, *f.*
330	Polish, adj.	польский	polnisch	polonais
331	polite form	вежливая форма	höfliche Anredeform	vousvoiement, *m.*
332	polite speech	вежливая речь	höfliche Redeweise/ Respektssprache, *f.*	langage poli, *m.*
333	political community	политическая община	politisches Gemeinwesen	communauté politique, *f.*
334	politics, n.	политика, *f.*	Politik, *f.*	politique, *f.*
335	poly-	поли- /много-	Poly- /Viel-	poly-
336	polyglot, adj.	многоязычный	mehrsprachig	polyglotte
337	polyglot, n.	полиглот, *m.*	Polyglotte, *m.*	polyglotte, *s.*
338	polysemy, n.	полисемия, *f.*/ многозначность, *f.*	Polysemie, *f.*/ Mehrdeutigkeit, *f.*	polysémie, *f.*
339	polysyllabic, adj.	многосложный	mehrsilbig	polysyllabique
340	polysynthetic languages, pl.	полисинтетические языки, *m.*, pl.	polysynthetische Sprachen, *f.*, pl.	langues poly- synthétiques, *f.*, pl.
341	polytonic languages, pl.	многотонные языки, *m.*, pl.	polytonische Sprachen, *f.*, pl.	langues polytoniques, *f.*, pl.
342	popular expression	просторечие, *n.*	volkstümliche Redewendung	expression populaire, *f.*/ expression vulgaire, *f.*
343	popular etymology	народная этимология	Volksetymologie, *f.*	étymologie populaire, *f.*
344	population, n.	население, *n.*	Bevölkerung, *f.*	population, *f.*
345	pornography, n.	порнография, *f.*	Pornographie, *f.*	pornographie, *f.*

No.	ENGLISH	RUSSIAN	GERMAN	FRENCH
346	portmanteau morpheme	морфемная смесь	unteilbare, zwei Morpheme enhaltende Form	forme indivisible contenant deux morphèmes, f.
347	portmanteau word	словесная смесь	Schachtelwort, n.	mot gigogne, m./ mot-valise, m./ amalgame, m.
348	Portuguese, adj.	португальский	portugiesisch	portugais
349	position, n.	позиция, f./ положение, n.	Stellung, f.	position, f./place, f.
350	position in sentence	место в предложении, n.	Satzstellung, f.	place dans la phrase, f.
351	position of neutralization	позиция нейтрализация, f.	Aufhebungsstellung, f.	position de neutralisation, f.
352	position of rest	состояние покоя, n./ нейтральное положение	Indifferenzlage, f./ Ruhelage, f.	position d'indifférence, f.
353	position of the tongue	подъем языка, n./ положение языка, m.	Zungenstellung, f.	position de la langue, f.
354	position of the lips	полежение губ, n.	Lippenstellung, f.	position des lèvres, f.
355	positional change	позиционное изменение	kombinatorischer Wechsel	changement combinatoire, m.
356	positional conditioning	позиционное обусловление	Stellungsbedingung, f.	conditionnement contextuel, m.
357	positional variant	позиционный вариант	Stellungsvariante, f.	variante de position, f.
358	positive degree	положительная степень	Grundstufe, f./positive Steigerungsstufe	degré positif, m.
359	positive sentence	положительное предложение	Positivsatz, m.	phrase positive, f.
360	positive sign (+)	знак плюса, m.	Pluszeichen, n.	signe plus, m.
361	possession, n.	владение, n./ обладание, n.	Besitz, m.	possession, f.

No.	ENGLISH	RUSSIAN	GERMAN	FRENCH
362	possessive, adj.	притяжательный	besitzanzeigend	possessif
363	possessive adjective	притяжательное прилагательное	possessives Adjektiv	adjectif possessif, *m.*
364	possessive case	притяжательный падеж	Genetiv, *m.*/Wesfall, *m.*/ zweiter Fall	possessif, *m.*
365	possessive pronoun	притяжательное местоимение	Possessivpronomen, *n.*/ besitzanzeigendes Fürwort	pronom possessif, *m.*
366	possessor, n.	владелец, *m.*/ обладатель, *m.*	Besitzer, *m.*	possesseur, *m.*
367	possibility, n.	возможность, *f.*	Möglichkeit, *f.*	possibilité, *f.*/ éventualité, *f.*
368	possible, adj.	возможный	möglich/eventuell	possible/éventuel
369	postcard, n.	открытка, *f.*/ почтовая карточка	Postkarte, *f.*	carte postale, *f.*
370	post-editing, n.	последующее редактирование	Nachbearbeitung, *f.*	corrections ultérieures, *f., pl.*
371	postfix, n.	постфикс, *m.*	Suffix, *n.*	suffixe, *m.*
372	post-graduate student (pre-doctoral)	аспирант, *m.*/ кандидат, *m.*	Doktorand, *m.*/ Cand. Phil.	licencié, *s.*
373	postdental, adj.	зазубный	postdental	postdental
374	postpalatal, adj.	занебный	postpalatal	postpalatal
375	postposition, n.	постпозиция, *f.*	Postposition, *f.*/ Nachstellung, *f.*	postposition, *f.*
376	postscript (P.S.), n.	постскриптум, *m.*	Postskriptum, *n.*/ Nachschrift, *f.*	post-scriptum, *m.*
377	post-tonic, adj.	заударный	nachtönig	post-tonique
378	postvelar, adj.	завелярный	postvelar	postvélaire
379	postulate, n.	постулат, *m.*	Grundvoraussetzung, *f.*	postulat, *m.*
380	potential, adj.	потенциальный/ возможный	möglich	potentiel/possible

No.	ENGLISH	RUSSIAN	GERMAN	FRENCH
381	potential vocabulary	потенциальный словарь	möglicher Wortschatz	vocabulaire potentiel, *m.*
382	power, n.	сила, *f.*	Kraft, *f.*	puissance, *f.*
383	powerful, adj.	сильный/мощный	kräftig/mächtig/stark	puissant
384	practical, adj.	практический	praktisch	pratique
385	prayer, n.	молитва, *f.*	Gebet, *n.*	prière, *f.*
386	prayer book	молитвослов, *m.*/ требник, *m.*	Gebetbuch, *n.*	livre de prières, *m.*/ eucologe, *m.*
387	preaching, n.	проповедование, *n.*	Predigen, *n.*	prédication, *f.*/sermon, *m.*
388	preaspiration, n.	предаспирация, *f.*	Vorbehauchung, *f.*	préaspiration, *f.*
389	preceding, adj.	предшествующий/ предыдущий	vorhergehend	précédent
390	precise, adj.	точный	genau	précis
391	precision, n.	точность, *f.*	Präzision, *f.*/ Genauigkeit, *f.*	précision, *f.*
392	preconception, n.	предвзятое мнение/ предвзятость, *f.*	Voreingenommenheit, *f.*	idée préconçue, *f.*
393	predecessor, n.	предшественник, *m.*	Vorgänger, *m.*	prédécesseur, *m.*
394	predetermination, n.	предопределение, *n.*	Vorherbestimmung, *f.*	détermination antérieure, *f.*
395	predicate, n.	предикат, *m.*/ сказуемое, *n.*	Prädikat, *n.*/ Satzaussage, *f.*	prédicat, *m.*
396	predicate adjective	именное сказуемое выраженное прилагательным	adjektivisches Prädikatsnomen	attribut prédicatif, *m.*
397	predicate complement	именное сказуемое	Prädikatsnomen, *n.*	complément prédicatif, *m.*
398	predicate noun	именное сказуемое выраженное существительным	substantivisches Prädikatsnomen	nom prédicatif, *m.*
399	predicative, adj.	предикативный	prädikativ	attributif

No.	English	Russian	German	French
400	predictability, n.	предсказуемость, *f.*	Vorhersagbarkeit, *f.*	prédictabilité, *f.*
401	predictable, adj.	предсказуемый	vorhersagbar	capable d'être prédit/ prévisible
402	predominant, predominating, adj.	приобладающий	vorherrschend	prédominant
403	preface, n.	предисловие, *n.*	Vorwort, *n.*	préface, *f.*
404	preference, n.	предпочтение, *n.*	Vorrang, *m.*/Vorzug, *m.*	préférence, *f.*
405	prefix, n.	префикс, *m.*/ приставка, *f.*	Präfix, *n.*/Vorsilbe, *f.*	préfixe, *m.*
406	prefixation, prefixion, prefixing, n.	префиксация, *f.*	Hinzufügung von Präfixen, *f.*	préfixation, *f.*
407	prehistoric, adj.	доисторический	prähistorisch/ vorgeschichtlich	préhistorique
408	prejudgement, n.	предрешение, *n.*	Vorurteil, *n.*	jugement prématuré, *m.*
409	prejudice, n.	предубеждение, *n.*	Voreingenommenheit, *f.*/ Vorurteil, *n.*	préjugé, *m.*
410	preliminaries, pl.	подготовительные мероприятия, *n.*, pl.	erste Schritte, *m.*, pl.	préliminaires, *m.*, pl.
411	preliminary, adj.	предварительный/ черновой	vorläufig/vorbereitend/ einleitend	préliminaire/préalable
412	preliminary classification	предварительная классификация	vorläufige Klassifizierung/vorläufige Einteilung	classement préliminaire, *m.*
413	premature, adj.	преждевременный	vorschnell/vorzeitig	prématuré
414	preparation, n.	подготовка, *f.*/ подготовление, *n.*	Vorbereitung, *f.*	préparation, *f.*
415	prepalatal, adj.	предалатальный	präpalatal	prépalatal
416	preponderance, n.	перевес, *m.*/ преобладание, *n.*	Übergewicht, *n.*	prépondérance, *f.*
417	preposition, n.	предлог, *m.*	Präposition, *f.*/ Verhältniswort, *n.*	préposition, *f.*

No.	ENGLISH	RUSSIAN	GERMAN	FRENCH
418	prepositional phrase	предложный оборот/ оборот речи с предлогом, *m.*	präpositionaler Ausdruck	locution prépositive, *f.*
419	prerequisite, n.	предпосылка, *f.*	Vorbedingung, *f.*	condition préalable, *f.*
420	prescriptive grammar	нормативная грамматика	präskriptive Grammatik/ normative Grammatik	grammaire normative, *f.*
421	presence, n.	наличие, *n.*/ присутствие, *n.*	Anwesenheit, *f.*/ Vorhandensein, *n.*	présence, *f.*
422	presentation, n.	представление, *n.*/ подача, *f.*	Darstellung, *f.*	présentation, *f.*
423	present-day, adj.	настоящий/ современный	heutig	actuel/d'aujourd'hui
424	present participle	причастие настоящего времени, *n.*	Präsenspartizip, *n.*/ Mittelwort der Gegenwart, *n.*	participe présent, *m.*
425	present perfect tense	перфект, *m.*	Perfekt(um), *n.*	parfait, *m.*
426	present tense	настоящее время	Präsens, *n.*/Gegenwart, *f.*	temps présent, *m.*
427	press, n.	пресса, *f.*/печать, *f.*	Presse, *f.*/Journalismus, *m.*/Zeitungswesen, *n.*	presse, *f.*
428	pressure, n.	давление, *n.*	Druck, *m.*	pression, *f.*
429	prestige, n.	престиж, *m.*	Prestige, *n.*	prestige, *m.*
430	prestige language	язык привилегированного класса, *m.*	Sprache der gehobenen Bevölkerungsschicht, *f*	langue de prestige, *f.*
431	preterite tense	прошедшее время	Präteritum, *n.*	prétérit, *m.*
432	pretonic, adj.	предударный	vortönig	prétonique
433	previous, adj.	предыдущий	vorhergehend	précédent/antérieur/ préalable
434	primary function	первичная функция	primäre Funktion	fonction primaire, *f.*
435	primary language	первобытный язык	ursprüngliche Sprache/ Ursprache, *f.*	langue originelle, *f.*/ langue primitive, *f.*

No.	ENGLISH	RUSSIAN	GERMAN	FRENCH
436	primary school	начальная школа	Grundschule, f./Volks-schule, f./Vorschule, f.	école primaire, f.
437	primary meaning	основное значение	Hauptbedeutung, f.	sens primaire, m.
438	primary signal system	первичная сигнальная система	⟨primäres Zeichen-system⟩	système de signes primaire, m.
439	primary stress	главное ударение	Hauptton, m./ Starkton, m.	accent principal, m.
440	prime, n.	первичный элемент	Primärelement, n.	élément, m.
441	primer, n.	букварь, m.	Fibel, f.	premier livre, m.
442	primitive peoples, pl.	малоразвитые народы, m., pl.	Naturvölker, n., pl.	peuples primitifs, m., pl.
443	primitive society	примитивное общество	primitive Gesellschaft	société primitive, f.
444	primitive system	простая система	einfaches System	système primitif, m.
445	primitive thought	примитивное мышление	primitives Denken	pensée primitive, f.
446	primitive verb	глагол-основа, m.	Stammzeitwort, n.	verbe-racine, m.
447	principal clause	главное предложение	Hauptsatz, m.	proposition principale, f.
448	principal parts of the sentence, pl.	главные члены предложения, m., pl.	Satzgrundbestandteile, m., pl.	parties principales de la phrase, f., pl.
449	principal parts of the verb, pl.	основные формы глагола, f., pl.	Stammzeiten des Ver-bums, f., pl.	parties principales du verbe, f., pl.
450	principal variant	основной вариант	Grundvariante, f.	variante fondamentale, f.
451	principle, n.	принцип, m.	Prinzip, n./Grundsatz, m.	principe, m.
452	principle of economy	принцип экономии, m.	ökonomisches Prinzip/ Einsparungsprinzip, n./ Sparsamkeitsgrundsatz, m./ Wirtschaftlichkeit, f.	principe d'economie, m.
453	principle of least effort	принцип наимень-шего усилия, m.	Prinzip des geringsten Kraftaufwandes, n.	principe du moindre effort, m.

No.	ENGLISH	RUSSIAN	GERMAN	FRENCH
454	principle of simplicity	принцип простоты, *m.*	Prinzip der Einfachheit, *n.*	principe de simplicité, *m.*
455	principle of bi-unique-ness	⟨принцип двусторон-ной единичности⟩, *m.*	⟨Prinzip der doppelten Ein-Eindeutigkeit⟩, *n.*	principe du caractère bi-unique, *m.*
456	principle of total accountability	принцип полной подотчетности, *m.*	Prinzip der vollkom-menen Erklärlichkeit, *n.*	principe de la respon-sabilité totale, *m.*
457	print (by hand), v.	писать печатными буквами	in Blockbuchstaben schreiben/in Druckschrift schreiben	écrire en caractères d'imprimerie
458	print (by machine), v.	печатать	drucken	imprimer
459	printed, adj.	печатный	gedruckt	imprimé
460	printed matter	печатный материал	Drucksache, *f.*	imprimés, *m.*, pl.
461	printer's error	опечатка, *f.*	Druckfehler, *m.*	faute d'impression, *f.*/ coquille, *f.*
462	printing, n.	печать, *f.*/шрифт, *m.*	Druck, *f.*	impression, *f.*/ typographe, *m.*
463	printing ink	печатная краска	Druckerschwärze, *f.*	encre typographique, *f.*
464	printing press	печатный станок/ печатная машина	Druckpresse, *f.*	presse, *m.*
465	priority, n.	очередность, *f.*	Priorität, *f.*/Vorzug, *m.*	priorité, *f.*
466	private school (in U.S.)	частная школа	Privatschule, *f.*	école privée, *f.*
467	privative, adj.	отрицательный	verneinend	privatif
468	privative opposition	привитивное противоположение	privative Opposition	opposition privative, *f.*
469	privilege, n.	привилегия, *f.*	Privileg, *n.*/Vorrecht, *n.*	privilège, *m.*
475	probable, adj.	вероятный	wahrscheinlich	probable
476	probability, n.	вероятность, *f.*	Wahrscheinlichkeit, *f.*	probabilité, *f.*
477	problem, n.	проблема, *f.*/задача, *f.*/ вопрос, *m.*	Problem, *n.*/Aufgabe, *f.*/ schwierige Frage	problème, *m.*/question, *f.*

No.	ENGLISH	RUSSIAN	GERMAN	FRENCH
478	procedure, n.	процедура, *f.*/ методика, *f.*	Arbeitsweise, *f.*/ Verfahren, *n.*	procédé, *m.*
479	process, n.	процесс, *m.*	Vorgang, *m.*	processus, *m.*/ déroulement, *m.*
480	proclitic, n.	проклитика, *f.*	Proklise, *f.*/Proklitika, *f.*	proclitique, *m.*
481	produce, v.	производить	hervorbringen/ergeben	produire
482	product, n.	продукт, *m.*/ произведение, *n.*	Produkt, *n.*/Erzeugnis, *n.*	produit, *m.*/production, *f.*
483	productive class	продуктивный класс	produktive Klasse	classe productive, *f.*
484	productivity, n.	продуктивность, *f.*	Produktivität, *f.*	productivité, *f.*
485	profanity, n.	богохульство, *n.*/ похабщина, *f.*	Fluchen, *n.*	juron, *m.*/blasphème, *m.*
486	professional jargon	профессиональный жаргон	Berufsjargon, *m.*/ Berufssprache, *f.*	jargon professionnel, *m.*
487	proficiency in a language	степень совершенства языка, *f.*	Sprachfertigkeit, *f.*/ Sprachkenntnis, *f.*	maîtrise d'une langue, *f.*
488	proficiency test	испытание компетентности, *n.*	Leistungstest, *m.*	épreuves de compétence, *f.*, pl.
489	profile, n.	профиль, *m.*	Profil, *n.*	profil, *m.*
490	program, n.	программа, *f.*/ план работы, *m.*	Programm, *n.*/ Arbeitsplan, *m.*	programme, *m.*
491	programmed teaching material	программированное обучение	programmiertes Lehrwerk	instruction programmée, *f.*
492	programming (for computer), n.	программирование, *n.*	Programmierung, *f.*/ Plankalkül, *m.*	programmation, *f.*
493	programming language	язык для программирования, *m.*	Programmiersprache, *f.*	code de programmation, *m.*
494	progress, n.	прогресс, *m.*	Fortschritt, *m.*	progrès, *m.*
495	progress of events	ход событий, *m.*	Gang der Dinge, *m.*	cours des événements, *m.*

No.	ENGLISH	RUSSIAN	GERMAN	FRENCH
496	progressive aspect	продолженный вид	Dauerform des Ver-bums, *f.*	aspect progressif, *m.*
497	progressive assimilation	прогрессивная ассимиляция	progressive Assimilation /vorwirkende Assimi-lation	assimiltion progressive, *f.*
498	prohibition, n.	запрещение, *n.*	Verbot, *n.*	défense, *f.*/interdiction, *f.* /prohibition, *f.*
499	project, n.	проект, *m.*	Projekt, *n.*/Entwurf, *m.*	projet, *m.*
500	prolongation, n.	продление, *n.*/ продолжение, *n.*	Ausdehnung, *f.*/ Verlängerung, *f.*	prolongation, *f.*
501	prolonged, adj.	длительный/ затянувшийся	ausgedehnt	prolongé
502	prominent, adj.	выдающийся	hervorragend	important
503	promise, n.	обещание, *n.*	Versprechen, *n.*	promesse, *f.*
504	pronominal, adj.	местоименный	pronominal	pronominal
505	pronoun, n.	местоимение, *n.*	Pronomen, *n.*/Fürwort, *n.*	pronom, *m.*
506	pronounceable, adj.	удобопроизносимый	aussprechbar	prononçable
507	pronouncement, n.	произнесение, *n.*	Äusserung, *f.*	déclaration, *f.*
508	pronunciation, n.	произношение, *n.*	Aussprache, *f.*	prononciation, *f.*
509	proof, n.	доказательство, *n.*	Beweis, *n.*	preuve, *f.*
510	proofreading, n.	читка корректуры, *f.*	Korrekturlesen, *n.*	correction d'épreuves, *f.*
511	proof-sheet, n.	корректура, *f.*	Korrekturbogen, *m.*/ Korrekturfahne, *f.*	épreuve, *f.*
512	propaganda, n.	пропаганда, *f.*	Propaganda, *f.*/ Werbung, *f.*	propagande, *f.*
513	proper adjective	собственное прилагательное	eigentliches Adjektiv	adjectif propre, *m.*
514	proper name	собственное имя	Eigenname, *m.*	nom propre, *m.*

No.	ENGLISH	RUSSIAN	GERMAN	FRENCH
515	proper noun	имя существительное собственное	Eigenname, *m.*	nom propre, *m.*
516	proper sense	правильный смысл	eigentlicher Sinn/ richtiger Sinn	sens propre, *m.*/sens correct, *m.*
517	proper usage	правильное употребление	richtiger Gebrauch	bon usage, *m.*
518	proper word	подходящее слово	passendes Wort	mot propre, *m.*
519	property, n.	свойство, *n.*	Eigenschaft, *f.*/Eigentum, *n.*/Zug, *m.*	propriété, *f.*/ caractéristique, *f.*
520	proportion, n.	пропорция, *f.*	Verhältnis, *n.*	proportion, *f.*
521	proposed, adj.	предложенный	vorgelegt	proposé
522	prose, n.	проза, *f.*	Prosa, *f.*	prose, *f.*
523	prosodeme, n.	просодема, *f.*	Prosodem, *n.*	prosodème, *m.*
524	prosodic, adj.	просодический	prosodisch	prosodique
525	prosodic features, pl.	просодические признаки, *m.*, pl.	prosodische Züge, *m.*, pl.	caractéristiques prosodiqes, *f.*, pl.
526	prosody, n.	просодия, *f.*	Prosodie, *f.*/Verslehre, *f.*	prosodie, *f.*
527	prosthesis, n.	протез, *m.*/ поставление префикса, *n.*	Prothese, *f.*/Vorsetzung einer Silbe, *f.*	prosthèse, *f.*
528	proto-language, n.	праязык, *m.*	Protosprache, *f.*/Ursprache	protolangue, *f.*/ langue-mère, *f.*
529	prototype, n.	прототип, *m.*	Musterbild, *n.*	prototype, *m.*
530	provable, adj.	доказуемый	beweisbar	prouvable
531	proven, adj.	доказанный	erwiesen	éprouvé
532	proverb, n.	пословица, *f.*	Sprichwort, *n.*	proverbe, *m.*
533	provincialism, n.	областное выражение	Provinzialismus, *m.*/ Lokalausdruck, *m.*	provincialisme, *m.*
534	proximity, n.	близость, *f.*	Nähe, *f.*	proximité, *f.*
535	pseudonym, n.	псевдоним, *m.*	Pseudonym, *n.*/ Deckname, *m.*	pseudonyme, *m.*

No.	English	Russian	German	French
536	psychiatry, n.	психиатрия, *f.*	Psychiatrie, *f.*	psychiatrie, *f.*
537	psycholinguistics, n.	психолингвистика, *f.*/ психолгия языка, *f.*	Psycholinguistik, *f.*/ Sprachpsychologie, *f.*	psycholinguistique, *f.*
538	psychoanalysis	психоанализ, *m.*	Psychoanalyse, *f.*	psychanalyse, *f.*
539	psychological, adj.	психологический	psychologisch	psychologique
540	psychology, n.	психология, *f.*	Psychologie, *f.*	psychologie, *f.*
541	psychotherapy, n.	психотерапия, *f.*	Psychotherapie, *f.*	psychothérapie, *f.*
542	public, adj.	общенародный/ коммунальный	öffentlich	public
543	public instructions, pl.	правила поведения в общественных местах, *n., pl.*	öffentliche Bekanntma- chungen, *f., pl.*	avis officiels, *m., pl.*
544	public library	публичная библиотека	öffentliche Bibliothek	bibliothèque municipale, *f.*
545	public opinion	общественное мнение	öffentliche Meinung	opinion publique, *f.*
546	public school (in U. S.)	государственная школа	Volksschule, *f.*	école communale, *f.*
547	publication, n.	издание, *n.*	Publikation, *f.*/ Veröffentlichung, *f.*/ Herausgabe, *f.*	publication, *f.*
548	publicity, n.	реклама, *f.*	Reklame, *f.*/Werbung, *f.*/ öffentliche Aufmerksamkeit	publicité, *f.*
549	published work	изданная работа	veröffentlichtes Werk	ouvrage publié, *m.*
550	publisher, n.	издатель, *m.*	Verleger, *m.*	éditeur, *m.*
551	publishing house	издательство, *n.*	Verlag, *m.*	éditions, *f., pl.*
552	pulsation, n.	пульсация, *m.*	Pulsschlag, *f.*	pulsation, *f.*
553	pulverization of dialects	пульверизация диалектов, *f.*	Dialektpulverisierung, *f.*	pulvérisation des dialectes, *f.*
554	pun, n.	каламбур, *m.*/ игра слов, *f.*	Wortspiel, *n.*	calembour, *m.*/ jeu de mots, *m.*
555	punched card	перфокарта, *f.*	Lochkarte, *f.*	carte perforée, *f.*

No.	ENGLISH	RUSSIAN	GERMAN	FRENCH
556	punched tape	перфолента, *f.*	Lochband, *m.*/ Lochstreifen, *n.*	bande perforée, *f.*/ ruban perforé, *m.*
557	punctual aspect	мгновенный вид/ точечный вид	punktuelle Aktionsart	aspect ponctuel, *m.*
558	punctuation, n.	пунктуация, *f.*	Interpunktion, *f.*/ Satzzeichensetzung, *f.*	ponctuation, *f.*
559	punctuation mark	знак препинания, *m.*	Satzzeichen, *n.*	signe de ponctuation, *m.*
560	pure form	чистая форма	reine Form	forme pure, *f.*
561	pure language	несмешанный язык	ungemischte Sprache	lange pure, *f.*
562	purification of language	очистка языка, *f.*	Sprachreinigung, *f.*	purification d'une langue, *f.*
563	purity, n.	чистота, *f.*	Reinheit, *f.*	pureté, *f.*
564	purport, n.	смысл, *m.*/ содержание, *n.*	Inhalt, *m.*/Sinn, *m.*	portée *f.*/signification, *f.*
565	purpose, n.	цель, *f.*/намерение, *n.*/ задача, *f.*	Zweck, *m.*/Ziel, *n.*/ Absicht, *f.*	dessein, *m.*/intention, *f.*/ but, *m.*/fin, *f.*
566	put into brackets, v.	поставить в скобки	in eckige Klammern setzen	mettre entre crochets

Q

No.	ENGLISH	RUSSIAN	GERMAN	FRENCH
001	quadrangle, n.	квадрат, *m.*	Quadrat, *n.*/Viereck, *n.*	quadrilatère, *m.*
002	quadruple, adj.	четверной/ четырехкратный	vierfach	quadruple
003	qualifier, n.	определяющий	bestimmender Ausdruck	qualificatif, *m.*
004	qualitative adjective	качественное прилагательное	attributives Adjektiv	adjectif qualificatif, *m.*
005	qualitative change	качественное изменение	qualitative Veränderung	changement qualitatif, *m.*

No.	English	Russian	German	French
006	qualitative reduction	качественная редукция	qualitative Reduktion	réduction qualitative, *m.*
007	quality, n.	качество, *n.*/тембр, *m.*	Qualität, *f.*/Klangfarbe, *f.*	qualité, *f.*/timbre, *m.*
008	quantifier, n.	указатель количества, *m.*	quantitätsbestimmender Ausdruck	quantificatif, *m.*
009	quantitative change	количественное изменение	quantitative Veränderung	changement quantitatif, *m.*
010	quantitative linguistics	количественная лингвистика	quantitative Sprachforschung	linguistique quantitative, *f.*
011	quantitative reduction	количественная редукция	quantitative Reduktion	réduction quantitative, *f.*
012	quantitative stress	количественное ударение/долготное ударение	Dauerakzent, *m.*/ quantitativer Akzent	accent quantitatif, *m.*
013	quantity, n.	количество, *n.*	Quantität, *f.*	quantité, *f*
014	quasi-linguistic, adj.	квази-лингвистический	quasi-linguistisch	quasi-linguistique
015	question, n.	вопрос, *m.*	Frage, *f.*	question, *f.*
016	question intonation	вопросительная интонация	Fragesatzintonation, *f.*/ Frageton, *m.*	intonation interrogative, *f.*
017	question mark (?)	вопросительный знак, *m.*	Fragezeichen, *n.*	point d'interrogation, *m.*
018	questionable, adj.	сомнительный	zweifelhaft	discutable
019	questionnaire, n.	вопросник, *m.*/ анкета, *f.*	Fragebogen, *m.*	questionnaire, *m.*
020	quiz, n.	контрольная работа/ предварительный экзамен	Prüfung, *f.*	examen, *m.*
021	quotation, n.	цитата, *f.*	Zitat, *n.*	citation, *f.*
022	quotation marks, pl. ("—")	кавычки, pl.	Anführungsstriche, *m.*, pl./Anführungs-zeichen, *m.*, pl./ Gansefüsschen, *n.*, pl.	guillemets, *n.*, pl.

No.	ENGLISH	RUSSIAN	GERMAN	FRENCH

R

No.	ENGLISH	RUSSIAN	GERMAN	FRENCH
001	race, n.	раса, *f.*	Rasse, *f.*	race, *f.*
002	radio, n.	радио, *n.*	Radio, *n.*/Rundfunk, *m.*	radio, *f.*/T.S.F., *f.*
003	radio announcer	диктор, *m.*	Radioansager, *m.*	speaker, *m.*
004	radio broadcast	радиопередача, *f.*	Radiosendung, *f.*/Rund-funksendung, *f.*	radiodiffusion, *f.*/ émission, *f.*
005	radical, n.	корень, *m.*	Wurzel, *f.*/Stammwort, *m.*	radical, *m.*
006	raising (articulation), n.	передвижение вверх, *n.*/повышение, *n.*	Hebung, *f.*	relèvement, *m.*
007	range of meaning	пределы значения, *m.*, pl.	Bedeutungsspanne, *f.*	domaine sémantique, *m.*
008	range of voice	диапазон голоса, *m.*	Stimmumfang, *m.*	diapason, *m.*
009	rank, n.	ранг, *m.*	Rang, *m.*	rang, *m.*
010	rank equivalence	эквивалентность по рангу, *f.*	Ranggleichheit, *f.*	équivalence de rang, *f.*
011	rank order	ранговый порядок	Rangordnung, *f.*	ordre de rang, *m.*
012	rapid, adj.	быстрый/скорый	schnell	rapide
013	rapid speech	быстрая речь	schnelles Sprechen/ schnelle Rede/ Allegroform, *f.*	parole rapide, *f.*
014	rare, adj.	редкий	seiten	exceptionnel/ peu commun
015	rarely used, adj.	малоупотребительный	selten gebraucht	rarement employé
016	rate of decay	скорость распадения, *f.*	Verfallsrate, *f.*	allure de la déchéance, *f.*
017	rate of illiteracy	процент неграмотности, *m.*	Ausmass des Anal-phabetentums, *n.*	taux de l'analphabétisme, *m.*
018	rate of replacement	скорость замена, *f.*/ скорость перехода, *f.*	Ersetzungshöhe, *f.*	taux de remplacement, *m.*

No.	ENGLISH	RUSSIAN	GERMAN	FRENCH
019	ratio, n.	пропорция, *f.*/ соотношение, *n.*	Verhältnis, *n.*	proportion, *f.*/raison, *f.*/ rapport, *m.*
020	rationalization, n.	рационализация, *f.*	Rationalisierung, *f.*	rationalisation, *f.*
021	raw data	сырые данные, pl.	Rohmaterial, *n.*/ unausgewertete Daten, *f.*, pl.	données brutes, *f.*, pl.
022	reaction, n.	реакция, *f.*	Reaktion, *f.*	réaction, *f.*
023	reading, n.	чтение, *n.*	Lesen, *n.*	lecture, *f.*
024	reading aloud	чтение вслух, *n.*	lautes Lesen	lecture à haute voix, *f.*
025	reading vocabulary	пассивный запас слов	Lesewortschatz, *m.*	vocabulaire pour la lecture, *m.*
026	reality, n.	действительность, *f.*	Realität, *f.*/ Wirklichkeit, *f.*	réalité, *f.*
027	realization, n.	реализация, *f.*/ актуализация, *f.*	Realisierung, *f.*/ Aktualisierung, *f.*	actualisation, *f.*
028	rearrangement, n.	перестановка, *f.*	Umordnung, *f.*	disposition nouvelle, *f.*/ combinaison nouvelle, *f.*
029	reason, n.	причина, *f.*	Grund, *m.*/Ursache, *f.*	raison *f.*
030	reasoning, n.	рассуждение, *n.*	Urteilen, *n.*	raisonnement, *m.*
031	recall, n.	восстановление в памяти, *n.*	Erinnerung, *f.*	rappel, *m.*
032	receiver, n.	получатель, *m.*/ приемник, *m.*	Empfänger, *n.*	récepteur, *m.*
033	recipe book	книга рецептов, *f.*	Rezeptbuch, *n.*	livre de recettes, *m.*
034	reciprocal, adj.	взаимный	reziprok/gegenseitig	réciproque
035	reciprocal assimilation	взаимная ассимиляция	reziproke Assimilation/ doppelseitige Assimilation	assimilation réciproque, *f.*
036	reciprocal pronoun	взаимное местоимение	reziprokes Pronomen	pronom réciproque, *m.*

No.	ENGLISH	RUSSIAN	GERMAN	FRENCH
037	reciprocal verb	взаимный глагол	reziprokes Verb	verbe réciproque, *m.*
038	recognition, n.	распознавание, *n.*	Erkennen, *n.*	reconnaisance, *f.*
039	recognition model	распознающая модель	Erkennungsmodell, *f.*	modèle de reconnaissance, *m.*
040	reconstruction, n.	реконструкция, *f.*/ перестройка, *f.*/ восстановление, *n.*	Rekonstruktion, *f.*	réconstruction, *f.*/ restitution, *f.*
041	record (phonograph), n.	пластинка. *f.*	Schallplatte, *f.*	disque, *m.*
042	record player	проигрыватель, *m.*	Schallplattenspieler, *m.*/ Plattenspieler, *m.*	tourne-disque, *m.*
043	recording speed	скорость записи, *f.*	Aufnahmegeschwindig-keit, *f.*	vitesse de l'enregistrement, *f.*
044	records (historical), pl.	записи, *f.,* pl.	geschriebene Urkunden, *f.,* pl.	archives, *m.,* pl./documentation écrite, *f.*
045	recurrent, adj.	повторяющийся	wiederkehrend	périodique
046	recursive, adj.	рекурсивный	rekursiv	récursif
047	redefinition, n.	переопределение, *n.*	Neudefinition, *f.*	définition nouvelle, *f.*
048	rediscovery, n.	переоткрытие, *n.*	Neuentdeckung, *f.*	redécouverte, *f.*
049	redistribution, n.	перераспределение, *n.*	Neuverteilung, *f.*	nouvelle répartition, *f.*/ redistribution, *f.*
050	reduced vowel	редуцированная гласная	reduzierter Vokal	voyelle réduite, *f.*
051	reduction, n.	редукция, *f.*	Reduktion, *f.*	réduction, *f.*
052	redundancy, n.	излишество, *n.*/ избыточность, *f.*	Redundanz, *f.*	redondance, *f.*
053	redundant features, pl.	недифференциальные признаки, pl.	irrelevante Merkmale, *m.,* pl./	traits non pertinant, *m.,* pl./traits redondants, *m.,* pl.
054	redundant word	излишнее слово	überflüssiges Wort	mot pléonastique, *m.*
055	reduplication, n.	редупликация, *f.*/ удвоение, *n.*	Reduplizierung, *f.*/ Verdoppelung, *f.*	redoublement, *m.*

No.	English	Russian	German	French
056	reference (in a book), n.	ссылка, *f.*	Verweis, *m.*	revoi, *m.*/repère, *m.*
057	reference (object referred to), n.	обозначаемый предмет	Verweisungsgegenstand, *m.*	signifié, *m.*
058	reference book	справочник, *m.*	Nachschlagewerk, *n.*	ouvrage à consulter, *m.*
059	references, pl.	источники, *m.*, pl./ библиография, *f.*	Quellennachweis, *m.*/ Literaturnachweis, *m.*/ Literaturverweis, *m.*	allusions, *f.*, pl.
060	referent (sign of reference), n.	обозначающий	Verweisungszeichen, *n.*	signifiant, *m.*
061	referential meaning	предметная отнесенность/ вещественное значение	Verweisungsbedeutung, *f*	sens référentiel, *m.*
062	reflection, reflex, n.	отражение, *n.*	Ableitungswort, *n.*	réflexe, *m.*
063	reflexive pronoun	возвратное местоимение	Reflexivpronomen, *n.*/ rückbezügliches Fürwort	pronoun réfléchi, *m.*
064	reflexive verb	возвратный глагол	reflexives Verb	verbe réfléchi, *m.*
065	reform, n.	реформа, *f.*	Reform, *f.*	réforme, *f.*
066	reformation, n.	переобразование, *n.*	Neugestaltung, *f.*	réformation, *f.*
067	reformulation, n.	переформулировка, *f.*	Reformulierung, *f.*	reformulation, *f.*
068	regimen, n.	управление, *n.*	Rektion, *f.*	régime, *m.*
069	region, n.	район, *m.*/область, *f.*	Gebiet, *n.*	région, *f.*
070	regional dialect	местный говор	lokale Mundart/ örtliche Mundart	patois, *m.*/dialecte régional, *m.*
071	regionalism, n.	местное выражение	örtliche Redeweise	régionalisme, *m.*
072	register (of voice), n.	регистр, *m.*	Register, *n.*/Tonlage, *f.*	registre, *m.*
073	register (speech subtypes), n.	особый язык	Sondersprache, *f.*	langue speciale, *f.*/ registre du langage, *m.*
074	regressive assimilation	регрессивная ассимиляция	regressive Assimilation/ nachwirkende Assimilation	assimilation régressive, *f.*/ assimilation anticipante, *f.*

No.	English	Russian	German	French
075	regular, adj.	регулярный/ закономерный	regelmässig	régulier
076	regular verb	правильный глагол	regelmässiges Verb	verbe régulier, *m.*
077	regularity, n.	закономерность, *f.*	Regelmässigkeit, *f.*	régularité, *f.*
078	regularity of sound laws	закономерность звуковых законов, *f.*	Ausnahmslosigkeit der Lautgesetze, *f.*	régularité des lois phonétiques, *f.*
079	reinforcement, n.	укрепление, *n.*	Verstärkung, *f.*	renforcement, *m.*
080	reissue, n.	переиздание, *n.*	Neuauflage, *f.*	réédition, *f.*
081	reiteration, n.	повторение, *n.*	Wiederholung, *f.*	réitération, *f.*
082	related field	смежная область	verwandtes Gebiet	discipline apparentée, *f.*
083	related languages, pl.	родственные языки, *m., pl.*	verwandte Sprachen, *f., pl.*	langues apparentées, *f., pl.*
084	relation(ship), n.	отношение, *n.*/связь, *f.*	Beziehung, *f.*/Relation, *f.*	relation, *f.*/rapport, *m.*
085	relational, adj.	реляционный	beziehungsmässig	relationnel
086	relational concept	реляционное понятие	beziehungsmässiger Begriff	concept relationnel, *m.*
087	relational meaning	реляционное значение	beziehungsmässige Bedeutung	sens relationnel, *m.*
088	relative adjective	относительное прилагательное	relatives Adjektiv	adjectif relatif, *m.*
089	relative clause	придаточное определительное предложение	Relativsatz, *m.*/ Beziehungssatz, *m.*	incidente, *f.*
090	relative frequency	относительная частота	relative Häufigkeit	fréquence relative, *f.*
091	relative pitch	относительная высота звука	relative Tonhöhe	hauteur relative, *f.*
092	relative pronoun	относительное местоимение	Relativpronomen, *n.*/ bezügliches Fürwort	pronom relatif, *m.*
093	relative stability	относительная устойчивость	relative Stabilität	stabilité relative, *f.*

No.	ENGLISH	RUSSIAN	GERMAN	FRENCH
094	relaxation, n.	ослабление, *n.*	Entspannung, *f.*	relaxation, *f.*
095	relearning, n.	переучивание, *n.*	Wiederlernen, *n.*	rapprendrement, *m.*
096	release, n.	размыкание, *n.*/ рекурсия, *f.*	Auslösung, *f.*	détente *f.*
097	relevance, n.	уместность, *f.*	**Relevanz**, *f.*/ Angemessenheit, *f.*	pertinence, *f.*
098	relevant features, pl.	релевантные признаки, *m.*, pl./ существенные признаки, *m.*, pl.	relevante Merkmale, *n.*, pl.	traits pertinents, *m.*, pl.
099	reliability, n.	надежность, *f.*	Zuverlässigkeit, *f.*	securité, *f.*
100	relic area	реликтовый район	Restgebiet, *n.*/ Sprachinsel, *f.*	îlot conservateur, *m.*
101	relic word	архаизм, *m.*	Reliktwort, *n.*/ Überbleibsel, *n.*	mot survécu, *m.*
102	religion, n.	религия, *f.*	Religion, *f.*	religion, *f.*
103	remainder, n.	остаток, *m.*	Rest, *m.*	reste, *m.*
104	remark, n.	замечание, *n.*	Bemerkung, *f.*	remarque, *f.*
105	remember, v.	помнить	sich erinnern	se rappeler
106	remind, v.	напоминать	erinnern	rappeler/évoquer
107	remnant, n.	остаток, *m.*	Überbleibsel, *n.*	vestige, *m.*
108	remote area	отдаленная область	entlegenes Gebiet	lieu reculé, *m.*
109	remote past tense	далекое прошедшее время	entfernte Vergangenheit, *f.*/Vorvergangenheit, *f.*	passé reculé, *m.*
110	remote relationship	отдаленное отношение	entfernte Verwandt- schaft	rapport elóigné, *m.*
111	repeated, adj.	повторный	wiederholt	répété
112	repetition, n.	повторение, *n.*	Wiederholung, *f.*	répétition, *f.*
113	repetition compound	повторное словосочетание	Wiederholungs- konstruktion, *f.*	composé par réduplication, *m.*

No.	English	Russian	German	French
114	replacement, n.	замена, *f.*/ подстановка, *f.*	Ersetzung, *f.*	remplacement, *m.*
115	replacive, n.	заместитель, *m.*	Ersetzungselement, *n.*	ce qui remplace
116	replica, n.	копия, *f.*/ репродукция, *f.*	Kopie, *f.*/Nachbildung, *f.*	reproduction, *f.*/copie, *f.*/ réplique, *f.*
117	reply, n.	ответ, *m.*	Antwort, *f.*	réponse, *f.*
118	report, n.	сообщение, *n.*/ доклад, *m.*	Bericht, *m.*	exposé, *m.*
119	reported speech	косвенная речь	indirekte Rede	discours indirect, *m.*
120	representation, n.	представление, *n.*	Darstellung, *f.*	représentation, *f.*
121	request, n.	просьба, *f.*	Bitte, *f.*	demande, *f.*/prière, *f.*/ requête, *f.*
122	requirement, n.	требование, *n.*	Anforderung, *f.*	condition requise, *f.*
123	research, n.	исследование, *n.*	Erforschung, *f.*/ Forschung, *f.*/ Nachforschung, *f.*	recherche, *f.*
124	resemblence, n.	сходство, *n.*	Ähnlichkeit, *f.*	ressemblance, *f.*
125	residue, n.	остаток, *m.*	Rest, *m.*/Restbestand, *m.*	reste, *m.*
126	resistance to change	сопротивление изменению, *n.*	Widerstand gegen Veränderung, *m.*	résistance au changement, *f.*
127	resonance, n.	резонанс, *m.*/ звонкость, *f.*	Resonanz, *f.*/ Klangfülle, *f.*	résonance, *f.*
128	resonance chamber	камера-резонатор, *m.*	Ansatzrohr, *n.*	chambre de résonance, *f.*
129	resonant, adj.	резонирующий	resonant/nachklingend	résonnant
130	resonants, pl.	сонанты, *m.*, pl.	Sonanten, *f.*, pl./ Sonorlaute, *m.*, pl.	sonantes, *f.*, pl.
131	resonator, n.	резонатор, *m.*	Resonator, *m.*	résonateur, *m.*
132	resources, pl.	ресурсы, *m.*, pl./ средства, *n.*, pl.	Hilfsmittel, *n.*	ressources, *f.*, pl.
133	respiration, n.	дыхание, *n.*	Atmen, *n.*	respiration, *f.*

No.	English	Russian	German	French
134	response, n.	реплика, *f.*	Antwort, *f.*	réponse, *f.*
135	restatement, n.	перефразировка, *f.*	Neuformulierung, *f.*	réaffirmation, *f.*
136	restoration, n.	восстановление, *n.*	Wiederherstellung, *f.*	restitution, *f.*
137	restraint, n.	ограничение. *n.*	Begrenzung, *f.*	restriction, *f.*
138	restricted class	замкнутый класс	beschränkte Klasse	classe restreinte, *f.*
139	restricted language	ограниченный язык	beschränkte Sprache	langue restreinte, *f.*
140	restricted system	ограниченная система	beschränktes System	système réduit, *m.*
141	restricted usage	ограниченное употребление	beschränkter Gebrauch/ restriktiver Gebrauch	usage restreint, *m.*
142	restriction, n.	ограничение, *n.*	Beschränkung, *f.*	restriction, *f.*
143	restrictive clause	определительное придаточное предложение	beschränkender Satz	proposition limitative, *f.*
144	result, n.	результат, *m.*	Ergebnis, *n.*/Resultat, *n.*	résultat, *m.*
145	result clause	следственное предложение	Ergebnissatz, *m.*	proposition résultante, *f.*
146	resume, n.	резюме, *n.*	Resümee, *n.*/ Zusammenfassung, *f.*	résumé, *m.*
147	retention, n.	сохранение, *n.*	Erhaltung, *f.*	conservation, *f.*
148	retranslation, n.	обратный перевод	Rückübersetzung, *f.*	retraduction, *f.*
149	retroflex consonants, pl.	ретрофлексные согласные, pl./ церебральные согласные, pl./ какуминальные согласные, pl.	retroflexe Konsonanten, *m.*, pl.	consonnes retrofléchies, *f.*, pl.
150	revealed structure	раскрытая структура	Auffindungsstruktur, *f.*	structure révélée, *f.*
151	reverberation, n.	отзвук, *m.*	Widerhall, *m.*	répercussion, *f.*
152	reverse dictionary	обратный словарь	rückläufiges Wörterbuch	dictionnaire inverse, *m.*
153	reverse order	обратный порядок	umgekehrte Ordnung	ordre inverse, *m.*

No.	ENGLISH	RUSSIAN	GERMAN	FRENCH
154	reversibility, n.	обратимость, *f.*	Umkehrbarkeit, *f.*	réversibilité, *f.*
155	review, n.	рецензия, *f.*	Rezension, *f.*/ Buchbesprechung, *f.*	compte rendu, *m.*/ critique, *m.*
156	revolutions per minute	обороты в минуту, *m.,* pl.	Umdrehungen pro Minute, *f.,* pl.	révolutions par minute, *f.,* pl.
157	rewrite rules, pl.	правила пере- писывания, *n.,* pl.	Äquivalenzregeln, *f.,* pl.	règles d'équivalence, *f.,* pl.
158	rhetoric, n.	риторика, *f.*	Rhetorik, *f.*	rhétorique, *f.*
159	rhetorical question	риторический вопрос	rhetorische Frage	question de pure forme, *f.*
160	rhetorical style	риторический стиль	rhetorischer Stil	style emphatique, *m.*
161	rhotacism, n.	ротацизм, *m.*	Rhotazismus, *m.*	rhotacisme, *m.*
162	rhyme, n.	рифма, *f.*	Reim, *m.*	rime, *f.*
163	rhymed couplet	рифмованное двустишие	gereimter Zweizeiler	rime plate, *f.*
164	rhyming, n.	рифмовка, *f.*	Reimen, *n.*	versification, *f.*
165	rhyming dictionary	словарь рифм, *m.*	Reimwörterbuch, *n.*	dictionnaire de rimes, *m.*
166	rhythm, n.	ритм, *m.*	Rhythmus, *m.*	rythme, *m.*
167	rhythmic(al), adj.	ритмический	rhythmisch	cadencé/rythmique
168	rib, n.	ребро, *n.*	Rippe, *f.*	côte, *f.*
169	riddle, n.	загадка, *f.*	Rätsel, *n.*	énigme, *f.*/devinette, *f.*
170	right, adj.	правильный	richtig	exact/correct/juste
171	right-handed person	праворукий, *m.*	Rechtshänder, *m.*	droitier, *s.*
172	right-to-left writing	письмо с права на лево, *n.*	von-rechts-nach-links Schreibweise, *f.*	écriture de droit à gauche, *f.*
173	rigorous, adj.	строгий	streng	rigoureux
174	rising tone	восходящий тон	steigender Ton	ton montant, *m.*
175	role, n.	роль, *f.*	Rolle, *f.*	rôle, *m.*

No.	ENGLISH	RUSSIAN	GERMAN	FRENCH
176	rolled r	вибрирующее р	gerolltes R, *n.*/ Zungen- R, *n.*	r roulé, *m.*
177	roman type	прямой светлый шрифт	Antiqua, *f.*	caractères romains, *m.,* pl.
178	Romany, adj.	цыганский	Zigeuner-	langue gitane/romand
179	root, n.	корень, *m.*	Wurzel, *f.*	racine, *f.*
180	root word	корневое слово	Wurzelnomen, *n.*	mot-racine, *m.*/ mot-souche, *m.*
181	root of the tongue	корень языка, *m.*	Zungenwurzel, *f.*	racine de la langue, *f.*
182	root isolating languages, pl.	корне-изолирующие языки, *m.,* pl.	wurzelisolierende Sprachen, *f.,* pl.	langues racines isolantes, *f.,* pl.
183	rounded vowels, pl.	лабиализованные гласные, pl.	gerundete Vokale, *m.,* pl.	voyelles arrondies, *f.,* pl.
184	rounding, n.	лабиализация, *f.*/ округление, *n.*	Rundung, *f.*	arrondissement, *m.*
185	row, n.	ряд, *m.*	Reihe, *f.*	rangée, *f.*/rang, *m.*
186	rubbing, n.	трение, *n.*	Reiben, *n.*	frottement, *m.*
187	rule, n.	правило, *n.*	Regel, *f.*	règle, *f.*
188	Rumanian, adj.	румынский	rumänisch	roumain
189	rural speech	деревянский говор	Bauerndialekt, *m.*/ ländliche Redeweise/ ländliche Sprache	langage rustique, *m.*
190	Russian, adj.	русский	russisch	russe

S

No.	ENGLISH	RUSSIAN	GERMAN	FRENCH
001	salutation, n.	приветствие, *n.*	Begrüssung, *f.*	salutation, *f.*
002	same, adj.	одинаковый	derselbe	même
003	sameness, n.	тождество, *n.*	Gleichheit, *f.*	identité, *f.*
004	sample, n.	образец, *m.*/пример, *m.*	Beispiel, *n.*	échantillon, *m.*/essai, *m.*

S 005 sample size — S 025 scope, n.

No.	ENGLISH	RUSSIAN	GERMAN	FRENCH
005	sample size	примерная величина	Anzahl der Beispiele, *f.*	dimension d'échantillon, *f.*
006	sandhi, n.	сандхи, *n.*	Sandhi, *n.*	sandhi, *m.*
007	satem languages, pl.	сатем-языки, *m.,* pl.	Satemsprachen, *f.,* pl.	langues satem, *f.,* pl.
008	sarcasm, n.	сарказм, *m.*	Sarkasmus, *m.*	sarcasme, *m.*
009	satire, n.	сатира, *f.*	Satire, *f.*	satire, f.
010	satisfy, v.	удовлетворять	erfüllen	remplir
011	saying, n.	поговорка, *f.*	Sprichwort, *n.*	adage, *m.*/maxime, *f.*/ proverbe, *m.*
012	scale, n.	шкала, *f.*	Skala, *f.*/Abstufung, *f.*	échelle, *f.*
013	scansion of a poem	скандирование стихотворения, *n.*	Skandieren eines Gedichts, *n.*	scansion d'un poeme, *f.*
014	scattering, n.	разброска, *f.*	Streuung, *f.*	éparpillement, *m.*
015	scheme, n.	схема, *f.*	Schema, *n.*	schéma, *m.*
016	scholar, n.	ученый, *m.*	Gelehrter, *m.*	savant, *m.*
017	scholastic institution	учебное заведение	Lehranstalt, *f.*	institution académique, *f.*
018	scholastic year	учебный год	akademisches Jahr/ Schuljahr, *n.*	année scolaire, *f.*
019	school, n.	школа, *f.*	Schule, *f.*	école, *f.*
020	science, n.	наука, *f.*	Wissenschaft, *f.*	science, *f.*
021	scientific language	научный язык	wissenschaftliche Sprache	langage scientifique, *m.*
022	scientific research	научное исследование	wissenschaftliche Forschung	récherche scientifique, *f.*
023	scientific-technical literature	научно-техническая литература	technische Fachliteratur	littérature technico-scientifique, *f.*
024	scientist, n.	ученый, *m.*	Wissenschaftler, *m.*	savant, *m.*
025	scope, n.	охват, *m.*/размах, *m.*	Umfang, *m.*	domaine propre, *m.*/ portée, *f.*

No.	ENGLISH	RUSSIAN	GERMAN	FRENCH
026	Scot(tish), adj.	шотландский	schottisch	écossais
027	scrap-book, n.	альбом газетных вырезок, *m.*	Einklebebuch, *n.*/ Sammelmappe, *f.*	album de découpures, *m.*
028	scrawl, n.	неразборчивое письмо	Gekritzel, *n.*/ Geschmiere, *n.*	griffonage, *m.*/ gribouillage, *m.*
029	scream, n.	крик, *m.*/визг, *m.*	Schrei, *m.*	cri perçant, *m.*/ hurlement, *m.*
030	scribbling, n.	каракули, pl.	Gekritzel, *n.*	gribouillage, *m.*/ griffonage, *m.*
031	scribe, n.	писец, *m.*	Schreiber, *m.*/Kopist, *m.*	scribe, *m.*
032	script, n.	письмо, *n.*/ рукописный шрифт	Schrift, *f.*/Handschrift, *f.*	écriture, *f.*
033	scroll, n.	свиток, *m.*	Papyrus, *m.*/ Papyrusrolle, *f.*	rouleau, *m.*
034	search, n.	поиски, pl./ отыскание, *n.*/ изыскание, *n.*	Nachforschung, *f.*/ Suche, *f.*	quête, *f.*/recherche, *f.*
035	second language learning	изучение второго языка, *n.*	Erlernung einer zweiten Sprache, *f.*	acquisition d'une seconde langue, *f.*
036	second person	второе лицо	zweite Person, *f.*	deuxième personne, *f.*
037	secondary, adj.	второстепенный	zweitrangig	secondaire
038	secondary meaning	второстепенное значение	Sekundärbedeutung, *f.*/ zweitrangige Bedeutung	sens dérivé, *m.*
039	secondary school	срёдняя школа	höhere Schule	école secondaire, *f.*
040	secondary sentence parts, pl.	второстепенные члены предложения, *m.*, pl.	zweitrangige Satzteile, *m.*, pl.	parties secondaires de la phrase, *f.*, pl.
041	secondary signal system	вторичная сигнальная система	⟨zweitrangiges Zeichensystem⟩	système de signes secondaire, *m.*
042	secondary stress	второстепенное ударение	Nebenton, *m.*	accent accessoire, *m.*/ accent secondaire, *m.*
043	secret language	тайный язык	Geheimsprache, *f.*	langage secret, *m.*

No.	English	Russian	German	French
044	section, n.	часть, *f.*	Teil, *m.*	section, *f.*
045	seeing, n.	зрение, *n.*	Sehen, *n.*	vue, *f.*/vision, *f.*
046	segment, n.	сегмент, *m.*/ отрезок, *m.*	Segment, *n.*	segment, *m.*
047	segmental phoneme	сегментная фонема	segmentäres Phonem	phonème segmental, *m.*
048	segmentation, n.	сегментация, *f.*/ деление, *n.*/ членение, *n.*	Segmentierung, *f.*/ Gliederung, *f.*/ Vergliederung, *f.*	segmentation, *f.*
049	selection, n.	подбор, *m.*/отбор, *m.*	Auswahl, *f.*	choix, *m.*
050	self-contained system	самостоятельная система	abgeschlossenes System/ vollständiges System	système indépendant, *m.*
051	semanteme, sememe, n.	семантема, *f.*	Bedeutungselement, *n.*	sémantème, *m.*
052	semantic ambiguity	семантическая двусмысленность	semantische Zweideutigkeit	ambiguïté sémantique, *f.*
053	semantic category	семантическая категория	Bedeutungskategorie, *f.*	catégorie sémantique, *f.*
054	semantic change	семантическое изменение	Bedeutungswandel, *m.*	changement sémantique
055	semantic content	семантическое содержание	Bedeutungsinhalt, *m.*	contenu sémantique, *m.*
056	semantic context	семантический контекст	Bedeutungszusammen- hang, *m.*	contexte sémantique *m.*
057	semantic expansion	семантическое расширение	Bedeutungserweiterung, *f.*	extension sémantique, *f.*
058	semantic feature	семантический признак	semantisches Merkmal	trait sémantique, *m.*
059	semantic group	семантическая группа	semantische Gruppe	groupe sémantique, *m.*
060	semantic innovation	семантическое новшество	semantische Neuerung	innovation sémantique, *f.*
061	semantic law	семантический закон	semantisches Gesetz	loi sémantique, *f.*

No.	ENGLISH	RUSSIAN	GERMAN	FRENCH
062	semantic level	семантический уровень	semantische Ebene	plan sémantique, *m.*
063	semantic narrowing	семантическое сужение	Bedeutungsverengerung, *f.*	restriction sémantique, *f.*
064	semantic overloading	семантическая перегрузка	semantische Überlastung	surchargement sémantique, *m.*
065	semantic range	семантическое поле/ понятийное поле/ концептуальное поле	Begriffsblock, *m.*/ Begriffsfeld, *n.*/ Begriffskomplex, *m.*/ Sinnbezirk, *m.*	domaine sémantique, *m.*
066	semantic structure	семантическая структура	semantische Struktur, *f.*	structure sémantique, *f.*
067	semantics, n.	семантика, *f.*	Semantik, *f.*/ Bedeutungslehre, *f.*	sémantique, *f.*
068	semasiology, n.	семасиология, *f.*	Semasiologie, *f.*/ Wortbedeutungslehre, *f.*	sémasiologie, *f.*
069	semi-, adj.	пол(у)-	Halb-	demi-
070	semicolon (;)	точка с запятой, *f.*	Semikolon, *n.*/ Strichpunkt, *m.*	point-virgule, *m.*
071	semiology, n.	семиология, *f.*	Semiologie, *f.*	sémiologie, *f.*
072	semiotics	семиотика, *f.*	Semiotik, *f.*	sémiotique, *f.*
073	semivowel, n.	полугласная, *f.*	Halbvokal, *m.*	demi-voyelle, *f.*
074	sender, n.	отправитель, *m.*	Sender, *m.*	expéditeur, *m.*
075	sense, n.	смысл, *m.*	Sinn, *m.*	sens, *m.*
076	sense of hearing	слух, *m.*	Gehör, *n.*	ouïe, *f.*
077	sense organs, pl.	органы чувств, *m.*, pl.	Sinnesorgane, *n.*, pl.	organes des sens, *m.*, pl.
078	sensitivity, n.	чувствительность, *f.*	Empfindlichkeit, *f.*	sensibilité, *f.*
079	sensory perception	сенсорное восприятие	Sinneswahrnehmung, *f.*	perception des sens *f.*
080	sentence, n.	предложение, *n.*	Satz, *m.*	phrase, *f.*

No.	ENGLISH	RUSSIAN	GERMAN	FRENCH
081	sentence analysis	анализ предложения, *m.*	Satzanalyse, *f.*	analyse de la phrase, *f.*
082	sentence arrangement	расположение частей предложения, *n.*	Satzanordnung, *f.*	agencement de la phrase, *m.*
083	sentence beginning	начало предложения, *n.*	Satzanfang, *m.*	début de la phrase, *m.*
084	sentence boundary	граница предложения, *f .*	Satzgrenze, *f.*	frontière de la phrase, *f.*
085	sentence component	компонент предложения, *m./* составляющая часть предложения	Satzglied, *n./*Satzteil, *m.*	composant de la phrase, *m.*
086	sentence connections, pl.	связи между предложениями, *f., pl.*	Satzverbindungen, *f., pl.*	liaison entre des phrases, *f.*
087	sentence construction	построение предложения	Satzbildung, *f.*	construction de la phrase, *f.*
088	sentence definition	определение предложения, *n.*	Satzdefinition, *f.*	définition de la phrase, *f.*
089	sentence division	членение предложения, *n.*	Satzteilung, *f.*	division de la phrase, *f.*
090	sentence final position	конечное положение в предложении	Satzschluss, *m.*	finale de la phrase, *f.*
091	sentence interpretation	толкование предложения, *n./* разбор предложения, *m.*	Satzinterpretation, *f.*	interprétation de la phrase, *f.*
092	sentence intonation	интонация предложения, *f.*	Satzbetonung, *f./* Satzintonation, *f./* Satzmelodie, *f.*	intonation de la phrase, *f.*
093	sentence introducer	зачинатель предложения, *m.*	Satzeinleitung, *f.*	ce qui introduit la phrase
094	sentence length	длина предложения, *f.*	Satzlänge, *f.*	longueur de la phrase, *f.*
095	sentence meaning	значение предложения, *n.*	Satzbedeutung, *f.*	sens de la phrase, *m.*

No.	ENGLISH	RUSSIAN	GERMAN	FRENCH
096	sentence part	часть предложения, *f.*/ член предложения, *m.*	Satzglied, *n.*/Satzteil, *m.*	partie de la phrase, *f.*
097	sentence pattern	модель предложения, *f.*	Satzmuster, *n.*	structure de la phrase, *f.*
098	sentence pause	пауза в предложении, *f.*	Satzpause, *f.*	pause dans la phrase, *f.*
099	sentence phonetics	фразовая фонетика	Satzphonetik, *f.*	phonétique syntaxique, *f.*
100	sentence position	позиция в предложении, *f.*/место в предложении, *n.*	Satzstellung, *f.*	position dans la phrase, *f.*
101	sentence punctuation	пунктуация предложения, *f.*	Satzzeichensetzung, *f.*	ponctuation de la phrase, *f.*
102	sentence predicate	фразовое сказуемое	Satzaussage, *f.*	attribut, *m.*/prédicat, *m.*
103	sentence rhythm	ритмика предложения, *f.*	Satzrhythmus, *m.*	rythme de la phrase, *m.*
104	sentence sense	смысл предложения, *m.*	Satzbedeutung, *f.*	sens de la phrase, *m.*
105	sentence stress	фразовое ударение	Satzakzent, *m.*	accent de la phrase, *m.*
106	sentence structure	структура предложения, *f.*/ строй предложения, *m.*	Satzstruktur, *f.*/ Satzbau, *m.*	structure de la phrase, *f.*
107	sentence subject	фразовое подлежащее	Satzgegenstand, *m.*	sujet de la phrase, *m.*
108	sentence termination	конец предложения, *m.*	Satzende, *n.*/ Satzschluss, *m.*	fin de la phrase, *f.*
109	sentence transformation	трансформация предложения, *f.*	Satztransformation, *f.*/ Satzumformung, *f.*	transformation de la phrase, *f.*
110	sentence type	тип предложения, *m.*	Satztyp, *m.*/Satzart, *f.*	classe de phrase, *f.*
111	separable compound	раздельный композит	trennbare Zusammensetzung	composé séparable, *m.*
112	separable prefix	раздельная приставка	trennbares Präfix	préfixe séparable, *m.*

No.	ENGLISH	RUSSIAN	GERMAN	FRENCH
113	separate, v.	отделять/разделять/ разлагать	abtrennen/zerteilen	séparer/diviser
114	separate, adj.	отдельный	getrennt	separé/détaché
115	separate word	отдельное слово	getrenntes Wort	mot séparé, *m.*
116	separation, n.	выделение, *n.*/ разделение, *n.*	Trennung, *f.*	séparation, *f.*
117	sequence, n.	последовательность, *f.*/ ряд, *m.*	Sequenz, *f.*/Folge, *f.*/ Abfolge, *f.*/ Reihenfolge, *f.*	séquence, *f.*/série, *f.*/ succession, *f.*
118	sequence of morphemes	последовательность морфем, *f.*	Morphemfolge, *f.*	sucession de morphèmes, *f.*
119	sequence of phonemes	последовательность фонем, *f.*	Phonemfolge, *f.*	succession de phonèmes, *f.*
120	sequence of pitches	тональная последовательность	Tonhöhenfolge, *f.*	succession de tons, *f.*
121	sequence of segments	последовательность сегментов, *f.*	Segmentfolge, *f.*	succession de segments, *f.*
122	sequence of sentences	последовательность предложений, *f.*	Satzfolge, *f.*	succession de phrases, *f*
123	sequence of sounds	последовательность звуков, *f.*	Lautfolge, *f.*	succession de sons, *f.*/ suite de sons, *f.*
124	sequence of tenses	последовательность времен, *f.*	Zeitenfolge, *f.*	concordance des temps, *f.*
125	sequential, adj.	последовательный	folgend	successif
126	Serbo-Croation, adj.	сербохорватский	serbo-kroatisch	serbo-croate
127	series, n.	ряд, *m.*/серия, *f.*	Reihe, *f.*	série, *f.*
128	series-generating component	⟨компонент устанавливающий новый фонемный ряд⟩, *m.*	⟨neue Reihe erzeugende Phonemkomponente⟩, *f.*	élément sériant, *m.*
129	sermon, n.	проповедь, *m.*	Predigt, *f.*	sermon, *m.*
130	set, n.	множество, *n.*	Menge, *f.*	ensemble, *m.*

No.	ENGLISH	RUSSIAN	GERMAN	FRENCH
131	set definition	определение множества, *n.*	Mengendefinition, *f.*	définition d'ensemble, *f.*
132	set expression	устойчивое словосочетание	feste Wortgruppe	locution fixe, *f.*
133	set intersection	пересечение множеств, *n.*	Durchschnitt von Mengen, *m.*	intersection des ensembles, *f.*
134	set member	член множества, *m.*	Mengenglied, *n.*	membre d'ensemble, *m.*
135	set theory	теория множеств, *f.*	Mengenlehre, *f.*/ Mengentheorie, *f.*	théorie des ensembles, *f.*
136	set union	объединение множеств, *n.*	Mengenvereinigung, *f.*	union des ensembles, *f.*
137	set-theoretic(al) model	теоретико-множественная модель	mengentheoretisches Modell	modèle d'après la théorie des ensembles, *m.*
138	sex words, pl.	половые слова, *m.*, pl.	Sexwörter, *n.*, pl.	mots de sexe, *m.*, pl.
139	shade of meaning	оттенок значения, *m.*/ смысловой оттенок	Spur von Bedeutung, *f.*	nuance de sens, *f.*
140	shape, n.	форма, *f.*	Form, *f.*	forme, *f.*
141	shared feature	взаимный признак/ общая черта	gemeinsame Eigenschaft/ gemeinsamer Zug	trait partagé, *m.*
142	shared meaning	обоюдное значение	gemeinsame Bedeutung	sens commun, *m.*
143	sharp, adj.	резкий	abgebrochen/scharf	abrupt
144	shift, n.	передвижение, *n.*	Verschiebung, *f.*	déplacement, *m.*
145	short, adj.	короткий/краткий	kurz	court/bref
146	short duration	краткая длительность/ краткая продолжительность	kurze Dauer	courte durée, *f.*
147	short form	краткая форма	Kurzform, *f.*	forme brève, *f.*
148	short sentence	короткое предложение	kurzer Satz	phrase brève, *f.*
149	short story	рассказ, *m.*/ короткий рассказ	Kurzgeschichte, *f.*	conte, *m.*/nouvelle, *f.*

No.	ENGLISH	RUSSIAN	GERMAN	FRENCH
150	short vowels, pl.	краткие гласные, pl.	kurze Vokale, *m.*, pl.	voyelles brèves, *f.*, pl.
151	shortened form	укороченная форма	Kurzform, *f.*/ verkürzte Form	forme réduite, *f*
152	shortening, n.	сокращение, *n.*/ укорочение, *n.*	Verkürzung, *f.*	raccourcissement, *m.*/ abrègement, *m.*
153	shorthand, n.	стенография, *f.*/ скоропись, *f.*	Kurzschrift, *f.*	sténographie, *f.*
154	shortness, n.	краткость, *f.*	Kürze, *f.*	brévité, *f.*
155	shouting, n.	крик, *m.*	Rufen, *n.*	clameur, *f.*/cri, *m.*
156	shwa, *n.* (ə)	шва. *m.*	Schwa, *n.*	chva, *m.*
157	sibilant consonants, pl.	свистящие согласные, pl./шипящие согласные, pl.	Zischlaute, *m.*, pl.	consonnes sifflantes, *f.*, pl.
158	sight, n.	зрение, *n.*	Sehen, *n.*	vision, *f.*/vue, *f.*
159	sign, n.	знак, *m.*	Zeichen, *n.*	signe, *m.*
160	sign language	язык знаков, *m.*/ язык жестов, *m.*	Zeichensprache, *f.*/ Gebärdensprache, *f.*	langage par signes, *m.*/ langage mimique, *m.*
161	sign of equality (=)	знак равенства. *m.*	Gleichheitszeichen, *n.*	signe d'équivalence, *m.*
162	sign of inequality (≠)	знак неравенства. *m.*	Ungleichheitszeichen, *n.*	signe d'inégalité, *m.*
163	sign system	сигнальная система	Zeichensystem, *n.*	système de signes, *m.*
164	signal, n.	сигнал, *m.*	Signal, *n.*	signal, *m.*
165	signalization, n.	сигнализация, *f.*	Signalisieren, *n.*	signalisation, *f.*
166	signature, n.	подпись, *n.*	Unterschrift, *f.*	signature, *f.*
167	significance, n.	важность, *f.*/ значение, *n.*	Bedeutung, *f.*/Wichtigkeit, *f.*/Bedeutsamkeit, *f.*	importance, *f.*
168	significant, adj.	значимый	bedeutsam	significatif
169	significant unit	значимая единица, *f.*	bedeutungstragende Einheit	unité significative, *f.*

No.	ENGLISH	RUSSIAN	GERMAN	FRENCH
170	(the) signified, n.	означаемое, *n.*	Signifikat, *n.*	signifié, *m.*
171	signifier, n.	означающее, *n.*	Signifikant, *n.*	signifiant, *m.*
172	silence, n.	молчание, *n.*	Schweigen, *n.*/ Stillschweigen, *n.*	silence, *m.*
173	silent film	немой фильм	Stummfilm, *m.*	film muet, *m.*
174	silent letter	немая буква/непро- износимая буква	stummer Buchstabe	lettre muette, *f.*
175	silent reading	чтение про себя, *n.*	lautloses Lesen	lecture de pensée, *f.*
176	silent syllable	непроизносимый слог	stumme Silbe	syllabe muette, *f.*
177	similar, adj.	похожий/сходный	ähnlich	ressemblant/semblable
178	similarity, n.	сходство, *n.*	Ähnlichkeit, *f.*/ Gleichheit, *f.*	ressemblance, *f.*
179	similarity in form	формальное сходство	Formähnlichkeit, *f.*	ressemblance de forme, *f.*
180	similarity in structure	структурное сходство	strukturelle Ähnlichkeit	ressemblance structurale, *f.*
181	similarity in meaning	смысловое сходство	Bedeutungsähnlichkeit, *f.*	ressemblance de sens, *f.*
182	simile, n.	сравнение, *n.*	Gleichnis, *n.*	comparaison, *f.*
183	simple, adj.	простой	einfach	simple
184	simple predicate	простое сказуемое	einfaches Prädikat, *n.*	prédicat simple, *m.*
185	simple sentence	простое предложение	einfacher Satz	phrase indépendante, *f.*
186	simple stop	простая смычная	einfacher Verschlusslaut	occlusive simple, *f.*
187	simple subject	простое подлежащее	einfaches Subjekt	sujet simple, *m.*
188	simple tense	простое время	einfache Zeitform	temps non composé, *m.*/ temps simple, *m.*
189	simplicity, n.	простота, *f.*	Einfachheit, *f.*	simplicité, *m.*
190	simplification, n.	упрощение, *n.*	Vereinfachung, *f.*	simplification, *f.*
191	simultaneous, adj.	одновременный	gleichzeitig	simultané

No.	ENGLISH	RUSSIAN	GERMAN	FRENCH
192	simultaneous translation	синхронный перевод	Simultanübersetzung, *f.*	traduction simultanée, *f.*
193	singing, n.	пение, *n.*	Singen, *n.*	chant, *m.*
194	singing voice	певучий голос	Gesangsstimme, *f.*	voix chanteuse, *f.*
195	single, adj.	одиночный/ однократный/ единичный	einzeln	seul/unique
196	single base transformation	однобазная трансформация	Ein-Satztransformation, *f.*/eine zugrundeliegende Satztransformation/einfache Transformation	⟨transformation à base unique⟩, *f.*
197	single constituent sentence	односоставное предложение	aus einem Bestandteil bestehender Satz	phrase monorème, *f.*
198	singular, adj.	единичный	einzig	individuel
199	singular number	единственное число	Singular, *m.*/Einzahl, *f.*	singulier, *m.*
200	sister languages, pl.	родственные языки одного поколения, *m.,* pl.	Schwestersprachen, *f.,* pl.	langues soeurs, *f,* pl.
201	situation, n.	ситуация, *f.*	Situation, *f.*	situation, *f.*
202	situational context	бытовой контекст	Situationskontext, *m.*/ Situationszusammenhang, *m.*	contexte social, *m.*
203	situational meaning	ситуационное значение	Situationsbedeutung, *f.*	sens situationnel, *m.*
204	situational language	ситуационная речь	Zwecksprache, *f.*	langage situationnel, *m.*
205	size, n.	размер, *m.*	Grösse, *f.*	grandeur, *f.*
206	size of opening	степень открытия, *f.*	Öffnungsgrad, *m.*	degré d'aperture, *m.*
207	sketch, n.	очерк, *m.*	Aufriss, *m.*/Entwurf, *m.*/ Skizze, *f.*	esquisse, *f.*
208	skull, n.	череп, *m.*	Schädel, *m.*	crâne, *m.*
209	slang, n.	арго, *n.*	Slang, *m.*	argot, *m.*/langue verte, *f.*
210	slant lines, pl. (//)	косые скобки, pl.	Querstriche, *m.,* pl./ schräge Linien, *f.,* pl.	lignes en biais, *f.,* pl.

No.	English	Russian	German	French
211	Slavic Slavonic, adj.	славянский	slawisch	slave
212	slice, n.	отрезок, *m.*	Schnitt, *m.*	tranche, *f.*
213	slip of the tongue	оговорка, *f.*	Versprechen, *n.*	lapsus, *m.*
214	slogan, n.	лозунг, *m.*	Slogan, *m.*/ Wahlspruch, *m.*	slogan, *m.*/devise, *f.*
215	slot, n.	клетка, *f.*/прорезь, *f.*	Fach, *n.*/Schlitz, *m.*	encoche, *f.*
216	slow, adj.	медленный	langsam	lent
217	slow speech	растянутая речь	langsame Rede/lang- sames Sprechen/ Lentoform, *f.*	parole lente, *f.*
218	slurred speech	невнятная речь	verschleifendes Sprechen	bredouillement, *m.*/ mauvaise articulation, *f.*
219	small, adj.	маленький	klein	petit
220	small area	небольшой район	Kleingebiet, *n.*	aire exigue, *f.*
221	small letter	строчная буква	kleiner Buchstabe/ Minuskel, *f.*	miniscule, *f.*/ petit caractère, *m.*
222	small talk	светский разговор	Geplauder, *n.*	menus propos, *m.*, pl./ papotage, *m.*
223	smooth off-glide	слабая рекурсия	weicher Abglitt	détente douce, *f.*/ métatase douce, *f.*
224	smooth on-glide	слабая экскурсия	weicher Anglitt	catastase douce, *f.*/ tenue douce, *f.*
225	smooth onset	слабый начальный приступ	weicher Einsatz	attaque douce, *f.*
226	smooth release	слабый конечный отступ	weiche Auslösung	détente douce, *f.*
227	smooth transition	закрытый переход	verschlossene Verbin- dung	liaison etroite, *f.*
228	so-called, adj.	так называемый	sogenannt	ainsi nommé/soi-disant/ pretendu
229	social change	социальное изменение	Gesellschaftswandel, *m.*	changement social, *m.*

No.	ENGLISH	RUSSIAN	GERMAN	FRENCH
230	social class	социальный класс	Gesellschaftsklasse, *f.*	classe sociale, *f.*/ couche sociale, *f.*
231	social contract	социальный договор	Gesellschaftsvertrag, *m.*	contrat social, *m.*
232	social dialects, pl.	социальные диалекты, *m.*, pl.	soziale Dialekte, *m.*, pl.	dialectes sociaux, *m.*, pl.
233	social differences, pl.	социальные различия, *n.*, pl.	soziale Unterschiede, *m.* pl.	différences sociales, *f.*, pl.
234	social environment	социальная среда	soziale Umwelt	milieu social, *m.*
235	social rank	общественное положение	Gesellschaftsstufe, *f.*	rang dans la société, *m.*
236	society, n.	общество, *n.*	Gesellschaft, *f.*	société, *f.*
237	sociolinguistics, n.	социолингвистика, *f.*	Sprachsoziologie, *f.*	sociolinguistique, *f.*
238	socio-linguistic structure	социально-языковая структура	gesellschaftlich-sprachliche Struktur	structure socio-linguistique, *f.*
239	soft breathing	тонькое придыхание	ruhiges Atmen	respiration douce, *f.*
240	soft consonants, pl.	мягкие согласные, pl.	weiche Konsonanten, *m.*, pl.	consonnes douces, *f.*, pl./ consonnes molles, *f.*, pl.
241	soft onset	слабый начальный приступ	leiser Einsatz	attaque douce, *f.*/ début doux, *m.*
242	soft palate	мягкое небо/небная занавеска	Gaumensegel, *n.*	voile du palais, *m.*/ palais mou, *m.*
243	soft sign	мягкий знак	weiches Zeichen	signe mou, *m.*
244	soft release	слабый конечный отступ	weiche Auslösung	détente douce, *f.*
245	soft sound	тихий звук	leiser Laut	son doux, *m.*
246	softening, n.	смягчение, *n.*	Erweichung, *f.*	adoucissement, *m.*
247	softly, adv.	тихо	leise	doucement
248	solecism, n.	солецизм, *m.*/грамматическая ошибка	Sprachfehler, *m.*/ Sprachschnitzer, *m.*	solécisme, *m.*/ faute de grammaire, *f.*

No.	ENGLISH	RUSSIAN	GERMAN	FRENCH
249	solution, n.	решение, *n.*	Lösung, *f.*	résolution, *f.*/solution, *f.*
250	sonant consonants, pl.	сонорные согласные, pl./ звонкие согласные, pl.	Sonorlaute, *m.,* pl./ stimmhafte Konsonanten, *m.,* pl.	consonnes sonores, *f.* pl.
251	song	песня, *f.*	Gesang, *m.*/Lied, *n.*	chanson, *f.*
252	sonority, n.	звучность, *f.*/ звонкость, *f.*	Sonorität, *f.*/ Schallstärke, *f.*	sonorité, *f.*
253	sort, n.	сорт, *m.*/тип, *m.*	Sorte, *f.*/Art, *f.*	sorte, *f.*/espèce, *f.*
254	sort, v.	сортировать	sortieren	assortir/ classer par catégories
255	sound, n.	звук. *m.*	Laut, *m.*	son, *m.*
256	sound analysis	анализ звуков, *m.*	Schallanalyse, *f.*	analyse phonétique, *f.*
257	sound and meaning	звук и смысл	Laut und Bedeutung	son et phonème
258	sound and phoneme	звук и фонема	Laut und Phonem	son et sens
259	sound and symbol	звук и символ	Laut und Symbol	son et symbole
260	sound chain	звуковая цепь	Lautkette, *f.*	chaîne de sons, *f.*
261	sound change, n.	звуковое изменение	Lautwandel, *m.*/ Lautwechsel, *m.*	changement phonétique, *m.*
262	sound chart	таблица звуков, *f.*	Lauttafel, *f.*	table des sons, *f.*
263	sound classification, n.	классификация звуков, *f.*	Lautklassifizierung, *f.*/ Lauteinteilung, *f.*	classement de sons, *m.*
264	sound combination, n.	звукосочетание, *n.*	Lautkombination, *f.*	combinaison de sons, *f.*
265	sound correspondence	звуковое соответствие	Lautentsprechung, *f.*	correspondance phonétique, *f.*
266	sound disappearance	исчезновение звука, *n.*	Lautschwund, *m.*	disparition d'un son, *f.*
267	sound duration	длительность звука, *f.*	Lautdauer, *f.*	durée d'un son, *f.*
268	sound features, pl.	звуковые признаки, *m.,* pl.	Schalleigenschaften, *f.,* pl./Schallmerkmale, *n.,* pl.	traits acoustiques, *m.,* pl.

No.	ENGLISH	RUSSIAN	GERMAN	FRENCH
269	sound film	звуковой фильм	Tonfilm, *m.*	film sonore, *m.*
270	sound frequency	частота звука, *f.*	Lautfrequenz, *f.*	fréquence d'un son, *f.*
271	sound image	звуковая картина	Klangfigur, *f.*/Lautbild, *n.*	image sonore, *f.*
272	sound imitation	звукоподражание, *n.*	Lautnachahmung, *f.*	imitation d'un son, *f.*
273	sound intensity	интенсивность звука, *f.*	Lautstärke, *f.*	intensité d'un son, *f.*
274	sound law, n.	звуковой закон	Lautgesetz, *n.*	loi phonétique, *f.*
275	sound name	название звука, *n.*	Lautbenennung, *f.*	nom d'un son, *m.*
276	sound notation	звуковая нотация	Lautbezeichnung, *f.*	notation phonétique, *f.*
277	sound perception	восприятие звуков, *n.*	Lautwahrnehmung, *f.*	perception des sons, *f.*
278	sound pitch	высота тона, *f.*	Lauthöhe, *f.*/Tonhöhe, *f.*/ Tonstufe, *f.*	hauteur d'un son, *f.*
279	sound quality	звукокачество, *n.*	Lautqualität, *f.*	timbre d'un son, *m.*
280	sound quantity	звукоколичество, *n.*	Lautquantität, *f.*	quantité phonétique, *f.*
281	sound recognition	распознание звуков, *n.*	Lauterkennung, *f.*	reconaissance d'un son, *f.*
282	sound repitition	повторение звука, *n.*	Lautwiederholung, *f.*	répétition d'un son, *f.*
283	sound segment	отрезок звука, *m.*	Lautabschnitt, *m.*	segment phonétique, *m.*
284	sound sequence	звуковая последовательность	Lautfolge, *f.*	succession de sons, *f.*
285	sound shift, n.	передвижение звуков, *n* .	Lautverschiebung, *f.*	déplacement phonétique, *m.*
286	sound signal	звуковой сигнал	Lautsignal, *n.*	signal sonore, *m.*
287	sound spectrograph	звуковой спектрограф	Lautspektrograph, *m.*	spectrographe de son, *m.*
288	sound split, n.	звуковое расподобление	Lautspaltung, *f.*	dédoublement d'un son, *m.*/ bifurcation d'un son, *f.*
289	sound structure	звуковая структура/ звуковой строй	Lautstruktur, *f.*/ Lautstand, *m.*	structure phonétique, *f.*
290	sound substance	звуковое вещество	Lautstoff, *m.*	substance phonique, *f.*

No.	ENGLISH	RUSSIAN	GERMAN	FRENCH
291	sound substitution	звуковая замена	Lautsubstitution, *f./* Lautersetzung, *f.*	substitution de son, *f.*
292	sound symbolism	звуковая символика	Lautsymbolismus, *m.*	symbolisme phonétique, *n.*
293	sound system	звуковая система	Lautsystem, *n.*	système phonétique, *m.*
294	sound transmission	передача звуков, *f.*	Lautübertragung, *f.*	transmission phonique, *f.*
295	sound timbre	тембр звука, *m.*	Klangfarbe, *f.*	timbre d'un son, *m.*
296	sound velocity	быстрота звука, *f.*	Schallgeschwindigkeit, *f.*	vélocité d'un son, *f.*
297	sound wave	звуковая волна	Lautwelle, *f.*	onde sonore, *f.*
298	soundproof, adj.	звуконепроницаемый/ звукоизоляпион- ный	schalldicht	insonorisé
299	source, n.	источник, *m.*	Quelle, *f./*Ursprung, *m.*	source, *f./*origine, *f.*
300	source language (translation)	язык-источник, *m.*	Sprache des Originals, *f.*	langue de départ, f.
301	source language (historical)	праязык, *m.*	Ursprache, *f.*	langue-mère, *f.*
302	source language (dialectology)	язык-источник, *m.*	Quellensprache, *f.*	langue de source, *f.*
303	source material	источники, *m.,* pl.	Quellenmaterial, *n.*	sources originelles, *f.,* pl./ recueil de textes originels, *m.*
304	space (between words), n.	пропуск, *m.*	Wortzwischenraum, *n./* Zwischenraum, *n.*	espace, *m.*
305	space and time	пространство и время	Raum und Zeit	espace et temps
306	space dimension	размерность пространства, *f.*	Raumdimension, *f.*	dimension d'éspace, *f.*
307	Spanish, n.	испанский	spanisch	espagnol, *m.*
308	speak fluently, v.	бегло говорить	fliessend sprechen	parler couramment
309	speaker, n.	говорящий, *m.*	Sprecher, *m.*	locuteur, *m.*
310	speaker and hearer	говорящий и слушатель	Sprecher und Hörer	locuteur et interlocuteur

No.	ENGLISH	RUSSIAN	GERMAN	FRENCH
311	speaking, n.	речь, *f.*	Sprechen, *n.*	action de parler, *f.*
312	speaking voice	разговорный голос	Sprechstimme, *f.*	voix oratoire, *f.*
313	speaking vocabulary	речевой словарь	Sprechwortschatz, *m.*	vocabulaire utilisé dans la parole, *m.*
314	special case	особый случай	Sonderfall, *m.*	cas spécial, *m.*
315	specialization, n.	специализация, *f.*	Spezialisierung, *f.*/ Spezialität, *f.*	spécialisation, *f.*
316	specialized linguistics	частная лингвистика	Sprachwissenschaft einer bestimmten Sprachgruppe, *f.*	linguistique spécialisée, *f.*
317	specialized meaning	особое значение	begrenzte Bedeutung	sens spécialisé, *m.*
318	specialized vocabulary	обособленный словарь	Spezialwortschatz, *m.*	vocabulairé spécialisé, *m.*
319	specific, adj.	специфический	spezifisch/bestimmt	précis
320	specification, n.	уточнение, *n.*	Spezifizierung, *f.*/ Vorschrift, *f.*	spécification, *f.*
321	spectrogram, n.	спектрограмма, *f.*	Spektrogramm, *n.*	spectrogramme, *m.*
322	spectrograph	спектрограф, *m.*	Spektrograph, *m.*	spectographe, *m.*
323	spectroscope, n.	спектроскоп, *m.*	Spektroskop, *n.*	spectroscope, *m.*
324	spectrum, n.	спектр, *m.*	Spektrum, *n.*	spectre, *m.*
325	speech, n.	речь, *f.*	Rede, *f.*/Sprechen, *n.*	parole, *f.*/discours, *m.*
326	speech act	речевой акт	Sprechakt, *m.*/ Redeakt, *m.*	acte de parole, *m.*
327	speech and song	речь и песня	Rede und Lied	parole et chant
328	speech apparatus	речевой аппарат	Sprechapparat, *m.*	appareil de la parole, *m.*
329	speech blunder	оговорка, *f.*	Sprachschnitzer, *m.*/ Sprachsünde, *f.*	faute de parole, *f.*
330	speech breathing	речевое дыхание	Phonationsatmung, *f.*	chuche, *m.*
331	speech center (brain), n.	речевой центр	Sprachzentrum, *n.*	centre du langage, *m.*

No.	ENGLISH	RUSSIAN	GERMAN	FRENCH
332	speech chain	речевая цепь	Sprechkette, *f.*/Sprech-kontinuum, *n.*	chaîne parlée, *f.*
333	speech communication	речевое общение	Sprachkommunikation, *f.*	communication par le langage, *f.*
334	speech community	языковая общность/ говорящий коллектив	Sprachgemeinschaft, *f.*	communauté linguistique, *f.*
335	speech continuum	речевой континуум	Sprechkontinuum, *n.*	continu linguistique, *m.*
336	speech defect	речевой дефект	Sprachfehler, *m.*/ Sprachstörung, *f.*	difficulté d'élocution, *f.*
337	speech form	языковая форма	Sprachform, *f.*	forme de parole, *f.*
338	speech habits, pl.	речевые навыки, *f.*, pl./ речевые привычки, *f.*, pl.	Sprachgewohnheiten, *f.*, pl.	habitudes articulatoires, *f.*, pl.
339	speech impediment	речевой дефект	Sprachfehler, *m.*/ Sprachstörung, *f.*	difficulté d'élocution, *f.*
340	speech island	языковой островок	Sprachinsel, *f.*	îlot linguistique, *m.*
341	speech measure	речевой такт	Sprechtakt, *m.*	période, *f.*
342	speech melody	мелодика речи, *f.*	Sprachmelodie, *f.*	mélodie du discours, *f.*
343	speech organs, pl.	органы речи, *m.*, pl.	Sprachwerkzeuge, *n.*, pl./ Sprechorgane, *n.*, pl.	organes dits de la parole, *m.*, pl./organes phona-toires, *m.*, pl.
344	speech pathology	патология речи, *f.*	Sprachpathologie, *f.*	pathologie de la parole, *f.*
345	speech pause	пауза в разговоре. *f.*	Sprechpause, *f.*	arrêt dans le discours, *m.*
346	speech production	производство речи, *n.*	Sprachhervorbringung, *f.*/Spracherzeugung, *f.*/ Sprechen, *n.*	production de la parole, *f.*
347	speech register	голосовой регистр	Tonlage der Stimme, *f.*	registre de la parole, *m.*
348	speech segment	отрезок речи, *m.*	Sprachabschnitt, *m.*	segment de la parole, *m.*
349	speech sign(al)	речевой сигнал/ устный знак	Sprachzeichen, *n.*/ Sprechsignal, *n.*	signal de la parole, *m.*/ signe verbal, *m.*

No.	ENGLISH	RUSSIAN	GERMAN	FRENCH
350	speech situation	речевая ситуация	Sprechsituation, *f.*	contexte social du langage, *m.*
351	speech sound	звук речи, *m.*	Sprachlaut, *m.*	son du langage, *m.*
352	speech stream	речевой поток	Redestrom, *m.*/ Sprachstrom, *m.*	courant de la parole, *m.*/ débit, *m.*
353	speech style	стиль речи, *m.*	Sprachstil, *m.*	style de langage, *m.*
354	speech synthesis	синтез речи, *m.*	Sprachsynthese, *f.*	synthèse de la parole, *f.*
355	speech synthesizer	речевой синтезатор/ речевое синтезирующее устройство	Sprechmaschine, *f.*	appareil pour synthétiser la parole, *m.*
356	speech tempo	темп речи, *m.*	Sprechtempo, *n.*	tempo de parler, *m.*
357	speech therapy	терапия речи, *f.*	Sprachtherapie, *f.*	thérapeutie linguistique, *f.*
358	spelling, n.	правописание, *n.*/ орфография, *f.*	Buchstabieren, *n.*/ Rechtschreibung, *f.*	orthographe, *f.*
359	spelling pronunciation	диктовочное произношение	orthographische Aussprache/ ⟨Schriftaussprache⟩, *f.*	prononciation orthographique, *f.*
360	spelling reform	реформа орфографии, *f.*	Rechtschreibereform, *f.*	réforme orthographique, *f.*
361	spirant consonants, pl.	спиранты, *m.*, pl.	Reibelaute, *m.*, pl./ Spirans, *m.*	consonnes spirantes, *f.*, pl.
362	split	расподобление, *n.*	Spaltung, *f.*	dédoublement, *m.*/ bifurcation, *f.*
363	spoken language	устная речь/ разговорный язык	gesprochene Sprache	langue parlée, *f.*
364	spoken word	устное слово	gesprochenes Wort	parole *f.*
365	spontaneous creation	непосредственный неологизм	spontane Neuschöpfung	création spontanée, *f.*
366	spontaneous sound-change	стихийное звукоизменение	spontaner Lautwandel	changement phonétique spontané, *m.*
367	spoonerism, n.	акрофоническая перестановка	Schüttelreim, *m.*/ Schüttelform, *f.*	contrepetterie, *f.*

No.	English	Russian	German	French
368	sporadic, adj.	спорадический	sporadisch	isolé/rare
369	spread, n.	распространение, *n.*	Verbreitung, *f.*	diffusion, *f.*/ propagation, *f.*
370	square, n.	квадрат, *m.*	Quadrat, *n.*/Viereck, *n.*	carré, *m.*
371	stability, n.	устойчивость, *f.*	Beständigkeit, *f.*	stabilité, *f.*
372	stable system	устойчивая система	stabiles System	système stable, *m.*
373	stabilization, n.	стабилизация, *f.*	Stabilisierung, *f.*	stabilisation, *f.*
374	staccato speech (style)	прерывистая речь	abgehackte Sprechweise	parole saccadée, *f.*
375	stage (theatre)), n.	сцена, *f.*	Bühne, *f.*	scène, *f*
376	stage of development	этап развития, *m.*	Entwicklungsstufe, *f.*	degré de développement, *m.*
377	stage pronunciation	театральное произношение	Bühnenaussprache, *f.*	prononciation théâtrale, *f.*
378	stammering, n.	заикание, *n.*	Gestammel, *n.*/Gestotter, *n.*/Stammeln, *n.*/ Stottern, *n.*	bégaiement, *m.*
379	standard, n.	норма, *f.*	Norm, *f.*/Standard, *m.*	norme, *f.*/modèle, *m.*
380	standard language	стандартный язык/ образцовый язык	Standardsprache, *f.*	langue courante, *f.*
381	standardization, n.	нормализация, *f.*/ стандартизация, *f.*	Standardisierung, *f.*/ Normalisierung, *f.*	normalisation, *f.*
382	starting point	исходный пункт	Anfangspunkt, *m.*/ Ausgangspunkt, *m.*	point de départ, *m.*
383	state, n.	состояние, *n.*	Zustand, *m.*	état, *m.*
384	statement, n.	повествовательное предложение	Aussagesatz, *m.*	phrase assertive, *f.*/ constatation, *f.*
385	static, n.	помехи, pl.	Störung, *f.*	parasites, *m.*, pl.
386	static linguistics	статическая лингвистика	statische Linguistik	linguistique statique, *f.*
387	statistical analysis	статистический анализ	statistische Analyse	analyse statistique, *f.*

No.	English	Russian	German	French
388	statistical distribution	статистическое распределение	statistische Verteilung	distribution statistique, *f.*/ répartition statistique, *f.*
389	statistical factor	статистический фактор	statistischer Faktor	facteur statistique, *m.*
390	statistical independence	статистическая независимость	statistische Unabhängigkeit	indépendance statistique, *f.*
391	statistical linguistics	статистическая лингвистика	statistische Linguistik	linguistique statistique, *f.*
392	statistics, n.	статистика, *f.*	Statistik, *f.*	statistique, *f.*
393	status, n.	состояние, *n.*/ положение, *n.*	Status, *m.*	position, *f.*/rang, *m.* status, *m.*
394	steady-state sounds, pl.	установочные звуки, *m.,* pl.	Stellungslaute, *m.,* pl.	articulations stables, *f.,* pl.
395	stem, n.	основа, *f.*	Stamm, *m.*	théme, *m.*/radical, *m.*
396	stem alternation	тематическое чередование	Stammabstufung, *f.*	alternance thématique, *f.*
397	stem inflection	флексия основы, *f.*/ внутренняя флексия	Stammflexion, *f.*	flexion thématique, *f.*
398	stencil, n.	восковка, *f.*	Matrize, *f.*	stencil, *m.*/pochoir, *m.*
399	stenography, n.	стенография, *f.*	Kurzschrift, *f.*/ Stenographie, *f.*	sténographie, *f.*
400	stich, n.	стих, *m.*	Vers, *m.*	vers, *m.*
401	stimulus, n.	стимул, *m.*	Stimulus, *m.*/Reiz, *m.*	stimulus, *m.*
402	stimulus and response	стимул и реакция	Stimulus und Reaktion/ Reiz und Antwort	stimulus et réponse
403	stop consonants, pl.	смычные согласные, pl./затворные согласные, pl.	Verschlusslaute, *m.,* pl./ Explosivlaute, *m.,* pl.	consonnes occlusives, *f.,* pl./consonnes momentanées, *f.,* pl.
404	storage, n.	хранение, *n.*/ накопитель, *m.*/ память, *f.*	Speicher, *n.*/ Speicherung, *f.*	stockage, *m.*/mémoire, *f.*

No.	English	Russian	German	French
405	story, n.	рассказ, *m.*	Erzählung, *f.*/ Geschichte, *f.*	histoire, *f.*/récit, *m.*/ conte, *m.*
406	straight line	прямая линия	gerade Linie	ligne droite, *f.*
407	strange, adj.	незнакомый/чужой	fremd/sonderbar	étrange
408	strategy, n.	стратегия, *f.*	Strategie, *f.*	stratégie, *f.*
409	stratification, n.	стратификация, *f.*/ наслоение, *n.*	Schichtung, *f.*	stratification *f.*
410	stratificational model	стратификационная модель	Stratifikationsmodell, *n.*/ ⟨Schichtungsmodell⟩, *n.*	modèle de langue stratificationnel, *m*
411	stratum, n.	слой, *m.*/ярус, *m.*	Schicht, *f.*	couche, *f.*
412	stream, n.	поток, *m.*	Fluss, *m.*/Durchfluss, *m.*/ Strömung, *f.*	courant, *m.*
413	street names, pl.	названия улиц, *n.*, pl.	Strassennamen, *m.*, pl.	noms des rues, *m.*, pl.
414	street sign	дорожный указатель	Strassenschild, *n.*	plaque indicatrice, *f.*
415	stress, n.	ударение, *n.*	Betonung, *f.*/Ton, *m.*/ Druck, *m.*	accent tonique, *f.*
416	stress alternation	чередование ударения, *n* .	Tonwechsel, *m.*	alternance accentuelle, *f.*
417	stress change	передвижение ударения, *n.*	Betonungswechsel, *m.*	changement d'accentuation, *m.*
418	stress degree	степень ударения, *f.*	Betonungsstufe, *f.*	degré d'accent, *m.*
419	stress distribution	распределение ударений	Druckverteilung, *f.*	distribution d'accent, *f.*
420	stress group	акцентная группа/ ударная группа	Nachdrucktakt, *m.*	groupe accentuel, *m.*
421	stress phoneme	фонема ударения, *f.*	Betonungsphonem, *n.*	phonème d'accent, *m.*
422	stress-timed rhythm	тоническая ритмика речи	akzentierender Rhythmus/akzentzählender Rhythmus	rythme de la parole mésuré par accents, *m.*
423	stressed syllable	ударный слог	betonte Silbe	syllabe accentuée, *f.*

No.	ENGLISH	RUSSIAN	GERMAN	FRENCH
424	stressed vowel	ударная гласная	betonter Vokal	voyelle accentuée, *f.*
425	stretched form	протяженная форма	Streckform, *f.*	forme allongée/ forme étirée, *f.*
426	stricture, n.	сужение, *n.*	Verengerung, *f.*	rétrécissement, *m.*
427	string, n.	цепь, *f.*	Kette, *f.*	chaîne, *f.*
428	strong aspiration	сильное придыхание	starke Aspiration	aspiration forte, *f.*
429	strong position	сильная позиция	starke Stellung	position forte, *f.*
430	strong ending	сильное окончание	starke Endung	terminaison forte, *f.*
431	strong stress	сильное ударение	starke Betonung	accent tonique, *m.*
432	strong verb	сильный глагол	ablautendes Zeitwort/ unregelmässiges starkes Verb(um)	verbe fort, *m.*
433	strophe, n.	строфа, *f.*	Strophe, *f.*	strophe, *f.*
434	structural analysis	структурный анализ	Strukturanalyse, *f.*	analyse structurale, *f.*
435	structural description	структурное описание	Strukturbeschreibung, *f.*	description structurale, *f.*
436	structural dialectology	структуральная диалектология	strukturelle Mundarten- forschung	dialectologie structurale, *f.*
437	structural layer	структуральный слой/ структуральный ярус	Strukturschicht, *m.*	couche structurale, *f.*
438	structural level	структурный уровень	Strukturebene, *f.*	niveau structural, *m.*
439	structural linguistics	структурная лингвистика	strukturelle Sprachfor- schung	linguistique structurale, *f.*
440	structural marker	структурный указатель	Strukturzeichen, *n.*	indice structural, *m.*
441	structural relationship	structorное отношение	Strukturbeziehung, *f.*	rapport structural, *m.*
442	structural semantics	структурная семантика	strukturelle Semantik	sémantique structurale, *f.*
443	structural stability	структурная устойчивость	Strukturstabilität, *f.*	stabilité structurale, *f.*

No.	English	Russian	German	French
444	structural typology	структурная типология	strukturelle Typologie	typologie par structure, *f.*
445	structuralism, n.	структурализм, *m.*	Strukturalismus, *m.*	structuralisme, *m.*
446	structurally conditioned, adj.	структурно обусловленный	strukturbedingt	conditionné par la structure
447	structure, n.	структура, *f./* устройство, *n.*	Struktur, *f.*/Bau, *m.*	structure, *f.*
448	study, n.	изучение, *n./* исследование, *n.*	Studium, *n./* Untersuchung, *f.*	étude, *f.*
449	stuttering, n.	заикание, *n.*	Gestammel, *n.*/Gestotter, *n.*/Stammeln, *n.*/ Stottern, *n.*	bégaiement, *m.*
450	style, n.	стиль, *m./*слог, *m.*	Stil, *m.*	style, *m.*
451	stylistic effect	стилистический эффект	stilistische Wirkung	effet stylistique, *m.*
452	stylistic punctuation	стилистическая пунктуация	stilistische Interpunktion	ponctuation stylistique, *f.*
453	stylistic variation	стилистическая вариация	stilistische Variation	variation stylistique, *f.*
454	stylistics, n.	стилистика, *f.*	Stilistik, *f.*	stylistique, *f.*
455	subclass, n.	подкласс, *m.*	Unterklasse, *f.*	sous-classe, *f.*
456	subdivision, n.	подразделение, *n.*	Unterteilung, *f.*	subdivision, *f.*
457	subgroup, n.	подгруппа, *f.*	Untergruppe, *f.*	sous-groupe, *m.*
458	subheading, n.	подзаголовок, *m.*	Untertitel, *m.*	sous-titre, *m.*
459	subject, n.	подлежащее, *n.*	Subjekt, *n./* Satzgegenstand, *m.*	sujet, *m.*
460	subject index	предметный указатель	Sachregister, *n./* Sachverzeichnis, *n.*	index de matières, *m.*
461	subject matter, n.	сюжет, *m./*тема, *f.*	Stoff, *m.*	sujet, *m./*thème, *m.*
462	subjective case	падеж подлежащего, *m.*	Nominativ, *m.*/Werfall, *m.*/erster Fall	cas sujet, *m.*

No.	ENGLISH	RUSSIAN	GERMAN	FRENCH
463	subjectivity, n.	субъективность, *f.*	Subjektivität, *f.*	subjectivité, *f.*
464	subjectless sentence	безличное предложение	subjektloser Satz	phrase sans sujet, *f.*
465	subjunctive mood	сослагательное наклонение	Konjunktiv, *m.*	subjonctif, *m.*
466	submorphemic, adj.	субморфемный/ подморфемный	submorphemisch	sub-morphémique
467	subordinate, adj.	придаточный/ подчиненный	abhängig/untergeordnet	subordonné
468	subordinate clause	придаточное предложение	Nebensatz, *m.*	proposition subordonnée, *f.*/incidente, *f.*
469	subordinating conjunc-tion	подчинительный союз	unterordnende Konjunktion	conjonction de subordi-nation, *f.*
470	subordination, n.	подчинение, *n.*	Unterordnung, *f.*	subordination, *f.*
471	subphonemic, adj.	субфонемный/ подфонемный	subphonemisch	sub-phonémique
472	subscript, n.	подстрочный знак	Unterschrift, *f.*	souscrit, *m.*
473	subscription, n.	подписка, *f.*	Abonnement, *n.*/ Subskription, *f.*	abonnement, *m.*
474	subsequent, adj.	последующий	folgend	subséquent/postérieur
475	subset, n.	подмножество, *n.*	Teilmenge, *f.*/ Untermenge, *f.*	sous-ensemble, *m.*
476	substance, n.	вещество, *n.*/ сущность, *f.*	Stoff, *m.*	substance, *f.*
477	substantive, n.	существительное, *n.*	Substantiv, *n.*/ Nennwort, *n.*	substantif, *m.*
478	substitution, n.	замена, *f.*/замещение, *n.*/подстановка, *f.*	Ersatz, *m.*/Ersetzung, *f.*/ Stellvertretung, *f.*	substitution, *f.*
479	substitution class	замещающий класс	Substitutionsklasse, *f.*	classe de substitution, *f.*
480	substitution drill	упражнение с подстановками, *n.*	Substitutionsübung, *f.*/ Umwandlungsübung, *f.*	exercice par substitu-tions, *m.*

No.	ENGLISH	RUSSIAN	GERMAN	FRENCH
481	substitution frame	заместительная рама	Substitutionsrahmen, *m.*	cadre de substitution, *m.*
482	substratum, n.	субстрат, *m.*/ нижний слой	Substratum, *n.*/ Unterschicht, *f.*	substrat, *m.*
483	subsystem, n.	подсистема, *f.*	Untersystem, *n.*	sous-système, *m.*
484	subtitle, n.	подзаголовок, *m.*	Untertitel, *m.*	sous-titre, *m.*
485	subtraction, n.	вычитание, *n.*	Subtraktion, *f.*/ Abziehen, *n.*	soustraction, *f.*
486	success, n.	удача, *f.*/успех, *m.*	Erfolg, *m.*	succès, *m.*
487	succession, n.	последовательность, *f.*	Folge, *f.*	succession, *f.*/suite, *f.*/ série, *f.*
488	successive cuts, pl.	последовательные разрезы, *m., pl.*	aufeinander folgende Schnitte, *m., pl.*	analyse par dissection, *f.*
489	sucking sound	всасывающий звук/ звук сосания, *m.*	Sauglaut, *m.*	son inverse, *m*
490	sufficient, adj.	достаточный	genügend	suffisant
491	sufficient condition	достаточное условие	genügende Bedingung/ hinreichende Bedingung	condition suffisante, *f.*
492	suffix, n.	суффикс, *m.*	Suffix, *n.*/Nachsilbe, *f.*	suffixe, *m.*
493	suffixation, suffixion, suffixing, n.	суффиксация, *f.*	Anhängen von Suffixen, *n.*	suffixation, *f.*
494	suitable, adj.	подходящий	passend/geeignet	convenable
495	sum, n.	сумма, *f.*	Summe, *f.*	somme, *f.*
496	summary, n.	резюме, *n.*/конспект, *m.*	Zusammenfassung, *f.*	sommaire, *m.*
497	superficial, adj.	поверхностный	oberflächlich	superficiel
498	superfluous, adj.	избыточный/ излишний	überflüssig	superflu
499	superlative degree	превосходная степень	superlative Steigerungsstufe	degré superlatif, *m.*

No.	English	Russian	German	French
500	superposition, n.	накладывание, *n.*	Übereinanderlagerung, *f.*	superposition, *f.*
501	superscript, n.	надстрочный знак	Überschrift, *f.*	suscription, *f.*
502	superstition, n.	суеверие, *n.*	Aberglaube, *m.*	superstition, *f.*
503	superstratum, n.	суперстрат, *m.*/ верхний слой	Superstratum, *n.*/ Oberschicht, *f.*	superstrat, *m.*
504	superstructure, n.	надстройка, *f.*	Oberbau, *m.*	superstructure, *f.*
505	supplement (to book), n.	приложение, *n.*	Nachtragsband, *m.*	supplément, *m.*
506	suppletive, n.	суплетив, *m.*/ заместитель, *m.*	Suppletivismus, *m.*	supplétif, *m.*
507	supraglottal, adj.	надгортанный	superglottal	supraglottique
508	suprasegmental phoneme	суперсегментная фонема	suprasegmentales Phonem	phonème suprasegmental, *m.*
509	surface structure	поверхностная структура	Oberflächenstruktur, *f.*	structure apparentée, *f.*
510	surname, n.	фамилия, *f.*	Familienname, *m.*/ Zuname, *m.*	nom de famille, *m.*/ surnom, *m.*
511	surprise, n.	удивление, *n.*	Überraschung, *f.*	surprise, *f.*/ étonnement, *m.*
512	survey, n.	конспект, *m.*/обзор, *m.*	Überblick, *m.*	aperçu, *m.*
513	suspicious pairs, pl.	подозретельные пары, *f.*, pl.	zweifelhafte Paare, *n.*, pl.	paires suspectes, *f.*, pl.
514	swear word, n.	ругательство, *n.*	Schimpfwort, *n.*/ Fluch, *m.*	juron, *m.*/gros mot, *m.*
515	Swedish, n.	шведский	schwedisch	suédois, *m.*
516	switching of code	перемена кода, *f.*	Codewechsel, *m.*	changement de code, *m.*
517	syllabary, n.	слоговая азбука	Silbenliste, *f.*	syllabaire, *m.*
518	syllabic alphabet	силлабический алфавит	syllabisches Alphabet	alphabet syllabique, *m.*
519	syllabic consonant	слоговая согласная	silbischer Konsonant	consonne faisant syllabe, *f.*

No.	ENGLISH	RUSSIAN	GERMAN	FRENCH
520	syllabic nucleus	слоговое ядро/ выдержка, *f.*	Silbenkern, *m.*	noyau syllabique, *m.*
521	syllabic peak	вершина слога, *f.*	Silbengipfel, *m.*	sommet de syllabe, *m.*
522	syllabic phoneme	слоговая фонема	silbisches Phonem	phonème syllabique, *m.*
523	syllabic script	слоговое письмо	Silbenschrift, *f.*	écriture syllabique, *f.*
524	syllabic stress	слоговое ударение	Silbenakzent, *m.*	accent syllabique, *m.*
525	syllabic writing system	силлабическое письмо	silbisches Schriftsystem	système d'écriture par syllabes, *m.*
526	syllabification, n.	слогораздел, *m.*	Silbentrennung, *f.*	syllabification, *f.*
527	syllable, n.	слог, *m.*	Silbe, *f.*	syllabe, *f.*
528	syllable boundary	граница слога, *f.*	Silbengrenze, *f.*	frontière de syllabe, *f.*
529	syllable division	слогораздел, *m.*	Silbenteilung, *f.*	division syllabique, *f.*
530	syllable final positon	конец слога, *m.*	Silbenende, *n.*	fin de syllabe, *f.*
531	syllable initial position	начало слога, *n.*	Silbenanfang, *m.*	initiale de syllabe, *f.*
532	syllable structure	структура слога. *f.*	Silbenstruktur, *f.*	structure syllabique, *f.*
533	syllable-internal, adj.	внутрислоговой	inlautend	à l'intérieur des syllabes
534	syllable-timed rhythm	силлабическая ритмика речи	silbenzählender Rhythmus	rythme de la parole mesuré par syllabes, *m.*
535	syllabus, n.	конспект, *m.*	Lehrplan, *m.*	programme, *m.*
536	symbol, n.	символ, *m.*	Symbol, *n.*	symbole, *m.*
537	symbolic language	символический язык	symbolische Sprache	langue symbolique, *f.*
538	symbolic logic	символическая логика	symbolische Logik	logique symbolique, *f.*
539	symbolic signalization	символическая сигнализация	symbolische Signalisierung	signalisation symbolique, *f.*
540	symbolism, n.	символизм, *m.*	Symbolismus, *m.*	symbolisme, *m.*
541	symbolization, n.	символизация, *f.*	Symbolisierung, *f.*/Versinnbildlichung, *f.*	symbolisation, *f.*

No.	ENGLISH	RUSSIAN	GERMAN	FRENCH
542	symmetrical, adj.	симетрический	symmetrisch/ gleichmässig	symétrique
543	symmetry, n.	симетрия, *f.*	Symmetrie, *f.*	symétrie, *f.*
544	synchronic, adj.	синхронический/ синхронный	synchronisch/gleichzeitig	synchronique
545	synchronic analysis	синхронный анализ	synchronische Analyse	analyse synchronique, *f.*
546	synchronic linguistics	синхронная лингвистика	synchronistische Sprach- forschung	linguistique synchro- nique, *f.*/linguistique statique, *f.*
547	synchronism, n.	синхронизм, *m.*	Gleichlauf, *m.*	synchronisme, *m.*
548	synchrony, n.	синхрония, *f.*	Synchronie, *f.*	synchronie, *f.*
549	syncopation, syncope, n.	синкопа, *f.*	Synkope, *f.*	syncope, *f.*
550	syncretism, n.	синкретизм, *m.*	Synkretismus, *m.*	syncrétisme, *m.*
551	syndetic, adj.	соединительный/ союзный	verbindend	syndétique
552	synharmony, n.	сингармонизм, *m.*	Vokalharmonie, *f.*	harmonie vocalique, *f.*
553	synonym, n.	синоним, *m.*	Synonym, *n.*	synonyme, *m.*
554	synonymy, n.	синонимия, *f.*	Synonomie, *f.*/ Gleichbedeutigkeit, *f.*	synonymie, *f.*
555	syntactic(al), adj.	синтактический	syntaktisch	syntaxique
556	syntactic ambiguity	синтактическая двусмысленность	syntaktische Zweideutig- keit	ambiguïté syntaxique, *f.*
557	syntactic category	синтактическая категория	syntaktische Kategorie	catégorie syntaxique, *f.*
558	syntactic change	синтактическое изменение	syntaktischer Wechsel	changement syntaxique, *m.*
559	syntactic class	синтактический класс	syntaktische Klasse	classe syntaxique, *f.*
560	syntactic combination	синтактическое сочетание	syntaktische Zusammensetzung	combinaison syntaxique, *f.*
561	syntactic construction	синтактическая конструкция	syntaktische Konstruktion	construction syntaxique, *f.*

No.	English	Russian	German	French
562	syntactic device	синтаксический механизм	syntaktisches Mittel	procédé syntaxique, *m.*
563	syntactic economy	синтаксическая экономия	syntaktische Ökonomie	économie syntaxique, *f.*
564	syntactic environment	синтаксическое окружение	syntaktische Umgebung	milieu syntaxique, *m.*
565	syntactic equivalence	синтаксическая эквивалентность	syntaktische Gleichwertigkeit	équivalence syntaxique, *f.*
566	syntactic expansion	синтаксическое расширение	syntaktische Erweiterung	élargissement syntaxique, *m.*
567	syntactic feature	синтаксический признак	syntaktische Eigenschaft	trait syntaxique, *m.*
568	syntactic freedom	синтаксическая свобода	syntaktische Freiheit	liberté syntaxique, *f.*
569	syntactic function	синтаксическая функция	syntaktische Funktion	fonction syntaxique, *f.*
570	syntactic government	синтаксическое управление	syntaktische Rektion	rection syntaxique, *f.*
571	syntactic group	синтаксическая группа	syntaktische Gruppe	groupe syntaxique, *m.*
572	syntactic innovation	синтаксическое нововведение	syntaktische Neuerung	nouveauté syntaxique, *f.*
573	syntactic level	синтаксический уровень	syntaktische Ebene	niveau syntaxique, *m.*
574	syntactic paradigm	синтаксическая парадигма	syntaktisches Paradigma	paradigme syntaxique, *m.*
575	syntactic relationship	синтаксическое отношение	syntaktische Beziehung	affinité syntaxique, *f.*
576	syntactic stress	синтагматическое ударение/ логическое ударение	Satzbetonung, *f.*	accent logique, *m.*
577	syntactic unit	синтаксическая единица	syntaktische Einheit	unité syntaxique, *f.*

No.	ENGLISH	RUSSIAN	GERMAN	FRENCH
578	syntagm, n.	синтагма, *f.*	Syntagma, *n.*	syntagme, *m.*
579	syntagmatic, adj.	синтагматический	syntagmatisch	syntagmatique
580	syntagmatic axis	синтагматическая ось	syntagmatische Achse	axe syntagmatique, *m.*
581	syntax, n.	синтаксис, *m.*	Syntax, *f.*/Satzlehre, *f.*	syntaxe, *f.*
582	synthesis, n.	синтез, *m.*	Synthese, *f.*	synthèse, *f.*
583	synthetic languages, pl.	синтетические языки, *m.*, pl.	synthetische Sprachen, *f.*, pl.	langues synthétiques, *f.*, pl.
584	system	система, *f.*	System, *n.*	système, *m.*
585	system balance	равновесие системы, *n.*	Gleichgewicht des Systems, *n.*	équilibre du système, *m.*
586	system of signs	система знаков, *f.*	Zeichensystem, *n.*	système de signes, *m.*
587	systematic, adj.	систематический	systematisch	systématique
588	systematicity of language	системность языка, *f.*	Sprachsystematie, *f.*/Systemhaftigkeit der Sprache, *f.*	nature systématique des langue, *f.*

T

001	table, n.	таблица, *f.*	Tabelle, *f.*	table, *f.*
002	table of contents	оглавление, *n.*/содержание, *n.*	Inhaltsverzeichnis, *n.*	table de matières, *f.*/sommaire, *m.*
003	table talk	застольная беседа	Tischgespräch, *n.*	propos de table, *m.*, pl.
004	tablet, n.	дощечка, *f.*	Inschriftstafel, *f.*/Gedenktafel, *f.*	plaque commémorative, *f.*
005	taboo word	слово-табу, *n.*	Tabu-Wort, *n.*	mot tabou, *m.*
006	tactics, n.	тактика, *f.*	Taktik, *f.*	tactique, *f.*
007	tabulation, n.	табулирование, *n.*	Tabellierung, *f.*	tabulation, *f.*
008	tactile language	осязательный язык	Tastsprache, *f.*	langage tactile, *m.*
009	tagmeme, n.	тагмема, *f.*	Tagmem, *n.*	tagmème, *m.*

No.	ENGLISH	RUSSIAN	GERMAN	FRENCH
010	tagmemic model	тагмемная модель	tagmemisches Modell	modèle tagmémique, *m.*
011	tale, n.	повесть, *f.*/рассказ, *m.*	Erzählung, *f.*	conte, *m.*/récit, *m.*
012	talk, n.	беседа, *f.*/разговор, *m.*/ речь, *f.*/доклад, *m.*	Gespräch, *n.*/Unterhaltung, *f.*/Vortrag, *m.*	mots, *m.*, pl./ conversation, *f.*/ entretien, *m.*
013	talkative, adj.	болтливый/ словоохотливый	gesprächig/redselig	bavard
014	talkie, n.	звуковой фильм	Tonfilm, *m.*	cinéma parlant, *m.*
015	talking, n.	говор, *m.*	Sprechen, *n.*	paroles, *f.*, pl./ propos, *m.*, pl.
016	talking, adj.	говорящий	sprechend	parlant
017	talking to oneself, n.	разговор с самим собой, *m.*	Selbstgespräch, *n.*	parler à soi-méme, (v.)
018	tamber, n.	тембр, *m.*/окраска, *f.*	Klangfarbe, *f.*	timbre, *m.*
019	tape, n.	лента, *f.*	Band, *n.*	bande, *f.*/ruban, *m.*
020	tape recorder	магнитофон, *m.*	Magnetophon, *n.*/ Tonbandgerät, *n.*	magnétophone, *m.*
021	tape recording	магнитофонная запись	Tonbandaufnahme, *f.*	enregistrement sur magnétophone, *m.*
022	target language (translation)	переводящий язык	Zielsprache, *f.*	langue d'arrivée, *f.*
023	task, n.	задание, *f.*/задача, *f.*	Aufgabe, *f.*	travail, *m.*/tâche, *f.*/ besogne, *f.*
024	taste, n.	вкус, *m.*	Geschmack, *m.*	goût, *m.*
025	tautology, n.	тавтология, *f.*	Tautologie, *f.*	tautologie, *f.*
026	taxonomic grammar, —— model	таксономическая грамматика/ таксономическая модель	taxonomische Grammatik/taxonomisches Modell	grammaire taxonomique, *f.*/modèle taxonomique, *m.*
027	teaching, n.	обучение, *n.*/ преподавание, *n.*	Lehren, *n.*/Unterricht, *m.*	enseignement, *m.*
028	teaching machine	обучающая машина	Lehrmaschine, *f.*	appareil pour enseigner, *m.*

No.	ENGLISH	RUSSIAN	GERMAN	FRENCH
029	teaching materials, pl.	учебные пособые, *n.*, pl.	Lehrmaterialien, *n.*, pl./ Unterrichtsmaterialien, *n.*, pl.	matériaux d'instruction, *m.*, pl.
030	teaching method	метод обучения, *m.*	Lehrmethode, *f.*	méthode de l'enseignement, *f.*
031	teaching problem	вопрос преподавания, *m.*	Lehrproblem, *n.*	problème d'enseignement, *m.*
032	teaching profession	преподавательская профессия	Lehrstand, *m.*	enseignement, *m.*
033	teaching staff	преподавательский состав	Lehrkörper, *m.*	corps de l'enseignement, *m.*
034	team, n.	коллектив, *m.*	Arbeitsgruppe, *f.*	équipe, *f.*
035	technical, adj.	технический	technisch	technique
036	technical language	технический язык	Fachsprache, *f.*	langage technique, *m.*
037	technical term	технический термин	Fachausdruck, *m.*	terme technique, *m.*
038	technique, n.	техника, *f.*	Technik, *f.*	technique, *f.*
039	technology, n.	технология, *f.*	Technologie, *f.*	technologie, *f.*
040	teen-age language	язык подростков, *m.*	Jugendsprache, *f.*	langage des adolescents, *m.*
041	teeth, pl.	зубы, *f.*, pl.	Zähne, *m.*, pl.	dents, *f.*, pl.
042	telecast, n.	телевизионная передача	Fernsehsendung, *f.*	émission de télévision, *f.*
043	telegram, n.	телеграмма, *f.*	Telegramm, *n.*	télégramme, *m.*/dépéche, *f.*
044	telegraph address	телеграфный адрес	Telegrammadresse, *f.*/ Drahtanschrift, *f.*	adresse télégraphique, *f.*
045	telegraph code	телеграфный код	Telegrammschlüssel, *m.*	code télégraphique, *m.*
046	telegraphese, n.	телеграфный стиль	Telegrammstil, *m.*	style télégraphique, *m.*
047	telegraphic, adj.	телеграфный	telegraphisch	télégraphique
048	teleology, n.	телеология, *f.*	Teleologie, *f.*	téléologie, *f.*

No.	ENGLISH	RUSSIAN	GERMAN	FRENCH
049	telepathy, n.	телепатия, *f.*	Gedankenübertragung, *f.* /Telepathie, *f.*	télépathie, *f.*
050	telephone, n.	телефон, *m.*	Telefon, *n.*/ Fernsprecher, *m.*	téléphone, *m.*
051	telephone call, ———— conversation	звонок по-телефону, *m.*	Telefonanruf, *m.*/ Telefongespräch, *n.*	appel téléphonique, *m.*/ communication téléphonique, *f.*
052	telephone directory	книга телефонных абонентов, *f.*	Telefonbuch, *n.*	annuaire, *m*
053	telephone number	номер телефона, *m.*	Telefonnummer, *f.*	numéro de téléphone, *m.*
054	telephone speech	телефонная речь	Telefonsprache, *f.*	langage téléphonique, *m.*
055	teleprinter, teletype, n.	телетайп, *m.*	Fernschreibeapparat, *m.*/ Fernschreiber, *m.*	téléimprimeur, *m.*/ télétype, *m.*
056	television, T.V., n.	телевидение, *n.*	Fernsehen, *n.*/ Bildfunk, *m.*	télévision, *f.*
057	television set	телевизор, *m.*	Fernsehapparat, *m.*	appareil de télévision, *m.*
058	tell, v.	сказать/рассказывать	sagen/erzählen	dire/raconter
059	tell time, v.	указать время	die Uhr lesen	dire l'heure
060	tempo, n.	темп, *m.*	Tempo, *n.*	tempo, *m.*
061	temporal, adj.	временной	temporal/ Zeit-	temporel
062	tenable, adj.	защитимый	haltbar/überzeugend	soutenable
063	tendency, n.	тенденция, *f.*/ наклонность, *f.*	Tendenz, *f.*/Neigung, *f.*	tendance, *f.*
064	tense, n.	время, *n.*	Tempus, *m.*/Zeitform, *f.*	temps, *m.*
065	tense, adj.	напряженный	gespannt	tendu
066	tension, tenseness, n.	напряжение, *n.*/ напряженность, *f.*	Spannung, *f.*/ Spannungsgrad, *m.*	tension, *f.*
067	tentative, adj.	пробный/ экспериментальный	probend/versuchend/ vorläufig	provisoire
068	term, n.	термин, *m.*	Terminus, *m.*	terme, *m.*/expression, *f.*

No.	ENGLISH	RUSSIAN	GERMAN	FRENCH
069	term of address	форма обращения, *f.*	Anredeform, *f.*	titre d'adresse, *m.*
070	term of derision	насмешка, *f.*	Hohn, *m.*/Spott, *m.*	terme de dérision, *m.*
071	term of endearment	ласкательная форма	Zärtlichkeitsform, *f.*/ Koseform, *f.*	terme d'attendrissement, *m.*
072	term of pain	выражение боли, *n.*	Ausdruck des Schmerzes, *m.*	terme de chagrin, *m.*
073	term of pleasure	выражение удовольствия, *n.*	Ausdruck des Wohlgefallens, *m.*	terme de plaisir, *m.*
074	term of surprise	выражение удивления, *n.*	Ausruf der Überraschung, *m.*/ Überraschungsschrei, *m.*	terme de surprise, *m.*
075	terminal, adj.	заключительный/ конечный/ окончательный	End- /Schluss-	final/ultime
076	terminal contour	конечная оболочка	Schlusstonhöhenkurve, *f.*	contour terminal, *m.*
077	terminal string	терминальная цепочка/конечная цепочка	Endkette, *f.*	chaîne finale, *f.*
078	termination, n.	окончание, *n.*	Endung, *f.*	terminaison, *f.*
079	terminology	терминология, *f.*	Fachausdrücke, *m., pl.*/ Terminologie, *f.*	terminologie, *f.*
080	ternary, adj.	тройной	dreifach	ternaire
081	terse, adj.	сжатый	bündig/markig	concis
082	tertiary stress	третичное ударение	Schwachton, *m.*	accent tertiaire, *m.*
083	test, n.	испытание, *n.*/проба, *f.*	Probe, *f.*	épreuve, *f.*
084	text, n.	текст, *m.*	Text, *m.*	texte, *m.*
085	text-book, n.	учебник, *m.*	Lehrbuch, *n.*/ Leitfaden, *m.*	manuel, *m.*
086	texture, n.	ткань, *f.*	Gefüge, *n.*	contexture, *f.*
087	theater, n.	театр, *m.*	Theater, *n.*/ Schauspielhaus, *n.*	théâtre, *m.*

No.	ENGLISH	RUSSIAN	GERMAN	FRENCH
088	theatrical speech	театральная речь	Bühnensprache, *f.*	langage du théâtre, *m.*
089	theme (stem), n.	основа. *f.*	Stamm, *m.*	thème, *m.*
090	theme (topic), n.	тема, *f.*	Thema, *n.*	thème, *m.*
091	theorem, n.	теорема, *f.*	Lehrsatz, *m.*	théorème, *m.*
092	theoretical, adj.	теоретический	theoretisch	théorique
093	theoretical language	теоретический язык	theoretische Sprache	langue théorique, *f.*
094	theory, n.	теория, *f.*	Theorie, *f.*	théorie, *f.*
095	therapy, n.	терапия. *f.*	Therapie, *f.*	thérapie, *f.*
096	thesaurus, n.	сокровищница, *f./* источник сведений	Thesaurus, *m.*	trésor, *m./*gros recueil, *m.*
097	thesis, n.	тезис, *m.*	These, *f./*Doktorarbeit, *f.*	thèse, *f.*
098	thick, adj.	толстый	dick	épais
099	thieves' jargon	воровской жаргон	Gaunersprache, *f./* Rotwelsch, *n.*	jargon de voleurs, *m.*
100	thing, n.	вещь, *f./*предмет, *m.*	Ding, *m./*Sache, *f.*	chose, *f./*objet, *m.*
101	thinking, n.	мышление, *n.*	Denken, *n.*	pensée, *f.*
102	third person	третье лицо	dritte Person	troisième personne, *f.*
103	thorn, n. (θ)	фита, *f.*	Thorn, *m.*	thorn, *m.*
104	thought, n.	мышление, *n./*мысль, *f.*	Denken, *n./*Gedanke, *m.*	pensée, *f./*idée, *f.*
105	thought process	умственный процесс	Denkprozess, *m.*	mouvement de la pensée, *m.*
106	thought transference	телепатия, *f.*	Telepathie, *f./* Gedanken- übertragung, *f.*	télépathie, *f.*
107	thought wave	мысленная волна	Gedankenwelle, *f.*	onde télépathique, *f.*
108	throat, n.	глотка, *f./*горло, *n.*	Kehle, *f./*Rachen, *m.*	gorge, *f./*gosier, *m.*
109	throat cavity	полость глотки, *f.*	Rachenhöhle, *f.*	cavité postérieure, *f.*
110	throaty, adj.	гортанный	guttural/ Kehl-	guttural

No.	ENGLISH	RUSSIAN	GERMAN	FRENCH
111	thumb, n.	большой палец	Daumen, *m.*	pouce, *m.*
112	thumb index	буквенный указатель	Daumenregister, *n.*	onglet, *m.*/touche,*f.*
113	thyroid gland	щитовидная железа	Schilddrüse, *f.*	thyroïde, *m.*
114	tie, n.	связь, *f.*	Verbindung, *f.*	lien, *m.*/attache, *f.*
115	tilde, n. (~)	тильда, *f.*	Tilde, *f.*	tilde, *m.*
116	timbre, n.	тембр, *m.*	Klangfarbe, *f.*	timbre, *m.*
117	time, n.	время, *n.*	Zeit, *f.*	temps, *m.*
118	time and space	время и пространство	Zeit und Raum	temps et espace
119	time axis	временная ось	Zeitachse, *f.*	axe du temps, *m.*
120	time depth (of a language)	давность, *f.*	Zeittiefe der Sprache, *f.*	date à laquelle remonte (d'une langue), *f.*
121	time dimension	размерность времени, *n.*	Zeitdimension, *f.*	dimension temporelle, *f.*
122	time division	деление времени, *n.*	Zeitverteilung, *f.*	division de temps, *f.*
123	time expression	выражение времени, *n.*	Zeitausdruck, *m.*	expression temporelle, *f.*/ locution temporelle, *f.*
124	time factor	фактор времени, *m.*/ роль времени, *f.*	Zeitfaktor, *m.*	facteur du temps, *m.*
125	time span, time interval	промежуток времени, *m.*/срок, *m.*	Zeitspanne, *f.*/ Zwischenzeit, *f.*	espace de temps, *m.*
126	time-telling, n.	указание времени, *n.*	die Uhr lesen (v.)	dire l'heure, (v.)
127	timeless verb	вневременной глагол	zeitloses Verb(um)	verbe atemporel, *m.*
128	title, n.	название, *n.*/ заголовок, *m.*/ заглавие, *n.*	Titel, *m.*	titre, *m.*
129	title of address	звание, *n.*	Anredetitel, *m.*	titre, *m.*
130	title of book	заглавие книги, *n.*	Buchtitel, *m.*	titre, *m.*/intitulé, *m.*
131	title of nobility	титул, *m.*	Adelsbrief, *m.*	titre de noblesse, *m.*

No.	English	Russian	German	French
132	title page	титульный лист	Titelblatt, *n.*/Titelseite, *f.*	page de titre, *f.*
133	tittle-tattle, n.	сплетни, pl./ болтовня, *f.*	Geschwätz, *n.*/ Geklatsch, *n.*	cancans, *m.*, pl./ commérages, *m.*, pl./ bavardages, *m.*, pl.
134	tmesis, n.	тмезис, *m.*	Tmesis, *f.*	tmèse, *f.*
135	toast, n.	тост, *m.*	Trinkspruch, *m.*	toast, *m.*
136	token, n.	знак, *m.*	Zeichen, *n.*	marque, *f.*/gage, *m.*
137	tomb, n.	могила, *f.*	Grab, *n.*/Grabgewölbe, *n.*/Grabstätte, *f.*	tombeau, *m.*
138	tombstone, n.	надгробная плитка/ надгробный камень	Grabstein, *m.*/Leichenstein, *m.*/Grabmal, *n.*	pierre tombale, *f.*
139	tome, n.	толстая книга	dicker Band	tome, *m.*
140	tonal stress	тональное ударение	melodische Betonung	accent mélodique, *m.*
141	tonality, n.	тональность, *f.*	Tonalität, *f.*	tonalité, *f.*
142	tone, n.	тон, *m.*	Ton, *m.*	ton, *m.*
143	tone and intonation	тон и интонация	Ton und Intonation	ton et intonation
144	tone and noise	тон и шум	Klingen und Rauschen	son et bruit
145	tone languages, pl.	многотонные языки, *m.*, pl.	polytone Sprachen, *f.*, pl.	langues à tons, *f.*, pl.
146	tone phoneme	фонема тона, *f.*	Tonphonem, *n.*	phonème de ton, *m.*
147	tone-deaf, adj.	тонально-глухой	ohne musikalisches Gehör/unfähig Tonhöhe zu unterscheiden	incapable de distinguer les tons
148	toneme, n.	тонема, *f.*	Tonem, *n.*	tonème, *m.*
149	tongue, n.	язык, *m.*	Zunge, *f.*/Sprache, *f.*	langue, *f.*
150	tongue blade	передняя часть языка	Zungenblatt, *n.*	plat de la langue, *m.*
151	tongue dorsum	спинка языка, *f.*	Zungenrücken, *m.*	dos de la langue, *m.*

No.	ENGLISH	RUSSIAN	GERMAN	FRENCH
152	tongue level	подъем языка, *m.*	Zungenhöhe, *f.*	niveau de la langue, *m.*
153	tongue position	положение языка, *m.*	Zungenstellung, *f.*	position de la langue, *f.*
154	tongue root	корень языка, *m.*	Zungenwurzel, *f.*	racine de la langue, *f.*
155	tongue side	боковая часть языка	Zungenseite, *f.*	côte de la langue, *m.*
156	tongue tip	кончик языка, *m.*	Zungenspitze, *f.*	point de la langue, *f.*
157	tongue twister	скороговорка, *f.*	Zungenbrecher, *m.*	phrase à decrocher la machoire, *f.*/mot imprononçable, *m.*
158	tonic, adj.	ударный	betont	tonique
159	tool, n.	орудие, *n.*/ инструмент, *m.*	Werkzeug, *n.*/ Instrument, *n.*/ Gerät, *n.*	outil, *m.*/instrument, *m.*
160	topic, н.	тема, *f.*	Thema, *n.*	sujet, *m.*
161	topical, adj.	актуальный	aktuell	d'actualité
162	topmost, adj.	самый верхний/ вершинный/ наивысший	höchst/oberst	le plus haut
163	toponymy, n.	торономия, *f.*	Toponymie, *f.*	toponymie, *f.*
164	total, adj.	весь/целый/ полный/совокупный	ganz/gesamt/völlig	total/complet/plein/entier
165	totality, n.	совокупность, *f.*/ целое, *n.*	Totalität, *f.*/Gänze, *f.*/ Gesamtheit, *f.*	totalité, *f.*/tout, *m.*/ ensemble, *m.*
166	touch, n.	осязание, *n.*	Tastsinn, *m.*	tact, *m.*/toucher, *m.*
167	touch typing	печатание в слепую, *n.*	Blindschreiben, *n.*	bonne dactylographie, *f.*
168	tower of Babel	вавилонская башня	Turmbau von Babel, *m.*	tour de Babel, *f.*
169	trace, n.	след, *m.*	Spur, *f.*	trace, *f.*/vestige, *m.*
170	traceable, adj.	проследимый	zurückführbar	découvrable
171	trachea, n.	трахея, *f.*	Luftröhre, *f.*	trachée, *f.*
172	trade language	лингва франка/ торговый язык	Handelssprache, *f.*/ Verkehrssprache, *f.*	lingua franca, *f.*/sabir, *m.*

No.	ENGLISH	RUSSIAN	GERMAN	FRENCH
173	trade mark, n.	фабричная марка	Schutzmarke, *f.*/ Warenzeichen, *n.*	marque de fabrique, *f.*
174	trade name	торговое название товара/название фирмы, *n.*	Markenname, *m.*/ Firmenname, *m.*	appelation commerciale, *f.*/marque déposée, *f.*
175	tradition, n.	традиция, *f.*/обычай, *m.*	Tradition, *f.*	tradition, *f.*
176	traditional grammar	традиционная грамматика/ обычная грамматика	herkömmliche Grammatik	grammaire traditionnelle, *f.*
177	tragedy, n.	трагедия, *f.*	Trauerspiel, *n.*	tragédie, *f.*
178	train of thought	ход мыслей, *m.*	Gedankenfolge, *f.*	chaîne de pensées, *f.*
179	training, n.	воспитание, *n.*	Erziehung, *f.*	formation, *f.*
180	trait, n.	штрих, *m.*/признак, *m.*	Zug, *m.*/Merkmal, *n.*	trait, *m.*
181	transactions, pl.	труды, *m.*, pl./ протоколы, *m.*, pl.	Abhandlungen, *f.*, pl./ Berichte, *m.*, pl.	actes, *m.,* pl.
182	transcription, n.	транскрипция, *f.*/ запись, *f.*	Transkription, *f.*/ Umschrift, *f.*	transcription, *f.*
183	transfer, n.	перенос, *m.*	Übertragung, *f.*	transfert, *m.*
184	transfer of function	перенос по функции. *m.*	Funktionsübertragung, *f.*	transfert de fonction, *m.*
185	transfer of meaning	перенос значения, *m.*	Bedeutungsübertragung, *f.*	transfert de sens, *m.*
186	transfer of name	перенос названия, *m.*	Nennungsübertragung, *f.*	transfert d'appélation, *m.*
187	transference, n.	перенесение, *n.*	Übertragung, *f.*	transferement, *m.*
188	transferred, adj.	переносный/ перенесенный	übertragen	transféré
189	transformation, n.	трансформация, *f.*/ превращение, *n.*	Transformation, *f.*/ Umformung, *f.*	transformation, *f.*
190	transformational grammar	трансформационная грамматика	Transformationsgrammatik, *f.*	grammaire transformationnelle, *f.*

No.	ENGLISH	RUSSIAN	GERMAN	FRENCH
191	transformational level	трансформационный уровень	Transformationsebene, *f.*	niveau de transformation, *m.*
192	transformational model	трансформационная модель	Transformations-modell, *m.*	modèle transformationnel, *m.*
193	transformational rule	правило превращения, *n.*	Transformationsregel, *f.*	règle de transformation, *f.*
194	transformed string	превращенная цепь	transformierte Kette	chaîne transformée, *f.*
195	transition, n.	переход, *m.*	Übergang, *m.*	transition, *f.*
196	transition area	переходная зона	Übergangsgebiet, *n.*/ Übergangszone, *f.*	aire intermédiare, *f.*
197	transitional probability	переходная вероятность	Übergangswahrschein-lichkeit, *f.*	probabilité transitionnelle, *f.*
198	transitional sound	переходный звук	Übergangslaut, *m.*/ Gleitlaut, *m.*	son transitoire, *m.*/ son de transition, *m.*
199	transitive verb	переходный глагол	transitives Verb(um)/ zielendes Verb(um)	verbe transitif, *m.*
200	transitivity, n.	транситивность, *f.*	Transitivität, *f.*	transitivité, *f.*
201	transitory, adj.	переходящий	vergänglich	transitoire
202	translatable, adj.	переводимый	übersetzbar	traduisible
203	translation, n.	перевод, *m.*	Übersetzung, *f.*	traduction, *f.*
204	translation problem	затруднение в переводе, *n.*	Übersetzungsschwierig-keit, *f.*	difficulté de traduction, *f*
205	translation machine	машина для перевода, *f.*	Übersetzungsmaschine, *f.*	machine à traduire, *f.*
206	translator, n.	переводчик, *m.*	Übersetzer, *m.*	traducteur, *m.*
207	transliteration, n.	транслитерация, *f.*	Transkription, *f.*/ Umschreibung, *f.*	transcription, *f.*
208	transmission, n.	передача, *f.*	Sendung, *f.*	transmission, *f.*
209	transposition, n.	перестановка, *f.*/ перемещение, *n.*	Umstellung, *f.*	transposition, f.
210	travel grant	путевое пособие/ путевые, pl.	Reisestipendium, *n.*	bourse de voyage, *f.*

No.	ENGLISH	RUSSIAN	GERMAN	FRENCH
211	treatise, n.	трактат, *m.*/ научный труд,	Abhandlung, *f.*	traité, *m.*
212	treatment, n.	трактовка, *f.*	Behandlung, *f.*	traitement, *m.*
213	tree, n.	дерево, *n.*	Baum, *m.*	arbre, *m.*
214	trend, n.	тенденция, *f.*	Neigung, *f.*/Tendenz, *f.*	tendance, *f.*
215	trial and error method	экспериментальный метод	Probe- und Irrtums- methode, *f.*	méthode de tatonnements, *f.*
216	triangle, n.	треугольник, *m.*	Dreieck, *n.*	triangle, *m.*
217	tribal languages, pl.	племенные языки, *m.*, pl.	Stammessprachen, *f.*, pl.	langues de tribus, *f.*, pl.
218	triconsonantal root	трехсогласный корень	dreikonsonantische Wurzel	racine à trois consonnes, *f.*
219	trilingual, adj.	трехъязычный	dreisprächig	trilingue
220	trill, n.	трель, *f.*/ дрожащий звук	Triller, *m.*/Zitterlaut, *m.*/ gerollter Laut	trille, *m.*/son roulé, *m.*
221	triphthong, n.	трифтонг, *m.*	Triphthong, *m.*/ Dreilaut, *m.*	triphthongue, *f.*
222	triple, adj.	тройной	dreifach	triple
223	trisyllabic, adj.	трехсложный	dreisilbig	trisyllabique
224	trite, adj.	избитый	abgedroschen	rebattu/usé
225	triumphal arch	триумфальная арка	Triumphbogen, *m.*	arc de triomphe, *m.*
226	trivial, adj.	мелкий/ незначительный	geringfügig/unbedeutend	banal/insignifiant
227	trochee, n.	трохей, *m.*/хорей, *m.*	Trochäus, *m.*	trochée, *m.*
228	trope, n.	троп, *m.*/образное выражение	Tropus, *m.*/ bildlicher Ausdruck	trope, *m.*
229	true, adj.	верный	wahr	vrai
230	truism, n.	трюизм, *m.*	Binsenwahrheit, *f.*/ Gemeinplatz, *m.*	truisme, *m.*
231	truncation, n.	урезывание, *n.*	Stützung, *f.*	mutilation, *f.*

No.	ENGLISH	RUSSIAN	GERMAN	FRENCH
232	truncated, adj.	сокращенный	abgestuzt	tronqué
233	truth, n.	правда, *f.*/истина, *f.*	Wahrheit, *f.*	verité, *f.*/véracité, *f.*/ vrai, *m.*
234	tune, n.	мелодия, *f.*	Melodie, *f.*	air, *m.*
235	tuning fork	камертон, *m.*	Stimmgabel, *f.*	diapason, *m.*
236	Turkic, n.	тюркский	türkisch	turquois
237	Turkish, adj.	турецкий	Turkei-türkisch	turc
238	turning point	поворотный пункт	Wendepunkt, *m.*	tournant, *m.*
239	twang, n.	гнусавый выговор	Näseln, *n.*	parler nasillard,*m.*
240	twin formations, pl.	парные образования, *n., pl.*	Zwillingsformeln, *f.,* pl.	formations jumelles,*f.,* pl.
241	two-dimensional, adj.	двуразмерный	zweidimensional	à deux dimensions
242	two-level theory (of grammar)	двухступенчатая модель	⟨zweistufiges Sprachmodell⟩	modèle à deux niveaux, *m.*
243	two-membered, adj.	двучленный	zweigliedrig	à deux membres
244	type (kind), n.	тип, *m.*/сорт, *m.*	Typus, *m.*/Art, *f.*	type, *m.*/genre, *m.*
245	type (printing), n.	литера, *f.*/шрифт, *m.*	Type, *f.*	caractère d'imprimerie, *m.*
246	type-face, n.	шрифт, *m.*	Schriftbild, *n.*	genre de caractère imprimé, *m.*
247	type-script, n.	машинопись, *f.*	getipptes Manuskript/mit Schreibmaschine geschriebenes Manuskript	texte dactylographié, *m.*
248	type-token relationship	отношение типа к знаку, *n.*	Beziehung des Typs und Zeichens, *f.*	rapport de type à exemple, *m.*
249	types of sentence construction	виды построения предложений, *m., pl.*	Arten der Satzkonstruktion, *f.,* pl.	modes de construction des phrases, *m.,* pl.
250	typewriter, n.	пишущая машинка	Schreibmaschine, *f.*	machine à écrire, *f.*
251	typewriting, n.	машинопись, *f.*	Maschinenschreiben, *n.*/ Tippen, *n.*	dactylographie, *f.*

No.	ENGLISH	RUSSIAN	GERMAN	FRENCH
252	typical, adj.	типичный	typisch	typique
253	typing, n.	машинопись, *f.*	Maschinenschreiben, *n./* Tippen, *n.*	dactylographie, *f*
254	typing error	опечатка, *f.*	Tippfehler, *m.*	faute de frappe, *f.*
255	typographical error	типографическая ошибка/опечатка, *f.*	Druckfehler, *m.*	coquille, *f.*
256	typography, n.	книгопечатание, *n.*	Typographie, *f.*	typographie, *f.*
257	typological classification	типологическая классификация	typologische Klassifizierung	classement typologique, *m.*
258	typology, n.	типология, *f.*	Typologie, *f.*	typologie, *f.*

U

No.	ENGLISH	RUSSIAN	GERMAN	FRENCH
001	ultra-	ультра- / сверх-	Ultra- / Über-	ultra
002	ultramodern, adj.	сверхсовременный	übermodern	ultramoderne
003	umlaut, n.	умлаут, *m./* перегласовка, *f.*	Umlaut, *m.*	métaphonie, *f.*
004	unabbreviated, adj.	несокращенный	ungekürzt/unverkürzt	non abrégé
005	unaccented, adj.	неударный	unbetont	non accentué
006	unacceptable, adj.	неприемлимый	unannehmbar	inacceptable
007	unaccountable, adj.	необъяснимый	unerklärlich	inexplicable
008	unaccustomed, adj.	непривыкший/ непривычный	ungewöhnt	inaccoutumé
009	unacquired, adj.	неприобретенный	unerworben	non acquis/naturel/inné
010	unaffected, adj.	неизменный	unbeeinflusst	immuable
011	unalterable, adj.	неизменяемый	unveränderlich	invariable
012	unambiguous, adj.	недвусмысленный	unzweideutig	sans ambiguïté
013	unaspirated, adj.	непридыхательный	nicht aspiriert/ unbehaucht	non aspiré

No.	ENGLISH	RUSSIAN	GERMAN	FRENCH
014	unassimilated, adj.	неассимилированный	nicht assimiliert	inassimilé
015	unattached, adj.	неприкрепленный	nicht verbunden	indépendant/non lié
016	unattainable, adj.	недостижимый	unerreichbar/ unerfüllbar	irréalisable
017	unattempted, adj.	неиспробованный	unversucht	non tenté
018	unattested, adj.	незасвидетельство- ванный	unbezeugt	non attesté
019	unavoidable, adj.	неизбежный	unvermeidbar	inévitable
020	unbalanced, adj.	неуравновешенный	unausgeglichen	mal equilibré
021	unbelievable, adj.	невероятный	unglaublich	incroyable
022	uncertain, adj.	сомнительный	unbestimmt	indéterminé
023	unchanging, adj.	неизменный	unveränderlich	invariable
024	unclassifiable, adj.	неподдающийся классификаций	nicht klassifizierbar	inclassifiable
025	unclear, adj.	неясный	unklar	peu clair
026	uncommon, adj.	необыкновенный	ungewöhnlich	peu commun/rare
027	uncompleted, adj.	неоконченный	unvollendet	inachevé
028	unconditioned, adj.	необусловленный	bedingungslos	non conditionné
029	unconnected, adj.	несвязанный/ несвязный	unverbunden	sans liaison
030	unconscious, adj.	бессознательный	unbewusst	inconscient
031	unconventional, adj.	нешаблонный/ оригинальный	ungewöhnlich	peu conventionnel/ original
032	uncoordinated, adj.	несогласованный	nicht beigeordnet	non coordonné
033	uncorrected, adj.	неисправленный	unverbessert	non corrigé
034	undated, adj.	недатированный	undatiert	sans dâte
035	undeclinable, adj.	несклоняемый	undeklinierbar	indéclinable
036	undefinable, adj.	неопределяемый	unbestimmbar	indéfinissable

No.	ENGLISH	RUSSIAN	GERMAN	FRENCH
037	undefined, adj.	неопределенный	unbestimmt	non défini
038	undependable, adj.	ненадежный	unzuverlässig	douteux/non digne de confiance
039	underdifferentiated, adj.	малодифференциро-ванный/ недостаточно дифференцирован-ный	unterdifferenziert	sous différencié
040	undergraduate, n.	студент, *m.*	Student, *m.*	étudiant non diplômé, *m.*
041	underived, adj.	непроизводный	unabgeleitet	non dérivé
042	underlined, adj.	подчеркнутый	unterstrichen	souligné
043	underlying, adj.	подлежащий/ исходный	zugrundeliegend	sous jacent
044	underscored, adj.	подчеркнутый	unterstrichen	souligné
045	undersigned, adj.	подписанный	unterzeichnet	sousigné
046	understand, v.	понимать	verstehen	comprendre
047	understandable, adj.	понятный	verständlich	compréhensible
048	understanding, n.	понимание, *n.*	Verständnis, *n.*	compréhension, *f.*/ entendement, *m.*
049	undescribed, adj.	неописанный	unbeschrieben	non étudié
050	undetermined, adj.	неопределенный	unbestimmt	indéterminé
051	undifferentiated, adj.	недифференцирован-ный	undifferenziert	non différencié
052	undisputed, adj.	неспорный/ несомненный	unbestritten	incontesté
053	undistinguishable, adj.	неразличимый	nicht unterscheidbar	indistinct
054	undivided, adj.	неразделенный	ungeteilt	indivisé
055	undoubted, adj.	бесспорный/ несомненный	unbezweifelt	indubitable
056	uneducated, adj.	необразованный/ неученный	ungebildet	inculte

No.	English	Russian	German	French
057	unequal, adj.	неравный/ неодинаковый	ungleich	inégal
058	unessential, adj.	несущественный	unwesentlich	non essentiel
059	uneven distribution, adj.	неравномерное распределение	unregelmässige Vertei-lung	distribution inégale, *f.*
060	unexpected, adj.	неожиданный	unvorhergesehen	inattendu
061	unexpressed, adj.	невыраженный	unausgesprochen	sous entendu/ non exprimé
062	unfamiliar, adj.	незнакомый	unbekannt	étranger
063	unfavorable, adj.	неблагоприятный	unvorteilhaft	défavorable
064	unfinished, adj.	неоконченный/ несовершенный	unvollendet	inachevé
065	unfolding, n.	развертывание, *n.*	Entfaltung, *f.*	déroulement, *m.*
066	unfounded, adj.	необоснованный	unbegründet	injustifié/sans fondement
067	ungrammatical, adj.	грамматически неправильный	ungrammatisch/falsch	contraire à la grammaire/ incorrect
068	ungrammatical sentence	грамматически неправильное предложение	falscher Satz	phrase incorrecte, *f.*
069	unidimensional, adj.	одномерный	eindimensional	unidimensionnel
070	unidirectional, adj.	однонаправленный	gerichtet	unidirectionnel
071	uniform, adj.	равномерный	gleichförmig	uniforme
072	uniform distribution	равномерное распределение	gleichförmige Verteilung	distribution uniforme, *f.*
073	uniformity, n.	однородность, *f.*/ равномерность, *f.*	Gleichförmigkeit, *f.*/ Gleichmässigkeit, *f.*	uniformité, *f.*
074	unilateral, adj.	односторонний	einseitig	unilatéral
075	unilingual, adj.	одноязычный	einsprachig	unilingue
076	unimportant, adj.	неважный	unwichtig	insignifiant

No.	ENGLISH	RUSSIAN	GERMAN	FRENCH
077	uninflected, adj.	неизменяющийся	undekliniert	sans flexion
078	uninfluenced, adj.	неподверженный влиянию	unbeeinflusst	non influencé
079	uninhabited, adj.	ненаселенный	unbewohnt	inhabité
080	unintelligible, adj.	непонятный	unverständlich	inintelligible
081	uninterrupted, adj.	непрерывный/ непрерыванный	ununterbrochen	continu/non interrompu
082	union, n.	союз, *m.*/ соединение, *n.*/ объединение, *n.*	Einheit, *f.*/Vereinigung, *f.*	union, *f.*
083	unique, adj.	уникальный/ единственный/ единичный	einzigartig	unique
084	uniquely defined, adj.	единично определенный	eindeutig definiert	défini uniquement
085	unit, n.	единица, *f.*	Einheit, *f.*	unité, *f.*
086	unit phoneme	единичная фонема	Einheitsphonem, *n.*	unité phonémique, *f.*
087	unity, n.	единство, *n.*/ единение, *n.*/ единица, *f.*	Einheit, *f.*	unité, *f.*
088	universal, adj.	универсальный/ всеобщий	universal/allgemein	universel
089	universal feature	универсальный признак	universales Merkmal	trait universel, *m.*/ absolu, *m.*
090	universal languages, pl.	всемирные языки, *m.*, pl.	Weltsprachen, *f.*, pl.	langues universelles, *f.*, pl.
091	universal law	универсальный закон	allgemeines Gesetz	loi universelle, *f.*
092	universal verb	универсальный глагол	Allerweltsverb, *n.*	verbe universel, *m.*
093	universality, n.	универяальность, *f.*/ всеобщность, *f.*	Universalität, *f.*/ Allgemeinheit, *f.*	universalité, *f.*
094	university, n.	университет, *m.*	Universität, *f.*/ Hochschule, *f.*	université, *f.*

No.	English	Russian	German	French
095	unjustifed, adj.	неоправданный	unberechtigt	injustifié/sans preuve
096	unknown, adj.	неизвестный	unbekannt	inconnu
097	unlearned, adj.	невыученный	nicht erlernt	inappris
098	unlike, adj.	непохожий/ несходный	unähnlich	dissemblable
099	unlikely, adj.	маловероятный	unwahrscheinlich	invraisemblable/ improbable
100	unlimited, adj.	неограниченный/ беспредельный	unbegrenzt	illimité
101	unmarked, adj.	немаркированный/ неотмеченный	merkmallos	non marqué
102	unmodified, adj.	неизмененный	unverändert	intact
103	unmistakable, adj.	безошибочный/ несомненный	unverkennbar	sans équivoque
104	unmixed, adj.	несмешанный	ungemischt	pur
105	unmotivated, adj.	немотивированный	unmotiviert	immotivé
106	unnamed, adj.	безымянный	unbenannt	innommé
107	unnatural, adj.	неестественный	unnatürlich	anormal
108	unnecessary, adj.	ненужный/излишний	unnötig	superflu/inutile
109	unobserved, adj.	незамеченный	unbemerkt	inaperçu
110	unobstructed passage	свободный проход	ungehinderter Durch- fluss/ungehemmter Durchfluss	passage sans obstacle, *m.*
111	unpaired phoneme	непарная фонема	nicht integriertes Phonem	phonème non intégré, *m.*
112	unpredictable, adj.	непредсказуемый	nicht vorhersagbar	imprévisible
113	unprefixed, adj.	бесприставочный	ohne Präfix/ ohne Vorsilbe	non préfixé
114	unproductive, adj.	непродуктивный	nicht produktiv	non productif

No.	ENGLISH	RUSSIAN	GERMAN	FRENCH
115	unpronounceable, adj.	непроизносимый	unaussprechbar	impronoçable
116	unproven, adj.	недоказанный	unbewiesen	inéprouvé
117	unpublished, adj.	неопубликованный/ неизданный	unveröffentlicht	inédit/non publié
118	unreadable, adj.	неразборчивый	unleserlich	illisible
119	unreal, adj.	нереальный	unwirklich	irréel
120	unrecognizable, adj.	неузнаваемый	unerkennbar	méconnaissable
121	unrecorded, adj.	незаписанный/ назафиксированный	unverzeichnet	non enregistré
122	unrelated languages, pl.	неродственные языки, *m.*, pl.	unverwandte Sprachen, *f.*, pl.	langues non apparentées, *f.*, pl.
123	unreliable, adj.	ненадежный	unzuverlässig	douteux
124	unrepeated, adj.	неповторный	nicht wiederholt	non repété
125	unresolved, adj.	неразрешенный	ungelöst	irrésolu
126	unrestricted, adj.	неограниченный	unbegrenzt	non limité
127	unrestricted class	открытый класс	offene Klasse	classe ouverte, *f.*
128	unrounded vowels, pl.	неокругленные гласные, pl.	ungerundete Vokale, *m.*, pl.	voyelles non arrondies, *f.*, pl.
129	unrounding, n.	делабиализация, *f.*	Entrundung, *f.*	délabialisation, *f.*/ désarrondissement, *m.*
130	unsatisfactory, adj.	неудовлетворитель-ный	nicht zufriedenstellend	peu satisfaisant
131	unscholarly, adj.	ненаучный	unwissenschaftlich	indigne d'un savant
132	unscientific, adj.	ненаучный	unwissenschaftlich	peu scientifique
133	unsolved, adj.	нерешенный	ungelöst	non résolu
134	unspecified, adj.	неуточненный/ неуказенный	nicht spezifiziert	non spécifié
135	unspoken, adj.	невысказанный	ungesagt/ungesprochen	non prononcé/inexprimé

No.	English	Russian	German	French
136	unstable, adj.	неустойчивый	labil/nicht stabil/ unbeständig	instable
137	unstable vowel	беглая гласная	flüchtiger Vokal/ schwindender Vokal	voyelle instable, *f.*
138	unstressed, adj.	безударный	unbetont	inaccentué/atone
139	unstressed syllable	безударный слог	unbetonte Silbe	syllabe inaccentuée, *f.*
140	unsuitable, adj.	неподходящий	ungeeignet	impropre
141	unsymmetrical, adj.	несимметричный	unsymmetrisch/ asymmetrisch	asymétrique
142	unsystematic, adj.	несистематичный	unsystematisch	non systématique/ sans méthode
143	untenable, adj.	незащитимый	unhaltbar	insoutenable
144	untested, adj.	непроверенный	unerprobt	non éprouvé
145	untraceable, adj.	непроследимый	nicht zurückführbar	indécouvrable
146	untranslatable, adj.	непереводимый	unübersetzbar	intraduisible
147	untrue, adj.	неверный/ложный	unwahr	inexact/faux
148	unusual, adj.	необыкновенный/ непривычный	ungewöhnlich	inusité/rare
149	unvoiced, adj.	глухой/незвонкий	stimmlos	sourd/muet
150	unvoiced consonants, pl.	глухие согласные, pl.	stimmlose Konsonanten, *m., pl.*	voyelles sourdes, *f., pl.*
151	unvoicing, n.	оглушение, *n.*	Stimmloswerden, *n.*	assourdissement, *m.*
152	unwritten languages, pl.	бесписьменные языки, *m., pl.*	schriftlose Sprachen, *f., pl.*	langues sans écriture, *f., pl.*
153	upbringing, n.	воспитание, *n.*	Erziehung, *f.*	formation, *f.*
154	upper bound	верхняя граница/ верхняя грань	obere Grenze	limite supérieure, *f.*
155	upper case letter	прописная буква/ заглавная буква	grosser Buchstabe/ Majuskel, *f.*	majuscule, *f.*
156	upper class	высший класс	gute Gesellschaft, *f.*/ Oberschicht, *f.*	classe supérieure, *f.*

No.	ENGLISH	RUSSIAN	GERMAN	FRENCH
157	upper jaw	верхняя челюсть	Oberkiefer, *m.*	mâchoire supérieure, *f.*
158	upper register	верхний регистр	höhere Tonlage	régistre supérieur, *m.*
159	upper teeth, pl.	верхние зубы, *f.,* pl.	Oberzähne, *m.,* pl.	dents supérieures, *f.,* pl.
160	uppermost, adj.	самый верхний/ высший/ наивысший	höchst/oberst	plus haut
161	urban speech	городской язык	städtische Sprache	langage urbain, *m.*
162	urgency, n.	неотложимость, *f.*	Dringlichkeit, *f.*	urgence, *f.*
163	usable, adj.	применимый	brauchbar	utilisable
164	usage, n.	употребление, *n.*	Gebrauch, *m.*	usage, *m.*/emploi, *m.*
165	use, v.	употреблять/ воспользоваться/ применять	benutzen/gebrauchen/ verwenden	employer/utiliser
166	useful, adj.	полезный	nützlich	utile
167	useful expressions, pl.	полезные выражения, *n.,* pl./бытовые выражения, *n.,* pl.	gebräuchliche Ausdrücke, *m.,* pl.	expressions usuelles, *f.,* pl.
168	useless, adj.	бесполезный	unbrauchbar	inutile
169	usual, adj.	обычный/ обыкновенный	gewönlich	usuel
170	usual word order	обычный порядок слов	gewöhnliche Wortfolge/ gewöhnliche Wortstellung	ordre de mots usuel, *m.*/ ordre de mots neutre, *m.*
171	utilization, n.	использование. *n.*	Nutzung, *f.*/ Gebrauch, *m.*	utilisation, *f.*/emploi, *m.*
172	utterance, n.	высказывание, *n.*	Äusserung, *f.*	énoncé, *f.*
173	uvula, n.	уɛула, *f.*/ маленький язычок	Zäpfchen, *n.*	luette, *f.*
174	uvular consonants, pl.	увулярные согласные, pl./язычковые согласные, pl.	uvulare Konsonanten, *m.,* pl./Halszäpfchen- laute, *m.,* pl.	consonnes uvulaires, *f.,* pl.
175	uvular r	увулярное p	Zäpfchen-R, *n.*	r grasséyé

No.	ENGLISH	RUSSIAN	GERMAN	FRENCH

V

No.	ENGLISH	RUSSIAN	GERMAN	FRENCH
001	vague, adj.	неопределенный	unbestimmt	indéfini
002	vague resemblance	отдаленное сходство	flüchtige Ähnlichkeit	ressemblance vague, *f.*
003	valence, n.	валентность, *f.*	Valenz, *f.*	valence, *f.*
004	validity, n.	обоснованность, *f.*	Gültigkeit, *f.*	validité, *f.*
005	value, n.	ценность, *f.*/ значение, *n.*	Wert, *m.*/Geltung, *f.*	valeur, *f.*
006	variability, n.	изменчивость, *f.*/ непостоянство, *n.*	Veränderlichkeit, *f.*/ Unbeständigkeit, *f.*	variabilité, *f.*/ inconstance, *f.*
007	variable, n.	переменное, *n.*	Veränderliche, *f.*	variable, *f.*
008	variable, adj.	изменчивый	veränderlich	variable
009	variable stress	разноместное ударение	freie Betonung	accent variable, *m.*
010	variant, n.	вариант, *m.*/ аллофон, *m.*	Variante, *f.*/Allophon, *n.*	variante, *f.*
011	variant forms, pl.	разновидные формы, *f.*, pl.	verschiedene Formen, *f.*, pl.	formes variantes, *f.*, pl.
012	variant meanings, pl.	разные значения, *n.*, pl.	verschiedene Bedeutungen, *f.*, pl.	sens variants, *m.*, pl.
013	variation, n.	вариация, *n.*/ варьирование, *f.*	Variation, *f.*	variation, *f.*
014	variety, n.	разнообразие, *n.*/ разновидность, *f.*	Verschiedenheit, *f.*/ Vielfalt, *f.*	variété, *f.*/diversité, *f.*
015	various, adj.	разный	verschieden	divers
016	vector, n.	вектор, *m.*	Vektor, *m.*	vecteur, *m.*
017	velar, adj.	велярный/ задненебный/ заднеязычный	velar/Hinterzungen-	vélaire
018	velar consonants, pl.	велярные согласные, pl./задненебные согласные, pl.	velare Konsonanten, *m.*, pl./Hinter- zungenlaute, *m.*, pl.	consonnes vélaires, *f.*, pl.

No.	ENGLISH	RUSSIAN	GERMAN	FRENCH
019	velar vowels, pl.	велярные гласные, pl./ заднеязычные гласные, pl.	velare Vokale, *m.*, pl./ Hinterzungenvokale, *m.*, pl.	voyelles vélaires, *f.*, pl./ voyelles postérieures, *f.*, pl.
020	velarization, n.	веляризация, *f.*	Velarisierung, *f.*	vélarisation, *f.*
021	velarized, adj.	веляризованный	velarisiert	vélarisé
022	velocity, n.	скорость, *f./* быстрота, *f.*	Geschwindigkeit, *f./* Schnelligkeit, *f.*	vélocité, *f.*
023	velum, n.	заднее небо	Gaumensegel, *n.*	voile du palais, *m./* palais mou, *m.*
024	ventriloquism, ventriloquy, n.	чревовещание, *n.*	Bauchredekunst, *f.*	ventriloquie, *f.*
025	verb, n.	глагол, *m.*	Verb, *n.*/Verbum, *n.*/ Zeitwort, *n.*	verbe, *m.*
026	verb class	класс глаголов, *m.*	Verbklasse, *f.*	classe de verbes, *f.*
027	verb of action	глагол действия, *m.*	Tatverb(um), *n.*	verbe d'action, *m.*
028	verb of motion	глагол движения, *m.*	Bewegungsverb(um), *n.*	verbe de mouvement, *m.*
029	verb of state	глагол состояния, *m.*	Zustandsverb(um), *n.*	verbe d'état, *m.*
030	verb phrase	глагольная фраза/ глагольная группа	Verbalphrase, *m./* Verbalgruppe, *f./* Verbgefüge, *n.*	groupe verbal, *m.*
031	verb tenses, pl.	времена глагола, *n.*, pl.	Verbtempora, *n.*, pl.	temps verbaux, *m.*, pl.
032	verbal (of words), adj.	устный/словесный	gesprochen/wortlich	oral
033	verbal (of verbs), adj.	глагольный	verbal	verbal
034	verbal adjective	отглагольное прилагательное	verbales Adjektiv	adjectif verbal, *m.*
035	verbal adverb	деепричастие, *n.*	verbales Adverb	adverbe verbal, *m.*
036	verbal behavior	словесное поведение	Sprachverhalten, *n.*	comportement verbal, *m.*
037	verbal inflection	глагольная флексия	verbale Flexion	flexion verbale, *f.*
038	verbal inhibition	слово-табу, *n.*	Tabu-Wort, *n.*	mot tabou, *m.*
039	verbal memory	словопамять, *f.*	Wortgedächtnis, *f.*	mémoire verbale, *f.*

No.	English	Russian	German	French
040	verbal noun	отглагольное существительное	verbales Substantiv	substantif verbal, *m.*/ nom verbal, *m.*
041	verbal predicate	глагольное сказуемое	verbales Prädikat	prédicat verbal, *m.*
042	verbalize (to use as verb), v.	превращать в глагол	in ein Zeitwort verwandeln	employer comme verbe
043	verbatim, adv.	дословно	Wort für Wort wortgetreu/wörtlich	mot pour mot/ textuellement
044	verbiage, n.	пустословие, *n.*	Wortschwall, *m.*	verbiage, *m.*
045	verbosity, n.	многословие, *n.*	Weitschweifigkeit, *f.*	verbosité, *f.*/prolixité, *f.*
046	vernacular, n.	местный говор/ обиходный язык	einheimische Sprache/ Volkssprache, *f.*	vernaculaire, *m.*/ langage vulgaire, *m.*
047	verification, n.	проверка, *f.*/ подтверждение, *n.*	Verifizierung, *f.*/Wahrheitsnachweis, *m.*	vérification, *f.*/ contrôle, *m.*
048	verse, n.	стих, *m.*	Vers, *m.*	vers, *m.*
049	verse intonation	интонация стиха, *f.*	Versintonation, *f.*	intonation du vers, *f.*
050	versification, n.	переложение в стихи, *n.*	Versemachen, *n.*	versification, *f.*
051	version, n.	версия, *f.*/перевод, *m.*	Version, *f.*/ Übersetzung, *f.*	version, *f.*/traduction, *f.*
052	versions of the Bible, pl.	библейские варианты, *m.*, pl.	Versionen der Bibel, *f.*, pl.	traductions de la Bible, *f.*, pl.
053	vertical, adj.	вертикальный	vertikal/senkrecht	vertical
054	vertical axis	вертикальная ось	vertikale Achse/ y-Achse, *f.*	axe vertical, *m.*
055	vertical line	вертикальная линия	vertikale Linie	ligne verticale, *f.*
056	vertical writing	вертикальное письмо	vertikale Schrift	écriture verticale, *f.*
057	vestige, n.	остаток, *m.*/след, *m.*/ пережиток, *m.*	Spur, *f.*/Überbleibsel, *n.*	vestige, *m.*/trace, *f.*
058	vibrant consonants, pl.	вибранты, *m.*, pl./ дрожащие согласные, pl.	Vibrante, *m.*, pl./Zitterlaute, *m.*, pl./gerollte Konsonanten, *m.*, pl.	vibrantes, *f.*, pl./ consonnes roulées, *m.*, pl.

No.	English	Russian	German	French
059	vibration, n.	колебание, *n.*	Schwingung, *f.*	vibration, *f.*
060	viewpoint, n.	точка зрения, *f./* взгляд, *m.*	Standpúnkt, *m.*	point de vue, *m.*
061	violation, n.	нарушение, *n.*	Verletzung, *f.*	violation, *f.*
062	visible speech	видимая речь	sichtbare Sprache	langage visible, *m.*
063	vision, n.	зрение, *n.*	Sehen, *n.*	vision, *f./*vue, *f.*
064	visual, adj.	визуальный/ зрительный	visuell	visuel
065	visual aids (in teaching), pl.	наглядные пособия, *n.,* pl.	Unterrichtshilfsmaterialien, *n.,* pl./Veranschaulichungsmittel, *n.,* sg.	aides visuelles, *f.,* pl.
066	visual image	зрительный образ	visuelles Bild	image visuelle, *f.*
067	visual memory	зрительная память	visuelles Gedächtnis	mémoire visuelle, *f.*
068	visual sign(al)	оптический знак	Sichtzeichen, *n.*	signe visuel, *m.*
069	vocabulary, n.	лексика, *f./*лексикон, *m./*словарный фонд/ запас слов, *m.*	Lexikon, *n./* Wortschatz, *m.*	vocabulaire, *m./* lexique, *m.*
070	vocabulary entry	словарная статья	Worteintragung, *f.*	article du lexique, *m.*
071	vocal, adj.	вокальный/звуковой	vokalisch/lautlich	vocalique/sonore
072	vocal character of language	звуковой характер языка	lautlicher Charakter der Sprache	caractère vocalique du langage, *m.*
073	vocal cords, vocal folds, pl.	голосовые связки, pl.	Stimmbänder, *n.,* pl.	cordes vocales, *f.,* pl.
074	vocal tract	голосовой механизм	Artikulationskanal, *m.*	chenal expiratoire, *m./* tractus vocal, *m.*
075	vocalic, adj.	вокальный	vokalisch	vocalique
076	vocalic phonemes, pl.	гласные фонемы, *f.,* pl.	vokalische Phoneme, *n.,* pl.	phonèmes vocaliques, *m.,* pl.
077	vocalism, n.	вокализм, *m./* огласовка, *f.*	Vokalismus, *m.*	vocalisme, *m.*

No.	ENGLISH	RUSSIAN	GERMAN	FRENCH
078	vocalization, n.	вокализация, *f.*/ озвончение, *n.*	Vokalisierung, *f.*/ Stimmgebung, *f.*	vocalisation, *f.*
079	vocative case	звательный падеж	Vokativ, *m.*/Ruffall, *m.*	vocatif, *m.*
080	voice (of person), n.	голос, *m.*	Stimme, *f.*	voix, *f.*
081	voice (of verb), n.	залог, *m.*	Modus des Verbs, *m.*	voix, *f.*
082	voice bar	голосовая полоса	Stimmleiste, *f.*	barre sonorisante, *f.*
083	voice box	гортань, *f.*	Kehlkopf, *m.*	larynx, *m.*
084	voice onset	начальный приступ голоса	Einsatz der Stimme, *m.*	début de voix, *m.*/ attaque de voix, *f.*
085	voice power	сила голоса, *f.*	Stimmkraft, *f.*	force vocale, *f.*
086	voice production	дикция, *f.*	Stimmerzeugung, *f.*	diction, *f.*/élocution, *f.*
087	voice quality	голосовой тембр	Stimmqualität, *f.*	qualité de voix, *f.*
088	voice range	голосовой диапозон	Stimmumfang, *m.*	diapason, *m.*/étendue, *f.*
089	voiced, adj.	звонкий	stimmhaft	sonore
090	voiced consonants, pl.	звонкие согласные, pl.	stimmhafte Konsonanten, *m.*, pl./Mediae, pl.	consonnes sonores, *f.*, pl.
091	voiceless, adj.	глухой	stimmlos	sourd/muet
092	voiceless consonants, pl.	глухие согласные, pl.	stimmlose Konsonanten, *m.*, pl./Tenues, pl.	consonnes sourdes, *f.*, pl.
093	voiceless vowels, pl.	глухие гласные, pl.	stimmlose Vokale, *m.*, pl.	voyelles sourdes, *f.*, pl.
094	voicelessness, n.	глухость, *f.*	Stimmlösigkeit, *f.*	sourditę, *f.*
095	voicing, n.	озвончение, *n.*	Stimmgebung, *f.*	sonorisation, *f.*
096	volume (book), n.	том, *m.*	Band, *m.*	tome, *m.*/volume, *m.*
097	volume control	регулятор громкости, *m.*	Lautstärkeregler, *m.*	régulateur de volume, *m.*
098	vowel, n.	гласная, *f.*/ гласный звук	Vokal, *m.*/Selbstlaut, *m.*	voyelle, *f.*
099	vowel alternation	чередование гласных, *n.*	Vokalwechsel, *m.*/ Ablaut, *m.*	alternance vocalique, *f.*

No.	ENGLISH	RUSSIAN	GERMAN	FRENCH
100	vowel change	перемена гласных, *f.*	Vokalwechsel, *m.*	changement vocalique, *m.*
101	vowel classification	классификация гласных, *f.*	Vokalklassifizierung, *f.*	classification de voyelles, *f.*
102	vowel cluster	стечение гласных, *n.*	Vokalgruppe, *f.*	groupe de voyelles, *m.*
103	vowel degree	ступень чередования гласных, *f.*	Ablautsstufe, *f.*	degré d'alternance, *m.*
104	vowel diagram	схема гласных, *f.*	Vokaldiagramm, *n.*	tableau des voyelles, *m.*
105	vowel formation	образование гласных, *n.*	Vokalartikulation, *f.*	formation des voyelles, *f.*
106	vowel gradation	аблаут, *m.*/чередование гласных, *n.*	Ablaut, *m.*	alternance vocalique, *f.*
107	vowel harmony	гармония гласных, *f.*	Vokalharmonie, *f.*	harmonie vocalique, *f.*
108	vowel insertion	вставка гласного, *f.*	Vokaleinschub, *m.*/ Vokaleinschiebung, *f.*	voyelle d'appui, *f.*
109	vowel length	длительность гласных, *f.*	Vokallänge, *f.*/ Vokalquantität, *f.*	quantité vocalique, *f.*
110	vowel mutation	метафония, *f.*/ перегласовка, *f.*	Umlaut, *m.*	métaphonie, *f.*
111	vowel omission	пропуск гласного, *m.*	Vokalauslassung, *f.*/ Vokalelision, *f.*	omission vocalique, *f.*
113	vowel quadrangle	четырехугольник гласных, *m.*	Vokalviereck, *n.*	quadrilatère des voyelles, *m.*
114	vowel quality	тембр гласного звука, *m.*	Vokalqualität, *f.*	timbre vocalique, *m.*
115	vowel point	вокалический значок	Vokalzeichen, *n.*	point-voyelle, *f.*
116	vowel reduction	редуцирование гласных, *n.*	Vokaldreduktion, *f.*/ Vokalreduzierung, *f.*	réduction vocalique, *f.*
117	vowel series	ряд гласных, *m.*	Vokalreihe, *f.*	série de voyelles, *f.*
118	vowel shift	передвижение гласных, *n.*/ смещение гласных, *n.*	Vokalverschiebung, *f.*	mutation vocalique, *f.*

No.	ENGLISH	RUSSIAN	GERMAN	FRENCH
119	vowel sound	гласный звук	Stimmlaut, *m.*	son vocalique, *m.*
120	vowel system	система гласных, *f.*	Vokalsystem, *n.*	système vocalique, *m.*
121	vowel triangle	треугольник гласных, *m* .	Vokaldreieck, *n.*	triangle des voyelles, *m.*
122	vulgarism, n.	вульгарное выражение	vulgärer Ausdruck/ gemeiner Ausdruck	expression triviale, *f.*

W

No.	ENGLISH	RUSSIAN	GERMAN	FRENCH
001	wandering word	скитающееся слово	Wanderwort, *n.*	mot de civilisation, *m./* mot errant, *m.*
002	warning, n.	предупреждение, *n.*	Warnung, *f.*	avertissement, *m.*
003	wave, n.	волна, *f.*	Welle, *f.*	onde, *f.*
004	wave theory	теория волн, *f.*	Wellentheorie, *f.*	théorie des ondes, *f.*
005	weak, adj.	слабый	schwach	faible
006	weak aspiration	слабое придыхание	schwache Behauchung	aspiration faible, *f.*
007	weak ending	слабое окончание	schwache Endung	terminaison faible, *f.*
008	weak position	слабая позиция	schwache Stellung	position faible, *f.*
009	weak stress	слабое ударение	Schwachton, *m.*	sous-accent, *m.*
010	weakening, n.	ослабление, *n.*	Schwächung, *f.*	affaiblissement, *m.*
011	weather expressions, pl.	климатические выражения, *n., pl.*	Wetterausdrücke, *m., pl.*	terminologie des conditions atmosphériques, *f., sg.*
012	weeping, n.	плач, *m.*	Weinen, *n.*	pleurs, *m., pl.*
013	well-formed, adj.	закономерный/ правильный	gut geformt/richtig	bien-formé
014	Welsh, n.	валлийский	walisisch	gallois, *m.*
015	whimpering, n.	хныканье, *n.*	Gewimmer, *n./* Gewinsel, *n.*	pleurnicherie, *f./* ton geignard, *m.*

No.	ENGLISH	RUSSIAN	GERMAN	FRENCH
016	whining, n.	скулеж, *m.*	Gewimmer, *n.*/ Gejammer, *n.*	gémissement, *m.*/ pleurnicherie, *f.*
017	whispered vowels, pl.	шепотные гласные, pl.	Flüstervokale, *m.*, pl.	voyelles chuchotées, *f.*, pl.
018	whispering, n.	шепот, *m.*	Flüstern, *n.*	chuchotement, *m.*
019	whistling, n.	свист, *m.*	Pfeifen, *n.*/Flöten, *n.*	sifflement, *m.*
020	whistling sound	свистящий звук	pfeifender Laut	son sifflant, *m.*
021	white noise	(белый) шум	Rauschen, *n.*	bruit, *m.*
022	whole, adj.	целый/весь	ganz/vollständig	entier/complet
023	(the) whole, n.	целое, *n.*/ совокупность, *f.*	Ganze, *n.*/Gesamtheit, *f.*/ Totalität, *f.*	tout, *m.*/ensemble, *m.*/ totalité, *f.*
024	wholeness, n.	цельность, *f.*	Ganzheit, *f.*	intégralité, *f.*
025	wide, adj.	широкий	breit	large
026	wide band filter	широкополосовой фильтр	Breitbandfilter, *m.*	filtre large, *m.*
027	wide vowels, pl.	широкие гласные, pl.	breite Vokale, *m.*, pl.	voyelles larges, *f.*, pl.
028	widening, n.	расширение, *n.*	Ausbreitung, *f.*	élargissement, *m.*
029	widespread, adj.	широко распространенный	ausgedehnt	très répandu
030	winking, n.	мигание, *n.*	Zwinkern, *n.*/Blinzeln, *n.*	clignement, *m.*/ clignotement, *m.*
031	wisecrack, n.	удачное замечание/ острота, *f.*	Bonmot, *n.*/ witzige Bemerkung	bon mot, *m.*
032	wish, n.	пожелание, *n.*	Wunsch, *m.*	désir, *m.*
033	witticism, n.	острота, *f.*/остроумное замечание	Witz, *m.*	mot d'esprit, *m.*
034	word, n.	слово, *n.*	Wort, *n.*	mot, *m.*/parole, *f.*/ terme, *m.*
035	word and thing	слово и вещь	Wort und Ding	mot et chose

No.	ENGLISH	RUSSIAN	GERMAN	FRENCH
036	word association	словесная ассоциация	Wortassoziation, f.	association de mots, f.
037	word book	словарь, m.	Wörterbuch, n.	vocabulaire, m.
038	word boundary	граница слова, f.	Wortgrenze, f.	frontière de mot, f.
039	word-by-word translation	дословный перевод	wortgetreue Übersetzung/wörtliche Übersetzung	traduction mot-à-mot, f.
040	word categories, pl.	категории слов, f., pl.	Wortkategorien, f., pl.	parties du discours, f., pl.
041	word change	словоизменение, n.	Wortänderung, f.	changement de mot, m.
042	word choice	выбор слова, m.	Wortwahl, f.	choix de mots, m.
043	word class	словесный класс	Wortklasse, f.	classe de mots, f.
044	word combination	словосочетание, n.	Wortkombination, f.	combinaison de mots, f.
045	word compounding, n.	словосложение, n.	Wortgefüge, n.	combinaison de mots, f.
046	word content	содержание слова, n.	Wortumfang, m.	contenu de mot, m.
047	word context	словесный контекст	Wortzusammenhang, m.	contexte de mots, m.
048	word correlates, pl.	соотносительные слова, n., pl.	entsprechende Wörter, n., pl.	mots en corrélation, m., pl.
049	word creation	словотворчество, n.	Wörterzeugung, f.	création de mots, f.
050	word derivation	словопроизводство, n.	Wortableitung, f.	dérivation des mots, f.
051	word etymology	этимология слова, f.	Wortgeschichte, f.	étymologie, f.
052	word family	словесное гнездо	Wortfamilie, f.	famille de mots, f.
053	word final position	конечное положение в слове	Wortendstellung, f.	finale de mot, f.
054	word formation	словообразование, n.	Wortbildung, f.	formation des mots, f.
055	word formative	словообразующий, m.	wortbildendes Element	élément formatif de mot, m.
056	word game	игра слов, f.	Wortspiel, n.	jeu de mots, m.
057	word history	история слов, f./ этимология, f.	Wortgeschichte, f.	histoire des mots, f.

No.	English	Russian	German	French
058	word image	образ слова, *m.*	Wortbild, *n.*	mot-image, *f.*
059	word inflection	флексия слова, *f.*/ словоизменение, *n.*	Wortflexion, *f.*	flexion de mot, *f.*
060	word initial position	начальное положение в слове	Wortanfangsstellung, *f.*	initiale de mot, *f.*
061	word list	список слов, *m.*	Wörterliste, *f.*, pl.	liste de mots, *f.*
062	word meaning	значение слова, *n.*	Wortbedeutung, *f.*	sens du mot, *m.*
063	word omission	пропуск слова, *m.*	Wortauslassung, *f.*	omission de mot, *f.*
064	word order	порядок слов, *m.*	Wortfolge, *f.*/ Wortstellung, *f.*	ordre des mots, *m.*
065	word pair	словопара, *f.*	Wortpaar, *n.*	paire de mots, *m.*
066	word play	игра слов, *f.*/ каламбур, *m.*	Wortspiel, *n.*	jeu de mots, *m.*
067	word position (in sentence)	позиция слова, *f.*	Wortstellung, *f.*	place du mot, *f.*
068	word root	корень слова, *m.*	Wortwurzel, *f.*	radical de mot, *m.*
069	word-sentence, n.	слово-предложение, *n.*	Wortsatz, *m.*	mot-phrase, *f.*
070	word sign	словесный знак	Wortzeichen, *n.*	mot-signe, *m.*
071	word square	словесный квадрат	Wortquadrat, *n.*	mot-carré, *m.*
072	word stem	основа слова, *f.*	Wortstamm, *m.*	radical, *m.*
073	word stock	словарный фонд	Wortschatz, *m.*	lexique, *m.*
074	word stress	словесное ударение	Wortakzent, *m.*	accent de mot, *m.*
075	word structure	структура слов, *f.*	Wortstruktur, *f.*	structure de mots, *f.*
076	word travels, pl.	скитания слов, *n.*, pl.	Wortreisen, *f.*, pl.	voyages des mots, *m.*, pl.
077	word usage	словоупотребление, *n.*	Wortgebrauch, *m.*	emploi de mot, *m.*
078	wording, n.	сформулировка, *f.*	Formulierung, *f.*	libellé, *m.*
079	work, n.	работа, *f.*/труд, *m.*/ произведение, *n.*/ сочинение, *n.*	Arbeit, *f*/Werk, *n.*	travail, *m.*/ouvrage, *m.*

No.	ENGLISH	RUSSIAN	GERMAN	FRENCH
080	world languages, pl.	всемирные языки, *m.*, pl.	Weltsprachen, *f.*, pl.	langues internationales, *f.*, pl.
081	writing, n.	писание, *n.*/письмо, *n.*/ письменность, *f.*	Schreiben, *n.*/Schrift, *f.*	écriture, *f.*
082	writing system	писменная система	Schriftsystem, *n.*	système d'écriture, *m.*
083	written, adj.	письменный/ написанный	geschrieben/schriftlich	écrit
084	written languages, pl.	письменные языки, *m.*, pl.	geschriebene Sprachen, *f.*, pl.	langues écrites, *f.*, pl.
085	written records, pl.	записи, *f.*, pl.	geschriebene Urkunden, *f.*, pl.	documentation écrite, *f.*/ archives, *m.*, pl.
086	wrong, adj.	неправильный/ ошибочный	falsch/unrichtig	faux/erroné/incorrect
087	wrong pronunciation	ошибочное произношение	falsche Aussprache	prononciation fausse, *f.*
088	wrong spelling	ошибочное правописание	falsches Buchstabieren	orthographe incorrecte, *f.*
089	wrong stress	неправильное ударение	unrichtige Betonung	accent faux, *m.*
090	wrong translation	ошибочный перевод	falsche Übersetzung	traduction erronée, *f.*
091	wrong word	неправильное слово/ не то слово	falsches Wort	mot faux, *m.*
092	wrong word order	неправильный порядок слов	falsche Wortstellung	ordre de mots faux, *m.*
093	wrong usage	ошибочное применение	falscher Gebrauch	emploi erroné, *m.*

X

No.	ENGLISH	RUSSIAN	GERMAN	FRENCH
001	X-ray photograph	рентгенограмма, *f.*	Roñtgenaufnahme, *f.*	radiographie, *f.*/cliché radiographique, *m.*

No.	English	Russian	German	French

Y

No.	English	Russian	German	French
001	Yiddish, adj.	новоеврейский/ идиш, *m.*, (n.)	jiddisch	yiddish
002	yield, n.	выработка, *f.*/ плоды, pl.	Ertrag, *m.*	rendement, *m.*
003	yo-heave-ho theory	теория ей-ухнем, *f.*	hau-ruck Theorie, *f.*	théorie oh hissé, *f.*

Z

No.	English	Russian	German	French
001	zero, n.	нуль, *m.*	Null, *f.*	zéro, *m.*
002	zero affix	нулевой аффикс	Nullaffix, *n.*	affixe zéro, *m.*
003	zero allomorph	нулевой алломорф	Nullallomorph, *n.*	allomorphe zéro, *m.*
004	zero allophone	нулевой аллофон	Nullallophon, *n.*	variante zéro, *f.*
005	zero ending	нулевое окончание	Nullendung, *f.*	désinence zéro, *f.*
006	zero grade	нулевая ступень	Nullstufe, *f.*	degré zéro, *m.*
007	zero indicator	нулевой показатель	Nullkennzeichen, *n.*	indicateur zéro, *m.*
008	zero inflection	нулевая флексия	Nullflexion, *f.*	flexion zéro, *f.*
009	zero member	нулевой член	Nullglied, *n.*	membre zéro, *m.*
010	zero morpheme	нулевая морфема	Nullmorphem, *n.*	morphème zéro, *m.*
011	zero probability	нулевая вероятность	Nullwahrscheinlichkeit, *f.*	probabilité nulle, *f.*
012	zero realization	нулевая реализация/ нулевая актуализация	Nullaktualisierung, *f.*/ Nullrealisierung, *f.*	réalisation zéro, *f.*
013	zone, n.	зона, *f.*	Zone, *f.*	zone, *f.*
014	zoonym, n.	зооним, *m.*/название животного, *n.*	Tiername, *m.*	nom d'animal, *m.*
015	zoosemiotics, n.	исследование языка животных, *n.*/ ⟨зоосемиотика⟩, *f.*	Tiersprachenforschung, *f.*/⟨Zoosemiotik⟩, *f.*	étude du langage des animaux, *f.*/ ⟨zoosemiotique⟩, *f.*

РУССКИЙ УКАЗАТЕЛЬ

абзац P 029
аблатив A 005
аблаут A 006, G 055, V 106
абруптивный-неабруптивный
    D 203
абсолютная высота тона A 020
абсолютная конструкция A 017
абсолютная форма A 019
абсолютное положение A 022
абсолютный исход A 018
абсолютный падеж A 016
абсолютный слух A 021, P 122
абсорбция A 023
абстракция A 028
абстракция высокого уровня
    H 037
автобиография A 301
автоматическая ручка F 166
автоматическое чередование
    A 302
автономная система A 305
автор A 300
авторское право C 367
агглютинирующие языки A 133
адекватность A 087
адекватность лингвистической
    модели L 187
административный жаргон
    O 036
адрес A 085
адресная книга D 160
азбука A 152
азбука глухонемых F 076, M 026
азиатский O 090
акроним A 063
акростих A 065
акрофоническая перестановка
    S 367
акрофония A 064
активное предложение A 071

активный A 069
активный орган A 253
активный словарь A 072
актуализация A 076, R 027
актуализация фонемы P 198
актуальный A 075, T 161
акустика A 057
акустическая фонетика A 055
акустическая классификация
    A 051
акустические признаки A 053
акустический A 049, P 259
акустический анализ A 050
акустический образ A 054
акустический сигнал A 056
акустический эффект A 052
акут A 078
акцент A 031
акцентная группа S 420
акцентуация A 034
алгебра A 142
алгоритм A 143
аллегория A 144, P 021
аллитерация A 145
аллограф A 146
алломорфа A 147
аллофон A 148, P 178, P 204, V 010
алфавит A 152
алфавитный порядок A 153
альбом газетных вырезок S 027
альвеола A 160
альвеолярные согласные A 159
альманах A 151
амальгама A 161
амальгамирующие языки A 162
амплитуда A 167
анаграмма A 169
анаколуф A 168
анализ A 181
анализ звуков S 256

анализ по компонентам C 204
анализ предложения S 081
анализ речи D 174
анализ содержания C 313
анализ языка L 013
аналитическая грамматика
    A 179
аналитические языки A 180
аналитическое сравнение A 178
аналог A 176
аналогические языки A 171
аналогическое изменение A 170
аналогичные отношения A 175
аналогичные формы A 174
аналогичный A 173
аналогия A 177
аналогия по форме F 144
анаптиксис A 183
анатомия A 184
анафора A 182
английский E 058
анекдот A 188
анкета Q 019
аномалия A 197
анонимный A 198
антиномия A 207
антитеза A 208
антология A 203
антоним A 209, C 387
антропологическая лингвистика
    A 204
антропология A 205
аорист A 210
аористический вид A 211
апикальные согласные A 215
апозиопесис A 218
апокопа A 216
апостроф A 219
апофония A 217
аппарат A 220, M 082

аранжировка A 246, O 087
арго S 209
ареальная группа A 244
ареальная лингвистика A 245
артикль A 250
артикуляторная классификация
   A 254
артикуляторная фонетика A 255
артикуляционная база B 029
артикуляция A 252
архаизм A 238, R 101
архаический A 237
археология A 236
архетип A 239
архив A 241
архифонема A 240
асимметричный A 272
асимметрия A 273
аспирант G 060, P 372
аспирантура G 061
аспирация A 261
ассимиляция A 263
ассонанс A 268
ассоциативное значение A 264
ассоциативное поле A 266
атлас A 275
атонцческий A 276
афазия A 213
афиша B 042, P 293
афоризм A 214
аффективная речь A 119
аффективное ударение A 120
аффикс A 124
аффиксация A 125
аффиксирующие языки A 126
аффрикаты A 127
база B 018, B 028
баллада B 015
банальность P 303
банальный C 168
барабан D 262
барабанная перепонка E 002
барабанный язык D 263
басня F 001
беглая гласная F 099, U 137
беглая речь F 109
бегло говорить S 308
беглость F 108
безграмотность I 016
беззвучный N 093
безконечное число I 124
безличное местоимение I 039

безличное предложение I 040,
   S 464
безличный I 038
безличный глагол I 041
безошибочный I 119, U 103
безударный A 276, U 138
безударный слог U 139
безымянный A 198, U 106
белиберда G 040
беллетристика F 040
белый стих B 062
белый шум W 021
бемольный-простой D 203
беседа C 353, D 173, I 207, T 012
бесконечный I 123
бесписьменные языки U 152
бесполезный U 168
беспредельный U 100
бесприставочный U 113
бессловный язык N 133
бессмысленный M 075, N 128
бессмысленный язык N 127
бессознательный U 030
бессоюзное сочинение P 037
бессоюзный A 274
бесспорный U 055
бесшумный N 093
библейские варианты V 052
библейский язык B 037
библиография B 038, R 059
библиотека L 166
библия B 035
билабиальные согласные B 039
бинарная конструция B 046
бинарная оппозиция B 047
бинарная система B 051
бинарность B 043
бинарный B 044
биография B 053
биолингвистика B 054
биология B 055
бихевиоризм B 033
благозвучие E 112
благоприятные условия F 031
благословение B 034, B 064
близкий C 098
близкое сходство C 100
близость A 121, P 534
блок-схема F 104
богохульство P 485
божество D 048
боковая часть языка T 155

боковые согласные L 107
болгарский B 107
болтливый T 013
болтовня C 055, G 053, T 133
большинство M 014, M 015
большой палец T 111
бранная речь I 252
бранное выражение E 165
бронхи B 104
брошюра B 102, P 014
будущее F 219
будущее время F 222
будущее немедленное I 025
будущее предварительное F 221
буква G 093, L 131
буквальное значение L 260
буквальный L 259
буквенное письмо A 154
буквенный указатель T 112
бумага P 016
быстрая речь F 030, R 013
быстродействующая память
   H 040
быстрота V 022
быстрота звука S 296
быстрый R 012
бытовая речь E 122
бытовой контекст S 202
бытовые выражения C 158
в конце концов E 121
в первую очередь F 086
вавилонская башня T 168
важность S 167
важный I 044
валентность V 003
валлийский W 014
варваризм B 017
вариант A 148, A 156, V 010
вариант фонемы P 178, P 193,
   P 204
вариация V 013
варьирование V 013
введение I 246
вводное предложение P 043
вводные слова P 044
вводящее слово I 245
вводящий A 206
вводящий в заблуждение M 160
вдох I 167
вдыхание I 167
вдыхательные согласные I 143

вопросительное слово I 235
вопросительный I 229
вопросительный знак I 234,
　Q 017
вопросник Q 019
воркование C 359
воровское арго F 098
воровской жаргон T 099
восклицание E 139
восклицательное предложение
　E 141
восклицательный знак E 140
восковка S 398
воспитание T 179
воспитанная речь C 410
воспользоваться U 165
воспоминание M 096
воспринимаемый P 118
восприятие P 119
восприятие звуков S 277
восстановление R 040
восстановление в памяти R 031
восстановление R 136
восточный O 090
восходящий тон A 258, R 174
восьмиричный O 030
впечатление I 047
вранье L 321
времена глагола V 031
временная ось T 119
временной T 061
время T 064, T 117
время и пространство T 118
всасывающий звук S 489
всемирные языки U 090, W 080
всеобщий U 088
всеобщность G 012, U 093
вспомогательное слово E 047
вспомогательные языки A 307
вспомогательный A 306
вспомогательный глагол A 308
вставка E 071, I 163
вставка гласного V 108
вставка звука A 183
вставка согласного C 291
встречаемость O 029
вступительное испытание E 063
вся жизнь L 169
всякая всячина H 064
вторичная сигнальная система
　S 041
второе лицо S 036
второстепенное значение S 038

второстепенное ударение S 042
второстепенные члены
　предложения S 040
второстепенный S 037
вуз C 131
вульгарное выражение V 122
вход и выход I 159
выбор C 065
выбор слова W 042
вывод C 233, D 028, I 121
выговор M 024
выдающийся P 502
выделение S 116
выдержка E 134, E 191, S 520
выдох E 162
выдыхание E 162
выкрик O 109
вымерший
вымерший E 188
вымысел F 039
вымышленный F 041
выпадение D 259
выпадение слогов D 260
выполнение E 146, P 127
выпуск I 275
выпускные экзамены F 062
выработка Y 002
выравнивание L 141
выравнивание по аналогии A 172
выравнивание по смежности
　A 284
выражение E 173, L 281
выражение боли T 072
выражение возраста A 131
выражение времени T 123
выражение на лице F 003
выражение удивления T 074
выражение удовольствия T 073
выразительная интонация E 177
выразительность E 179
выразительный язык E 178
высказывание U 172
высокая частота H 035
высокие гласные H 043
высокий H 034
высокий регистр тона H 041
высокий тон H 042
высокой тональности H 038
высокой тональности-низкой
　тональности D 203
высота H 020
высота тона P 289, S 278
высшее учебное заведение G 061

высший H 044, U 160
высший класс U 156
выученное поведение L 115
выход O 115
вычисление C 003
вычислительная техника I 138
вычислительный центр C 224
вычитание S 485
вышеупомянутый F 134
газета N 083
газетная заметка I 279
газетные объявления по
　категориям C 088
газетный стиль N 084
гаплология H 004
гармоническая ассимиляция
　N 109
гармония гласных V 107
гектограф M 137
генеалогическая классификация
　G 005
генеалогия G 007
генеалогия языков L 070
генезис G 019
генерализованная
　трансформация D 241
генетика G 021
географическая классификация
　G 026
географическая лингвистика
　G 029
географическое название G 030
географическое препятствие
　G 025
географическое разнообразие
　G 031
географическое расположение
　G 028
географическое схождение
　G 027
география G 032
геометрия G 033
героическая поэма H 023
героический эпос H 023
герундий G 036
герц C 431
гибкость F 101
гипербола H 093
гипотаксис H 098
гипотеза H 099
гипотетическая форма H 101
гипотетические данные H 100

грамматическое чередование G 069
грамматическое ядро G 074
грамматичность G 091
грамматичный G 066
граммофон P 260
грамотность L 258
грамотный L 266
граница B 081, L 174
граница морфемы M 217
граница предложения S 084
граница слова W 038
граница слога S 528
граница фонемы P 180
гранка G 001
графема G 093
графемика G 094
график D 110, G 092
графическая ассимиляция G 096
графическая передача G 097
графический G 095
графическое слово G 098
графология G 100
греческий G 106
громкий голос L 300
громкоговоритель L 302
громкость L 301
грудная клетка C 060
грудобрюшная преграда D 118
грудь C 060
группа C 110, G 109
группировка G 110
губа L 249
губно-губные согласные B 039
губно-зубной L 005
губные согласные L 002
давление P 428
давно не издававшаяся O 108
давно не печатающийся O 108
давнопрошедшее время P 094, P 309
давность T 120
далекий F 029
далекое будущее D 199
далекое прошедшее время R 109
дальний D 198, F 029
данные D 005
дата D 007
дательный падеж D 009
датирование D 008
датировка языков L 058

датский D 001
движение M 255, M 262
движения губ L 250
движущая сила M 201
двоеточие C 135
двоичная единица B 052, B 058
двоичная система B 051
двоичная шкала B 048
двоичный B 044
двоичный знак B 052, B 058
двоичный код B 045
двоичный символ B 050
двойная стрелка D 239
двойное изображение D 267
двойное отрицание D 245
двойное притяжательное D 246
двойное членение D 269
двойной B 044, D 264
двойные согласные D 250, G 002
двойственное число D 266
двойственность D 268
двоякое значение D 244
двугласный D 145
двугубные согласные B 039
двуразмерный T 241
двусложный D 219
двусмысленность A 164
двусоставное предложение B 049
двустишие D 200
двусторонний B 040
двусторонняя единственность B 059
двухбазная трансформация D 241
двухступенчатая модель T 242
двухфокусная артикуляция D 240
двучленный T 243
двуязычие B 041
дебаты D 014
девиз M 258
девичья фамилия M 011
дедуктивное рассуждение D 029
дедукция D 028
деепричастие V 035
деепричастный P 060
действие A 066, O 058
действительность R 026
действительный A 075
действительный залог A 073
действующее лицо A 132
действующий A 069
декодирование D 025
делабиализация U 129

делать выдержки A 024
делать грамматический разбор P 049
деление D 226, S 048
деление времени T 122
делимый D 225
демография D 055
дентальные согласные D 064
деревенский говор R 189
дерево T 213
деривационный аффикс D 073
деривация D 072
десигнат D 089
десигнатель D 088
дескриптивная лингвистика D 084
десны G 114
десятилетие D 015
десятичный D 017
детали M 155
деталь D 092
детская речь B 002, I 120
детские стишки N 173
детский рассказ N 175
детский сад K 005, N 174
детский язык C 062, N 172
дефект слуха H 017
дефективная дистрибуция D 032
дефис H 095
деятель A 074, A 132
диагональная линия D 109
диаграмма D 110, G 092, L 178
диакритический знак D 107
диалект D 111
диалектальная география D 114
диалектная область D 112
диалектологический атлас D 113
диалектология D 115
диалог D 116, I 207
диапазон D 119
диапазон голоса R 008
диарема D 054
диасистема D 121
диафон D 117
диафрагма D 118
диахроническая фонология D 104
диахроническая лингвистика D 103
диахронический D 101
диахронический анализ D 102

недостающее звено M 168
недостижимый U 016
неединичность N 132
неестественный U 107
неэффективный I 112
нежелательный O 006
независимая переменная I 088
независимая фонема I 087
независимое развитие I 086
независимость I 084
незаметный I 034
незамеченный D 190, U 109
незамещаемый N 106
незаписанный U 121
незасвидетельствованный
    U 018
незащитимый U 143
незвонкий U 149
незнакомый S 407, U 062
незначительный I 165, N 054,
    T 226
неизбежный I 115, N 038, U 019
неизвестный U 096
неизданный U 117
неизмененный U 102
неизменный I 028, I 249, P 142,
    U 010, U 023
неизменяемость I 248
неизменяемый I 249, U 011
неизменяющийся U 077
неисправленный U 033
неиспробованный U 017
нейтрализация N 070
нейтрализация фонематических
    сопоставлений N 071
нейтрализованный N 072
нейтральная интонация N 138
нейтральное положение P 352
нейтральный N 066
нейтральный гласный звук
    N 069
нейтральный звук N 068
неконечный N 115
некролог N 042, O 002
нексус N 087
нелинейный N 120
неличный глагол N 116
нелогичный I 017
немаркированный U 101
немая буква S 174
немая гласная M 287
немая согласная M 284

немецкий G 034
немой D 270
немой фильм S 173
немой (человек) M 286
немотивированный U 105
ненадежный U 038, U 123
ненаправленный N 111
ненапряженный D 203, L 112
ненаселенный U 079
ненаучный U 131, U 132
ненужный U 108
необоснованный U 066
необразованный U 056
необратимый I 266
необусловленный U 028
необходимые и достаточные
    условия N 039
необходимый E 098, I 102, N 038
необъяснимый I 117, U 007
необыкновенный U 026, U 148
необычайный E 194
необязательный O 067
неограничивающий N 126
неограниченный U 100, U 126
неограниченный список O 053
неодинаковый U 057
неоднородный H 026
неодушевленный I 058
неожиданный U 060
неоконченный U 027, U 064
неокругленные гласные U 128
неологизм C 123, M 194, N 057
неописанный U 049
неоправданный U 095
неопределенная фонема D 254
неопределенная форма глагола
    I 125
неопределенное время глагола
    I 082
неопределенное движение I 098
неопределенное местоимение
    I 081
неопределенный I 079, I 089,
    U 037, U 050, V 001
неопределенный артикль I 080
неопределяемый U 036
неопубликованный U 117
неотвлеченное существительное
    C 238
неотделимый I 162
неотложимость U 162
неотмеченный U 101

неотчетливый I 103
неотъемлемый N 129
непарная фонема N 118, N 122,
    U 111
непереводимый U 146
непересекающиеся N 119
непереходный глагол I 244
неповторный U 124
неподверженный влиянию U 078
неподвижное ударение F 094
неподвижный порядок слов
    F 095
неподдающийся классификации
    U 024
неподходящее название M 161
неподходящий U 140
неподчинение N 107
непознаваемый чувствами E 195
неполная ассимиляция P 054
неполное предложение I 070
неполный I 069
непонятный U 080
непосредственный неологизм
    S 365
непостоянность I 037
непостоянство V 006
непостредственно составляющие
    I 024
непохожий U 098
неправда F 018
неправильно поставленный
    M 162
неправильное предложение
    A 195
неправильное представление
    M 157
неправильное применение M 156
неправильное произношение
    M 164
неправильное слово W 091
неправильное толкование M 159
неправильное ударение W 089
неправильное употребление
    M 175
неправильность I 264
неправильный A 194, E 094,
    F 016, I 055, I 075, I 262
    W 086
неправильный глагол A 196,
    I 263
неправильный перевод M 173

неправильный порядок слов W 092
непредписывающий N 124
непредсказуемый U 112
непрерывный U 081
непрерывность C 328
непрерывный C 325, C 329, D 203, U 081
непрерывный процесс C 330
непривыкший U 008
непривычный U 008, U 148
непридыхательный U 013
неприемлемый U 006
неприкрепленный U 015
неприкрытый O 122
неприличные слова F 167
неприличные выражения O 017
неприменимый I 059
непринужденная речь N 035
неприобретенный U 009
неприступный I 053
непроверенный U 144
непродуктивный N 125, U 114
непроизводный U 041
непроизносимая буква M 285, S 174
непроизносимый U 115
непроизносимый слог S 176
непрослеживаемый U 145
непрошедший глагол N 123
неравенство I 113
неравномерное распределение U 059
неравный U 057
неразборчивое письмо S 028
неразборчивый I 014, U 118
неразделенный U 054
неразличимый U 053
неразличительный I 265, N 112
неразрешенный U 125
нерв N 058
нервная система N 059
нервный N 062
нереальный U 119
нерезкий D 203, M 090
нерешающий I 072
нерешенный U 133
нерешительный I 077
неродовой G 004
неродственные языки U 122
несвязанный U 029
несвязный U 029

несимметричный U 141
несистематичный U 142
несклоняемый I 078, U 035
неслышный I 060
несмежный D 169, N 108
несмешанный U 104
несмешанный язык P 561
несовершенное прошедшее I 071
несовершенный U 064
несовершенный вид I 035
несовместимый I 068
несогласный D 203
несогласованный I 032
несокращенный U 004
несомненность C 041
несомненный U 052, U 055, U 103
несообразный I 074
несоответствие D 177, D 185, I 073
несоприкасающийся D 169
несоразмерный I 067
несоставляющий контраста N 110
неспорный U 052
неспособность I 052
нестандартный N 130
несущественный N 114, U 058
несходный U 098
несходство D 194
нетипичный A 288, N 131
неточность I 054
неточный I 046, I 055, I 116
неударный U 005
неудовлетворительность I 056
неудовлетворительный U 130
неудовольствие D 191
неузнаваемый U 120
неуказенный U 134
неуравновешенный U 020
неустановленная фонема M 035
неустойчивость I 168
неустойчивый U 136
неуточненный U 134
нейтрализация фонем P 195
неученый U 056
нечеловеческий N 117
нечетное число O 032
нечленораздельная речь I 066
нешаблонный U 031
неясный O 018, U 025
нижненемецкий L 307

нижние гласные L 312
нижний слой S 482
нижняя граница L 313
нижняя грань L 313
нижняя губа L 317
нижняя челюсть L 316
низкая частота L 306
низкие гласные L 312
низкий голос L 311
низкий регистр тона L 310
низкий тон L 309
низкого тона L 308
низкой тональности D 203
нисходящий тон F 015
новая функция N 075
новелла N 161
новизна N 080
нововведение I 158
новое использование N 077
новое образование N 074
новое слово N 078
новоеврейский Y 001
новости N 081
новшество I 158
новые языки M 193
новый N 073, N 159
ноздря N 148
номенклатура N 097
номер телефона T 053
номинализация N 102
норвежский N 146
норма N 134, S 379
нормализация N 144, S 381
нормализация языка L 091
нормальное дыхание N 136
нормальное распределение N 137
нормальный N 135
нормативная грамматика N 145, P 420
нос N 147
носитель языка N 029
носовая полость N 013
носовой N 012
носовой-ртовый D 203
носовые гласные N 016
носовые согласные N 014
нотация N 149
ноты M 279
нужда N 040
нулевая актуализация Z 012
нулевая вероятность Z 011
нулевая морфема Z 010

пассивный запас слов R 025
пассивный орган P 081
пассивный словарь P 084
патефон P 260
патефонная пластинка P 261
патология P 096
патология речи S 344
пауза B 092, H 024, P 103
пауза в разговоре S 345
пауза в предложении S 098
певучий голос S 194
педагогика P 107
педагогический P 106
педагогическое училище N 140
педантичный P 108
пение S 193
первичная сигнальная система
  P 438
первичная функция P 434
первичный элемент P 440
первобытный язык P 435
первое издание F 087
первое лицо F 089
первоначально O 094
первый F 085
первый и последний F 160
пергамент P 038
перевернутая буква B 011
перевернутые запятые I 256
перевес P 416
перевод T 203, V 051
переводимый T 202
переводчик I 226, T 206
переводы библии B 036
переводящий язык T 022
перегласовка M 283, U 003, V 110
перегрузка O 119
передача B 101, T 208
передача звуков S 294
передвижение S 144
передвижение вверх R 006
передвижение вниз L 318
передвижение вперед F 196
передвижение гласных V 118
передвижение звуков S 285
передвижение назад B 009
передвижение согласных C 297
передвижение ударения S 417
передненебный F 194
переднеязычные гласные P 009
переднеязычный F 193
передние гласные F 195

передняя артикуляция F 192
передняя часть языка B 060,
  T 150
передовая статья E 013
пережиток V 057
переиздание R 080
перекрестная ссылка C 400
переложение в стихи V 050
перемена A 155, C 045
перемена гласных V 100
перемена кода C 114, S 516
переменное V 007
перемещение D 184, P 148, T 209
перемещение ударения A 032
перенесение T 187
перенесенный T 188
перенос C 018, T 183
перенос значения M 070, T 185
перенос названия T 186
перенос по функции T 184
переносное значение F 049
переносный T 188
переносный смысл F 049
переобразование R 066
переопределение R 047
переоткрытие R 048
переписка C 381
перераспределение R 049
перерыв P 103
переселение M 134
пересечение I 237
пересечение множеств S 133
пересказ P 036
перестановка P 148, R 028, T 209
перестановка звуков M 117
перестройка R 040
переучивание R 095
переформулировка R 067
перефразировка R 135
переход T 195
переходная вероятность T 197
переходная зона F 191, T 196
переходная полоса M 032
переходный M 031
переходный глагол T 199
переходный звук G 042, T 198
переходный язык M 033
переходящий T 201
перечисление E 066
перечислительная интонация
  E 067
период A 129

период развития P 130
периодика M 007
периодический P 133
периодическое издание P 134
периферический P 135
периферия M 030, P 138
перифраза P 139
перифрастическое спряжение
  P 140
перо P 110
перпендикулярный P 149
персидский P 152
перспектива O 113, P 160
перфект P 123, P 425
перфокарта P 125, P 555
перфолента P 126, P 556
песнь C 011
песня S 251
петля L 295
печатание в слепую T 167
печатать P 458
печать P 427, P 462
печатная краска P 463
печатная машина P 464
печатный P 459
печатный материал P 460
печатный станок P 464
пещерный житель C 030
пик P 104
пиктография P 286
писание W 081
писатель A 300
писать печатными буквами
  P 457
писец S 031
письменная система W 082
письменность W 081
письменные языки W 084
письменный W 083
письмо L 132, S 032, W 081
письмо понятиями I 007
письмо рисунками P 286
письмо с лева на право L 122
письмо с права на лево R 172
пишущая машинка T 250
пищевые названия F 117
плавность речи F 004
плавные согласные L 254
плагиат P 299
плакат P 293
план O 112, P 300
план выражения E 174

символическая сигнализация S 539
символический язык S 537
симетрический S 542
симетрия S 543
симуляция языка L 090
сингармонизм S 552
синкопа S 549
синкретизм S 550
синоним S 553
синонимия S 554
синтагма Р 129, S 578
синтагматическая ось S 580
синтагматический S 579
синтагматическое ударение S 576
синтаксис S 581
синтактическая группа S 571
синтактическая двусмысленность S 556
синтактическая единица S 577
синтактическая категория S 557
синтактическая конструкция S 561
синтактическая парадигма S 574
синтактическая свобода S 568
синтактическая функция S 569
синтактическая эквивалентность S 565
синтактическая экономия S 563
синтактический S 555
синтактический класс S 559
синтактический механизм S 562
синтактический признак S 567
синтактический уровень S 573
синтактическое изменение S 558
синтактическое нововведение S 572
синтактическое окружение S 564
синтактическое отношение S 575
синтактическое расширение S 566
синтактическое сочетание S 560
синтактическое управление S 570
синтез S 582
синтез речи S 354
синтетические языки S 583
синхронизм S 547
синхронический S 544
синхрония S 548

синхронная лингвистика S 546
синхронный S 544
синхронный анализ S 545
синхронный перевод S 192
система S 584
система гласных V 120
система знаков S 586
система коммуникации С 171
система согласных С 299
система фонем Р 203
систематический М 120, S 587
системность языка S 588
ситуационная речь S 204
ситуационное значение S 203
ситуация S 201
сказать Т 058
сказуемое Р 395
скандирование стихотворения S 013
сквернословие F 056
скитания слов W 076
скитающееся слово W 001
склад ума А 283, М 106
склонение D 023
склоняемый D 024
скобки В 085
скольжение G 042
скопление С 110
скопление согласных С 289
скороговорка Т 157
скоропись S 153
скорость V 022
скорость замена R 018
скорость записи R 043
скорость перехода R 018
скорость распадения R 016
скорый R 012
скрещивание языков L 055
скрытый С 226, С 393, О 018
скулеж W 016
слабая екскурсия S 224
слабая позиция W 008
слабая рекурсия S 223
слабое окончание W 007
слабое придыхание W 006
слабое ударение W 009
слабый W 005
слабый конечный отступ S 226, S 244
слабый начальный приступ S 225, S 241
славянский S 211

след Т 169, V 057
следственное предложение R 145
следствие С 280, С 368, Е 016
следующий F 116, N 086
слепой В 065
слепота В 066
слитное предложение С 334
слияние С 260, F 218, М 108
слияние согласных С 289
слияние фонем Р 194
словарь D 128, W 037
словарь рифм R 165
словарная статья D 129, V 070
словарная форма С 077
словарный состав детей С 063
словарный фонд L 163, V 069, W 073
словесная ассоциация W 036
словесная смесь Р 347
словесное гнездо W 052
словесное поведение V 036
словесное ударение W 074
словесный О 069, V 032
словесный знак W 070
словесный квадрат W 071
словесный класс W 043
словесный контекст L 198, W 047
словник G 044
слово W 034
слово и вещь W 035
слово написанное через дефис Н 096
слово образованное на случай N 105
словоизменение I 129, W 041, W 059
словообразование W 054
словообразовательный аффикс D 073
словообразующий F 161, W 055
словоохотливый Т 013
словопамять V 039
словопара W 065
словопроизводство W 050
словосложение W 045
словосочетание Р 274, W 044
словотворчество W 049
словоупотребление W 077
слово-ключ К 003
слово-предложение О 047, W 069
слово-призрак G 039, Р 166

суперсегментная фонема S 508
суперстрат S 503
супплетив S 506
суффикс S 492
суффиксация S 493
существенные признаки R 098
существенный E 098
существительное S 477
существо E 062
существование E 151
сущность N 036, S 476
сфера D 230
сформулировка W 078
схема C 054, D 110, O 112, S 015
схема гласных V 104
схема логической программы
     F 104
сходный L 171, S 177
сходство R 124, S 178
сходящееся развитие языков
     C 352
схождение C 351
сцена S 375
сцепление C 025, C 225
сцепленный I 204
счет C 388
съезд C 254, C 262
сырые данные R 021
сюжет S 461
таблица T 001
таблица звуков S 262
табулирование T 007
тавтология T 025
тагмема T 009
тагмемная модель T 010
тайнопись C 408
тайный язык S 043
так называемый S 228
таксономическая грамматика
     T 026
таксономическая модель T 026
тактика T 006
тарабарщина G 052
твердое небо H 007
твердые согласные H 005
твердый знак H 008
творительный падеж I 176
театр T 087
театральная речь T 088
театральное произношение S 371
тезис T 097
текст T 084

текущая проблема C 421
телевидение T 056
телевизионная передача T 042
телевизор T 057
телеграмма T 043
телеграфный T 047
телеграфный адрес T 044
телеграфный код T 045
телеграфный стиль A 002, T 046
телеология T 048
телепатия E 195, M 103, T 049,
     T 106
телетайп T 055
телефон T 050
телефонная речь T 054
телодвижение G 037
тема T 090, T 160, S 461
тематическое чередование S 396
тембр Q 007, T 018, T 116
тембр гласного звука V 114
тембр звука S 295
темное л D 002
темные гласные D 003
темп T 060
темп речи S 356
тенденция D 258, T 063, T 214
теорема T 091
теоретико-множественная
     модель S 137
теоретические знания B 074
теоретический T 092
теоретический язык T 093
теория T 094
теория ай-ай-ай O 107
теория аф-аф B 083
теория волн W 004
теория динь-динь D 144
теория ей-ухнем Y 003
теория информации I 140
теория множеств S 135
теория связи C 172
теория скрещивания C 402
терапия T 095
терапия речи S 357
термин T 068
терминальная цепочка T 077
терминология T 079
терминология родства K 008
территория распространения
     диалекта D 112
тесная связь C 099
техника T 038

техника собирания сырого
     материала E 025
технический T 035
технический термин T 037
технический язык T 036
технология T 039
течение D 258, F 103, P 078
течение времени P 079
тильда T 115
тип S 253, T 244
тип предложения S 110
типичный C 051, T 252
типографическая ошибка T 255
типологическая классификация
     T 257
типология T 258
тире D 004
тире и точка D 237
титул T 131
титульный лист T 132
тихий звук S 245
тихо S 247
ткань T 086
тмезис T 134
тождественная степень E 087
тождество I 005, S 003
толкование E 147, I 225
толкование предложения S 091
толстая книга T 139
толстый T 098
том V 096
тон T 142
тон и интонация T 143
тон и шум T 144
тональная оболочка P 291
тональная последовательность
     P 292, S 120
тонально-глухой T 147
тональное ударение M 282, P 290,
     T 140
тональность T 141
тонема T 148
тоническая ритмика речи S 422
тонкое придыхание S 239
тонкое различие F 074
тороним G 030
торонимика P 294
торономия T 163
торговое название товара T 174
торговый язык C 156, T 172
тост T 135
точечный вид P 557

энтропия E 064
энциклопедия E 050
эпентеза E 071
эпиграмма E 075
эпиграф E 076
эпилог E 077
эпитафия E 078
эпитет E 079
эпическая поэма E 072
эпоним E 081
эпопея E 082
эпоха A 129, E 080, P 131
эргатив E 092
эрудиция E 096
эстетика A 118
эстетический A 117
эстонский E 099
этап развития S 376
этимологические диалектальные
    различия E 105
этимологический дублет E 106
этимологическое правописание
    E 107
этимология E 108, W 057
этимология слова W 051
этимон E 109
этническая группа E 101
этнография E 102
этнологическая лингвистика
    E 103
этнология E 104
эффективность E 018
эффективный E 017
эхо E 006
явный O 025
явление P 171
ядерное предложение K 002
ядро K 001, N 163
язык L 009, T 149
    барабанный язык D 263
    бессловный язык N 133
    бессмысленный язык N 127
    военный язык M 135
    выразительный язык E 178
    гипотетический язык H 103
    городской язык U 161
    господствующий язык D 234
    детский язык C 062, N 172
    журнальный язык J 008
    заумный язык N 127
    иностранный язык F 129
    литературный язык L 264
    машинный язык M 001

мета-язык M 111
научный язык S 021
несмешанный язык P 561
обиходный язык V 046
обонятельный язык O 041
образцовый язык S 380
общий язык C 161
ограниченный язык R 139
однопадежный язык O 044
осязательный язык T 008
первобытный язык P 435
переводящий язык T 022
переходный язык M 033
поэтический язык P 316
праязык P 039, P 528
разговорный язык I 134,
    S 363
рекламный язык A 116
родной язык M 253, N 028
символический язык S 537
смешанный язык H 092, M 179
стандартный язык S 380
тайный язык S 043
теоретический язык T 093
технический язык T 036
торговый язык C 156, T 172
церковный язык L 269
человеческий язык H 084
членораздельный язык A 251
юридический язык L 123
язык взрослых A 101
язык для программирования
    P 493
язык жестов G 038, S 160
язык животных A 190
язык знаков S 160
язык и география L 021
язык и действительность L 037
язык и диалект L 020
язык и индивидуальность L 031
язык и климат L 016
язык и культура L 019
язык и лингвистика L 023
язык и литература L 024
язык и логика L 025
язык и математика L 026
язык и мета-язык L 027
язык и музыка L 028
язык и мышление L 043
язык и наследственность L 022
язык и наука L 039
язык и национальность L 029
язык и общение L 018

язык и общество L 040
язык и письмо L 044
язык и познание L 017
язык и политика L 034
язык п потребность L 030
язык и психология L 035
язык и раса L 036
язык и религия L 038
язык и речь L 041
язык и символизм L 042
язык и физиология L 033
язык и философия L 032
язык и цивилизация L 015
язык и языкознание L 023
язык как система знаков L 048
язык по общему соглашению
    L 047
язык по сигнальной системе
    L 048
язык подростков A 099, T 040
язык привилегированного
    класса P 430
язык с конечным числом
    состояний F 082
язык цветов F 105
язык-источник S 300, S 302
язык-посредник I 209
язык-потомок D 010
язык-предок A 186, P 039
(языки)
    агглютинирующие языки
        A 133
    амальгаммрующие языки
        A 162
    аналитические языки A 180
    аналогические языки A 171
    аффиксирующие языки A 126
    бесписьменные языки U 152
    всемирные языки U 090,
        W 080
    вспомогательные языки A 307
    древние языки A 187
    естественные языки N 033
    живые языки L 272
    заброшенные языки N 053
    известные языки K 010
    изолирующие языки I 272
    иноземные языки E 153
    исскуственные языки A 257
    классические языки C 085
    корне-изолирующие языки
        R 182

DEUTSCHES REGISTER

Calque C 008
Cand. Phil. P 372
Casus obliquus O 013
Cedille C 032
charakteristisch C 051
charakteristik C 052
Chiffre C 070, C 113
Chiffrieren C 116, E 049
chinesisch C 064
Chronogramm C 067
Chronologie C 069
chronologische Reihenfolge C 068
Code C 111
Code und Nachricht C 112
Codewechsel S 516, C 114
Corpus C 369
danebenstehend A 088
dänisch D 001
dankende Erwähnung A 048
Darstellung P 422, R 120
Dasein E 062, E 151
Daten D 005
Datenverarbeitung D 006
Datierung D 008
Dativ D 009
Dativobjekt I 099
Datum D 007
Dauer D 274, L 126
Dauerakzent Q 012
Dauerform des Verbums P 496
Dauerlaute C 326
dauernd L 106, P 142
Dauerphonem L 128
Dauerspeicher P 143
Daumen T 111
Daumenregister T 112
dazwischen liegend I 208
Dazwischenschreiben I 205
Debatte D 014
Dechiffrierung D 025
Deckname P 535
Deckwort C 115
Deduktion D 028
deduktives Urteil D 029
defektiv D 031
defektive Verteilung D 032
defektives Verb(um) D 033
definitiv D 039
Definition D 038
Dehnung L 129
deiktisch D 047
Deklination D 023
deklinierbar D 024

Dekodierung D 025
Demographie D 055
Demonstrativartikel D 056
Demonstrativpronomen D 057
Demonstrativ(um) D 058
Denken T 101, T 104
Denkmal M 211
Denkprozess T 105
Denkreim M 182
Denkspruch M 056
Denominativ(um) D 059
dentale Konsonanten D 064
derivativ D 074
derivatives Affix D 073
Derivatum D 075
derselbe S 002
derzeitig C 309
Designant D 086
Designator D 088
deskriptive Linguistik D 084
deskriptives Adjektiv D 082
deskriptives Attribut D 083
Detail D 092
Determinante D 094
deutlich D 204, L 125, O 025
deutsch G 034
Deutung I 225
deverbativ D 096
Devise M 258
dezimal D 017
Diachronie D 106
diachronisch D 101
diachronische Analyse D 102
diachronische Phonologie D 104
diachronische Sprachwissenschaft
    D 103
diachronische Syntax D 105
diagonale Linie D 109
Diagramm D 110, G 092
diakritisches Zeichen D 107
Dialekt D 111
Dialektatlas D 113
Dialektgebiet D 112
Dialektgeographie D 114
Dialektologie D 115
Dialektpulverisierung P 553
Dialog D 116
Diaphon D 117
Diasystem D 121
dichotome Phonologie D 123
Dichotomie D 122
Dichotomie-Skala D 124
Dichte D 061

Dichte der Isoglossen D 062
Dichter P 315
dichterische Freiheit P 317
Dichtersprache P 316
Dichtung P 320
dick T 098
dicker Band T 139
die Uhr lesen T 059
diffus D 203
Dihärese D 108
Diktaphon D 125
Diktat D 126
Diktiergerät D 125
Dimension D 141
Diminutiv D 142
Ding T 100
Dingwort C 238
Diphthong D 145
Diphthongierung D 146
Diplom D 147
direkte Anrede D 148
direkte Bedeutung D 150
direkte Methode D 151
direkte Rede D 149
direktes Objekt D 152
disjunktiv D 183
diskrete Einheit D 178
Diskussion D 180
Dissertation D 193
Dissimilation D 195
Dissonanz D 196
Distichon C 389, D 200
distinktiv D 202
distinktive Merkmale D 203
distributionelle Ähnlichkeit
    D 213
distributionelle Beschränkungen
    D 212
distributiv D 214
distributive Zahl D 216
distributives Adjektiv D 215
distributives Pronomen D 217
Disziplin B 089, D 166
Divergenz D 221
Doktorand G 060, P 372
Doktorarbeit D 193, T 097
Doktrin D 227
Dokument D 228
Dokumentation D 229
Dolmetscher I 226
dominierender Knoten D 235
Doppelartikulation D 240
Doppelkonsonanten D 250, G 002

guttural T 110
Gutturale G 115
Gymnasium G 063
Halb- S 069
Halbvokal S 073
Hals N 041
Halszäpfchenlaute U 174
haltbar T 062
Haltung A 283
Handbuch H 002, M 025
handelnde Person A 132
Handelssprache C 156, T 172
Handfläche P 013
Handlung A 066
Handschrift H 003, M 027, S 032
Handschriftenkunde G 100, P 007
Haplologie H 004
Harmonik H 009
harte Konsonanten H 005
harter Gaumen H 007
hartes Zeichen H 008
hau-ruck Theorie Y 003
Hauch B 094
Hauchlaute B 096
häufig vorkommend F 188
Häufigkeit F 184
Häufigkeit des Vorkommens F 186
Häufigkeitszählung F 185
Hauptbedeutung P 437
Hauptsatz M 013, P 447
Hauptsprache D 234
Hauptteil M 015
Hauptton P 439
Hauptwort N 156
Hausaufgabe H 067
hebräisch H 019
Hebung R 006
Heimatland H 066
Heimschule B 069
heisere Stimme H 062
Heldengedicht E 072, H 023
hell D 203
helle Vokale B 099
Hemmung I 146
Herausgabe P 547
Herausgeber E 012
herkömmliche Grammatik T 176
Herkunft D 080, E 192, L 179,
 O 092, P 040
Herleitung D 028
herrschend D 232
Hertz C 431
heruntermachend P 109
hervorbringen P 481

hervorragend P 502
heterogen H 026
Heulen H 080
heuristisch H 027
heutig P 423
Hiatus H 028
Hierarchie H 031
hierarchische Struktur H 030
Hieroglyphe H 032
Hieroglyphenschrift H 033
Hilfs- A 306
Hilfsmittel R 132
Hilfssprachen A 307
Hilfsverb(um) A 308
Hilfswort A 037, E 047, F 202
Hilfszeitwort A 308
Hindernis I 030, O 022, O 023
Hinderung O 023
hinreichende Bedingung S 491
hintere Konsonanten B 004
hintere Vokale B 007
hinteres L D 002
Hintergrundsgeräusch B 008
Hinterzungen- D 236, V 017
Hinterzungenlaute V 018
Hinterzungenvokale V 019
Hinweis C 109, I 093
hinweisend D 047
hinweisendes Fürwort D 057
Hinzufügung A 083
Hinzufügung von Affixen A 125
Hinzufügung von Präfixen P 406
historisch-vergleichende Methode
 C 179
historische Dialektologie H 047
historische Dokumentation H 048
historische Methode H 050
historische Morphologie H 051
historische Phonetik H 053
historische Phonologie H 052, H 054
historische Rekonstruktion H 057
historische Semantik H 058
historische Sprachwissenschaft
 H 049
historische Syntax H 059
historischer Vorgang H 056
historischer Wechsel H 046
historisches Präsens H 055
hoch H 034
hochdeutsch H 036
Hochfrequenz H 035
Hochschule C 131, G 061, U 094
Hochsprache C 410
höchst T 162, U 160

Hochton H 042
höfliche Anredeform P 331
höfliche Redeweise P 332
Höhe H 020
hohe Tonlage H 041
hohe Vokale H 043
höher H 044
höher Tonumfang H 041
höhere Abstraktionsstufe H 037
höhere Schule G 063, H 039, S 039
höhere Tonlage U 158
Höhle C 031
Höhlenbewohner C 030
Höhlenmensch C 030
Hohn T 070
Hokuspokus H 063
holländisch D 275
homogen H 068
Homogramm H 069
Homonym H 070
Homonymie H 071
Homophon H 072
homorgan H 073
hörbar A 290
Hörbarkeit A 289
Hören H 015
Hörfehler H 017
Hörgerät H 016
horizontal H 075
horizontale Linie H 077
horizontale Schrift H 078
Hörmechanismus H 018
Humor H 087
humoristisch H 088
humorvoll H 088
hybride Bildung H 091
Hyperbel H 093
Hypernormalisierung O 116
Hyperurbanismus H 094
Hypotaxe H 098
Hypothese H 099
hypothetische Form H 101
hypothetische Sprache H 103
hypothetische Unterlagen H 100
hypothetisches Gebilde H 102
Idee I 002
Ideenassoziation A 267
Identifizierung I 004
identisch I 003
Identität I 005
Ideogramm I 006
Ideolekt I 008
Idiom I 009
idiomatischer Ausdruck I 010

Morphemvariante A 147, M 216
Morphemverteilung M 222
Morphologie A 038, M 246
morphologisch M 231
morphologische Analogie M 233
morphologische Analyse M 234
morphologische Bedingung M 238
morphologische Ebene M 241
morphologische Einteilung M 236
morphologische Homonymie M 240
morphologische Klassifizierung
    M 236
morphologische Korrelation M 239
morphologische Matrix M 242
morphologische Typologie M 245
morphologische Veränderung M 235
morphologische Wechselreihe M 232
morphologische Wortbildung M 237
morphologischer Vorgang M 243
Morphonem M 247
morphonemische Darstellung M 250
morphonemische Ebene M 249
morphonemische Regeln M 251
morphonemischer Wechsel M 248
Morphophonologie M 252
Motivierung M 257
Motorik K 006
Motto M 258
Mouillierung P 010
Multiplikativum M 270
Mund M 260
Mund- O 069
Mundart D 111
Mundartenforschung D 115
Mundhöhle O 071
Mundlaut O 075
mündlich O 069
mündliche Konsonanten O 073
mündliche Vokale O 076
Mundverschluss O 072
Murmellaut N 069
Murmelstimme M 273
Musik M 275
musikalisch M 276
musikalische Bezeichnung M 279
Musikinstrument M 277
Muskel M 274
Muster A 246, P 098
Musterbeispiel P 022
Musterbild P 529
Mustererkennung P 101
mustergültiges Beispiel C 084
Musterübereinstimmung P 099
Musterübung P 100

Muttersprache M 254, N 028
Mythe M 293
Mythologie M 294
Nachahmung I 023, M 136
Nachbearbeitung P 370
Nachbildung R 116
Nachdruck E 038
Nachdruckstakt S 420
Nachforschung R 123, S 034
Nachfrage I 160
Nachklangserscheinung E 006
nachklingend R 129
Nachname N 025
Nachrede G 053
Nachricht I 137, M 109
Nachricht und Code M 110
Nachrichten N 081
Nachrichtensendung N 082
Nachrichtenweg C 170
Nachruf O 002
Nachschlagewerk R 058
Nachschrift P 376
Nachsilbe S 492
Nachstellung P 375
Nachteil D 161
nachteilig D 162
nachtönig P 377
Nachtragsband S 505
nachwirkende Assimilation R 074
Nachwirkung A 128
Nachwort E 077
nah C 098
Nahassimilation C 322
Nähe P 534
nähere Auskunft P 066
nähere Zukunft I 025
Name N 001, N 002
Namensgebungsfunktion N 003
Namenkunde O 048
Nasal- N 012
nasal-oral D 203
nasale Konsonanten N 014
nasale Vokale N 016
Nasalieren N 018
nasalisiert O 095
Nasalität N 017
Nasallaute N 014
Nase N 147
Näseln N 015, T 239
Nasenloch N 148
Nasenraum N 013
national N 019
Nationalbewusstsein N 022
nationale Aussprache N 020
nationale Sprachen N 023

Nationalität N 024
Natur N 036
Natur- N 031
natürlich N 031
natürliche Sprachen N 033
natürliches Geschlecht N 032
Naturvölker P 442
Naturwissenschaften N 034
Nebenbedeutung C 276
Nebeneinanderstellung J 013
Nebenordnung P 037
Nebenprodukt O 111
Nebensatz D 069, S 468
Nebenton S 042
Nebenwort A 037, F 202
Negation N 043
negativ N 044
negative Frage N 048
negative Partikel N 046
negative Transformation N 051
negatives Affix N 045
negatives Merkmal M 151
negatives Pronomen N 047
negatives Verb N 052
Negativsatz N 049
Neigung G 105, T 063, T 214
Nekrolog N 042, O 002
Nennform I 125
Nennwort S 477
Nennungsübertragung T 186
Neologismus N.057
Nerv N 058
Nerven- N 062
Nervensystem N 059
Netz N 061
neu N 073, N 159
Neuauflage R 080
Neubildung N 074
Neudefinition R 047
neue Funktion N 075
neue Reihe erzeugende Phonem-
    komponente S 128
Neuentdeckung R 048
neuere Sprachen M 193
Neuerung I 158, M 194, N 057
neues Wort N 078
Neuformulierung R 135
Neugebrauch N 077
neugeschaffene Schriftsprachen
    N 079
Neugestaltung R 066
Neuheit N 080
Neurologie N 063
Neurose N 064

neutral N 066
neutraler Vokal N 069
neutralisiert N 072
Neutralisierung N 070
Neutrum N 065
Neuverteilung R 049
nicht aneinander grenzend D 169
nicht aspiriert U 013
nicht assimiliert U 014
nicht beigeordnet U 032
nicht benachbart N 108
nicht distinktiv N 112
nicht einschränkend N 126
nicht endlich N 115
nicht erhöht D 203
nicht erlernt U 097
nicht erniedrigt D 203
nicht gerichtet N 111
nicht integriertes Phonem U 111,
   N 118
nicht klassifizierbar U 024
nicht konsonantisch D 203
nicht linear N 120
nicht linguistisch N 121
nicht menschlich N 117
nicht nasalasiert D 203
nicht normal N 130
nicht präskriptiv N 124
nicht produktiv N 114
nicht schneidend N 119
nicht spezifiziert U 134
nicht stabil U 136
nicht standard N 130
nicht umkehrbar I 266
nicht unterscheidbar U 053
nicht verbunden U 015
nicht vertauschbar N 106
nicht vokalisch D 203
nicht vorhersagbar U 112
nicht wiederholt U 124
nicht wörtliche Übersetzung F 179
nicht zufriedenstellend U 130
nicht zulässig O 006
nicht zurückführbar U 145
nicht zutreffend I 059
Nichtübereinstimmung I 073
Nichtvergangenheitsverb(um) N 123
Nichtvorhandensein A 009
Nichtvorhandensein einer grammatischen Kategorie A 010
nichtzielendes Verb I 244
niederdeutsch L 307
Niederfrequenz L 306
niederländisch D 275
nomadisch N 095

Nomen N 156
Nomenklasse N 157
Nomenklatur N 097
nominal A 096, N 098
nominale Flexion N 100
nominale Klasse N 099
Nominalgruppe N 158
Nominalisierung N 102
Nominalphrase N 158
Nominalsatz N 101
Nominativ N 104, S 462
Norm N 134, S 379
normal D 203, N 135
normale Aussprache N 139
normale Buchstabierung N 141
normale Intonation N 138
normale Schreibweise C 165
normale Verteilung N 137
normale Wortstellung N 143
normaler Gebrauch N 142
normales Atmen N 136
Normalisierung N 144, S 381
normative Grammatik N 145, P 420
norwegisch N 146
Notation N 149
Notiz M 097
Notizbuch N 150
Notizen N 151
notwendig N 038
notwendige und hinreichende Bedin-
   gungen N 039
Notwendigkeit N 040
Novelle N 161
Nuance N 162
Null Z 001
Nullaffix Z 002
Nullaktualisierung Z 012
Nullallomorph Z 003
Nullallophon Z 004
Nullendung Z 005
Nullflexion Z 008
Nullglied Z 009
Nullkennzeichen Z 007
Nullmorphem Z 010
Nullrealisierung Z 012
Nullstufe Z 006
Nullwahrscheinlichkeit Z 011
Numerierung N 168
numerisch N 170
Numerus N 166
Numeruskongruenz A 138
Nummer I 275
nützlich U 166
Nutzung U 171

oben erwähnt F 122
Oberbau S 504
oberdeutsch H 036
obere Grenze U 154
oberer H 044
Oberflachenstruktur S 509
oberflächlich S 497
Oberkiefer U 157
Oberschicht S 503, U 156
oberst T 162, U 160
Oberton H 009, O 123
Oberwelle H 009
Oberzähne U 159
obig F 122
Objekt O 003, O 004
Objektfall O 009
objektiv O 007
Objektivität O 010
obligatorisch O 011
obligatorische Transformation O 012
obsolet O 021
obszöne Wörter F 167
obszöne Ausdrücke O 017
Ode O 034
offen O 052
offenbar O 122
Offenbarung M 020
offene Klasse U 127
offene Liste O 053
offene Silbe O 054
offene Verbindung O 055, P 312
offene Vokale O 056
offener Übergang O 055, P 312
offensichtlich A 221, O 122
öffentlich P 542
öffentliche Aufmerksamkeit P 548
öffentliche Bekanntmachungen P 543
öffentliche Bibliothek P 544
öffentliche Meinung P 545
Öffnung A 212, O 057
Öffnungsgrad D 041, S 206
ohne musikalisches Gehör T 147
ohne Präfix U 113
ohne Vorsilbe U 113
Ohr E 001
Ohrenphonetik A 295
Ohrmuschel A 299
Ökonomie E 007
Ökonomie in der Sprache E 008
ökonomisches Prinzip P 452
oktal O 030
Oktave O 031
Onomatopöie O 049
Ontologie O 051
Operationsdefinition O 059

Sprachforschung L 218, L 229
Sprachfortschritt L 086
Sprachfunktionen L 069
Sprachgebiet L 046
Sprachgebrauch L 226
Sprachgefühl L 045, L 209
Sprachgemeinschaft L 195, S 334
Sprachgenealogie L 070
Sprachgeographie A 245, G 029, L 207
Sprachgeschichte L 073
Sprachgewandheit F 004
Sprachgewohnheiten L 208, S 338
Sprachgrenze L 096
Sprachgruppe L 071
Sprachinsel R 100, S 340
Sprachhervorbringung S 346
Sprachkausalität L 192
Sprachkenntnis L 085, P 487
Sprachkode L 052 .
Sprachkommunikation S 333
Sprachkreuzung L 055
Sprachlaboratorium L 075
Sprachlaut S 351
sprachliche Bedeutung L 220
sprachliche Funktion L 206
sprachliche Ontogenese L 213
sprachliche Untergruppe L 223
sprachliche Vorgeschichte L 214
sprachlicher Vorläufer A 186
sprachliches Grundelement L 215
sprachliches Zeichen L 219
Sprachmaterialien L 056, L 199
Sprachmelodie S 342
Sprachminderheit L 211
Sprachminorität L 211
Sprachmodelle L 079
Sprachökonomie L 066
Sprachorgan A 253
Sprachpathologie S 344
Sprachpolitik L 083
Sprachpsychologie P 537
Sprachreform L 088
Sprachreinheit L 087
Sprachreinigung P 562
Sprachschnitzer S 248, S 329
Sprachschranke L 049
Sprachsimulieren L 090
Sprachsoziologie S 237
Sprachstandardisierung L 091
Sprachstil S 353
Sprachstörung L 074, S 336, S 339
Sprachstrom S 352
Sprachstruktur L 092
Sprachsünde S 329

Sprachsynthese S 354
Sprachsystem L 094
Sprachsystematie S 588
Sprachtheorie L 224
Sprachtherapie S 357
Sprachtiefe L 060
Sprachuniversalien L 228
Sprachunterricht L 095
Sprachveränderung L 050, L 193
Sprachverbreitung L 065
Sprachverfall L 059
Sprachvergleich L 053, L 196
Sprachverhalten V 036
Sprachvertrautheit F 022
Sprachverwandtschaft L 011, L 089, L 188
Sprachwandel L 050, L 193
Sprachwechsel L 093
Sprachwerkzeuge S 343
Sprachwidrigkeit B 017
Sprachwirklichkeit L 216
Sprachwissenschaft L 229, P 173
Sprachwissenschaft einer bestimmten Sprachgruppe S 316
Sprachwissenschaft einer bestimmten Sprache L 243
Sprachwissenschaftler L 185
sprachwissenschaftlich L 186, P 172
sprachwissenschaftliche Daten L 056, L 199
sprachwissenschaftliche Typologie L 225
Sprachzeichen S 349
Sprachzentrum S 331
Sprechakt S 326
Sprechapparat S 328
Sprechen S 311, S 325, S 346, T 015
  eintöniges Sprechen M 209
  langsames Sprechen S 217
  schleppendes Sprechen D 257
  schnelles Sprechen F 030, R 013
  unzusammenhängendes Sprechen I 066
  verschleifendes Sprechen S 218
Sprechen im Chor C 066
sprechend T 016
Sprecher S 309
Sprecher der Muttersprache N 029
Sprecher und Hörer S 310
Sprechkette S 332
Sprechkontinuum S 332, S 335
Sprechlaut P 176
Sprechmaschine S 355
Sprechmelodie I 242
Sprechorgane S 343

Sprechpause S 345
Sprechsignal S 349
Sprechsituation S 350
Sprechstimme S 312
Sprechtakt B 095, S 341
Sprechtempo S 356
Sprechweise L 281
Sprechwortschatz S 313
Sprengung E 169
Sprichwort A 080, B 114, P 532, S 011
Sprossvokal E 071
Spur T 169, V 057
Spur von Bedeutung S 139
staatlich N 019
Staatsangehörigkeit N 024
stabiles System S 372
Stabilisierung S 373
Stabilitätsgrad D 045
Stabreim A 145
Stadium P 170
städtische Sprache U 161
Stamm S 395, T 089
Stammabstufung S 396
Stammbaum F 027, G 006
Stammeln S 378, S 449
Stammessprachen T 217
Stammflexion S 397
stammverwandtes Wort P 048
Stammwort R 005
Stammzeiten des Verbums P 449
Stammzeitwort P 446
Standard S 379
Standardisierung S 381
Standardsprache S 380
ständig P 142
Standpunkt P 324, V 060
stark P 383
Stärke F 120
starke Aspiration S 428
starke Betonung S 431
starke Endung S 430
starke Stellung S 429
Starkton I 001, P 439
statische Linguistik S 386
Statistik S 392
statistische Analyse S 387
statistische Linguistik S 391
statistische Unabhängigkeit S 390
statistische Verteilung S 388
statistischer Faktor S 389
Status S 393
steigender Ton A 258, R 174
Steigerungsstufe D 043
Stelle D 139, L 279

INDEX FRANÇAIS

BIBLIOGRAPHY / БИБЛИОГРАФИЯ / BIBLIOGRAPHIE

* indicates an original work listed elsewhere in translation.
* указывает на подлинник уже внесенный в перевод.
* bedeutet einen Originaltitel, dessen Übersetzung anderweitig angeführt ist.
* indique le texte originel d'un ouvrage dont la version traduite est notée autre part.
** indicates a translated work listed elsewhere in the original.
** указывает на перевод уже внесенный в подлинник.
** bedeutet ein übersetztes Werk, dessen Originaltitel anderweitig angeführt ist.
** indique la version traduite d'un ouvrage dont le texte originel est noté autre part.

Standard Dictionaries and Reference Grammars

Betteridge, H. T. (ed.) *The New Cassell's German Dictionary* (New York, 1962).

Dubois, M. (ed.) *Larousse Modern French-English and English-French Dictionary* (Paris, 1960).

Duden, K. *Der Grosse Duden 1. Rechtschreibung* (Mannheim, 1961).

Grebe, P. (ed.) *Der Grosse Duden IV. Grammatik* (Mannheim, 1965).

Grevisse, M. *Le Bon Usage. Grammaire Francaise* (Gembloux, 1964).

Schulz, D. and Griesbach, H. *Grammatik der Deutschen Sprache*, 2nd rev. ed. (Munich, 1962).

Smirnitsky, A. I. *Russian-English Dictionary* (New York, 1959).

World Book Encyclopedia Dictionary, 2 vols. (Chicago, 1963).

Грамматика русского языка, I-III (АН СССР, Москва, 1960).

Мюллер, В. К. *Англо-русский словарь* (Москва, 1962).

Ожегов, С. И. *Словарь русского языка* (Москва, 1963).

Орфографический словарь русского языка (АН СССР, Москва, 1963).

Словарь русского языка I-IV (АН СССР, Москва, 1957).

Dictionaries of Technical Terms

Hamp, E. P. *Glossary of American Technical Usage 1925-1950.* Permanent Internation Committee of Linguists (Utrecht-Antwerp, 1963).*

Hofmann, J. B. und Rubenbauer, H. *Wörterbuch der grammatischen und metrischen Terminologie* (Heidelberg, 1963).

Knobloch, J. *Sprachwissenschaftliches Wörterbuch,* Lieferung 1,2 (Heidelberg, 1961-63).

Marouzeau, J. *Lexique de la Terminologie Linguistique* (Paris, 1961).*

Paternost, J. *Russian-English Glossary of Linguistic Terms* (Pennsylvania State University, 1965).

Vachek, J. *Dictionnaire de linguistique de l'ecole de Prague.* Permanent International Committee of Linguistics (Utrecht/Antwerp, 1960).*

Вахик, И. *Лингвистический словарь пражской школы* (Москва, 1964).**

Марузо, Ж. *Словарь лингвистических терминов, перевод с французского* (Москва, 1960).**

Русско-англо-немецко-французский словарь терминов по автоматическому управлению (АН СССР, Институт автоматики и телемеханики, Москва, 1963).

Словарь-минимум для чтения научной литературы на английском языке (АН СССР, Кафедра иностранных языков, Москва, 1959).

Хэмп, Э. *Словарь американской терминологии, перевод с английского А. А. Иванова* (Москва, 1964).**

Books

Akhmanova, O. S., Mel'chuk, I. A., Frumkina, R. M. and Paducheva, E. V. *Exact Methods in Linguistic Research,* translated from the Russian by David G. Hays and Dolores V. Mohr (University of California Press, 1963). [34]

Ammer, K. *Einführung in die Sprachwissenschaft,* Band I (Halle, 1958).

Arens, H. *Sprachwissenschaft* (München, 1955).

Bally, C. *Linguistique Générale et Linguistique Français* (Bern, 1944).

Bierwisch, M. *Grammatik des Deutschen Verbs,* Studia Grammatica II (Berlin, 1965).

Bloomfield, L. *Language* (New York, 1933).

Chomsky, N. *Syntactic Structures* (The Hague, 1957).*

Delavenay, E. *La Machine à Traduire* (Paris, 1959).

De Saussure, F. *Cours de Linguistique Générale* (Paris, 1931).*

De Saussure, F. *Course in General Linguistics,* translated from the French by Wade Baskin (New York, 1959).**

Etudes phonologiques dédiées à la mémoire M. le Prince Trubetzkoy (Alabama Linguistic and Philological Series 2, 1964).

Fonagy, I. *Die Metaphern in der Phonetik* (The Hague, 1963).

Gipper, H. *Bausteine zur Sprachinhaltsforschung* (Düsseldorf, 1963).

Gleason, H. A. *An Introduction to Descriptive Linguistics,* 2nd rev. ed. (New York, 1961).*

Grammont, M. *Traité de phonétique* (Paris, 1950).

Gray, L. H. *Foundations of Language* (New York, 1939).

Hall, R. A. *Introductory Linguistics* (Philadelphia, 1964).

Halle, M. *The Sound Pattern of Russian* (The Hague, 1959).*

Harris, Z. *Structural Linguistics* (Chicago, 1963).

Hartmann, P. *Allgemeinste Strukturgesetze in Sprache und Grammatik* (The Hague, 1961).

Hartmann, P. *Grammatik und Grammatizität* (The Hague, 1962).

Hjelmslev, L. *Prologomena to a Theory of Language,* translated from the Danish by Francis J. Whitfield (Baltimore, 1953).*

Hockett, C. *A Course in Modern Linguistics* (New York, 1958).

Hockett, C. F. *A Manual of Phonology* (Baltimore, 1955).

Homburger, L. *Le Langage et les Langues* (Paris, 1951).

Hughes, J. P. *The Science of Language* (New York, 1962).

Information Processing. (Proceedings of the International Conference on Information Processing, UNESCO, Paris, 1959).

For Roman Jakobson. Essays on the occasion of his sixtieth birthday (The Hague, 1956).

Jakobson, R. and Halle, M. *Fundamentals of Language* (The Hague, 1956).

Jakobson, R. und Halle, M. *Grundzüge der Sprache,* übersetzt von Otto von Essen (Berlin, 1965).

Jakobson, R., Fant, C. G. M., and Halle, M. *Preliminaries to Speech Analysis*-M.I.T. Acoustics Laboratory Technical Report No. 13 (1952).*

Jakobson, R. *Selected Writings,* Vol. I (The Hague, 1962).

Jespersen, O. *Essentials of English Grammar* (Alabama Linguistic and Philological Series 1, 1964).

Jesperson, O. *Language, its Nature, Development, and Origin* (London, 1950).

Lehmann, W. P. *Historical Linguistics* (New York, 1962).

Leroy, M. *Les Grands Courants de la Linguistique Moderns* (Bruxelles, 1963).

Lévy-Brühl, L. "Des rapports de la linguistique et de la sociologie", *Actes du 4-ème Congrès international des linguistes* (Copenhague, 1938).

Malblanc, A. *Stylistique comparée du français et de l'allemand* (Paris, 1961).

Malmberg, B. *La Phonétique* (Paris, 1962).*

Malmberg, B. *Phonetics,* translated from the French by L. M. Parker (New York, 1963).**

Malmberg, B. *Structural Linguistics and Human Communication* (New York, 1963).

Martinet, A. *Économie des Changements Phonétique: Traité de Phonologie Diachronique* (Paris, 1955).

Martinet, A. *Éléments de Linguistique Générale* (Paris, 1960).

Martinet, A. *Elements of General Linguistics,* translated by Elisabeth Palmer (Chicago, 1964).**

Martinet, A. *Grundzüge der Allgemeinen Sprachwissenschaft,* übersetzt von Fritz Ernst (Stuttgart, 1963).**

Marouzeau, J. *La Linguistique ou Science du Langage* (Paris, 1950).

Meillet, A. *Introduction à l'étude comparative des langues indo-européennes* (Alabama Linguistic and Philological Series 3, 1964).

Meillet, A. *Linguistique Historique et Linguistique Générale* (Paris, 1921).

Mounin, G. *La Machine à Traduire* (La Haye, 1964).

Mues, W. *Vom Laut zum Satz* (Heidelberg, 1964).

Ornstein, J. and Gage, W. *The ABC's of Languages and Linguistics* (Philadelphia, 1964).

Panov, D. Ju. *Automatic Translation,* translated from the Russian by R. Kisch (New York, 1960).

Perrot, J. *La Linguistique* (Paris, 1961).

Pilch, H. *Phonemtheorie,* Teil I (Basel, 1964).

Potter, S. *Modern Linguistics* (New York, 1964).

Pottier, B. *Introduction à l'étude des Structures Grammaticales Fondamentales* (Nancy, 1964).

Sapir, E. *Language: An Introduction to the Study of Speech* (New York, 1921).*

Schlauch, M. *The Gift of Tongues* (New York, 1942).

Sturdevant, E. H. *An Introduction to Linguistic Science* (Yale University Press, 1960).

Tesnière, L. *Éléments de Syntaxe Structurale* (Paris, 1959).

Trends in European and American Linguistics, 1930-1960 (Permanent International Committee of Linguists, Utrecht/Antwerp, 1961).

Troubetzkoy, N. S. *Principes de Phonologie* traduction d'allemand par J. Cantineau (Paris, 1949).

Trubetskoy, N. S. *Grundzüge der Phonologie* (Prague, 1939).*

Uldall, H. J. *Outline of Glossematics* (Copenhagen, 1957).*

Vendryes, J. *Le langage* (Paris, 1950).

Vinay, J. P. and Darbelnet, J. *Stylistique Comparée du français et de l'anglais* (Paris, 1958).

von Essen, O. *Allgemeine und angewandte Phonetik* (Berlin, 1962).

Wartburg, W. *Einführung in Problematik und Methodik der Sprachwissenschaft* (Tubingen, 1962).

Wartburg, W. *Problèmes et Méthodes de la Linguistique,* traduction d'allemand par Pierre Maillard (Paris, 1946).

Weinreich, U. *Languages in Contact. Findings and Problems* (New York, 1953).

Weisgerber, L. *Die sprachliche Gestaltung der Welt* (Düsseldorf, 1962).

Whorf, B. L. *Language, Thought, and Reality* (New York, 1956).

Аванесов, Р. И. *Фонетика современного русского языка* (Москва, 1956).

Агаян, Е. Б. *Введение в языкознание* (Ереван, 1959).

Артемов, В. А. *Экспериментальная фонетика* (Москва, 1956).

Ахманова, О. С. *О психолингвистике: материалы к курсам языкознания* (Москва, 1957).

Ахманова, О. С. *Очерки по общей и русской лексикологии* (Москва, 1957).

Ахманова, О. С. *Современные синтактические теории* (Москва, 1963).

Ахманова, О. С., Мельчук, И. А., Фрумкина, Р. М., и Падучева, Е. В. *О точных методах исследования языка* (Москва, 1961).*

Брызгунова, Е. *Практическая фонетика и интонация русского языка* (Москва, 1960).

Ъугадов, Р. А. *Введение в науку о языке* (Москва, 1958).

Виноградов, В. В. *Стилистика. Теория поэтической речи. Поэтика* (АН СССР, Москва, 1963).

Виноградов, В. В. (ред.) *Теоретические проблемы современного советского языкознания* (АН СССР, Москва, 1964).

Вопросы грамматического строя (Москва, 1955).

Вопросы терминологии (материалы Всесоюзного терминологического совещания) (Москва, 1962).

Глисон, Г. *Введение в дескриптивную лингвистику,* перевод с английского Е. С. Кудрякова и В. П. Мурат (Москва, 1959). [5]

Дегтерева, Т. А. (ред.) *Принципы научного анализа языка: сборник* (Москва, 1959).

Дегтерева, Т. А. (ред.) *Проблемы изучения языка* (Москва, 1957).

Дегтерева, Т. А. (ред.) *Проблемы общего и частного языкознания: сборник* (Москва, 1960).

Дегтерева, Т. А. *Пути развития современной лингвистики, I-III* (Москва, 1961-1964).

Де Соссюр, Ф. *Курс общей лингвистики, перевод с французского* (Москва, 1933).**

Звегинцев, В. А. *История языкознания XIX-XX веков в очерках и извлечениях.* Т.I,II (Москва, 1964).

Звегинцев, В. А. *Очерки по общему языкознанию* (Москва, 1963).

Звегинцев, В. А. (ред.) *Хрестоматии по истории языкознания* (Москва, 1956).

Зиндер, Л. Р. *Общая фонетика* (Ленинград, 1960).

Иванов, В. В. (ред.) *Вопросы структуры языка* (Москва, 1964).

Карпов, Л. А. (ред.) *Вопросы общего языкознания* (Ленинград, 1964).

Кузнецова, П. С. (ред.) *Машинный перевод.* Сборник статей (Москва, 1957).

Мартине, А. *Основы общей лингвистики, перевод с французского В. В. Шеворошкина.* Новое в лингвистике III, 366-566 (1963).**

Мартине, А. *Принцип экономии в фонетических изменениях, перевод с французского* (Москва, 1960).**

Мейе, А. *Введение в сравнительное изучение индоевропейских языков, перевод с французского* (Москва-Ленинград, 1938).**

Мучник, И. П. *Введение в языкознание: сборник задач и упражнений* (Москва, 1961).

Новое в лингвистике Вып. I-IV (Москва, 1960-1965). В. А. Звегинцев, ред.

Панов, Д. Ю. *Автоматический перевод* (АН СССР, Москва, 1960).

Ревзин, И. И. *Модели языка* (АН СССР, Москва, 1962).

Реформатский, А. А. *Введение в языкознание* (Москва, 1960).

Сепир, Э. *Язык, перевод с английского* (Москва, 1934).**

Серебренников, Б. А. и Суник, О. П. (ред.) *Морфологическая типология и проблема классификации языков* (АН СССР, Москва-Ленинград, 1965).

Трубетской, Н. С. *Основы фонологии, перевод с немецкого А. А. Холодовича* (Москва, 1960).**

Успенский, В. А. *Принципы структурной типологии* (Москва, 1962).

Чикобава, А. С. *Проблема языка как предмета языкознания* (Москва, 1959).

Шаумян, С. К. (ред.) *Проблемы структурной лингвистики* (АН СССР, Москва, 1963).

Шаумян, С. К. *Проблемы теоретической фонологии* (Москва, 1962).

Шаумян, С. К. (ред.) *Трансформационный метод в структурной лингвистике* (АН СССР, Москва, 1964).

Шенгели, Г. *Техника стиха* (Москва, 1960).

Articles

Benveniste, E. "La classification des langues", *Conférences de l'Institute de Linguistique de l'Université de Paris XI, Années 1952-1953*, pp. 33-50 (Paris, 1954).*

Fries, C. "Meaning and linguistic analysis", *Language* 30(1). 57-68 (1954).*

Gleason, H. A. "A File for a technical dictionary", *Georgetown University Monograph Series on Language and Linguistics* 14.115-122 (1961).

Greenberg, J. H. "A quantitative approach to the morphological typology of language", *International Journal of American Linguistics* 26(3).178-194 (1960).*

Gudschinsky, S. "The ABC's of lexicostatistics", *Word* 12 (1956).

Harris, Z. "Co-occurrence and transformation in linguistic structure", *Language* 33(3, part 1).283-340 (1957).

Haugen, E. "Directions in modern linguistics", *Language* 27 (1951).*

Hoijer, H. "Lexicostatistics: A Critique", *Language* 32(1).49-60 (1956).*

Householder, F. W. "On Linguistic terms", in Sol Saporta (ed.), *Psycholinguistics* (New York, 1961).

Hjelmslev, L. "Dans quelle mesure les significations des mots peuvent-elles être considérées comme formant une structure?" *Proceedings of the Eighth International Congress of Linguists,* pp. 636-654 (Oslo, 1958).

Hjelmslev, L. "La notion de rection" *Acta Linguistica* 1 (1939).

Hjelmslev, L. "La stratification du langage" *Word* 10 (1954).

Isačenko, A. V. "Versuch einer Typologie der slavischen Sprachen", *Linguistica Slovaca* 1.64-76 (Bratislava, 1939-40).*

Jakobson, R. "Typological studies and their contribution to historical comparative linguistics", *Proceedings of the Eighth International Congress of Linguists,* pp. 17-25 (Oslo, 1958).*

Jakobson, R. and Halle, M. "Phonology in relation to phonetics" in J. Kaiser (ed.), *Manual of Phonetics* (Amsterdam, 1957).*

Kubler, G. "Terminologie und Lexikographie", *Lebende Sprachen* 11.5-6 (1966).

Malmberg, B. "Questions de methode en phonetique synchronique", *Studia Linguistica X,* No. 1 (1956).*

Nida, E. A. "Analysis of meaning and dictionary making", *International Journal of American Linguistics* 24(4).279-292 (1958).*

Swadesh, M. "Lexicostatistic dating of prehistoric ethnic contacts", *Proceedings of the American Philosophical Society* 96.452-463 (1952).*

Swadesh, M. "Towards greater accuracy in lexicostatistic dating", *International Journal of American Linguistics* 21.121-137 (1955).*

Ullmann, S. "Descriptive semantics and linguistic typology", *Word* 9(3).225-240 (1953).*

Whorf, B. "Linguistics and Logic" in *Language, Thought, and Reality* (New York, 1956).*

Whorf, B. "Science and Linguistics" in *Language, Thought, and Reality* (New York, 1956).*

Whorf, B. "The relation of habitual thought and behavior to language", in *Language, Thought, and Reality* (New York, 1956).*

Worth, D. S. "Transform analysis of Russian instrumental constructions", *Word* 14(2-3).247-290 (1958).*

Ахманова, О. С. "К вопросу об основных понятиях метаязыка лингвистики", *Вопросы языкознания,* 1, 115-121 (1961).

Ахманова, О. С. "Основная терминология дескриптивной лингвистики", *Лексикографический Сборник* 6.131-138 (Москва, 1963).

Ахманова, О. С. и Веселицккий, В. В. "О современной лингвистической терминологии", *Лексикографический Сборник* 5.167-168 (Москва, 1962).

Ахманова, О. С. и Полторацкий, А. И. "Словари лингвистической терминологии", *Лексикографический Сборник* 5.188-190 (Москва, 1962).

Бенвенист, Э. "Классификация языков", перевод с французского В. А. Матвеенко, *Новое в лингвистике* III, 36-59 (1963).**

Гринберг, Дж. "Квантитативный подход к морфологической типологии языков", перевод с английского Е. С. Кудряковой и В. П. Марат, *Новое в лингвистике* III, 60-94 (1963).**

Ельмслев, Л. "Пролегомены к теории языка", перевод с английского Ю. К. Лекомцева, *Новое в лингвистике* I, 264-389 (1960).**

Исаченко, А. "Опыт типологического анализа славянских языков", перевод с немецкого В. В. Шеворошкина, *Новое в лингвистике* III, 106-121 (1963).**

Мальмберг, Б. "Проблема метода в синхронной фонетике", перевод с французского В. В. Шеворошкина, *Новое в лингвистике* II, 340-389 (1962).**

Найда, Е. А. "Анализ значения и составление словарей", перевод с английского Т. Н. Сергеевой, *Новое в лингвистике* II, 45-71 (1962).**

Никофоров, В. К. "О системности термина", *Вопросы языкознания* 1, 111-114 (1966).

Сводеш, М. "Лексикостатистическое латирование доисторических этническихконтактов", перевод с английского И. П. Токмаковой, *Новое в лингвистике* I, 23-52 (1960).**

Сводеш, М. "К вопросу о повышении точности в лексикостатистическом датировании", перевод с английского И. П. Токмаковой, *Новое в лингвистике* I, 53-87 (1960).**

Ульдалль, Х. И. "Основы глоссематики", перевод с английского Вяс. Вс. Иванова, *Новое в лингвистике* I, 390-436 (1960).**

Ульман, С. "Дескриптивная семантика и лингвистическая типология", Перевод с английского Е. С. Турковой, *Новое в лингвистике* II, 17-44 (1962).**

Уорс, Д. С. "Трансформационный анализ конструкций с творительным падежом в русском языке", перевод с английского Ф. А. Дрейзина и Т. М. Николаевой, *Новое в лингвистике* II, 637-683 (1962).**

Уорф, Б. Л. "Лингвистика и логика", перевод с английского Л. Н. Наман, *Новое в лингвистике* I, 183-198 (1960).**

Уорф, Б. Л. "Наука и яеыкознания", перевод с английского Е. С. Кудряковой и В. П. Мурат, *Новое в лингвистике* I, 169-182 (1960).**

Уорф, Б. Л. "Отношение норм поведения и мышления к языку", перевож с английского Л. Н. Наман и Е. С. Турковой, *Новое в лингвистике* I, 135-168 (1960).**

Фельдман, Н. И. "О границах перевода в иноязычно-русских словарях", *Лексикографический Сборник* 2.81-109 (1957).

Фельдман, Н. И. "Об анализе смысловой структуры в двуязычных словарях", *Лексикографический Сборник* 1.9-35 (1957).

Фриз, Ч. "Значение и лингвистический анализ", перевод с английского С. А. Григорьевой, *Новое в лингвистике* II, 98-116 (1962).**

Халле, М. "Фонологическая система русского языка", перевод с английского Д. М. Сегал, *Новое в лингвистике* II, 299-339 (1962).**

Хауген, Э. "Направления в современном лингвистике", перевод с английского С. А. Григорьевой, *Новое в лингвистике* I, 244-263 (1960).**

Хойер, Г. "Лексикостатистика (Критический разбор)", перевод с английского И. П. Токмаковой, *Новое в лингвистике* I, 88-107 (1960).**

Хомский, Н. "Синтактические структуры", перевод с английского К. И. Бабицкого, *Новое в лингвистике* II, 412-527 (1962).**

Хэррис, З. С. "Совместная встречаемость и трансформация в языковой структуре", перевод с английского Т. Н. Молошной, *Новое в лингвистике* II, 528-636 (1962).**

Якобсон, Р. "Типологические исследования и их вклад в сравнительно-историческое языкознание", перевод ё английского Е. С. Кудряковой и В. П. Марат, *Новое в лингвистике* III, 95-105 (1963).**

Якобсон, Р. и Халле, М. "Фонология и ее отношение к фонетике", перевод с английского А. А. Зализняка и Е. В. Падучевой, *Новое в лингвистике* II, 231-278 (1962).**

Якобсон, Р., Фант, Г. М., и Халле, М. "Введение в анализ речи", перевод с английского А. А. Зализняка и Е. В. Падучевой, *Новое в лингвистике* II, 173-230 (1962).**

Journals

Acta Linguistica (Budapest).
Cahiers Ferdinand de Saussure (Genève).
Cahiers de Linguistique Théorique et Appliquée (Bucarest).
Indogermanische Forschungen (Berlin).
IRAL (Heidelberg).
JPRS—Joint Publications Research Service (Washington).
Journal of Linguistics (London).
Language (Baltimore).
Les Langues Modernes (Paris).
Lebende Sprachen (Berlin).
Lingua (Amsterdam).
Linguistics (The Hague).
La Linguistique (Paris).
Die Neueren Sprachen (Frankfurt).
Orbis (Louvain).
Philologica Pragensia (Praha).
Revue Internationale de la Documentation (La Haye).
Die Sprache (Wien).
Studia Linguistica (Copenhague).
La Traduction Automatique (Paris).
Travaux de Linguistique et de Littérature (Strasbourg).
Word (New York).
Zeitschrift für Phonetik, Sprachwissenschaft, und Kommunikationsforschung (Berlin).
Zeitschrift für Vergleichende Sprachforschung (Göttingen).

Вопросы языкознания (Москва).
Машинный перевод и прикладная лингвистика (Москва).